Higher Education to 2030

VOLUME 2

GLOBALISATION

CENTRE FOR EDUCATIONAL RESEARCH AND INNOVATION

ORGANISATION FOR ECONOMIC CO-OPERATION AND DEVELOPMENT

The OECD is a unique forum where the governments of 30 democracies work together to address the economic, social and environmental challenges of globalisation. The OECD is also at the forefront of efforts to understand and to help governments respond to new developments and concerns, such as corporate governance, the information economy and the challenges of an ageing population. The Organisation provides a setting where governments can compare policy experiences, seek answers to common problems, identify good practice and work to co-ordinate domestic and international policies.

The OECD member countries are: Australia, Austria, Belgium, Canada, the Czech Republic, Denmark, Finland, France, Germany, Greece, Hungary, Iceland, Ireland, Italy, Japan, Korea, Luxembourg, Mexico, the Netherlands, New Zealand, Norway, Poland, Portugal, the Slovak Republic, Spain, Sweden, Switzerland, Turkey, the United Kingdom and the United States. The Commission of the European Communities takes part in the work of the OECD.

OECD Publishing disseminates widely the results of the Organisation's statistics gathering and research on economic, social and environmental issues, as well as the conventions, guidelines and standards agreed by its members.

This work is published on the responsibility of the Secretary-General of the OECD. The opinions expressed and arguments employed herein do not necessarily reflect the official views of the Organisation or of the governments of its member countries.

ISBN 978-92-64-05660-2 (print)
ISBN 978-92-64-07537-5 (PDF)

Series: Educational Research and Innovation

Also available in French: *L'enseignement supérieur à l'horizon 2030, Volume 2 : Globalisation*

Photo credits: Cover © Stockbyte/Getty images.

Corrigenda to OECD publications may be found on line at: *www.oecd.org/publishing/corrigenda*.

Foreword

Higher education and research play a key role in countries' response to globalisation. At the same time, even if no global model of the higher education system is currently emerging, higher education is increasingly becoming globalised. Higher education is thus simultaneously a response to, and a scene for, global competition, collaboration, mobility and cross-cultural encounters.

This book analyses recent trends in tertiary education systems that relate to globalisation and draws up several possible future scenarios for their evolution. It looks at three main sets of questions: cross-border higher education, that is, the mobility of students, faculty, programmes and institutions; the trends in the governance of tertiary education as a result of globalisation, notably as it relates to funding, quality assurance, and privatisation; and, finally, the perceived and actual forces fuelling competition and collaboration at the global level, including international rankings and the emergence of China and India as global players.

Like its companion volumes in this series, on demography (volume 1) and technology (volume 3) respectively, this report will help higher education policy makers and stakeholders to better understand globalisation-related trends in higher education – and imagine several possible and plausible futures.

Completed just before the recession, this book is a very timely opportunity to enlighten policy and decision making during the recovery. Business as usual cannot be the right answer. More than ever, it is essential to be forward-looking, innovative, and to question the continuation of some recent trends. Informing and framing this forward-looking discussion is precisely the mission of the Centre for Educational Research and Innovation (CERI) project on the future of higher education, led by Senior Analyst Stéphan Vincent-Lancrin.

This project has benefited from the support of all our member countries, but I would particularly like to thank Austria, France and Portugal, which have generously hosted expert and stakeholder meetings in relation to this strand of the project.

Stéphan Vincent-Lancrin and Analyst Kiira Kärkkäinen are the editors of the book. Therese Walsh and Ashley Allen-Sinclair provided assistance and helped in preparing the manuscript. I would further like to thank all the book's authors who have provided original and complementary insights into this complex subject as well as Dirk van Damme, head of CERI, for his strong support to the project and Tom Schuller, former head of CERI, from whose valuable advice the project on the future of higher education has benefited.

Barbara Ischinger
Director for Education

Table of Contents

List of Figures

Higher Education to 2030
Volume 2: Globalisation
© OECD 2009

Executive Summary

Higher education drives and is driven by globalisation. It trains the highly skilled workers and contributes to the research base and capacity for innovation that determine competitiveness in the knowledge-based global economy. It facilitates international collaboration and cross-cultural exchange. Cross-border flows of ideas, students, faculty and financing, coupled with developments in information and communication technology, are changing the environment where higher education institutions function. Co-operation and competition are intensifying simultaneously under the growing influence of market forces and the emergence of new players. How will global higher education evolve over the next 20 years? How can governments and institutions meet the challenges and make the most of the opportunities?

Higher Education to 2030: Globalisation, the second in a four-volume series, addresses these issues both from a quantitative and a qualitative standpoint. Increased global competition in higher education, simultaneous to cross-border collaboration is illustrated not only on a global scale, but also at a regional level through developments in Europe. Though the emphasis is on the OECD area, the reflections have a worldwide scope with particular emphasis on the potential of China and India. The book explores significant trends in higher education provision, financing and governance, including a specific focus on the future role of market forces, mobility, and quality assurance in higher education.

The reviewed trends point towards the possible following key developments in the future:

Cross-border higher education, implying mobility of students, faculty and institutions, will grow

Student mobility has increased significantly over the past decade, supported by internationalisation policies within Europe and in some other countries. Institutional rankings and pressure on financing are likely to continue to boost student mobility and global competition for international students – increasingly of Chinese or Indian origin, and attracted by English-speaking destinations. Geographical mobility of faculty, predominantly south-to-north and east-to-west, is likely to continue, driven by salary and superior infrastructure. Moreover, other types of cross-border mobility may become more important in the future, as has been shown by the sharp rise of programme and institution mobility over the past decade, especially in a few Asian countries. In the future, the increase in institutional mobility could take several different paths. It might level off due to the related costs and risks. Alternatively, the market could expand if host countries gradually become exporters of higher education services. In addition to the commercial approach, development of cross-border higher education through partnerships or along linguistic, religious or strategic lines could be envisaged in the future.

Academic research will become increasingly international and will continue to be affected by both collaborative and competitive forces

Cross-border collaboration in research has grown along with the development of information and communication technologies. The number of internationally co-authored articles more than doubled over the past two decades. International funding for university research has also increased, even if it still represents a small share of research funding. However, international rankings based heavily on research criteria are likely to further increase global competition, especially for research talent, as numerous countries are attempting to build so-called world-class universities. This raises the major issue of where academic research takes place. When taking into account the diverse objectives of higher education, the model of concentrating resources in a few institutions is not necessarily superior to the model of supporting excellent research departments across the different institutions and regions in a given country.

Higher education systems in Asia and Europe will gradually increase their global influence, although North America will continue to hold a clear advantage especially with regard to research

Over the past two decades, even if from lower starting points, the growth in scientific output has been faster in Asia and Europe than in North America. China and India, the two largest academic systems in the world, will have an increasingly important role to play in the future, even though they are unlikely to rival OECD systems in terms of quality in the medium term. A significant challenge for both countries is to create a sufficiently deep and extensive national research infrastructure. In European higher education, the Bologna Process has initiated reforms aimed at increasing global competitiveness through regional co-operation, providing an interesting example for other regions. While this has already led to some convergence of degree structures and to common frameworks for quality assurance and qualifications, the emergence of a fully integrated European higher education system is not yet in sight. Further harmonising of systems will imply finding a balance with the simultaneous trend towards institutional diversity.

Private higher education provision and financing will increase worldwide, especially outside the OECD area

On average, the growth of private higher education and, especially research funding, has been faster than that of public funding in the OECD area, although in the majority of OECD countries higher education is still largely funded by the public purse. With the exception of Japan and Korea, the persistent reliance on the State is even more marked in higher education provision, since the private sector caters to an increasing number of students in only a small number of OECD countries, namely in eastern Europe, Portugal and Mexico. Worldwide, however, both private higher education provision and funding have seen significant increases over the past decades. This growth is likely to continue, especially in developing countries where rapid demographic growth will continue to boost higher education demand.

Growth of market-like mechanisms will be more marked in higher education governance through the use of performance-based and competitive allocation of funds

The increase of competitive research funding in many OECD countries, together with an emerging range of merit-based grants and loans worldwide, reflects the global quest for accountability, efficiency and effectiveness. However, while demand-side financing has growth prospects, especially in higher education systems that already combine a mixture of public and private elements, traditional supply-side models of allocating government funding are still largely predominant in most OECD countries. Taking into account specific economic, social and cultural contexts, an essential challenge for higher education systems is to combine the encouragement of efficiency and excellence with the promotion of equity and access.

Focus on quality assurance will strengthen in response to the growing importance of private and cross-border higher education, institutional rankings and the quest for accountability

The overall emphasis on quality assurance has started to move towards assessing educational and labour market outcomes instead of inputs, but there are still notable differences between audit and evaluation approaches across regions. At the same time, one can observe the emergence of cross-border accreditation and a general strengthening of co-operation across borders: several regional networks of quality assurance agencies have been established and there is an increasing interest in establishing common regional criteria and methodologies, particularly in Europe. The emergence of a common quality assurance framework on a global scale does not, however, seem likely in the near future.

The book starts by illustrating trends and developments in the global environment of higher education and reflecting on how higher education might look in the future. While the thematic focus is on cross-border education and academic research, the specific cases of emerging Asian giants and European co-operation are examined in more detail. The book then shifts its focus to the themes of higher education provision, financing and governance that have a crucial impact on the capacity of countries, institutions and individuals in the context of globalisation.

Chapter 1 (Marginson and van der Wende) provides a comprehensive framework for understanding the dynamics of higher education and globalisation. It examines positions and strategies of different countries in the global environment, with a specific focus on research capacity and performance. The chapter concludes by reflecting on challenges and opportunities related to cross-border higher education and global public goods.

Chapter 2 (Vincent-Lancrin) explores developments in cross-border higher education, particularly with regard to student and institutional mobility. After depicting the main past trends and recent developments, the chapter sketches different paths cross-border education may take in the future, taking into account economic, political and cultural considerations.

Chapter 3 (McBurnie and Ziguras) examines the prospects for cross-border mobility of institutions and programmes through four scenarios. Drawing on current trends in student demand, programme delivery and government policies, the focus is on Australia and South East Asia, the leading regions in the development of cross-border programme and institution mobility at present.

Chapter 4 (Marginson and van der Wende) reflects on the interrelated dynamics of higher education and globalisation through three concrete examples. It first examines the policy developments within Europe, after which it takes a critical look at global institutional rankings and cross-border faculty mobility worldwide.

Chapter 5 (Vincent-Lancrin) focuses on past macro-level trends in academic research in OECD countries. It provides an overview of current characteristics of academic research both in terms of funding and activities in relation to research performed by other sectors. The chapter concludes by highlighting challenges and sketching scenarios for future academic research.

Chapter 6 (Altbach) examines the characteristics and future potential of higher education systems in China and India. After a historical overview, it discusses the role of the two countries as international higher education players in relation to cross-border mobility and academic research. The chapter concludes by looking at the internal challenges confronting Chinese and Indian higher education, namely access, equity and private provision.

Chapter 7 (Witte, Huisman and Purser) provides an example of regional co-operation as a strategic choice in the context of globalisation by taking a detailed look into the Bologna Process in Europe. After reviewing the complexity of the process and taking a stock of the main reforms related to it, the chapter discusses continuing challenges and alternative scenarios for the future of European higher education.

Chapter 8 (Teixeira) discusses the emergence of private higher education institutions on a global scale. It first recalls the history of private higher education, in particular against the background of the evolution of the modern State. The chapter then illustrates the driving forces behind the recent growth in private provision in several regions of the world and concludes by discussing the potential roles for private higher education in the future.

Chapter 9 (Vincent-Lancrin) analyses past macro-level trends regarding the relative importance of public and private higher education within the OECD area. It first examines the role of public and private provision through changes in student enrolments and then focuses on changes in higher education financing from the perspectives of institutions, students and governments.

Chapter 10 (Salmi) explores how higher education could develop in a financially sustainable way in the future. After discussing the main trends likely to impact future higher education financing, it presents the main characteristics of higher education financing today, with emphasis on funding sources and allocation mechanisms. The chapter assesses three scenarios for the future of higher education financing from a sustainability perspective.

Chapter 11 (Lewis) reviews the evolution of higher education quality assurance worldwide. It first examines different quality assurance models and differences in their use across regions. The chapter then reflects on a number of emerging trends with regard to quality assurance approaches and methodology as well as to cross-border quality assurance.

Chapter 1

The New Global Landscape of Nations and Institutions

by

Simon Marginson* and Marijk van der Wende**

This chapter provides a conceptual framework for understanding the dynamics between higher education and globalisation. It then reviews a range of related strategic elements relevant to both countries and higher education institutions. Against this background, the chapter reflects the relative global positions of different higher education systems, with a particular focus on research capacity and performance. The chapter concludes by reflecting on how globalisation is altering the traditional relationship between higher education and national environment.

* Centre for the Study of Higher Education, the University of Melbourne.
** Center for Higher Education Policy Studies (CHEPS), University of Twente, and the Vrije Universiteit Amsterdam.

1.1. Introduction

Higher education systems, policies and institutions are being transformed by globalisation, which is "the widening, deepening and speeding up of worldwide interconnectedness" (Held *et al.*, 1999, p. 2). Higher education was always more internationally open than most sectors because of its immersion in knowledge, which never showed much respect for juridical boundaries. Higher education has now become central to the changes sweeping through OECD and emerging nations, in which worldwide networking and exchange are reshaping social, economic and cultural life. In global knowledge economies, higher education institutions are more important than ever as mediums for a wide range of cross-border relationships and continuous global flows of people, information, knowledge, technologies, products and financial capital. "Not all universities are (particularly) international, but all are subject to the same processes of globalisation – partly as objects, victims even, of these processes, but partly as subjects, or key agents, of globalisation" (Scott, 1998, p. 122). Even as they share in the reinvention of the world around them, higher education institutions, and the policies that produce and support them, are also being reinvented.

A generation ago, international relations were largely marginal to the day-to-day operations of higher education institutions and systems, except in scientific research. Now the growing impact of the global environment is inescapable. In many nations international mobility, global comparison, bench-marking and ranking, and the internationalisation of institutions and systems are key policy themes, and governments and university leaders are preoccupied by strategies of cross-border co-operation and competition. For certain institutions, especially in the English-speaking world, international operations have become the primary mode of development. In Europe, the negotiation of the common Higher Education Area and European Research Area has made explicit the processes whereby a large section of the global higher education environment is being formed. Global research circuits have been wired into the rapidly developing higher education systems of China, Singapore and Korea; and the first two are already players in the global degree markets.

This chapter lays out the multitude of higher education and globalisation issues as follows: Section 1.2 discusses the factors shaping definitions and policy interpretations of globalisation; Sections 1.3 and 1.4 examine the global strategic environment for higher education and the variations between national systems and institutions in experiences of globalisation; finally, Sections 1.5 and 1.6 draw out the meta-policy implications of globalisation in two areas: the partial disembedding of institutions from their national contexts, and the growing role of global public and private goods in education and research.

1.2. Interpretations of globalisation in higher education

In this era globalisation combines economic and cultural change. On one hand globalisation entails the formation of worldwide markets operating in real time in common financial systems, and unprecedented levels of foreign direct investment and cross-border mobility of production. On the other hand it rests on the first worldwide systems of communications, information, knowledge and culture, tending towards a single world community as Marshall McLuhan (1964) predicted.[1] Continuously extending networks based on travel, mobile phones, broad-band Internet and other information and communications technologies (ICTs), are creating new forms of inter-subjective human association, of unprecedented scale and flexibility; spanning cities and nations with varied cultures and levels of economic development;[2] and enable the complex data transfers essential to knowledge-intensive production. It is the processes of communications and information, where the economic and cultural aspects are drawn together, that above all constitute what is new about globalisation; and inclusion/exclusion in relation to ICT networks and knowledge have become a key dividing line in shaping relations of power and inequality (Castells, 2000; Giddens, 2001).

In this chapter the term "globalisation" is designed to be neutral as far as possible and free of ideological baggage or particular national associations. "The widening, deepening and speeding up of worldwide interconnectedness" is here understood as a geo-spatial process of growing inter-dependence and convergence, in which worldwide or pan-regional (for example European) spheres of action are enhanced. This takes different forms and contains many projects. Globalisation can be variously understood as the roll-out of worldwide markets; the globalisation "from below" of environmental, consumer rights and human rights activists; and the exchange of knowledge and cultural artefacts within a common space (Torres and Rhoads, 2006). Hitherto Anglo American economic and cultural contents have tended to dominate, but we can today imagine an increasingly plural environment with American, European, Chinese, Islamic and other globalisations, as illustrated for example by the impact of the Arabic TV network Al-Jazeera. Nevertheless, like any process on-going and incomplete, the fuller possibilities of globalisation are difficult to grasp; and the English-language content of global convergence is more obvious than the convergence itself with its potential for reciprocal forms.

Higher education and globalisation

Higher education is implicated in all the changes related to globalisation. Education and research are key elements in the formation of the global environment, being foundational to knowledge, the take-up of technologies, cross-border association and sustaining complex communities. Though higher education institutions often see themselves as objects of globalisation they are also its agents (Scott, 1998). Research universities are intensively linked within and between the global cities that constitute the major nodes of a networked world (Castells, 2001; McCarney, 2005). Characteristically global cities have a high density of participation in higher education; there is a strong positive correlation between the higher education enrolment ratio of a nation or a region, and its global competitive performance (Bloom, 2005, pp. 23-24). Correspondingly, nations and regions that are relatively decoupled from the globally networked economy are typified by a low density of higher education.

Being deeply immersed in global transformations, higher education is itself being transformed on both sides of the economy/culture symbiosis. Higher education is swept up in global marketisation. It trains the executives and technicians of global businesses; the main student growth is in globally mobile degrees in business studies and computing; the sector is shaped by economic policies undergoing partial global convergence, and the first global university market has emerged.

Even larger changes are happening on the cultural side (*e.g.* Teichler, 2004, p. 23). While higher education may be a second level player in the circuits of capital and direct creation of economic wealth, it is pivotal to research and knowledge, constitutive in language, information and cross-cultural encounters, and has many connections with media and communications. Information and knowledge are highly mobile, readily slipping across borders, so that the cultural sphere of higher education, in which research and information are produced, is actually more globalised than the economic sphere. Above all there is the ever-extending Internet, supporting intellectual goods whose use value far exceeds the cost of their distribution and consumption. Advanced higher education is now unimaginable without it (Smeby and Trondal, 2005, p. 453). The Internet facilitates world wide databases and collaboration between academic faculty, stimulating more face-to-face and electronic meetings. Cross-border e-learning, combining ICTs and teaching, has not displaced existing educational institutions as some expected but continues to grow, with open potential for new kinds of pedagogy and access (OECD, 2005b).

At the same time, globalisation in higher education is *not* a single or universal phenomenon; it plays out very differently according to the type of institution. While it is no longer possible for nations or for individual higher education institutions to completely seal themselves off from global effects, research-intensive universities, and the smaller number of vocational universities organised as global international businesses, tend to be the most implicated in globalisation. Likewise, nor is every national system engaged with every other to the same extent or intensity. Globalisation can also vary according to policy, governance and management. Nations, and institutions, have space in which to pilot their own global engagement. But this self-determination operates within limits, that constrain some nations and institutions more than others, and complete abstention by national systems of higher education is no longer a strategic choice.

A good example of the globalisation process lies in the spread of new public management (NMP) in higher education. In nations throughout the world the responses of systems and institutions to globalisation have been conditioned by on-going reforms to national systems, and related reforms in the organisation and management of the institutions themselves, that draw on the techniques of the new public management.[3] In the last two decades these reforms have been the strongest single driver of change in many countries.

The new public management tends towards universality in the United Kingdom, Australia and New Zealand, in much of eastern Europe and Asia, and in parts of the developing world. In developed nations and the relatively robust policy systems of emerging nations such as China, Singapore and Malaysia, the reforms are often motivated by desires for global competitiveness but generated from within the nation. The new public management has been applied less completely in western Europe and North America. But it has influence everywhere. Numerous studies attest to its impact (Marginson and Considine, 2000). For example Musselin (2005) finds that in Europe, universities are moving away from the Humboldt model in which the idea of the university was more important than the material linkages between its components. Institutional regulation is becoming stronger and professional regulation weaker. Closer managerial control is associated with tensions between faculty links to the institution and faculty responsiveness to the global discipline (Musselin, 2005, pp. 147-49). In many European nations "higher education institutions are more and more involved in the management of their faculty staff, developing new tools and making decisions about position creations, suppression or transformations: their intervention in faculty careers is more and more frequent" (p. 143). Performance reporting and assessment cements a "stronger link between each academic and his/her institution" (p. 145). Academic self-regulation is partly preserved but overall faculty autonomy is reduced and "they must cope with 'external' constraints" (p. 146).

Globalisation is much more than a phenomenon encompassing markets and competition between institutions and between nations. Yet, while the new public management and marketisation (Marginson, 1997) are not reducible to a function of globalisation *per se*, in important ways reforms based on new public management have become generatively joined to a particular kind of globalisation. The transmission of reform templates is global in scale, and has rendered the different national systems more similar to each other in form and organisational language. One justification for reform is that competition, performance funding and transparency render institutions and systems more prepared for the global challenge. In the United Kingdom, Australia and New Zealand the new public management has undoubtedly facilitated an entrepreneurial, revenue-directed approach to cross-border relations. The new public management reforms have also facilitated the spread of selected Anglo-American practices elsewhere. For example, the academic profession in the United States is undergoing the partial replacement of tenured labour by part-time teaching and non-faculty functions (Rhoades, 1998; Altbach, 2005, pp. 152-53; AAUP, 2009). The same trend is observable elsewhere (Enders and Musselin, 2008) and can to some extent be attributed to the imitation of a dominant model.

However, because the new public management is nationally nuanced and nationally controlled its implications for globalisation, and globalisation's implications for it, vary from nation to nation, much as do the implications of globalisation itself. Nations use the new public management reform template selectively, filtering it through their own history and mechanisms. For example Finland has adopted institutional devolution, quasi-market competition in the system, and performance-managed staffing (Valimaa, 2004b, p. 118). It is focused on global research excellence and performance and compares the performance of its universities with those of other nations (Valimaa, 2005, p. 9). But the Finnish state "is not willing to relinquish its authority and power upwards or downwards" (p. 8), and there is little brain drain. Perhaps it is Finland's unique language, and its distinctive social policy tradition, that provides partial cultural insulation from global effects. In the Nordic countries, moves to greater internal system differentiation have relatively modest implications, playing out as they do in the context of strong egalitarian traditions in small systems (Valimaa, 2004a; Valimaa, 2005, p. 11). Nevertheless, in the Nordic nations as elsewhere, the new public management is associated with some loosening of traditional academic practices and a stronger executive steering capacity. This has facilitated a quickened global engagement, and routed some cross-border activity via institutions as institutions rather than their several academic faculty.

"Globalisation" and "internationalisation"

In this chapter "internationalisation" is understood in the literal sense, as inter-national. The term refers to any relationship across borders between nations, or between single institutions situated within different national systems. This contrasts with globalisation, the processes of worldwide engagement and convergence associated with the growing role of global systems that criss-cross many national borders. Internationalisation can involve as few as two units, whereas globalisation takes in many nations and is a dynamic process drawing the local, national and global dimensions more closely together (Marginson and Rhoades, 2002). Globalisation is more obviously transformative than internationalisation. Globalisation goes directly to the communication hubs and to the economic, cultural and political core of nations; remaking the heartlands where national and local identities are formed and reproduced; while also refashioning the larger higher education environment across and between the nations. Internationalisation is an older, more limited practice. It assumes that societies defined as nation-states continue to function as bounded economic, social and cultural systems even when they become more interconnected. "Conceptually, internationalisation was for a long time mainly seen as concentrating on the cross-border mobility of individual students and scholars and not as a strategy that affected higher education institutions or systems" (van der Wende, 2001, p. 432). Internationalisation allows scholars to selectively appropriate what they will from other realms without placing their own identities in question (Teichler, 2004, p. 11). Internationalisation in this sense takes place in the borderlands between nations and leaves the heart of those nations largely untouched. In contrast globalisation has a fecund potential to remake the daily practices of people working in higher education, expressed mostly in the research universities and in the most globalised areas such as research, science, policy and executive leadership.

Globalisation cannot be regarded simply as a higher form of internationalisation. Scott (1998) suggests that globalisation transcends national identities and carries the potential to be actively hostile to nation-states. In some respects globalisation in higher education is an alternative to the old internationalisation, even a rival to it. Yet they do not necessarily exclude each other. Internationalisation is by no means obsolete and it continues and multiplies greatly in a more global age. It is fostered within inter-dependent global systems and encourages their extension and development. Much of what begins as internationalisation has implications for globalisation, and adds to the accumulation of challenges to national policy autarky. One difference between globalisation and internationalisation is whether national systems become more *integrated* as suggested by globalisation, or more *interconnected* as with internationalisation (Beerkens, 2004). But thickening connections readily spill over into the evolution of common systems.

A case in point is Europeanisation in higher education. It has one set of origins in the growth of international mobility of people and ideas; another set of origins in the international co-operation between EU countries in their economic, social and cultural activities; and a third set of origins in the explicit commitment to a common European higher education zone in order to facilitate such international activities within Europe. At the same time international co-operation in higher education is expected to enhance the global competitiveness of Europe as a whole (van der Wende, 2004). This might appear to leave unchallenged the role of nation states, their control over higher education systems, and nation-centred assumptions about the public good role of higher education. But reality has become more complex. Competition in higher education and research is starting to play a more important role within the EU; and some elements of the Bologna and Lisbon processes, reinforced by supra-national political mechanisms such as the EU itself, constitute a partial integration across European nations. It is becoming difficult to distinguish between the notions of "interconnectedness" (the inter-governmentalist view) and "integration" (the supra-nationalist view). As the inter-governmentalist sees it, the multilateral Bologna countries participate for their own benefit and remain in full control, although larger countries may hold stronger and more influential positions in the process. As the supra-nationalist sees it, the Bologna Process is about spill-overs and collective goods facilitated by the common system architecture, such as common degree structures. Just as the growth of cross-border trade within Europe has fed economic integration, constituting a form of globalisation (Fligstein and Merand, 2002) so it is in higher education. Though member states remain distinguishable entities, Europeanisation implies a gradual de-nationalisation and integration of certain regulatory systems (Beerkens, 2004). Europeanisation in higher education, which began in internationalisation and continues to be sustained by it, has led to a form of globalisation on a regional scale with consequences yet to be fully manifest. Trends to internationalisation and to globalisation continually reinforce each other.

This suggests that instead of the relationship between globalisation and internationalisation being mutually exclusive, linear or cumulative; it is better understood as dialectical. Arguably the dialectic between the two different kinds of cross-border relations, international and global, is foundational to the contemporary university as an institution. The university was originally normed by pan-European mobility and scholarly Latin; that is, by global forms and relationships. Today worldwide disciplinary networks often constitute stronger academic identities than do domestic locations (Kaulisch and Enders 2005, p. 132). But from the beginning, each university was also locally idiosyncratic and was open to other powers; and in the 19th and 20th centuries higher education became a primary instrument of nation-building and population management (Scott, 1998). Today higher education is subject to national culture and government, while it is also imagined as a primary instrument of the "competition state" in the global setting (Beerkens, 2004), and is drawn haphazardly into the formal and informal processes of globalisation.

Conclusions on interpretations of globalisation

The new public management has helped to frame the context of globalisation in higher education, in shaping and colouring the growing convergences between national systems, but there remains considerable scope for national and institutional variations in organisational techniques, to achieve local and international policy objectives. Globalisation and internationalisation in higher education are potentially conflicting, while at the same time interactive and mutually generative. For example in higher education policy, one possible response to the globalisation of societies, cultures, economies and labour markets is to take measures encouraging a more controlled internationalisation of higher education, rendering institutions more effective in response to the global challenge; as by definition, internationalisation is a process more readily steerable by governments than is globalisation. By the same token, single governments have only a partial purchase on global developments through the medium of internationalisation. This poses policy questions about the multi-lateral ordering of higher education, and highlights the strategic importance of regional forms of association as in Europe.

1.3. Mapping the global environment of nations and institutions

National higher education systems and institutions across the world do not experience global flows and relationships in a uniform, even, consistent or entirely predictable manner. Nations and institutions have varying potentials to absorb, modify and resist global elements at home and to engage and act across borders in a global setting which affects them in different ways. Vaira (2004) discusses the filtering of global effects in national higher education systems. Douglas (2005) makes the point that "all globalisation is local" in that global convergences are subject to local, sub-national and national influences and countervailing forces, including governmental regulation and academic cultures. Hence the effects of globalisation are also differentiated by institutional type. Accordingly, national policy makers and the executive leaders of institutions now face a complex strategic environment. They pursue their own pathways, articulated through national tradition and open to their own strategy making, yet they no longer have full command over their destinies. A base level of global flows and forces in higher education is inescapable. Some impact institutions directly, others are mediated. The old policy-making circuit linking national/state government to institution has been partly broken open. Institutions and nations vary in the extent to which they are engaged with and open to global flows. Again, the extent of engagement is partly (but only partly) under their control. Nevertheless, the nation remains the major influence in the sector. International agencies play a minor role, multilateral negotiation in higher education is still unusual except in Europe, and a single worldwide policy setting in higher education is a distant prospect.

Global transformations

In higher education there are three kinds of potential global transformation, with varying implications for nation-states and for government/institution relations:

1. *Integrationist global transformation.* Global processes of an integrationist type that are distinct from national ones, that once established are difficult for national agents to block or modify, for example the development of Internet publishing; the formation of a global market in high value scientific labour, distinguishable from and to some extent over-determining the separate national labour markets.

2. *Nationally-convergent global transformation.* Global systems and relationships that engender a pattern of common changes in national higher education systems, leading again towards convergence and integration. Examples include the use of English as the language of academic exchange, and the convergence of approaches to PhD training. The question here is not just whether cross-border effects are manifest at the national level but whether these effects lead to global homogenisation.

3. *Nationally-parallel global transformation.* Parallel reforms by the different autonomous national governments, again, following common ideas and templates, which tend to produce some convergence and also facilitate inter-connectivity between different national higher education systems. One example is the selective changes inspired by the templates of the new public management, though as noted there is much scope for national and local nuancing. Note that this cross border "parallelisation" is facilitated by homogeneity in a national system and retarded by intra-system diversity.[4]

Changes generated under national auspices, nationally-parallel transformations, can lead to a tipping point that facilitates global integrationist or nationally-convergent transformations. Likewise nationally-convergent transformations can establish favourable conditions for integrationist transformations. Europeanisation, combining some integrationist and more nationally-parallel transformations, is opening higher education to larger changes than originally envisaged, as the element of convergence seems to be increasing over time.

Global "relativisation"

Integrationist and nationally-convergent transformations suggest globalisation has "relativised" nations and higher education institutions (Waters, 1995). They are referenced to the requirements and measures of informal global standards facilitated by worldwide publication and by the uneven tendencies to convergence and harmonisation in degree structures, recognition and quality assurance. International trade and market competition, for example in the education of foreign students and online programmes (OECD, 2004a; 2005b), encourages cross-border comparison between systems and institutions. International benchmarking of institutions and disciplines is ubiquitous. Performance counts in research and global university rankings take global relativisation further and centre it at the institutional level. In each nation governments, media and public are fascinated by the comparative global performance of "their" institutions, which becomes treated as a matter of significant national interest. But in locating institutions this way, government and public are complicit in modelling higher education as a worldwide competition of individual institutions in which differences in national context and potential are obscured. This model has a material grounding in a networked world in which the larger institutions in each nation have discrete websites, and direct faculty-to-faculty and leader-to-leader relationships, as expressed in messaging, knowledge transfers, trade and people mobility, have moved partly beyond the ken and control of national regulation. In this domain global integrationist transformations are working their way across the higher education world.

In turn this has transformative implications for relations between institutions and government. Nation-states cannot fully comprehend all the cross-border linkages of institutions and are unwise to try. As noted, the more autonomous evolution of institutions has been encouraged also by corporatisation and partial devolution under the auspices of the new public management, characterised by steering from the middle distance and more plural income raising. Some institutions operate relatively independently across borders. Here there is considerable variation by nation, and by institutional type. Research-intensive universities (especially major ones) and private institutions (especially commercial entities) normally enjoy the most global autonomy. Some non-profit institutions become differentiated between a publicly regulated segment at home and their commercial segment abroad (see Section 1.4), magnifying their freedom to operate outside the nation while limiting the wash-back effects at home engendered by global transformation.

The nation still matters

The implications of the partial "disembedding" of institutions from their national locations is explored below. Still, at this time the implications are more in the realm of the potential than the actual. The degree of separation from the nation should not be overstated. The great majority of institutions continue to be nationally embedded and dependent on governmental legitimation and resource support. The nation-state is not fading away: it remains the main site of economic activity. Fligstein (2001) estimates that about 80% of production is nation-bound, and the site of policy making in higher education and other sectors. Most governments devolve, and some deregulate, but none legislate themselves out of higher education. The fact that global economic competition is seen as knowledge-driven has magnified national policy interest in the sector. In most, though not all, nations, government remains the principal financer and the national public sector the main provider, though the role of the private sector is growing (Altbach and Levy, 2006). In some nations the cross-border relations of institutions continue to be largely administered by the national authorities, though this approach may tend to inhibit global responsiveness; and in all nations governments indirectly affect the cross-border dealings of institutions via resource levels and incentives and the frames for communication, co-operation and mobility (Teichler, 2004, p. 21). The concerns of policy makers are to render higher education more competent for the global era, to leverage its benefits for national development, to lift performance and value for money and to devise an appropriate set of steering instruments and behavioural incentives, with balances between competition and co-operation, to achieve these ends.

Recent European studies of the impact of multilateral processes and agreements in higher education confirm the continued autonomy of national policy-making and viability of national steering. Vlk's (2006) findings support the claim that it is still the nation-state, whether directly via domestic policy or by participation in international agreements such as GATS or supranational structures such as the EU, which ultimately decides how the national higher education systems will function; though the increasing interconnectedness of various policy levels, especially in Europe, means that state steering is more complex and driving forces not always so transparent. In a comparison of the Bologna Process in England, France, the Netherlands, and Germany, Witte (2006) found that from 1998 to 2004 there was a weak convergence between the four nations towards the English system. Although the changes leading to convergence all occurred within the framework of the Bologna Process, this does not necessarily mean that they were caused by it. Rather, the Bologna Process often serves to enable, sustain and amplify developments with larger historical momentum or serving particular interests at the national level. This suggests that actors align themselves with the global context and international perceptions when those perceptions are consistent with nationally-grounded preferences. At the same time, the global referencing reflex now inbuilt into higher education mentalities means that when they support national preferences, international perceptions have a considerable legitimating power. Even in cases where those international perceptions are selective and biased, or wrong in fact, they are rarely questioned. In his study of global university consortia Beerkens (2004) finds that despite the high expectations of, and strong focus on, the role of these consortia as entities in their own right, whether they are successful or not seems to be largely defined by the extent to which the institutions concerned are embedded in their national systems. National regulation and requirements might hinder institutions in their global operations, yet the national resource environment and national identity remain vital to them. Likewise a major European study on institutional strategies for internationalisation concludes that:

> Despite all the research demonstrating the growing importance of internationalisation, and even more the rhetoric in this respect, higher education institutions' behaviour (including their internationalisation strategies) are (still) mostly guided by national regulatory and funding frameworks. For internationalisation in particular, historical, geographic, cultural and linguistic aspects of the national framework are of great importance (Luijten-Lub, 2005, p. 239).

Not all higher education institutions are globally active

Likewise the rise of global referencing does not obviate the national identity of institutions. Studies of international student choice-making indicate that except for a small group of institutions, the Harvards, Berkeleys and Oxfords, that are household names in many nations, the national identity of institutions remains more important in determining their reputation than their individual identity (OECD, 2004a, p. 266). The degree of global engagement of institutions should not be overstated either. Research and doctoral training are the quintessential international and global fields and this continually reinforces the global orientation of networked research-intensive universities. But many first degree, sub-degree and vocational training institutions have no active global agenda as such. Though the populations they serve are directly or indirectly affected by global economic and cultural flows, for them their local or sub-national regional mission is a logical strategy within the global setting. On the other hand, not all sub-university institutions confine themselves to local operations. Many North American public community colleges (Levin, 2001) and Australian vocational education and training institutions sell places to international students. Some have established offshore operations in Asian nations. A significant proportion of international training in business studies, computing and English language learning is provided in private commercial non-university institutions.

Global strategy making

Figure 1.1 identifies four distinct but overlapping zones in which strategies and policies are formed, by governments, institutions and both. These are inter-governmental negotiations (quadrant 1 top left), institutions' global dealings (2 top right), national system setting by governments (3 bottom left), and local institutional agendas (4 bottom right).

Figure 1.1. **Four zones of strategy making by nations and higher education institutions**

Two decades ago nearly all the action was in the bottom half of the diagram. That is no longer the case: global strategy making has become important to many nations and institutions. Here they share the global higher education landscape with international and regional agencies, educational corporations, non-government organisations, and other groups and individuals with an active interest in cross-border relationships. Within the global higher education landscape, nations and institutions are both "positioned" and "position-taking" (Bourdieu, 1993). Nations and institutions are positioned by their inherited geographies, histories, economies, polities and cultures, including their education and research systems. In the longer term nations and institutions can augment their global capacity in some of these areas by their own efforts. In the short term they must make do with what they have. Every "position" within the global landscape suggests global "position-taking" moves corresponding to it. Nations with a strong research base can more develop themselves as providers of international doctoral education: high quality vocational institutions in Germany or Finland can readily play an international role in industry training; English-language nations can readily create an education export industry, and so on. Nevertheless, within and beyond these correspondences, there is much scope for imaginative strategy and for capacity building that will open up future strategic options. There are a host of possible networks and other global strategic permutations. Arguably, outcomes are less determined in the global setting, where the possibilities are more open, than the national setting. For example, national institutional hierarchies tend to be fairly stable with little room for upward mobility especially at the top. However second level institutions can build a new role through global production and alliances. In turn these institutions can leverage their global role to elevate their standing in the nation of origin (again indicating how the openness of the global environment has the potential to destabilise inherited certainties).

For governments and globally active institutions, there are two related objectives of global strategy: 1) to maximise capacity and performance within the global landscape, and 2) to optimise the benefits of global flows, linkages and offshore operations back home in the national and local settings. The achievement of these policy objectives depends on a realistic understanding of the global landscape, of the location of nation and institution within it, and of the possibilities for strategy. It also rests on the potential and capacity of system and institutions to operate in cross-border settings, and the degree of effective global engagement. These elements are now considered.

Mapping the global landscape

The global higher education landscape is a relational landscape. Continually moving, it is constituted by two elements: by the pattern of similarities and differences between nations and institutions; and by the cross-border flows of people, messages, knowledge, ideas, technologies and capital between them. For the most part global differences and global flows in higher education can be observed on an empirical basis, though the tools for doing this are only partly developed. *Differences* between nations and institutions are both horizontal and vertical in character. Vertical differences are differences in capacities, resources and status. Horizontal differences are institutional, organisational and systemic differences in kind that in themselves have no necessary implications for hierarchies of power.[5] Under certain historical circumstances horizontal differences have vertical implications, such as the advantages accruing to English-language nations in this era. Some but not all vertical and horizontal differences are calculable, for example in Tables 1.1 and 1.2. Horizontal and vertical differences are significant because they translate into variations in the outcomes from higher education, and the cross-border effects that one nation or institution generates in other nations or institutions. This pattern of differences forms the set of global power relations in higher education. These power relations are determining but not fixed, being open to change over time.

Cross-border *flows* constitute both lines of communication and also lines of influence and effect, which are sometimes but not always mutual in character. Again, the cross-border flows are partly accessible to observation and calculation,[6] though to make sense of these flows they need to be placed in their real world contexts, including the pattern of horizontal and vertical differences. Global flows in higher education are affected by global relations of power. Global traffic often flows in a-reciprocal fashion, benefiting some nations and institutions more than others. For example, strong nations and hegemonic research universities have a gravitational power of attraction, pulling towards them cross-border flows of faculty talent and doctoral students, tuition fees and research and philanthropic funding. In weaker systems global brain circulation becomes a brain drain transferring long-term academic capacity to the strong nations. At the same time, as the fluid metaphor of "flows" suggests (Marginson and Sawir, 2005), cross-border flows are continually undergoing and generating change. Global flows tends to loosen global relations of power; they contribute to the innovative and transformative character of globalisation, and impart to the global higher education landscape a certain openness, dynamism, instability and unpredictability.

Differences in global potential and capacity

As noted, global capacity is a function of both global "position" and of "position-taking" strategies. The capacity of nations and institutions to operate globally depends on both their absolute potential to do so, and the voluntary decisions they take to optimise raw potential as the ability (capacity) to operate globally. Raw national and institutional *potential* in higher education is framed by such elements as the size and wealth of the economy; the systems, resources and techniques of government; cultures and languages; the skills and talents of people; and the inherited educational system itself and its academic cultures including the size and resources of the national system and of institutions, research capacity in the different fields of inquiry. National and institutional *capacity* to operate globally is also shaped by such factors as on-going investment in higher education; the communications infrastructure sustaining global connectivity; the size and shape of research programmes; the qualities of steering instruments, organisational cultures and incentives; the subsidies allocated to cross-border programmes such as research training, academic visits and research collaborations; the entrepreneurial spirit in institutions; the character of institutional autonomy and academic freedom, which are necessary conditions for identifying and maximising the full range of global opportunities. The level and type of national funding is crucial, particularly in basic research which cannot be sustained by market forces and depends on the public funding of academically determined priorities. There is also an element difficult to define and measure but often key to developing imaginative global strategies: the spirit of sympathetic global engagement, a spirit grounded in a strong sense of one's own national identity and institutional project but also characterised by a vigorous curiosity about other cultures and nations and instinctive empathy for their higher education institutions and personnel.

The global implications of national system size and of language of use, especially the global role of English, are discussed below. Meanwhile Table 1.1 (see below) provides a small number of indicators of material global potential and capacity in the OECD nations, in areas open to data gathering. Columns 2 and 3 illustrate the differences in economic resources. In 2006, Gross National Income (GNI) varied from USD 13 195.7 billion in the United States to USD 10.2 billion in Iceland in power purchasing parities (PPPs). Gross National Income per head, a rough measure of wealth intensity within each nation,[7] varied from USD 50 070 in Norway, USD 40 840 in Switzerland and USD 44 070 in the United States[8] to an OECD low of USD 8 410 in Turkey. There is much variation in investment in tertiary educational capacity, from 2.9% of Gross Domestic Product (GDP) in the United States in 2005 to 0.9% in Slovak Republic and Italy. These data show that private sources of funding play a large role in some countries: the United States (1.9% of GDP),

Korea (1.8%), Canada (1.1%), Japan (0.9%), Australia (0.8%) and New Zealand (0.6%). It cannot be assumed that nations with high private investment in tertiary education are either more or less well equipped to engage globally, but high private spending suggests that cross-border relations might be affected by a more plural group of actors.

The differences between nations in the material base are associated also with differences in the competence of school students in mathematics (column 6), though the correlation is loose,[9] and in national research capacity as measured in quantitative terms by the number and intensity of researchers within the population (columns 7 and 8). Research capacity is particularly significant in global terms because of the key role played by research in attracting inward flows of faculty and doctoral students, and underpinning both outward flows of knowledge and ideas, and the ability to make use of knowledge flowing into the country. The United States has more than a third of all researchers in the OECD nations, though its proportion of research degree graduates within the population (1.3%) was in 2005 lower than Switzerland (3.1%), Portugal (2.6%), Germany (2.4%), Sweden (2.2%) and several other nations. Table 1.1 also provides data on China's GNI and the size of its research workforce. On both measures China is now second only to the United States.

Column 9 provides data on the number of broadband subscriptions per 100 persons, in all categories of broadband access. This is one indicator of global connectivity, the capacity for global engagement, as broadband is essential to full utilisation of the Internet. Within the OECD group this ratio varies from a high of 35.1 in Denmark to only 4.3 in Mexico (where the price of broadband is very high). Turkey, Poland, the Slovak Republic and Greece also have relatively low levels of broadband Internet access.

Differences in the level of global engagement

Global *engagement* includes elements such as the short-term and longer-term movement of faculty, students and other personnel in and out of the nation and its individual institutions for educational purposes; the pattern of research collaborations across borders; the volume of messaging and data transfer; the flows of financial capital in the form of investments offshore and revenues for cross-border educational services; and so on. The final two columns of Table 1.1 provide partial data in one of these domains: cross-border student mobility, incorporating foreign students as a proportion of total enrolment (albeit an imperfect measure of mobility because it includes resident foreigners), and the outward movement of student nationals.

There are marked variations between OECD nations in this form of global engagement (Table 1.1). Foreign enrolment exceeds 10% of tertiary students in Luxembourg, New Zealand, Australia, Switzerland, the United Kingdom, Austria, Canada, Belgium, Germany and France but is negligible in Poland, Korea, Turkey, and the Slovak Republic. In 2003, the outward movement of student nationals exceeded 5% in Luxembourg, Iceland, the Slovak Republic, Ireland, Greece, Norway and Austria but was low in the United States, Australia and Mexico. In part this is because these nations do not share in the European mobility schemes. However that is not the full explanation. The English-speaking nations of the United States, the United Kingdom and Australia are relatively attractive to foreign students but have largely one-way student flows with limited external engagement by nationals. Foreign student enrolment is more than ten times the level of outward movement. In the outcome few nations support sizeable student movement each way, with both columns showing more than 4% only in Austria, Norway, Switzerland, Luxembourg and Iceland.

Table 1.1. **Selected indicators of global potential, capacity and engagement, OECD countries and selected other countries**

	Gross National Income (GNI)	Gross National Income (GNI) per head	Share of GDP spent on tertiary education institutions		Mean PISA maths score	Total research persons	Ratio of research degree graduates to total population	Broadband Internet	Foreign tertiary students as share of students	Tertiary students abroad* as share of students
			Public	Private						
	2006	2006	2005	2005	2003	2006	2005	2007	2006	2003
	USD, PPP (billion)	USD, PPP	%	%		FTE	%	Per 100 persons	%	%
United States	13 195.7	44 070	1.0	1.9	483	1 334 628**	1.3	23.3	3.5**	0.2
Japan	4 195.9	32 840	0.5	0.9	534	709 691	0.9	22.1	3.2	1.6
Germany	2 692.3	32 680	0.9	0.2	503	282 063	2.4	23.8	11.4	2.8
United Kingdom	2 037.2	33 650	0.9	0.4	m	183 535	2.0	25.8	17.9	1.2
France	1 974.9	32 240	1.1	0.2	511	192 790**	1.1**	24.6	11.2	2.5
Italy	1 704.9	28 970	0.6	0.3	466	70 332**	1.0	17.2	2.4	2.2
Spain	1 244.2	28 200	0.9	0.2	485	115 798	1.0	18.0	2.9	1.5
Canada	1 184.4	36 280	1.4	1.1	532	112 624**	0.8**	26.6	14.6	m
Korea	1 113.0	22 990	0.6	1.8	542	199 990	1.1	30.5	0.7	2.8
Mexico	1 249.2	11 990	0.9	0.4	385	33 484**	0.1	4.3	m	0.9
Australia	702.5	33 940	0.8	0.8	524	73 344**	1.7	23.3	20.9	0.6
Turkey	61.7	8 410	m	m	423	42 663	0.2	6.0	0.8	2.5
Netherlands	620.0	37 940	1.0	0.3	538	45 852	1.5	34.8	6.1	2.4
Poland	543.4	14 250	1.2	0.4	490	59 573	0.9	8.8	0.5	1.3
Belgium	357.0	33 860	1.2	0.1	529	33 924	1.2	25.7	12.1	3.1
Sweden	311.7	34 310	1.5	0.2	509	55 729	2.2	30.3	9.8	3.6
Austria	298.4	36 040	1.2	0.1	506	30 452	2.0	19.6	15.5	5.5
Greece	344.1	30 870	1.4	n	445	19 907	0.7	9.1	2.5	8.4
Switzerland	305.9	40 840	1.4	m	527	25 400**	3.1	31.0	19.2	4.7
Czech Republic	214.9	20 920	0.8	0.2	516	26 267	1.2	14.6	6.3	2.4
Portugal	211.3	19 960	0.9	0.4	466	20 242**	2.6	14.4	4.6	3.0
Norway	233.3	50 070	1.3	m	495	20 989**	1.2	31.2	6.7	7.1
Denmark	196.7	36 190	1.6	0.1	514	28 653	1.2	35.1	8.4	3.3
Hungary	170.8	16 970	0.9	0.2	490	17 547	0.7	13.6	3.3	2.1
Ireland	148.2	34 730	1.0	0.1	503	12 167	1.2	18.1	m	8.7
Finland	174.7	33 170	1.7	0.1	544	40 411	2.0**	30.7	2.9	3.5
New Zealand	107.7	25 750	0.9	0.6	523	15 568**	1.1	18.3	28.5	3.5
Slovak Republic	92.0	17 060	0.7	0.2	498	11 776	1.3	7.6	0.9	9.1
Luxembourg	28.1	60 870	0.8**	m	493	2 346	m	26.7	42.2	211.6
Iceland	10.2	33 740	1.1	0.1	515	1 917**	0.3	32.2	4.5	22.3
OECD total	–	–	**0.9**	**1.0**	**489**	**3 791 009**	**m**	**20.0**	–	–
Country mean	–	–	**1.1**	**0.4**	**500**	–	**1.3**	–	**9.6**	**4.0**
China	6 119.1	4 660	m	m	m	1 223 756	m	m	m	1.8
India	2 726.3	2 460	0.7	0.2**	m	m	m	m	0.1**	0.9
Brazil	1 647.5	8 700	0.8	m	m	m	1.3	m	m	0.5
Russian Federation	1 814.9	12 740	0.8	m	m	464 357	m	m	0.9	0.3
Indonesia	737.2	3 310	0.3**	0.4**	m	m	m	m	m	1.0
Argentina	456.8	11 670	0.7**	0.4**	m	35 040	m	m	0.2**	0.4
Egypt	366.5	4 940	m	m	m	m	m	m	m	0.3
Malaysia	317.4	12 160	2.7**	0.9**	m	m	m	m	4.4**	6.5
Chile	185.6	11 300	0.3***	1.5***	m	m	m	m	0.3**	1.1
Israel	168.1	23 840	1.0	0.9	m	m	1.3	m	m	3.3

m = missing data
* Students enrolled in countries that report to the OECD (the OECD members plus selected comparators, which include China, India and Indonesia).
** Earlier year used
*** Year of reference 2006

Sources: OECD (2005a, 2005d, 2006a, 2007a, 2007b, 2008a and 2008c); World Bank (2006 and 2008).

Conclusions on mapping the global environment of nations and institutions

Globalisation in higher education is articulated in national and local contexts and is highly variable. The nation-state remains the site of policy making and is essential to the global capacity of non-profit institutions. At the same time globalisation has relativised the national and local settings: in an open information environment and global research system, some global effects are inevitable; and global comparisons and connections are now essential to national governments and research-intensive universities (though not to all other institutions). Here there is a disjunction between on one hand the worldwide character of cultural and economic relations, with instant mobility of messages and data, and the greater (albeit variable) ease of movement of people, institutions and programmes; and on the other hand the predominantly national character of policy and governance, and the nationally shaped academic labour markets and career structures (Enders and de Weert, 2004a, 2004b; Musselin, 2005). There is a "jurisdictional gap", a "discrepancy between a globalised world and national, separate units of policy making" (Kaul *et al.*, 1999, p. xxvi). One effect of this jurisdictional gap is to restrict the policy imagination. It is perhaps not surprising that nation-bound policy agencies have failed to compile all the data needed to understand cross-border differences, flows and effects in global higher education (Kelo *et al.*, 2006; Marginson, forthcoming A), though mapping the global landscape on a comprehensive basis would greatly assist national policy makers and institutions.

1.4. Global power relations in higher education and research

Global English

Many students from non-English-speaking nations want to acquire English and degrees from English-speaking systems, while comparatively few English-speaking students want to acquire other languages and degrees from non-English-speaking nations. The driver here is the vertical patterning of language and degree status. English is the premier language of business and the professions and the only global language of science, research and academic publication. The erstwhile worldwide roles of Latin, French, German and Russian have declined. French remains important in Francophone Africa, and German continues to be widely known in Central Europe and relatively well known in university circles in Japan; Arabic is a common medium of academic discussion in many nations; and Spanish an important regional language in Central and South America with a growing importance in the United States; nevertheless, in an increasing number of institutions throughout the world faculty have formal or informal incentives to publish in English-speaking journals. "It is English that stands at the very centre of the global knowledge system. It has become the *lingua franca par excellence* and continues to entrench that dominance in a self-reinforcing process" (Held *et al.*, 1999, p. 346; Crystal, 2003). The global academic role of English is as much driven by the weight of the Anglo-American bloc within the world economy, the cultural industries and the Internet, as by specific developments in higher education. The special status of English extends beyond the language itself to the works generated in it. Books prepared originally in English are much more likely to be translated into other languages than the other way round (Held *et al.*, 1999, p. 346).

Because knowledge conceived and discussed in English enjoys a privileged status *vis-à-vis* all other knowledge, much academic work of great social and scientific importance, originating in languages other than English, is excluded from the common global knowledge circuits, with incalculable consequences for economic and social development and for human rights. This is especially serious in relation to the study of society and the humanities, given the global impacts of works in French, German and Spanish (to name only three European languages) in the modern era alone.

English is also spreading as a medium of instruction in non English-speaking nations, particularly in programmes designed to attract foreign students. It is widely used in India and the Philippines, and in Singapore and Hong Kong (China), which have close historical links with English-speaking nations. In Malaysia, English has been reintroduced in the school sector and is dominant in the growing private tertiary college sector. It is also in growing use as a medium of instruction in the education export industry in China. Within Europe, English is increasingly used as the language of instruction in selected programmes, especially at Masters level and those targeting students from Asia. Nations where English is widely used include the Netherlands, Finland, Iceland, Sweden and Denmark, and also Singapore and Hong Kong China. German institutions are also extending the facility to prepare doctoral theses in English, and Japan provides about 80 English language programmes (OECD, 2005a, p. 255), but the spread of English as a medium of instruction and/or examination is more significant in the smaller European nations. As a second language English is much more widely used throughout the academic world. For example a survey of 1998-99 ERASMUS teachers and coordinators found that almost 90% of those from non-English-speaking countries spoke English; while the second language, French, was spoken by less than half of the respondents (Enders and Teichler 2005, p. 101). The second language use of English provides the benefits of a common global language without the cultural lacunae. At the same time English is itself becoming more diverse, with distinctive "Englishes" inflected by local language and culture, especially in Asian nations, though whether this finds its way into the research literature remains to be seen.

At this point in history, national and institutional capacity in English, especially in the sciences, is essential to global effectiveness in higher education. But the dominance of English is not guaranteed forever. As Table 1.2 shows, English is only one of the languages spoken by one billion people; the other is Putonghua ("Mandarin" Chinese). Two pairings of related and mutually intelligible languages are spoken by more than half a billion people: Hindi/Urdu, and Spanish/Portuguese. Another three languages are spoken by over 200 million people: Russian, Arabic and Bengali. Another four languages have more than 100 million speakers. These languages are too large to disappear. From this perspective, providing that China develops Putonghua as a language of scientific research it could become globally significant. Another possibility lies in the accumulation of China's economic role. It may be that Putonghua becomes used widely as a medium of transactions in many fields. In this case it could well become a normal part of higher education for students all over the world, enhancing its potential as a vehicle for common knowledge.

In addition to the number of speakers, the geographic spread or concentration of a language across countries may be important to its global significance. In that respect, Spanish, Arabic or French may have more assets than Putonghua, Hindi or Urdu to reach global significance. If regionalisation looms larger, some world regions (Latin America, nations using Arabic, and Francophone Africa) may assume a distinctive linguistic base, with one other language being used alongside English as a medium of exchange and

Table 1.2. **Spoken languages with more than 100 million voices worldwide**

Language/language group	Number of voices (millions)
English	1 000
Putonghua ("Mandarin")	1 000
Hindi/Urdu	900
Spanish/Portuguese	450/200
Russian	320
Arabic	250
Bengali	250
Malay-Indonesian	160
Japanese	130
French	125
German	125

Source: Linguasphere Observatory (2006).

marker of identity. It is possible also that English will stay dominant in the sciences while greater global plurality is maintained in the social sciences and humanities.

An Americanised global sector?

The most striking vertical difference in the global landscape is the special and hegemonic role played by American higher education, led by the powerful American doctoral sector. The United States constitutes 17 of the world's top 20 research universities in terms of research performance, and 53% of the top 100 (SJTUIHE, 2007) and draws and holds talented doctoral students, postdoctoral researchers and established faculty from everywhere. The norms diffusing from the United States to the global field reflect a distinctive American approach to competition and social markets in higher education: a high fee high aid mixed public/private system segmented by institutional type in which the public sector commands three quarters of enrolments but non-profit and for-profit private sector models are important. American tradition is different to that of the other English-speaking nations but in the last two decades changes in system-organisation and financing have brought Australia, New Zealand and the United Kingdom closer to United States' practice. To worldwide American power in the research universities is joined the secondary global role of the United Kingdom, especially through Oxford, Cambridge and the rest of the Russell Group of universities and through continued British authority in matters of culture, language and in developing governmental techniques.[10] In this context, for many in higher education around the world, globalisation appears as an American or Anglo-American process (Altbach, 2006; Rhoads and Torres, 2006), especially in the research university domain where in many ways national identity is shaped.

The concentration of research, resources and prestige in major universities constitutes institutions of key importance in their nations and powerful engines of globalisation on the world scale. The research performance of universities signifies their capacity to produce global knowledge goods and their status in the eyes of other institutions, prospective students and financial capital. The research performance of nations underpins their flexibility and innovative capability as networked global economies and helps them to attract highly skilled migrants, helping to determine the direction, volume and intensity of people flows in the global environment. Every nation wants strong research universities. Every research university wants to boost its reputation. All are focused on policies to elevate capacity and performance.

The comprehensive research-intensive university evolved in western Europe, the United Kingdom and the British foundations including those in North America. Combining teaching functions with research and scholarly activities, often though not always carried out by the same personnel, it has become globally hegemonic as the most powerful and imitated form of higher education, though there are many other models of university, of higher education and of research organisation (Marginson and Ordorika, 2007). The most prestigious universities concentrate research activities on a large scale. Research and doctoral training are also the most globalised higher education activities, particularly in the scientific disciplines which have long functioned on a worldwide basis. The research standing of institutions is a key marker in the global higher education landscape, more so since the advent of global research rankings in 2003. To the public and policy-makers global higher education often appears as a global market of research-intensive universities, in which the map of producers is highly stratified and institutions from the United States are dominant. Though in reality, only a small proportion of worldwide higher education institutions falls within this description. Research and scholarly activities are both collaborative and competitive, and innovative (even iconoclastic) as well as authoritative. Global comparisons of measured research performance, especially when the unit of measurement is the whole institution rather than the discipline, tend to strengthen the element of competition and the status of the established institutions. It is a radical over-simplification of higher education, but no less influential for that, and reflects an important reality of the sector.

The Shanghai Jiao Tong University Institute of Higher Education (SJTUIHE) has published annual data comparing research in the world's 500 leading universities since 2003. The SJTUIHE data comprise Nobel Prizes, Fields Medals in Mathematics, measures of publication in global journals, citations, the number of high citation ("HiCi") researchers located in the top 250-300 persons in each scientific field as classified by the Thomson ISI database, and per faculty output. In 2005, American research universities housed 4 031 of the HiCi researchers, compared to 260 in Germany, 258 in Japan, 185 in Canada, 159 in France, 113 in Switzerland, 111 in Australia, 61 in Sweden, 21 in China, 11 in India and none for example in Indonesia (ISI, 2008). The SJTUIHE data, illustrated in Table 1.3, show that the United States enjoys a global role in terms of institutional power that far exceeds its share of scientific output and unlike the latter shows no sign of relative decline. In 2007 the United States housed 54 of the SJTIHE world's top 100 research universities, led by Harvard. The United Kingdom provides the University of Cambridge at number two and is the second strongest nation with eleven of the top 100. With Canada (four) and Australia (two) the English-speaking nations constitute 71% of this group. A further 22 are in western Europe, six in Japan and one in each of Israel and Russia.[11] Leading European nations are Germany (six), France and Sweden (four each) and Switzerland (three) and the Netherlands (two). China and India have none of the top 100. China including Hong Kong has 25 of the top 500; five are in Chinese Taipei. India has just two of the top 500.[12]

Table 1.3 also maps each nation's share of global economic capacity against its share of the SJTUIHE 2007 top 100 and top 500 research universities. National economic capacity is calculated by multiplying Gross National Income with Gross National Income per head, thereby taking into account both quantitative economic weight and the intensity of wealth. Each nation's share of global economic capacity is calculated by comparing its national

Table 1.3. **Countries' share of the top 500 and 100 research universities as measured by Shanghai Jiao Tong University, compared to their share of world economic capacity**

	Gross National Income (GNI)	Population	Gross National Income (GNI) per head	Share of world economic capacity	Share of top 500 research universities	Share of top 100 research universities
	2006	2006	2006	2006	2007	2007
	USD, PPP (billion)	Millions	USD, PPP	%	%	%
United States	13 195.7	299.4	44 070	41.1	32.9	53.5
United Kingdom	2 037.2	60.6	33 650	4.8	8.3	10.9
Germany	2 692.3	82.4	32 680	6.2	7.9	5.9
Japan	4 195.9	127.8	32 840	9.7	6.5	5.9
Canada	1 184.4	32.6	36 280	3.0	4.4	4.0
France	1 974.9	61.3	32 240	4.5	4.6	4.0
Sweden	311.7	9.1	34 310	0.8	2.2	4.0
Switzerland	305.9	7.5	40 840	0.9	1.6	3.0
Australia	702.5	20.7	33 940	1.7	3.4	2.0
Netherlands	620.0	16.3	37 940	1.7	2.4	2.0
Italy	1 704.9	58.8	28 970	3.5	4.0	0.0
Israel	168.1	7.0	23 840	0.3	1.4	1.0
Austria	298.4	8.3	36 040	0.8	1.4	0.0
Finland	174.7	5.3	33 170	0.4	1.0	1.0
Denmark	196.7	5.4	36 190	0.5	0.8	1.0
Norway	233.3	4.7	50 070	0.8	0.8	1.0
Russian Federation	1 814.9	142.5	12 740	1.6	0.4	1.0
China*	6 119.1	1 311.8	4 660	2.0	2.8	0.0
Spain	1 244.2	44.1	28 200	2.5	1.8	0.0
Korea	1 113.0	48.4	22 990	1.8	1.6	0.0
Belgium	357	10.5	33 860	0.9	1.4	0.0
China Hong Kong	268.9	6.9	39 200	0.7	1.0	0.0
Chinese Taipei	x	x	x	0.0	1.2	0.0
New Zealand	107.7	4.2	25 750	0.2	1.0	0.0
Brazil	1 647.5	189.3	8 700	1.0	1.0	0.0
South Africa	421.7	47.4	8 900	0.3	0.8	0.0
India	2 726.3	1 109.8	2 460	0.5	0.4	0.0
Ireland	148.2	4.3	34 730	0.4	0.6	0.0
Poland	543.4	38.1	14 250	0.5	0.4	0.0
Singapore	194.1	4.5	43 300	0.6	0.0	0.0
Hungary	170.8	10.1	16 970	0.2	0.4	0.0
Turkey	61.7	73.0	8 410	0.0	0.2	0.0
Greece	344.1	11.1	30 870	0.8	0.4	0.0
Mexico	1 249.2	104.2	11 990	1.1	0.2	0.0
Argentina	456.8	39.1	11 670	0.4	0.2	0.0
Chile	185.6	16.4	11 300	0.1	0.4	0.0
Czech Republic	214.9	10.3	20 920	0.3	0.2	0.0
Portugal	211.3	10.6	19 960	0.3	0.4	0.0
All other nations**	10 613.0	2 494.3	4 255	3.2	0.0	0.0
World total	**60 209.9**	**6 538.1**	**9 209**	**100.0**	**100.0**	**100.0**

x = included in another row.
*   China Hong Kong is listed separately.
**   Population and GNI data include Chinese Taipei.
    World economic capacity is measured as an aggregate of the individual nations' economic capacity, defined as GNI multiplied by GNI per head. All nations without any top 500 research universities are treated as one unit.

Source: World Bank (2008); SJTUIHE (2007).

economic capacity to the global total. The nations whose university systems are above average performers in research terms, relative to national economic capacity are Israel, Sweden, Switzerland, the United Kingdom, the Netherlands, Canada, Finland, Denmark, Australia, Norway, the United Kingdom and the United States. In nearly all cases, superior national performance relative to economic capacity is correlated to relatively high public investment in research in higher education. Further, except in the United States, the private sector plays a relatively minor role in the nations in the high performance group, while several nations that underperform relative to economic capacity have large private sectors and a highly stratified research effort, including Japan, Korea, Poland, Brazil and Mexico. This underlines the dependence of research capacity on public investment.

The United States performs very well in its share of the top 100 research universities but underperforms in its share of the top 500, suggesting that resources and status have been concentrated in globally leading research universities, possibly at the expense of the potential of regional knowledge economies. Germany does well in its share of the top 500, indicating a broad-based research capacity across the national system, but not so well in its share of the top 100 research universities relative to economic capacity. Japan underperforms at both levels. The Americanisation in higher education may thus be driven by a small segment of the United States system and does not necessarily reflect its average performance.

It is noteworthy that there are no lines of policy accountability for "Americanisation". It is not managed by the United States government. It is constituted by the sum of the on-going cross-border dealings of American institutions and faculty, interacting as they do with institutions and personnel in other nations. American global engagement in higher education, underpinned by material power and cultural authority and the sense of right project they bring, mixing profit-taking with gratuitousness and gift economy, generates in other nations a mix of admiration, opportunism and resentment. Like Europeanisation, Americanisation has global effects. However, unlike Europeanisation, Americanisation it is not an explicitly political process.

The United States as a magnet for talented researchers

The effects of Americanisation can be a policy matter for some non-United States governments to consider. For them the key problem is often that Americanisation is sustained by highly unbalanced global flows of people and cultural transfer. The United States is an overwhelming "brain-gainer" in relation to the rest of the world, whereas most other nations face a net loss of research personnel to the United States. There is high foreign mobility into the United States' research system at every stage: doctoral training, postdoctoral posts and established faculty involved in both short-term visits and longer-term migration into the United States. The United States plays a particularly significant global role in drawing researchers from East Asia and South Asia.

American research universities are unique in the extent to which they focus on the doctoral level in recruiting foreign students. Whereas in 2006, just 4.2% of international students in Australia and 11.6% of those in the United Kingdom were doctoral students, in the United States in 2006, 15.7% of all international students in higher education were enrolled at doctoral level, and, in 2005, 30.8% in research-intensive universities. Thus whereas in 2006 the United Kingdom had 40 193 foreign students enrolled in advance research programmes, Spain 14 783, Australia 11 988, Switzerland 7 626 and Sweden 4 414, in 2005 the American doctoral sector enrolled 102 084 foreign doctoral students. Three quarters of the foreign doctoral students in the United States receive scholarships or other subsidies, mostly from their American universities, which is not the case in other countries (OECD, 2007a; IIE, 2007; *OECD Education Database*). As in many other nations,[13] the proportion of doctoral graduates who are foreign-born has grown. Between 1977 and 1997 the foreign share of American PhDs rose from 13.5 to 28.3%. In mathematics and computer science it rose from 20.2 to 43.9%, in engineering from 32.1 to 45.8% (Guellec and Cervantes, 2002, pp. 77-78). In 2006, the share of international students graduating from advanced research programmes was 28% in the United States (OECD, 2008c).

During their studies foreign students make a key contribution to American universities as research and/or graduate teaching assistants. And growth in the foreign student proportion of American PhDs has been matched by their propensity to stay. From 1987 to 2001 the stay rate for foreign doctoral graduates rose from 49 to 71% (OECD, 2004c, p. 159).[14] Though not all work in higher education, between 1975 and 2001 there was a sharp rise in foreign born with United States doctoral degrees as a proportion of faculty labour, from 12 to 21% (NSB, 2006, p. A5-45).

At the postdoctoral stage the United States offers the majority of posts worldwide. Whereas recent studies in Europe suggest that postdoctoral mobility is stable (Enders and de Weert, 2004a, pp. 146-47) in the United States a high and increasing proportion of postdoctoral personnel holding United States doctoral degree are foreign born: 41% in 2001 compared to 21% in 1985 (NSB, 2006, p. A5-47). The United States followed by the United Kingdom also draws the largest number of visiting faculty. Between 1994-95 and 2004-05 international scholarly visitors to the United States rose from 59 981 to 89 634, by 49.0% (IIE, 2006),[15] two-thirds of them in science and engineering. For most OECD countries two to four scholars and researchers hold positions in the United States for every 100 at home. In 2003-04 the ratio of visiting scholars to those at home was highest for Korea (13 per 100) and the Russian Federation (8). Between 1995 and 2004 the number of visiting scholars rose by annual rates of 9% from Korea, 6% from India and 4% from China (OECD, 2006b, p. 30).

The advantage of the United States in global doctoral and postdoctoral markets creates many long term benefits for the United States. For example between 1985 and 1996 the number of foreign students primarily supported as research assistants rose from 2000 to 7600 (Guellec and Cervantes, 2002, p. 89). About half the foreign doctoral graduates stay in the United States after graduation, many in faculty positions, augmenting the capacity of the United States as a global knowledge economy. Other doctoral graduates return to their nations of origin, making their countries of origin benefit of their newly acquired knowledge (OECD, 2006a), or migrate elsewhere, but also probably carrying with them some degree of commitment to American norms in higher education. Many eventually find themselves in positions of governmental or institutional leadership, no doubt easing global nationally-parallel transformations whereby nations implement different and parallel reforms following common ideas and templates. Also, with regard to academic profession in particular, for example the 1992 Carnegie survey of the academic profession in fourteen nations identified the United States as the main exporter of academic labour, supplying three of the nations surveyed – Hong Kong, Korea and Israel – with more than 18% of their staff (Welch, 2005, pp. 78-79).[16] The outcome is that American knowledge goods and models of higher education and research may have continuous effects in other national systems.

Uneven global knowledge flows

Because research is highly globalised, one of the measures of performance is the extent to which systems and institutions make effective use of cross-border collaboration to accumulate foreign knowledge and researchers at home. Between 1988 and 2005 the annual number of science and engineering articles, which are mostly produced in universities, rose from 466 419 to 709 541. The number of joint patent applications by researchers residing in two different countries doubled between the mid-1980s and mid-1990s (Guellec and Cervantes, 2002, p. 85). Between 1988 and 2001 the incidence of scientific articles published by authors of more than one nationality rose from 8 to 18%.[17] The incidence of citation of foreign articles also increased (Vincent-Lancrin, 2009; Laudel, 2005). A significant proportion of these collaborations are founded on the pairing of American faculty with foreign doctoral students and their growth reflects the expansion of foreign study in the United States. These trends are also sustained by the growing role of disciplinary publications with world reach *via* the Internet, often at the expense of local and national publication in non-English speaking countries (Bensimon and Ordorika, 2006; Marginson, 2007b). There has also been a growth of cross-national research projects and some pluralisation of funding sources across borders.

Some American universities are committed to working with partner universities in emerging nations to build capacity, for example by facilitating access to journals, databases, equipment and research training, partly counter-balancing the brain drain. However, an aid-based approach does not create a reciprocal global engagement. Anglo-American practices are underpinned by a distinctive approach to language and cultural diversity. Anglo-American universities, except in Canada and the indigenous institutions in New Zealand, are more sanguine about mono-cultural and mono-linguistic environments than their counterparts elsewhere (*e.g.* OECD, 2008b). In one sense this is readily explained: given the worldwide dominance of United States and United Kingdom universities in a networked sector, while institutions in other nations have little choice but to acknowledge English-language outputs, English-language institutions do not face an equivalent imperative. But there are also philosophical differences: in the United States and the United Kingdom "diversity" is understood in social rather than cultural terms for example as the access of non dominant groups to higher education. A fuller global diversity is not seen as an essential goal in itself. Daniel Drache and Marc Froese (2005) summarise the differences between Anglo-American and European outlooks as follows:

> The European Union looks to build linkages and networks between state regulatory policy, Brussels and cultural producers. This tripartite approach is difficult at the best of times, but it has been quite effective nonetheless. The European Union is linguistically and socially diverse and its internal stability depends on a pluralistic approach to the global commons. It regards freedom of expression as important to protect as part of its commitment to the social market…. The Anglo-American model is sharply contrasting in its regulatory and market dimensions. It should be noted that despite the fact that Britain is a member of the European Union, its elites share many ideas with their American counterparts. Simply put, this model values diversity as a function of competition and not the other way round. Consumers choose their cultural diet from a buffet of options. And just like many buffets, portion size is more important than quality and breadth (Drache and Froese, 2005, pp. 26-27).

One outcome is that most American institutions are not very globalised except at the point of entry into the research ranks. The Carnegie survey of the academic profession found that whereas more than 90% of scholars from other nations believed that it was necessary to read foreign books and journals, only 62% of American scholars agreed (Altbach, 2005, pp. 148-49). American scholars and students cross borders less than most of their counterparts. Altbach remarks that though American scholars are "at the centre of the world academic system", and this "imposes special responsibilities on them" (p. 150), and despite the fact that American universities are relatively sophisticated in data retrieval technologies with the United States constituting the world's largest single pool of broadband Internet subscribers (Drache and Froese 2005, p. 16), "American academics do not often cite works by scholars in other countries in their research. The American research system is remarkably insular, especially when compared to scientific communities in other countries… The American system accepts scholars and scientists from abroad, but only if they conform to American academic and scientific norms" (Altbach, 2005, p. 149). Though there are many individual exceptions to these generalisations, and though scholarly parochialism is by no means confined to the United States, what makes this pattern of insular globalisation and one way cross-border flows troublesome in many nations is the global weight of American higher education.

In 2005 scientists and social scientists in the United States published a number of papers in recognised international journals accounting almost a third of world output, and the United States "accounted for 41% of citations in the world scientific literature" (Vincent-Lancrin, 2009). In 2005, the volume of the science and engineering papers from the United States was 205 320, while from Japan it was 55 471, the United Kingdom 45 572, Germany 44 145, France 30 309 and Switzerland 8 749. By contrast, in Indonesia, a middle level developing nation with two thirds of the population of the United States, there were 207 papers in 2001. There were 14 608 from India and 41 596 from China (NSF, 2006 and 2008). Table 1.4 has full country data for the OECD nations, plus data for all other nations producing more than 1 000 papers in 2005 and four emerging nations with populations of more than 100 million but little scientific infrastructure.

Improving global research university performance

Longstanding policy means of leveraging international activity to develop national research capacity include scholarships, living allowances and travel support for the doctoral training of nationals abroad, the funding of short-term academic visits and exchanges; academic incentives to publish in leading journals which are now largely English-language journals; and the subsidisation of national researcher participation in cross-border research partnerships, networks and other kinds of collaborative projects.

In doctoral training, it is necessary to maintain a balance between augmenting the intellectual experience of student nationals and the potential for knowledge transfer from other nations via doctoral study and the pattern of longer-term collaborations, and nurturing local research capacity given that in many nations doctoral students are responsible for a large share of the total research effort: for example in Australia in 2004 research students carried out 57.2% of all funded research in higher education (ABS, 2006). The optimum national research system uses a multi-locational approach to doctoral training, concentrating students both at home and in several major locations of research activity abroad. The United Kingdom and a number of western European nations achieve this. Emerging nations face the uphill climb to establish a national research infrastructure

Table 1.4. **Output of published articles in science and engineering (including medicine and social sciences), OECD countries and selected other countries**

	Total population	Published S&E articles		Proportion of total world output of S&E articles		Change in number of articles
	2006	1988	2005	1988	2005	1988-2005
	Millions	Number	Number	%	%	1988 = 100
United States	299.4	177 682	205 320	38.1	28.9	115.6
Japan	127.8	34 435	55 471	7.4	7.8	161.1
United Kingdom	60.6	36 509	45 572	7.8	6.4	124.8
Germany	82.4	29 292	44 145	6.3	6.2	150.7
France	61.3	21 409	30 309	4.6	4.3	141.6
Canada	32.6	21 391	25 836	4.6	3.6	120.8
Italy	58.8	11 229	24 645	2.4	3.5	219.5
Spain	44.1	5 432	18 336	1.2	2.6	337.6
Australia	20.7	9 896	15 957	2.1	2.2	161.2
Netherlands	16.3	8 581	13 885	1.8	2.0	161.8
Korea	48.4	771	16 396	0.2	2.3	2 126.6
Sweden	9.1	7 573	10 012	1.6	1.4	132.2
Switzerland	7.5	5 316	8 749	1.1	1.2	164.6
Belgium	10.5	3 586	6 841	0.8	1.0	190.8
Poland	38.1	4 030	6 844	0.9	1.0	169.8
Finland	5.3	2 789	4 811	0.6	0.7	172.5
Denmark	5.4	3 445	5 040	0.7	0.7	146.3
Austria	8.3	2 241	4 566	0.5	0.6	203.7
Turkey	73.0	507	7 815	0.1	1.1	1 541.4
Greece	11.1	1 239	4 291	0.3	0.5	346.3
Norway	4.7	2 192	3 644	0.5	0.5	166.2
Mexico	104.2	884	3 902	0.2	0.5	441.4
New Zealand	4.2	2 075	2 983	0.4	0.4	143.8
Czech Republic	10.3	2 746	3 169	0.6	0.4	115.4
Hungary	10.1	1 714	2 614	0.4	0.4	152.5
Portugal	10.6	429	2 910	0.1	0.4	678.3
Ireland	4.3	790	2 120	0.2	0.3	268.4
Slovak Republic	5.4	m	955[**]	m	0.1[**]	m
Iceland	0.3	69	174[**]	m	m	252.2
Luxembourg	0.5	m	m	m	m	m
China	1 311.8	4 619	41 596	1.0	5.9	900.5
Russian Federation[*]	142.5	m	14 412	m	2.0	m
India	1 109.8	8 882	14 608	1.9	2.1	164.5
Chinese Taipei	22.8	1 414	10 841	0.3	1.5	766.7
Brazil	189.3	1 766	9 889	0.4	1.4	560.0
Israel	7.0	4 916	6 309	1.1	0.9	128.3
Argentina	39.1	1 423	2 930[**]	0.3	0.5[**]	205.9
Singapore	4.5	410	3 609	0.1	0.5	880.2
South Africa	47.4	2 523	2 392	0.5	0.3	94.8
Chile	16.4	682	1 203[**]	0.1	1.9[**]	176.4
Egypt	74.2	1 130	1 658	0.2	0.2	146.7
Indonesia	223.0	59	207[**]	m	m	350.8
Pakistan	159.0	235	282[**]	0.1	m	120.0
Bangladesh	156.0	95	177[**]	m	m	186.3
Nigeria	144.7	886	332[**]	0.2	0.1[**]	37.5
World total	**6 538.1**	**466 419**	**709 541**	**100.0**	**100.0**	**152.1**

m = missing data

[*] The number of articles from the Russian Federation was 31 625 in 1988, 6.8% of world output. The number of articles from Russia declined from 21 612 (3.8%) in 1994 to 14 412 (2.0%) in 2005.

[**] 2001 instead of 2005

Sources: NSF (2006 and 2008); World Bank (2008).

with depth and breadth sufficient to reproduce national research cadre. Achieving this generates many long term benefits as it augments research capacity in corporations and government agencies as well as universities; while optimising the diversity of inputs into the universities and the national knowledge economy. But returns are slow and the sunk costs appear expensive. The easier course is continued reliance on foreign universities for doctoral places. Arguably Chinese Taipei and Singapore (and before that Korea) have succeeded in moving to a multi-locational system, and China appears likely to do so, whereas Malaysia and Thailand remain overly dependent on foreign training.

The complication however is that research careers are exceptionally global and transferable and national research capacity readily slips through the policy grasp. With the gravitational pull of the research-strong American universities and the vast array of career opportunities that the United States provides for foreign talent, there is no certainty that doctoral students engaged in foreign training will return to the fledgling research system back home. As noted, "brain drain" to the United States is a live policy issue also in many developed nations.

New powers in higher education?

Personnel from American universities have a positive citation balance and a positive revenue balance (OECD, 2004a) with other university systems, just as the American film industry has a positive balance of trade with every other nation in the world. However, there are signs of pluralisation in film that "nobody could have foreseen a few decades ago", as demonstrated for example by the rise of India's Bollywood[18] as well as the animation industry in Japan, film in China and television production in Mexico, Venezuela and Brazil (Drache and Froese, 2005, pp. 7-8 and 24). In film, in both China and India the size and scope of the domestic market provides the platform for a future global role. Likewise, the growing importance of Korea, China and India in research and higher education and the development of the European research area, may herald a more diversified research environment.

As shown in Table 1.5, OECD Europe excluding the United Kingdom published 28.9% of the world's scientific papers in science and engineering in 2005, compared to 41.5% in the English-speaking countries (excluding Ireland). Table 1.4 also compares country outputs in 2005 with those of 1988 and indicates a pattern of pluralisation. Between 1988 and 2005 the number of articles from North America rose by 18% compared to 62% in western Europe and 181% in Asia. In 1999 the total output of scientific papers from western Europe moved

Table 1.5. **Countries in which the number of scientific papers in science and engineering grew particularly sharply between 1988 and 2005**

	1988	2005	Change from 1988-2005 1988 = 100
Korea	771	16 396	2 126.6
Turkey	507	7 815	1 541.4
China*	4 619	41 596	900.5
Singapore	410	3 609	880.2
Portugal	429	2 910	678.3
Brazil	1 766	9 889	560.0
Mexico	884	3 902	441.4

* The number of papers produced in Chinese Taipei increased from 1 414 to 10 841 (766.7).

Source: NSF (2008).

past that of North America. The United States' share of world scientific papers in science and engineering fell from 38.1 to 28.9%[19] (Vincent-Lancrin, 2009, p. 16; NSF, 2006 and 2008).

There has also been a dramatic increase in the number of papers from certain nations including Korea, China, Singapore and Turkey. Between 1988 and 2005 the output of South Korean papers in science and engineering, including social science, increased from 771 to 16 396, from 0.2 to 2.3% of world output. Over the same time papers from China grew from 4 619 (1.0%) to 41 596 (5.9%), Chinese Taipei's share rose from 0.3 to 1.5%, Singapore's share from 0.1 to 0.5% (see Table 1.5).

The emergence of two more national systems on the American scale, as illustrated in Table 1.6, plus the European Higher Education Area, could have profound implications for the worldwide higher education landscape. This may be even more so if the new systems are culturally coherent on a global scale and are major producers of basic research. Emerging economies outside the OECD now produce half of the world's economic wealth. China has 1.3 billion people and GNI of 6 119 billion in USD (PPP) with annual GDP growth rate of 10.7 in 2006. According to some projections, China's GDP will overtake United States PPP GDP by 2015 (Maddison, 2007). In 2003, the rate of Internet use in China was 63 per 1 000 people which is average for "lower middle income" as classified by the World Bank (2006). The same year China had 8.6 million broadband subscribers (Drache and Froese, 2005, p. 16). India has 1.1 billion people and its economy is also growing significantly, with Gross Domestic Product (GDP) growth rate of 9.2 in 2006. In both nations tertiary participation is expanding rapidly: the gross enrolment ratio rose from 3.0% in 1991 to 21.6% in 2006 in China and from 6.1% to 11.8% in India.

Table 1.6. **Selected indicators on selected countries and regions**

				United States	China	India	OECD Europe
Economic capacity	Gross National Income (GNI)	USD PPP (billions)	2006	13 196	6 119	2 726	13 976
	Gross National Income (GNI) per head	USD PPP	2006	44 070	4 660	2 460	25 977
	Annual Gross Domestic Product (GDP) growth	%	2006	2.9	10.7	9.2	4.0*
	Share of GDP spent on tertiary education	%	2006	2.9	m	0.9	1.3*
Demographic capacity	Total population	Millions	2006	299.4	1 311.8	1 109.8	538
	Annual Growth	%	2006	1.0	0.6	1.4	0.7
Participation in higher education	Gross enrolment ratio (GER)	%	2006	81.8	21.6	11.8	63.9*
	Change in GER	(1991 = 100)	1991-2006	111.5	729.1	194.1	207.0*
Research capacity	Research Persons (FTE)	Number	2006	1 334 628	1 223 756	m	1 340 333
	Share of top 500 research universities	%	2007	32.9	2.8	0.4	40.8
	Share of published science and engineering (S&E) articles	%	2005	28.9	5.9	2.1	35.3
	Change in number of published S&E articles	(1988 = 100)	1988-2005	115.6	900.5	164.5	166.4
Linguistic potential	Majority language	Speakers in the world (millions)	2006	1 000	1 000	900	n.a.
	Spread of majority language	Worldwide use	Current	Strong	Limited	Limited	n.a.
International mobility	Foreign tertiary students	% of students	2005	3.5***	m	0.1***	8.7**
	Tertiary students abroad	% of students	2003	0.2	1.8	0.9	13.7**

m = missing data

n.a. = not applicable

* Country mean

** Includes intra-European mobility

*** Earlier year used

Sources: Linguasphere Observatory (2006); NSF (2008); OECD (2007a and 2008a); SJTUIHE (2007); UIS (2008); World Bank (2008).

China looks likely to fulfil the conditions of becoming a new higher education power. Higher education in China is undergoing a major state-driven development in quantity and quality terms, in extraordinarily rapid time. From 1998 and 2004, a period of only six years, the total number of undergraduate admissions in China multiplied by *four times*, and in 2004 total enrolments in higher education reached 20 million, rendering Chinese higher education the largest system in the world. A further 8% increase was planned for 2005 (Liu, 2006, p. 1). China is committed to lifting the quality and global competitiveness of its leading research universities and a large-scale programme of state investment in universities is underway, led by the special programmes of state assistance under the 211 Project involving the leading 100 universities and the 985 Project which supports 38 universities. Both programmes provide block funding on the basis mainly of universities' strategic plans. Private higher education is also growing rapidly and in 2004 enrolled 1.4 million students, about 10% of the national total, although "private higher education still has a long way to go in terms of quality when compared with the public institutions" (Liu, 2006, p. 6).

China now accounts for half the R&D expenditure of the non-OECD nations (Vincent-Lancrin, 2009) and was the fifth largest producer of scientific papers in science and engineering in the world in 2005, compared to its fourteenth position in 1988 (NSF, 2008). The number of doctoral degrees awarded by universities in China rose from 19 in 1983 to 18 625 in 2003. Recent years have seen sharp annual growth in PhD intakes signalling the prospect of further rapid growth in domestic graduates. This would lessen China's intrinsic dependence on PhD training abroad, without necessarily reducing doctoral mobility per se, while reinforcing China's own role as a global centre of research activity: graduate students are first authors of about half of all journal articles published (Liu, 2006, pp. 2-6). While many foreign educational providers are active in China, a public-private partnership model instead of an open competition between local and foreign providers is preferred by the Chinese government. This strengthens the element of national steering also in the formation of global relationships.

India does not share the cultural integration of regional diversity that imparts national coherence in China and the United States, and has a lesser global economic and technological integration than China (Vicziany, 2004, pp. 93-96). Despite India's concentrations of technology-intensive industry and its global role as supplier of ICT labour, government dependent basic research has been slower to develop than in East Asia and Singapore. Between 1988 and 2001 the number of scientific papers increased from 8 882 to 14 608, constituting an increase from 1.9 to 2.1% of world output (NSF, 2008). Nevertheless tertiary education in India has three global advantages: 1) communicative competence via ICT systems and the widespread use of English, 2) flexibility in cross-border dealings via local autonomy, which facilitates engagement (the upside of non-centralisation), and, alongside a rather conservative orthodox university sector, 3) a technical education sector with 774 072 students in 2002 and a high degree of flexibility in provision. Technical education ranges from higher technological institutions (HTIs), some with autonomy and "deemed-to-be university status", and engineering colleges that grant doctoral degrees, to polytechnic diploma programmes and certificate programmes in industrial training institutes (ITIs) (Natarajan, 2005, pp. 156-57). The best vocational education in India is highly innovative. Among the autonomous institutions the research-intensive commercialised Indian Institutes of Technology (IITs) have attracted much attention. At least 40% of IIT graduates seek employment overseas (Bhushan, 2006, p. 6).

System size and regionalisation

Though the dominance of the United States and the emerging potential of China suggest that system size is a vector of global strategy there is no simple correlation between system size and research performance. Smaller European nations such as Sweden, Switzerland and Finland have outstanding research universities relative to national economic capacity and can attract international researchers and funds. China as yet has failed to translate national system size into a high quantity or quality of research, though this may change. Nor is there a simple correlation between size and global connectivity. The motivation and ability to connect is impacted also by factors other than size such as the national resource environment. In a study of conditions affecting the export and import of cross-border education Garrett (OBHE, 2005) notes that scarce government funding can push institutions into cross-border entrepreneurship as happened in the United Kingdom and Australia. Despite these considerations, all else being equal system size is one important factor shaping the strategic options and imperatives for systems and institutions.

Size affects the potential for global autonomy and the necessity for engagement and alliances. Larger nations are less dependent on cross-border provision to reproduce personnel and sustain a critical mass of activity; and have more scope to design a complex internal division of labour on the basis of institutional mission. Musselin (2005) notes that in larger European nations such as France and Germany academic labour markets tend to be more self-sufficient and the inward movement of foreign staff is more a policy choice than absolute necessity. This does not mean that larger nations can ignore the global dimension but it enables a broader range of possible global strategies and readier movement from reactive to proactive mode. The extreme case is the United States, where the size of the system and the professional labour markets underpins the attraction of foreign talent but institutions are under little pressure to adopt foreign perspectives. Middle sized and smaller nations, especially nations where national higher education capacity is incomplete in relation to needs, face different imperatives. They can scarcely afford to abstain from global engagement, yet must struggle to maintain their policy identity and autonomy vis-à-vis the larger players. This does not mean that smaller size signifies absolute global weakness or no strategic options. Singapore, Switzerland and the enclave of Hong Kong in China (Postiglione, 2005) have specialised in knowledge-intensive industries and cross-border services; in all three cases higher education capacity is both relatively strong and characterised by high rates of two-way mobility.

Globally successful middle-sized and smaller nations tend to be more dependent on global linkages than are their larger counterparts. Smaller nations must be ahead of the field to retain individual control over their own destiny. The alternative or additional strategy is to develop strong regional networks, which could create aggregate system size large enough to allow a potentially similar scope of activities to that of the larger countries. For example European OECD countries as an entity have a GNI and research personnel equivalent to that of the United States and a population almost twice the size of the US population (see Table 1.6). Furthermore, more than 40% of the world's top 500 research universities are located in the OECD European countries, which produced 35% of world's science and engineering articles in 2005. This is not to say that the knowledge economy in Europe is suddenly in a position to surpass that of the United States as the Lisbon Strategy imagined. The knowledge economy in the United States is underpinned not only by front rank universities that are integrated informally but effectively into a common system, but by American economic, technological, cultural, political and military advantage. Nevertheless, the global position of higher education and research in Europe is advancing (see Marginson and Van Der Wende, 2009).

The potency of Americanisation in national systems suggests regionalisation strategies in response. So far only European nations have established a common higher education area; but Southeast Asian nations in ASEAN (Association of Southeast Asian Nations) are working on mobility and recognition arrangements, and have established joint cross-border programmes; and Argentina, Brazil, Paraguay, and Uruguay are extending their educational co-operation within MERCOSUR (Mercado Común del Sur – southern Common Market) to other South American nations.

Conclusions on global power relations

In the global higher education setting there is significant scope for strategy making, more so than in many national settings. The distribution of capacities and resources between nations and institutions in many respects determines their global position and potential but the possibilities are not closed. Though higher education in the United States plays a hegemonic role there is space for national self-determination, albeit a space that varies from case to case, and there are some signs of global pluralisation. In sum, six interacting elements frame the possible global trajectories of systems, and individual institutions, and the potential benefits they gain from global operations: 1) the geographical and economic position of nations and institutions; 2) national history, system organisation, regulation, policy and resourcing in higher education; 3) institutional history, resources and academic and organisational cultures; 4) the global capacities of institutions and of agents such as governmental personnel; 5) national positioning-taking strategies in the global setting; and 6) institutional positioning-taking. All else being equal higher education capacity in the global environment is positively correlated to national wealth, the quality and quantity of constructive government support for higher education institutions, system size and competence in English. The intensity of global engagement is also affected by resource incentives. Some smaller nations are notably successful in their global strategies but at the price of high dependence on global flows. Outside the United States strategies of regionalisation have potential strategic benefits.

1.5. Tendencies to "disembedding" from national governance

Notions of the governance of higher education were long based on theories about the interplay of identified actors: the state, the market and the academic oligarchy (Clark, 1983). This interplay was typically, although not explicitly, conceptualised and framed in a national context. However various authors (van der Wende, 1997; Cloete et al., 2002; Verhoeven, 2005) now argue that this classic interplay of actors and forces is increasingly affected by internationalisation and globalisation, suggesting new theoretical questions (van der Wende, 2002). How does the fact that the State engages in cross-border or even supra-national co-operation affect its coordination of national higher education systems? What are the implications of the fact that competition and "the market" are now defined at an international or global level? Does the fact that the "academic oligarchy", in terms of both individual academics (disciplinary networks) and their institutions (university consortia), engage in international or global networks, impact governance? Many of these questions have yet to be answered in a comprehensive way. But it is possible to make observations on changing patterns of governance in the more global era. Beerkens (2004) defines globalisation as "a process in which basic social arrangements within and around the university become disembedded from their national context due to the intensification of transnational flows of people, information and resources".[20] One hypothesis posed by the changing patterns and forces is that higher education institutions are becoming and will become "disembedded" from their national contexts because some driving forces of globalisation exceed the strength of national factors. The disembedding hypothesis characterises the relationship between global and national elements not as symbiotic (as in the notion of the national domain as a filter of global effects) but as zero-sum.

Potential for mission shift

There is evidence of the potential for disembedding in several areas.

The first is funding. Pressure on national public funding for higher education in certain countries has encouraged or forced institutions to seek additional income from cross-border sources. This includes most institutions in the United Kingdom, Australia and New Zealand, and some four-year institutions and community colleges in the United States affected by state budget cuts. Australian universities have increased their revenue from full-fee paying international students from 5.8% of university income in 1995 to 14.5% in 2004 (DEST, 2006). In the United Kingdom between 1995 and 2000, income from full-fee paying students increased by 27.9%, compared to an increase in total income of 8.6%. International student revenues provided 9.9% of all income in the United Kingdom in 2002 (OECD, 2004a). Although these percentages are not yet overwhelming, the growth of cross-border education has the potential to place in doubt institutions' national missions. An interesting example is Oxford University. In early 2005 it was reported that "Oxford University is planning to cut the number of home and EU undergraduates from 10 400 to 8 500 and to expand its non-EU overseas undergraduates from 825 to 1 400 in order to improve its financial situation and at the same time to provide a more multi-cultural learning environment". In the same source the more general shift from national mission to cross-border activity was confirmed: "international students are quite simply what makes it possible for the academic enterprise to continue... public investment and fees do not cover the cost of teaching UK and EU undergraduates" (ACA Newsletter, March 2005).

In the case of Oxford the international mission threatens to reduce opportunities for domestic students. Alternately, a lack of domestic students may lead to an enhanced international mission, as both rest on zero-sum disembedding. In a period of demographic decline in the population of young people in some countries in Europe, such instances could multiply. For example, an agricultural university located in an EU country where the agricultural sector has lost its significance and domestic student numbers are low might survive by catering for students from other EU member countries, especially by adapting its programmes to food production and safety. Would the national tax payer agree to keep funding this university, and on what basis? One answer could be that the European higher education area constitutes a single public domain. Another answer could be that there is a continuing national interest in contributing to the quality of food production, by training students for work countries from which the nation imports agricultural products. A third answer could be that continuing to operate the university helps to sustain a national research capacity in such a critical area as food quality and safety. As well as pointing to the potential for disembedding, these examples also suggest that notions of the "public interest" and "public good" exceed traditional national territory, in two different ways: by drawing cross-border factors including trade into the scope of the national public interest;

and more radically, by extending the zone of public interest beyond national borders themselves.

A second set of examples of potential disembedding lies in research, where funding is becoming more available and accessible at international and supranational levels, such as EU Framework programmes. Research themes and teams are more often internationally defined and composed.

Beyond national jurisdiction

A third example is again related to cross-border education. By operating either virtually or physically across national borders, institutions exceed the boundaries of their enabling legislation. Governmental powers to regulate services performed abroad by their national institutions, and services performed by foreign institutions at home, tend to be undeveloped or limited; partly because of inadequate regulatory reach, and partly because institutions that are public providers in their national context tend to operate as private entities abroad and are thereby complicit in "disembedding" themselves from the national context. The resulting lacuna in regulation raises many issues in areas such as quality assurance, funding and the recognition of qualifications. Regulation by both exporter and importer nations is partial, and though there is much variation from case to case the two regulatory systems do not always synchronise effectively. The nations which are most active in cross-border locations, the United Kingdom and Australia, have both moved to scrutinise the offshore operations of their own institutions, but surveillance is incomplete and it is not always clear where foreign institution stops and local partner begins: in this respect effective scrutiny of quality rests on a close understanding between importer nation and exporter nation.

The regulation of foreign providers by importing governments varies. Hong Kong, Malaysia and Singapore treat foreign provision as part of national higher education effort and scrutinise it accordingly. The Malaysian government has brought in a small number of foreign institutions to provide market stimulus for local providers in the full fee private sector, the main venue for capacity expansion and a significant export earner in its own right. Singapore aims to be a "global hub" for education and is using supervised foreign partnerships both to import educational expertise and to assist in structuring a differentiated map of institutions and programmes, ranging from elite research and business courses[21] to mass degrees. In some other importing countries regulation of the quality of foreign providers is underdeveloped. In India selected private institutions are accorded the status of "deemed universities", enabling them to offer degrees, and foreign providers are formally eligible for accreditation by the All India Council for Technical Education. Meanwhile in the last decade a wide range of commercial foreign provision has taken root in partnership with local agents. Foreign institutions range from prestige providers such as the US Wharton Business School and the London School of Economics, to professional associations in the hotel industry. No bricks and mortar foreign campuses have been established and there is little franchising: twinning predominates, though the UK Oxford Brookes University in Kolkata and the US Fairfax University at Pune provide full degree programmes on a partnership basis.[22] The growth of foreign provision is sustained by the strong demand for transnational education. However, in a largely unregulated environment with *de facto* free entry there are significant risks for students (Bhushan, 2006).

A fourth example is cross-border accreditation. There are many cases of institutions seeking accreditation outside their national context (Altbach, 2003; OECD, 2004b: OECD/World Bank, 2007), for several reasons: an absolute lack of accreditation opportunities at home; using international accreditation to enhance relative national position; using international accreditation to evade the requirements or prohibitions of national accreditation; or enhancing global recognition *via* accreditation by a reputable foreign accreditation body. National accreditation agencies also have various motivations for "exporting" their services (Eaton, 2003). The small group of would-be global accreditation agencies has a vested interest in expanding the role of global referencing in accreditation, thereby fostering a global space and encouraging more radical disembedding.

Disembedding varies by function and by institution

The disembedding of institutions from their national context often begins in nationally-convergent and nationally-parallel transformations, such as the creation of funding incentives to raise monies from international students, but has the potential to partly transfer the institution into the global dimension, generating integrationist effects that are difficult to control or reverse at the national level. At the same time, in order to assess the extent to which institutions are disembedded from their national contexts, the scale and magnitude of these developments should be considered. At this time in most nations, the education of foreign students plays a marginal role in relation to nationally based institutions and it has rarely been a driver of new missions or pedagogical orientations even in the United Kingdom and Australia. On the other hand, in most nations the global market plays a larger and potentially more transformative role in doctoral education, through the exit of their own nationals to doctoral programmes abroad and/or the doctoral education of foreign students on home soil. Worldwide doctoral education, like research more generally, is one area that has been clearly globalised and where the disembedding potential is particularly obvious.

The potential for disembedding is also a function of the role of particular institutions within diversified national systems. Despite some shifts in resource sources and student composition, elite institutions continue to be the national standard bearers of prestige and high quality. Globalisation has often had a greater direct impact on second tier institutions. They might have to merge or otherwise reorganise in order to address new forms of competition, for example from foreign for-profit institutions; and being locked out of the elite segment in the nation, as noted they might leverage globalisation to improve their strategic options at home. One case in point is Mexico where several private sector higher education institutions have a much stronger global orientation in undergraduate studies than the Universidad Autonoma Nacional de Mexico (UNAM), which is the leading public sector research university and the dominant provider in Mexico overall. (In post-graduate studies, UNAM is one of the most globally oriented institutions in Latin America though.) In many nations private sector institutions have more freedom to vary their mission, clientele and global engagement.

Conclusions on disembedding from national governance

When some institutions are more disembedded than others, a national system of higher education becomes a more complex amalgam in which institutions have varying degrees of national accountability, which stretches the capacity of existing steering instruments. Moreover, if policy and governance do not keep pace with shifting missions and expanding cross-border activities, institutions will be *de facto* disembedded to the extent that significant parts of their operations fall altogether outside national governance structures and regulatory frameworks. Here governments and institutions are in uncharted waters. Few means of international or global governance have developed. One of the small number of examples is the UNESCO/OECD *Guidelines for Quality Provision in Cross-border Higher Education* (OECD, 2005c). As well as the fact that national policy, funding, regulatory and quality frameworks are falling short in their reach, there are larger questions at stake. Where are the partly disembedded institutions accountable for their international activities and outreach? Should the creation of global public goods be seen as part of their public service remit? But who are their global stakeholders; and why and how should they be held accountable to them? These challenges are more than technical, they are conceptual and political. National public higher education systems were always held to coincide with national priorities, legislation and territory. In the wake of the trends to more extensive and intensive cross-border activities, the very notion of "public" education, and related to that notions of priority, responsibility and accountability, are in question. The traditional responsibilities and roles of national governments have to be reconsidered. "Public sphere", "public interest" and "public good(s)" are obtaining new dimensions and meanings.

1.6. Global private and public goods

In industries focused solely on cross-border trade the global setting is imagined naturally as a trading environment and national and cross-national regulation assessed in terms of their potential to affect flows of goods and capital. Matters are more complicated in higher education, where global trade is part but not the sum of cross-border relations and much of the decision making takes place in governments or is otherwise framed by public interest. In higher education cross-border flows of people, technologies, communications, ideas and knowledge are important in their own right, as well as significant in relation to trade. In many nations and institutions the non trading global flows are more significant than the trade flows. Higher education produces a complex mix of private and public goods in both national and global dimensions (Marginson, forthcoming B). The global private goods include the degrees obtained when crossing national borders and those outcomes of commercial research traded across borders prior to their entry into the public domain. These private goods pose new problems of quality assurance and consumer protection across nations. However, a more far-reaching challenge to national policy is posed by global public goods.

The nature of public goods

This plurality in the goods produced in higher education derives in part from the intrinsic nature of information and knowledge, which constitute "public goods" in the technical economic sense whether produced in public sector institutions or not. As defined by Paul Samuelson (1954) "public goods" (including services) are goods that are non-rivalrous and non-excludable.[23] Knowledge, especially basic research, is an almost pure public good (Stiglitz, 1999). As Samuelson also noted, public and part-public goods tend to be underprovided in economic markets. Yet such goods are also central to the workings of advanced economies, societies and polities.

An immense array of information and knowledge generated in higher education, notably the outcomes of basic research, is openly accessible and subject to nominal charges well below its use value and below its costs of production. Once research findings and online courseware are released they can be copied many times without losing further value and their broadest distribution optimises the common good. The essential private goods in teaching and learning are not the content of courseware (which once the product is out there becomes a natural public good) but the brands, positional advantages, networking and high quality teaching (if provided) in elite institutions. Likewise, in research the volume of freely exchanged knowledge in the public domain far exceeds that of tradable intellectual property; though many public knowledge goods enter the chain of value-creation in other industrial sectors. This highlights the importance of open source models of ICT use in order for these national and global public goods to become universally accessible, and thereby maximising their utility, to industry and to national and global society, as public goods.[24]

Global public goods

Global public goods are goods that have a significant element of non-rivalry and/or non-excludability and are available across populations on a global scale. They affect more than one group of countries, are broadly available within countries, and are inter-generational; that is, they meet needs in the present generation without jeopardising future generations (Kaul *et al.*, 1999, pp. 2-3). Global public goods in higher education include collective global goods, and also positive or negative global externalities. Collective global goods are obtained by nations and/or institutions from cross-border systems common to the world or a meta-national region, for example regulation, systems and protocols that improve cross-border recognition and mobility. One example is the Washington Accords in Engineering, whereby each member of a group of nations have agreed to recognise the vocational qualifications of all the others' Engineering graduates and professionals, enhancing the potential of individual Engineers to move freely between workplaces across borders, and expanding the pool of labour available to each nation. Thus a low-cost informal global system of Engineering credentialing, regulated by common documentation and process, is to have benefits in each participant nation. Global externalities arise when education in one nation significantly affects people in other nations; for better, such as the positive contribution of research flowing across national borders; or for worse, such as the net "brain drain" of national faculty. In their positive form, like other public goods, global public goods tend to be underprovided in markets. The process of WTO-GATS negotiation, that has been designed to facilitate trade also in education, is a not a spontaneous development out of the market itself but has proceeded from the different policy spheres on a multi-lateral basis. This kind of regulatory systems, and the creation of interfaces between national regulatory spaces on the global scale, are classic public goods.

However, multilateral forums can directly create global higher education public goods, for example collective worldwide recognition systems and academic freedom protocols, and UNESCO, the OECD (2004b) and EU have all advanced the discussion of these elements. Cross-border externalities are more difficult to regulate. There is no agreed basis for identifying, measuring, costing and financing "downstream effects" between one nation and another even in the sphere of the environment where such effects are acknowledged. Only brain drain is an active issue and policy tools for measuring and redressing it are as yet underdeveloped and even then, it is sometimes difficult to know whether we face brain drain or brain circulation.

The creation of new global public goods in higher education occurs both in the space created by the partial disembedding of higher education institutions, and alongside the more traditional creation of public outcomes at the national level. In one respect it bypasses national governments and brings new non-government actors into play; in another respect it is dependent on national and regional authorities and on inter-governmental negotiation. Like globalisation itself, global private and public goods are at the same time *substitutes* for nation-states and traditional practices in higher education, *supplementary*, and also *complementary* in that they are associated symbiotically with the governmental and institutional frameworks that are the vehicles for global transformations. Again, the relationship between national and global elements is ambiguous, with both zero-sum and positive-sum aspects.

However the strategic possibilities and problems of global public goods are largely unexplored. The absence of an agreed analytical and policy framework for operationalising global public goods (especially externalities) in the national interest, let alone the mutual interest, predisposes national policy makers to neglect those goods (Kaul *et al.*, 1999; Kaul *et al.*, 2003). It is another example of the jurisdictional gap between global effects, especially integrationist effects, and national policy framework. While there has been a major expansion of global public goods in the global era, the difficulty is that most of the time they are underrecognised. Kaul and colleagues pose the problem as follows: "In the international sphere, where there is no government, how are public goods produced?" (Kaul *et al.*, 1999, p. 12; Marginson, 2007a). The answer is, either spontaneously through the operations of human activities such as research or travel, or deliberately by inter-national and multi-lateral negotiation, often (but not always) involving international organisations. However, international organisations have little instrumental power and the notion of a single global sphere of interest is little developed, so that multi-lateral negotiations are mostly read by the participant nations in terms of national public goods, not global public goods. It is likely that negotiations concerning responses to climate change and global warning will encourage a more explicit recognition of global public goods but whether this will become associated with global state-like structures, and the possible longer-term implications for global public goods in higher education and research, all remain to be seen.

Cross-border student security as a universal global public good

One set of practical examples lies in the absence of universal social and economic protections for temporarily mobile populations such as students, executives and administrators, and faculty. People travelling across borders for education purposes may not exercise the full rights enjoyed by local citizens, such as access to government services and legal representation, and economic freedoms such as maintaining bank accounts, securing loans or purchasing property; and their opportunities for redress in relation to injury may be restricted. For example, a recent study suggests that in Australia many cross-border students enter the lower sub-strata of the workforce and can experience discriminatory or exploitative work practices during the period of study in excess of the difficulties experienced by local students (Nyland, forthcoming). Questions of the economic and social security of cross-border populations in higher education can extend also to social welfare, health care, housing rights, and freedom from discrimination.

These issues invoke problems of national and international law, policy and governance that have immediate practical importance for many people, but are inherently difficult to address because they push beyond nation-state frameworks. Precisely because such issues of cross-border security are generated in cross-border movement, single national governments normally face limited "ownership" and domestic political pressure to address them. For the nations sending students abroad for education, the problems of their citizen-students tend to be addressed only in exceptional circumstances by foreign missions and through bilateral negotiation with the nation(s) of education. For nations that receive students for the purposes of education, these are not their own citizens, though in Europe, in effect some benefits of citizenship are extended to students from other European nations. The rights of these non-citizen students are sometimes treated as consumer rights, for example in Australian legislation; or rights to pastoral care during their education as in New Zealand; but not as the full range of human and civil rights; though foreign students and visiting faculty often contribute to social and cultural life, some pay taxes, and some later become citizens. Nor have the international agencies addressed the social and economic security of people in education and other sectors who move across national borders, except in relation to categories such as refugees. For example, while the International Labour Organisation (ILO) includes migration within its concerns, it explicitly excludes students from its definition of migrants (Deumert *et al.*, 2005).

However governments alone do not have a monopoly on global public goods, more so given the absence of global democracy and global governance. For example cross-border students draw on the support of community-based organisations, student clubs and informal networks as part of the framework of security. Non-government associations, institutions and commercial companies also have claims on people's loyalties, also operate across borders and can also be meta-national and global in effect (Sen, 1999). Higher education institutions, not to mention networks and consortia, are important global actors in their own right. A framework for enhancing global public and private goods in higher education should take this plurality of actors into account.

Conclusions on *global public goods*

Though globalisation enhances the potential for both global private goods and global public goods in higher education, it has proven difficult for national governments to design policies so as to optimise the flows of both kinds of good simultaneously. Global public goods receive only sporadic attention, more in their negative form as brain drain than in their positive forms. Nations can control the externalities they generate with effects on others, these are nationally-parallel global effects; but not the externalities they are subjected to by higher education in other nations which are integrationist global effects. National governments can secure regulatory control over integrationist externalities and collective global goods only in the framework of multilateral negotiations.

But though the regulation of trade in education is negotiated in WTO/GATS there is no global policy space in which to consider global public goods in higher education. There is a role here for international agencies, not as surrogate for a supra-national public interest but in setting the ring for cross-border negotiations. Ultimately, however, issues such as cross-border student security would be most effectively addressed by a multilateral commitment to an on-going common higher education space, itself a global public good and a means to enhance the production of many other private and public goods. In other words it would be beneficial to extend the logic of Europeanisation on a broader scale. This would have the potential to enhance the outcomes of higher education overall, though arguably at the price of further advancing the disembedding of higher education from its different national contexts. In addition to governments and international agencies, such a global higher education public space could be designed so as to incorporate civil agents, autonomous institutions, disciplinary communities, professions and market actors involved in cross-border relations in the sector.

1.7. General conclusions

Economic and cultural globalisation has ushered in a new era in higher education. Cross-border dealings and strategies have become more important than before for all governments and systemic agencies, for all research universities and for some non-research institutions. For the first time in history every research university is part of a single worldwide network and the world leaders in the field have an unprecedented global visibility and power. Research is more internationalised than before and the mobility of doctoral students and faculty has increased, particularly movement into the United States and movement within Europe. In many nations and regions, especially in Europe and East Asia, governments are focusing on policies designed to concentrate research fire-power and this is likely to aggregate into an upward movement in worldwide investment in university research (see more detailed discussion in Marginson and Van Der Wende, 2009).

Global higher education is more ontologically open than are national systems, with a bewildering range of opportunities for innovations, alliances and markets. To maximise effectiveness in the global environment, on one hand it is essential to retain a strong sense of identity and purpose; on the other hand it is essential to be open to and engaged with others. One reason why American higher education is so globally successful is its particular combination of decentralisation and centralisation. Its institutions are engaged in a plethora of unregulated exchanges with institutions throughout the world, maximising the scope for American initiative and influence, and minimising the capacity of other nations to restrain them by inter-governmental negotiation. But American higher education institutions are more coordinated than it might appear. They share a resilient common culture, and a sense of national project and American way of doing, that binds them to each other without much direction.

To be effective in the global environment means being prepared to change. Global exchange is transformative and all policies and institutional habits are ripe for reconsideration in the light of the global challenge. Globalisation is often annexed to policy shifts. Governments in many nations are wrestling with the question of whether competition at home improves competitiveness abroad, and which combination of competition with collaboration will deliver the best results outside the border. At the regional level Europe is preoccupied with the same question. Yet perhaps these dilemmas are ultimately more apparent than real, and more in the realm of policy discourses than the gritty policy mechanisms. Though from time to time ideology is comforting what matters is what works. No doubt some cross-border activities of institutions need to be brought into the domain of national policy, while at the same time systems and institutions with a history of insularity or dependence need to become more autonomous, open and proactive to be globally effective. How they become engaged is a more open matter. The how is less important than the outcome. On some occasions deregulation serves; sometimes state investment in expanded capacity, and sometimes both are needed. The more difficult question is to devise coherent means of coordinating institutions with a sufficiently light touch so as to progress their autonomous global capacities while achieving the common strategic purpose.

Another complication is that the role of national purpose itself is in doubt. Globalisation has broken open the old role of government in higher education centred on bounded nation-states. The factors at play are on one hand the new public management, on the other hand the growth of cross-border communications and activities in which institutions deal directly with parties outside the nation. Though institutions continue to be nested in national/local identity and resources, they have been partly disembedded from the national policy context and the potential of global private and public goods has increased. In other words, national government remains a key player in higher education but its negotiating space has become more complex and its reach over higher education is no longer complete. Its functions are shared with many other parties, including other national governments, multilateral agencies and institutions themselves. Some cross-border activity of institutions takes them beyond their national legislative charter into a void where global governance is little developed and where the collective global interest is unexpressed. To what extent can global research and knowledge transfer, recognition regimes and mobility of personnel be understood through the prism of national self-interest? How are downstream cross-border externalities in higher education (positive or negative) to be measured, costed and optimised?

Future developments in the globalisation of higher education are difficult to predict. There are many variables, meta-policy questions and issues. The variables include the potential for pluralisation of power in global higher education; the future mobility of people, information and ideas; language of use and the extent of cultural plurality in global exchange; and the future forms of academic labour. The meta-policy questions include the evolution of multilateralism in higher education, the development of Europeanisation and other forms of regionalism in the sector, and the extent to which policy in national and multilateral forums generates tendencies to inclusiveness on the national and global scale, in response to the tendencies to bifurcation and stratification triggered by global developments and national responses. The more immediate issues include the policy handling of university rankings and the evolution of the high priced researcher market.

Notes

1. Guy Neave's description of globalisation as "quickening exchange" is suggestive of both its economic and cultural aspects (Neave, 2002, p. 332).

2. For example in the first quarter of 2002, 24 billion text messages were sent globally; 70% of households in Korea already have broad-band Internet connections (Drache and Froese, 2005, pp. 16 and 22).

3. The templates of the new public management include the modelling of national systems as economic markets; government-steered competition between institutions, and executive-steered competition between academic units; part-devolution of responsibility for administering and often for raising finances; incentives to reduce costs per unit, and to engage in entrepreneurial behaviour; new or augmented price signals; incentives to link with business and industry; performance measures and output-based funding; and relations with funding agencies and managers based on quasi-corporate forms such as contracts, accountability and audit.

4. Teichler (2004, pp. 18-19) discusses this in more detail.

5. Such differences include variations in customary institutional sizes and configurations (single city site, multi-site, dispersed network); differences in the types of institutional specialisation on offer; differences in the segmentation between types of institutions (graduate research institutes, research-intensive universities, predominantly teaching universities, vocational universities,

training colleges); differences in the extent of vertical differentiation between institutions, and the roles of competition and market forces; differences in the balance between public and private institutions, and the cost of education for students; differences in languages of instruction and scholarship, and in disciplinary traditions and academic cultures; differences in managerial cultures (bureaucratic, administrative, entrepreneurial), in performance measures and in organisational systems.

6. For example the global flows of people in higher education include students involved in short-term exchange; first degree and professional Masters students accessing foreign degrees or involved in cross-border joint degrees; doctoral students; post-doctoral researchers; academic faculty involved in teaching, research, conferences and seminars and other forms of collaboration and exchange; administrators and executives on short-term visits for negotiating agreements with other universities, or learning about other systems, or marketing degree programmes; academic or non-academic staff involved in offshore provision, etc. Some global flows are already accessible to systematic data collection. In the case of certain flows such as the movement of students into foreign degree programmes, the data are widely collected and are accessible to comparative analysis (OECD, 2005a, pp. 250-73); albeit subject to caveats.

7. Gross National Income per head neglects, however, distributional factors and fails to distinguish between investment and unproductive consumption.

8. Leaving aside the idiosyncratic case of Luxembourg with a per capita GNI of USD 60 870.

9. For example the United States falls slightly below the PISA country mean in school mathematical competence despite its very high level of national economic resources.

10. Arguably the core ideas of the new public management (NMP) are a British rather than US creation (see for example the account of the genesis of the Thatcher reforms in the UK in Cockett, 1995) though the idealised NPM templates in higher education reflect the norms of the American non-profit and for-profit private sectors (for more discussion of the last point see among others Marginson and Ordorika, 2007; Marginson, 2008).

11. There are 101 universities in the "top 100" group: using the SJTUIHE metrics there is a tie for 100th place.

12. Other measures of research outcomes confirm this picture. Nobel prizes go to the developed nations and "rich countries, home to 15% of the world's population, are responsible for over 90% of the patents granted" (Bloom, 2005, pp. 25 and 35).

13. France is an exception. In the 1990s the proportion of doctoral graduates who were foreign declined from one third to one fifth, while the recruitment of foreigners to permanent university posts declined. On the other hand there was an increase in the proportion of the staff of the research institutes that was foreign (Musselin, 2004, p. 156).

14. Stay rates are high among the large number of graduates in engineering, computing and technologies (Gupta *et al.*, 2003). While in 1985 50.0% of foreign science and engineering doctoral degree holders planned to stay, by 1995 it had reached 70.6% (OECD, 2002, p. 49).

15. Notably however the number of visiting scholars faltered in the first two years after 11 September 2001, falling from 86 015 in 2001-02 to 82 905 in 2003-04. Between 2001 and 2003 the rate of refusal of visa applications for short-term visits by high-skilled personnel rose from 7.8 to 15.9%; there was a concurrent increase in the refusal rate in relation to applications for student visas (NSB, 2006, p. 337).

16. The next largest exporter, the United Kingdom, is much less important. France and Germany also play a small role as exporters of academic labour (Welch, 2005, pp. 78-9). Most nations are net importers of academic labour however.

17. In the United States the share of internationally co-authored articles doubled since 1988, rising to 23% in 2005. In western Europe collaboration, much of it with a regional flavour, rose from 17 to 33% between 1988 and 2001; in Asia the movement was from 11 to 21%.

18. India's Bollywood produces over 800 films in 25 different Indian languages each year from many regional centres, compared to 200 films each year in the United States. Selected Bollywood and "cross-over" products are breaking into mainstream global markets (Drache and Froese, 2005, pp. 7-8 and 24).

19. Since 1992 in the United States and the late 1990s in the United Kingdom, Canada and the Netherlands the number of scientific articles has flattened (NSB 2006, A 5-35). Nevertheless, between 1993 and 2005 the number of books produced by American university presses rose by 23% (for an extended discussion of these trends see Vincent-Lancrin, 2009).

20. This definition finds some support also in the work of Held *et al.* (1999) and others.

21. Singapore is housing several foreign business schools on a partnership basis and has commissioned the University of New South Wales in Australia to establish a full-scale undergraduate campus.

22. One survey found that in 2004, 131 private institutions in India were collaborating with foreign providers (50% from the United States and 45% from the United Kingdom); the bulk of these partnerships being located in the States of Tamil Nadu, Maharashtra, Delhi and Andhra Pradesh; with 42% of programmes in hotel management, 34% offering MBAs and 15% in Medical Technology. The Apollo Group is operating in India in partnership with the K.K. Modi Group (Bhushan, 2006).

23. Goods are non-rivalrous when they can be consumed by any number of people without being depleted, for example knowledge of a mathematical theorem. Goods are non-excludable when the benefits cannot be confined to individual buyers, for example law and order, or social tolerance. Goods with neither quality are classified as private goods.

24. Strategies to maximise public goods can be pursued by institutions as well as governments. MIT moved early to use the Internet this way, providing its courseware on the basis of open access, promoting itself as the intellectual originator of learning and thereby strengthening its brand more tangibly than simply using rhetorical advocacy or images associated with desire fulfilment like any non-university advertiser. In this manner MIT aligned its strategies to the intrinsic nature of knowledge and information and to its own nature as a knowledge forming organisation. Other institutions tried and failed to make money by offering teaching light online programmes in which web-based courseware were presented as the principal private goods, even though most such contents can already be downloaded from the Internet free of charge (Marginson, 2004).

Bibliography

Altbach, P. (2003), "American Accreditation of Foreign Universities: Colonialism in Action", *International Higher Education*, Vol. 32, pp. 5-7.

Altbach, P. (2005), "Academic Challenges: The American Professoriate in Comparative Perspective", in A. Welch (ed.), *The Professoriate: Portrait of a Profession*, Springer, Dordrecht, pp. 147-65.

Altbach, P. (2006), "The Dilemmas of Ranking", *International Higher Education*, Vol. 42, p. 3.

Altbach, P. and D. Levy (2006), *Private Higher Education: A Global Revolution*, Sense Publishers, Rotterdam.

American Association of University Professors (AAUP) (2009), "Trends in Faculty Status, 1975-2005", AAUP Factsheet, accessed on 13 July 2009, *www.aaup.org/NR/rdonlyres/9218E731-A68E-4E98-A378-12251FFD3802/0/Facstatustrend7505.pdf*.

Australian Bureau of Statistics (ABS) (2006), Research and Experimental Development, Higher Education Organisations, Australia, 2004, Catalogue Number 8110.0, ABS, Canberra.

Beerkens, H.J.J.G. (2004), Global Opportunities and Institutional Embeddedness: Higher Education Consortia in Europe and Southeast Asia, Center for Higher Education Policy Studies, University of Twente, accessed on 10 February 2006. *http://doc.utwente.nl/50803/1/thesis_Beerkens.pdf*

Bensimon, E. and I. Ordorika (2006), "Mexico's Estímulos: Faculty Compensation Based on Piecework", in R.A. Rhoads and C.A. Torres (eds.), *The University, State, and Market: The Political Economy of Globalization in the Americas*, Stanford University Press, Stanford, CA, pp. 250-74.

Bhushan, S. (2006), *Foreign Education Providers in India: Mapping the Extent of Regulation*, The Observatory on Borderless Higher Education, Accessed on 2 April 2006 at *www.obhe.ac.uk*.

Bloom, D. (2005), "Raising the Pressure: Globalization and the Need for Higher Education Reform", in G. Jones, P. McCarney and M. Skolnik (eds.), *Creating Knowledge: Strengthening Nations: The Changing Role of Higher Education*, University of Toronto Press, Toronto, pp. 21-41.

Bourdieu, P. (1993), *The Field of Cultural Production*, Polity Press, Cambridge; Columbia University Press, New York.

Castells, M. (2000), *The Rise of the Network Society, 2nd Edition, Volume I of The Information Age: Economy, Society and Culture*, Blackwell, Oxford.

Castells, M. (2001), *The Internet Galaxy: Reflections on the Internet, Business and Society*, Oxford University Press, Oxford.

Clark, B. (1983), *The Higher Education System: Academic Organisation in Cross-national Perspective*, University of California Press, Berkeley and Los Angeles.

Cloete, N., R. Fehnel, P. Maassen, H. Perold and T. Gibbon (2002), *Higher Education Policy, Institutions and Globalisation. New dynamics in South Africa after 1994*, Kluwer Academic Publishers, Dordrecht.

Cockett, R. (1995), *Thinking the Unthinkable: Think-Tanks and the Economic Counter-Revolution 1931-1983*, Harper-Collins, London.

Crystal, D. (2003), *English as a Global Language*, 2nd Edition, Cambridge University Press, Cambridge.

Currie, J. (2005), "Globalisation's Impact on the Professoriate in Anglo-American Universities", in A. Welch (ed.), *The Professoriate: Portrait of a Profession*, Springer, Dordrecht, pp. 21-34.

Department of Employment, Education and Training (DEST) (2006), Selected Higher Education Statistics, accessed 10 April 2006, *www.dest.gov.au/sectors/higher_education/publications_resources/ statistics/selected_higher_education_statistics/default.htm*

Deumert, A., S. Marginson, C. Nyland, G. Ramia and E. Sawir (2005), "Global Migration and Social Protection: The Social and Economic Security of Foreign Students in Australia", *Global Social Policy*, Vol. 5, No. 3, pp. 329-52.

Douglas, J.A. (2005), *All Globalization is Local: Countervailing Forces and the Influence on Higher Education Markets*, University of California, Berkeley.

Drache, D. and M. Froese (2005), *Globalization and the Cultural Commons: Identity, Citizenship and Pluralism after Cancun*, Research paper, Department of Political Science, York University, Canada.

Eaton, J. (2003), "The International Role of U.S. Recognized Accrediting Organizations", *International Higher Education*, Vol. 31, pp. 10-12.

Enders, J. and E. de Weert (2004a), "Science, Training and Career: Changing Modes of Knowledge Production and Labour Markets", *Higher Education Policy*, Vol. 17, pp. 135-52.

Enders, J. and E. de Weert (eds.) (2004b), *The International Attractiveness of the Academic Workplace in Europe*, Herausgeber und Bestelladresse, Frankfurt.

Enders, J. and U. Teichler (2005), "Academics' View of Teaching Staff Mobility: The ERASMUS Experience Revisited", in A. Welch (ed.), *The Professoriate: Portrait of a Profession*, Springer, Dordrecht, pp. 97-112.

Enders, J. and C. Musselin (2008), "Back to the Future? The Academic Professions in the 21st Century", in *Higher Education 2030, Volume 1: Demography*, OECD Publishing, Paris.

Fligstein, N. (2001), "The Architecture of Markets: An Economic Sociology of Twenty-first-century Capitalist Societies", Princeton University Press, Princeton, NJ.

Fligstein, N. and F. Merand (2002), "Globalization or Europeanization? Evidence on the European Economy since 1980", *Acta Sociologica*, Vol. 45, pp. 7-25.

Garrett, R. (2005b), *The Global Education Index 2005, Part 2: Public Companies – Relationships with Non-profit Higher Education*, OBHE, London, accessed 22 June 2007, *www.obhe.ac.uk/documents/ view_details?id=46*.

Giddens, A. (2001), *The Great Globalization Debate*, Zellerbach Distinguished Lecture, University of California, Berkeley, 25 October.

Guellec, D. and M. Cervantes (2002), "International Mobility of Highly Skilled Workers: From Statistical Analysis to Policy Formulation", *International Mobility of the Highly Skilled*, OECD Publishing, Paris, pp. 71-98.

Gupta, D., M. Nerad and J. Cerny (2003), "International PhDs: Exploring the Decision to Stay or Return", *International Higher Education*, Vol. 31, No. 8, accessed on 10 February 2006, *www.bc.edu/bc_org/avp/ soe/cihe/newsletter/News31/text008.htm* .

Held, D., A. McGrew, D. Goldblatt and J. Perraton (1999), *Global Transformations: Politics, Economics and Culture*, Stanford University Press, Stanford.

Institute for International Education (IIE) (2006), Data on US international education, accessed 17 August 2006, *http://opendoors.iienetwork.org/?p=69736*.

Institute for International Education (IIE) (2007), Data on US international education, accessed July 2008, *http://opendoors.iienetwork.org/page/113118/*.

Institute for Scientific Information, Thomson-ISI (2008), Data on highly cited researchers, ISIHighlyCited.com, accessed July 2008, *http://isihighlycited.com/*.

Kaul, I., P. Conceicao, K. le Goulven and R. Mendoza (eds.) (2003), *Providing Global Public Goods: Managing Globalisation*, Oxford University Press, New York.

Kaul, I., I. Grunberg and M. Stern (eds.) (1999), *Global Public Goods: International Co-operation in the 21st Century*, Oxford University Press, New York.

Kaulisch, M. and J. Enders (2005), "Careers in Overlapping Institutional Contexts: The Case of Academe", *Career Development International*, Vol. 10, No. 2, pp. 130-44.

Kelo, M., U. Teichler and B. Wachter (eds.) (2006), *Eurodata: Student Mobility in European Higher Education*, Lemmens Verlags & Mediengesellschaft, Bonn.

Laudel, G. (2005), "Migration Currents among the Scientific Elite", *Minerva* 43, pp. 377-95.

Levin, J. (2001), *Globalising the Community College: Strategies for Change in the Twenty-first Century*, Houndmills, Palgrave Macmillan.

Linguasphere Observatory (2006), *Linguasphere Table of the World's Major Spoken Languages 1999-2000*, data maintained by GeoLang, World Language Documentation Centre, accessed 22 June 2007 at: *www.geolang.com/* .

Liu, N. (2006), "The Differentiation and Classification of Chinese Universities and the Building of World-Class Universities in China", Presentation at the seminar at Leiden University, 16 February, *www.leidenslatest.leidenuniv.nl/content_docs/presentation_prof._liu.ppt#364,4*, Dream of Chinese for WCU.

Luijten-Lub, A. (2005), "Dutch Higher Education Institutions Working on Europeanisation, Internationalization and Globalization", in J. Huisman and M.C. van der Wende (eds.), *On Co-operation and Competition II. Institutional Responses to Internationalization, Europeanisation and Globalization*, Lemmens, Bonn.

Maddison, A. (2007), Chinese Economic Performance in the Long Run. Second Edition, Revised and Updated, Development Centre Studies 960–2030 AD, OECD Publishing, Paris.

Marginson, S. (1997), *Markets in Education*, Allen and Unwin, Sydney.

Marginson, S. (2004), "Don't Leave me Hanging on the Anglophone: The Potential for Online Distance Education in the Asia-Pacific Region", *Higher Education Quarterly*, Vol. 58, No. 2/3, pp. 74-113.

Marginson, S. (2007a), "The Public/private Division in Higher Education: A Global Revision", *Higher Education 53*.

Marginson, S. (2007b), "Global Position and Position-Taking: The Case of Australia", *Journal of Studies in International Education*, Vol. 11, No. 1, pp. 5-32.

Marginson, S. (2008), "Global Field and Global Imagining: Bourdieu and Relations of Power in Worldwide Higher Education", *British Journal of Educational Sociology*, Vol. 29, No. 3, pp. 303-16.

Marginson, S. (forthcoming A), "The Academic Profession(s) in the Global Era", chapter prepared for J. Enders and E. de Weert (eds.), *The Academic Profession and the Modernization of Higher Education: Analytical and Comparative Perspectives*.

Marginson, S. (forthcoming B), *University Strategies in the Global Higher Education Environment* [working title], manuscript in preparation, University of Melbourne Centre for the Study of Higher Education, Melbourne.

Marginson, S. and M. Considine (2000), *The Enterprise University: Power, Governance and Reinvention in Australia*, Cambridge University Press, Cambridge.

Marginson, S. and I. Ordorika (2007), "El central volumen de la fuerza" (The hegemonic global pattern in the reorganization of elite higher education and research), paper prepared for the United States Social Sciences Research Council (SSRC), SSRC, New York.

Marginson, S. and G. Rhoades (2002), "Beyond National States, Markets, and Systems of Higher Education: A Glonacal Agency Heuristic", *Higher Education*, Vol. 43, pp. 281-309.

Marginson, S. and E. Sawir (2005), "Interrogating Global Flows in Higher Education", *Globalization, Societies and Education*, Vol. 3, No. 3, pp. 281-310.

Marginson S. and M. Van Der Wende (2009), "Europeanisation, International Rankings and Faculty Mobility: Three cases in Higher Education Globalisation", in *Higher Education 2030, Volume 2: Globalisation*, OECD Publishing, Paris.

McCarney, P. (2005), "Global Cities, Local Knowledge Creation: Mapping a New Policy Terrain on the Relationship between Universities and Cities", in G. Jones, P. McCarney and M. Skolnik (eds.), *Creating Knowledge: Strengthening Nations: The Changing Role of Higher Education*, University of Toronto Press, Toronto, pp. 205-24.

McLuhan, M. (1964), *Understanding Media*, Abacus, London.

Musselin, C. (2004), "The Academic Workplace: Up to Now it is not as Bad… But! Country Report France", in J. Enders and E. de Weert (eds.), *The International Attractiveness of the Academic Workplace in Europe*, Herausgeber und Bestelladresse, Frankfurt, pp. 141-59.

Musselin, C. (2005), "European Academic Labour Markets in Transition", *Higher Education,* Vol. 49, pp. 135-54.

Natarajan, R. (2005), "The Role of Technical Education in Enabling the Creation of a Knowledge Economy and Society: The Indian Experience", in G. Jones, P. McCarney and M. Skolnik (eds.), *Creating Knowledge: Strengthening Nations: The Changing Role of Higher Education*, University of Toronto Press, Toronto, pp. 155-66.

National Science Board (NSB) (2006), Science and Engineering Indicators 2004, accessed on 9 April 2006, *www.nsf.gov/statistics/seind04/*.

Neave, G.Y. (2002), "Editorial: Academic Freedom in an Age of Globalization", *Higher Education Policy*, Vol. 15, pp. 331-35.

NSF (2006), *Science and Engineering Indicators 2006*, Arlington, VA.

NSF (2008), *Science and Engineering Indicators 2008*, Arlington, VA.

Nyland, C., (forthcoming), "International Student-Workers: A New Vulnerable Workforce", in Marginson, S., Nyland, C., Ramia, G., Forbes-Mewett, H., Sawir, E. and Smith, S., *Student Security in the Global Education Market: The case of Australia.*

OECD (2002), *Dynamizing National Innovation Systems*, OECD Publishing, Paris.

OECD (2004a), *Internationalisation and Trade in Higher Education: Opportunities and Challenges*, OECD Publishing, Paris.

OECD (2004b), *Quality and Recognition in Higher Education: The Cross-border Challenge*, OECD Publishing, Paris.

OECD (2004c), *OECD Science, Technology and Industry Outlook*, OECD Publishing, Paris.

OECD (2005a), *Education at a Glance: OECD Indicators*, OECD Publishing, Paris.

OECD (2005b), *E-learning in Tertiary Education: Where do we stand?*, OECD Publishing, Paris.

OECD (2005c), *Guidelines for Quality Provision in Cross-border Higher Education*, OECD Publishing, Paris.

OECD (2005d), OECD Broadband Statistics, December 2005, accessed on 15 August 2006, *www.oecd.org/documentprint/0,2744,en_2649_34223_36459431_1_1_1_1,00.html.*

OECD (2006a), *Main Science and Technology Indicators*, OECD Publishing, Paris.

OECD (2006b), "Background report. Higher Education: Quality, Equity and Efficiency", prepared for the meeting of OECD Education Ministers, 27-28 June, Athens.

OECD (2007a), *Education at a Glance: OECD Indicators*, OECD Publishing, Paris.

OECD (2007b), OECD Broadband Statistics, December 2007, accessed in July 2008, oecd.org/sti/ict/broadband

OECD (2008a), *Main Science and Technology Indicators*, OECD Publishing, Paris.

OECD (2008b), *OECD Thematic Review of Tertiary Education: Synthesis Report, Volume 3*, OECD Publishing, Paris.

OECD (2008c), *Education at a Glance: OECD Indicators*, OECD Publishing, Paris.

OECD/World Bank (2007), *Cross-border Tertiary Education: A Way towards Capacity Development*, OECD and the World Bank, Paris and Washington DC.

Postiglione, G. (2005), "China's Global Bridging: The Transformation of University Mobility between Hong Kong and the United States", *Journal of Studies in International Education*, Vol. 9, No. 1, pp. 5-25.

Rhoades, G. (1998), *Managed Professionals*, SUNY Press, New York.

Rhoads, R. and C. Torres (eds.) (2006), *The University, State, and Market: The Political Economy of Globalization in the Americas*, Stanford University Press, Stanford.

Samuelson, P. (1954), "The Pure Theory of Public Expenditure", *Review of Economics and Statistics*, Vol. 36, No. 4, pp. 387–89.

Scott, P. (1998), "Massification, Internationalization and Globalization", in P. Scott (ed.), *The Globalization of Higher Education*, The Society for Research into Higher Education/Open University Press, Buckingham, pp. 108-29.

Sen, A. (1999), "Global Justice: Beyond International Equity", in I. Kaul, I. Grunberg and M. Stern (eds.), *Global Public Goods: International Co-operation in the 21st century*, Oxford University Press, New York, pp. 116-25.

Shanghai Jiao Tong University Institute of Higher Education (SJTUIHE) (2007), *Academic Ranking of World Universities*, accessed July 2008, *http://ed.sjtu.edu.cn/ranking.htm*.

Smeby, J. and J. Trondal (2005), "Globalization or Europeanization? International Contact among University Staff", *Higher Education*, Vol. 49, pp. 449-66.

Stiglitz, J. (1999), "Knowledge as a Global Public Good", in I. Kaul, I. Grunberg and M. Stern (eds.), *Global Public Goods: International Co-operation in the 21st Century*, Oxford University Press, New York, pp. 308-25.

Teichler, U. (2004), "The Changing Debate on Internationalization of Higher Education", *Higher Education*, Vol. 48, pp. 5-26.

Torres, C. and R. Rhoads (2006), "Introduction: Globalization and Higher Education in the Americas", in C. Torres and R. Rhoads (eds.), *The University, State and Market: The Political Economy of Globalization in the Americas*, Stanford University Press, Stanford.

UNESCO Institute of Statistics (UIS) (2008), Education Statistics, accessed in July 2008, *http://stats.uis.unesco.org/unesco/ReportFolders/ReportFolders.aspx*

Vaira, M. (2004), "Globalization and Higher Education Organizational Change: A Framework for Analysis", *Higher Education*, Vol. 48, pp. 483-510.

Valimaa, J. (2004a), "Nationalisation, Localization and Globalization in Finnish Higher Education", *Higher Education*, Vol. 48, pp. 27-54.

Valimaa, J. (2004b), "The Academic Workplace: Country Report Finland", in J. Enders and E. de Weert (eds.), *The International Attractiveness of the Academic Workplace in Europe*, Herausgeber und Bestelladresse, Frankfurt, pp. 115-40.

Valimaa, J. (2005), "Globalization in the Concept of Nordic Higher Education", in A. Arimoto, F. Huang and K. Yokoyama (eds.), *Globalization and Higher Education*, International Publications Series 9, Research Institute for Higher Education, Hiroshima University, Accessed 10 February 2006, *http://en.rihe.hiroshima-u.ac.jp/pl_default_2.php?bid=63653*.

Verhoeven, J.C., G. Kelchtermans and K. Michielsen (2005), McOnderwijs in Vlaanderen. Internationalisering en commercialisering van het hoger onderwijs, Wolters Plantijn.

Vicziany, M. (2004), "Globalization and *Hindutva*: India's Experience with Global Economic and Political Integration", in G. Davies and C. Nyland (eds.), *Globalization in the Asian Region*, Edward Elgar, Cheltenham, pp. 92-116.

Vincent-Lancrin, S. (2009), "What is Changing in Academic Research? Trends and Prospects", in *Higher Education 2030, Volume 2: Globalisation*, OECD Publishing, Paris.

Vlk, A. (2006), "Higher Education and GATS: Regulatory Consequences and Stakeholders' Responses", CHEPS/Universiteit Twente, accessed 22 June 2007, *http://doc.utwente.nl/57133/1/thesis_Vlk.pdf*.

Waters, M. (1995), *Globalization*, Routledge, London.

Welch, A. (2005), "Challenge and Change: The Academic Profession in Uncertain Times", in A. Welch (ed.), *The Professoriate: Portrait of a Profession*, Springer, Dordrecht, pp. 1-19.

Wende, M.C. van der (1997), "Missing Links", in T. Kälvermark and M.C. van der Wende (eds.), *National Policies for Internationalisation of Higher Education in Europe*, National Agency for Higher Education, Stockholm.

Wende, M.C. van der (2001), "The International Dimension in National Higher Education Policies: What has Changed in Europe in the Last Five Years?", *European Journal of Education*, Vol. 36, No. 4, pp. 431-41.

Wende, M.C. van der (2002), "The Networked University: The Impact of Globalization and New Technologies", Lecture at the CHEPS PhD summer school, Barcelona.

Wende, M.C. van der (2004), "Introduction", in J. Huisman and M.C. van der Wende (eds.), *On Co-operation and Competition. National and European Policies for Internationalisation of Higher Education*, ACA Papers on International Co-operation, Lemmens, Bonn.

Witte, J. (2006), "Change of Degrees and Degrees of Change", Comparing Adaptations of European Higher Education Systems in the Context of the Bologna Process, Dissertation, CHEPS.

World Bank (2006), World Bank Data and Statistics, accessed on 15 August 2006, *http://web.worldbank.org/WBSITE/EXTERNAL/DATASTATISTICS/0,,contentMDK:20399244XXXXmenuPK:1192694XXXXpagePK:64133150XXXXpiPK:64133175XXXXtheSitePK:239419,00.html*.

World Bank (2008), World Bank Data and Statistics, accessed in July 2008, *http://go.worldbank.org/4C55Z0H7Z0*.

Chapter 2

Cross-border Higher Education:
Trends and Perspectives

by

Stéphan Vincent-Lancrin*

This chapter examines the future of cross-border higher education, notably student mobility. After pointing out several major trends in cross-border higher education and describing the main internationalisation strategies, it argues that international student mobility should continue to increase in the medium term and offers a prospective analysis of the evolution of the internationalisation strategies adopted by countries and institutions, examining in particular their convergence or the continued diversity of approaches.

* OECD, Directorate for Education, Centre for Education Research and Innovation (CERI). This chapter develops previous work on cross-border higher education carried out in collaboration with Kurt Larsen (World Bank) and Keiko Momii (National Institute for Educational Policy Research, Japan), who are gratefully acknowledged.

2.1. Introduction

The internationalisation of higher education has steadily increased since the 1990s. The ongoing harmonisation of higher education systems on a European scale, *via* the Bologna Process, and the repercussions of this process in Asia, Africa and Latin America attest to the growing significance of this international dimension. The emergence of worldwide university rankings and the media coverage which surrounds them also signal the appearance of a new global higher education area which is transforming the practices of higher education institutions, political decision-makers and students (Salmi and Saroyan, 2007; Salmi, 2009; Marginson and van der Wende, 2009a; Hazelkorn, 2007; Harfi and Mathieu, 2006; Sadlak and Nian, 2007). However, the considerable increase in cross-border higher education – i.e. anything to do with the international mobility of students and teachers, educational programmes or higher education institutions (Knight, 2004) – constitutes another major aspect of this evolution.

A growing number of people choose to study abroad, enrol in foreign programmes or institutions located in their country or simply to use the Internet to follow courses provided by universities or other higher education institutions based abroad. The number of foreign students in the OECD area rose by 90% between 1998 and 2007 to reach 2.5 million. Academic mobility is also on the increase. In the United States, it rose by 77% between 1994 and 2007 to reach 106 000 international academics in 2007 (IIE, 2008). This also applies to Japan and Korea, where this mobility more than doubled in the last decade, and to Europe (Vincent-Lancrin, 2009; Marginson and van der Wende, 2009b).

This evolution is the result of several factors which, albeit different, are not mutually exclusive: the countries' desire to stimulate academic and cultural exchanges; the greater mobility of qualified people and professionals within a global economy; the desire of higher education institutions to accrue additional income or raise their profile and visibility on the national and international stage; or even the need to benefit from an economically active population with a higher level of education in emerging or ageing economies (OECD, 2008a).

Although this international mobility may appear as a tradition in the academic world, its dynamic has deeply changed. Twenty years ago, it mostly reflected political, geostrategic, cultural and development aid motivations: the countries encouraged mobility as a way to open up to the world, hoping to create elite international networks. Universities welcomed foreign students but did not make any special effort to recruit them. Nowadays, cross-border education also corresponds to short term economic motivations: it is often perceived as an economic development lever by governments and as a competitive advantage by the institutions.

Cross-border higher education has evolved differently depending on the OECD country and region. Generally speaking, student mobility has been induced by political action in Europe and by significant demand in the Asia Pacific region. North America has always been a magnet for foreign students: it is only in recent years that the US has adopted a more proactive approach to the recruitment of international students. Furthermore, the education institutions themselves have decided to open sites or provide courses abroad, thereby enabling the residents of the host countries to enrol in a foreign institution without leaving their national territory. This evolution has been facilitated by the substantial autonomy granted to higher education institutions in certain countries as well as by the policies adopted by the host countries (OECD, 2004a).

The major trends in cross-border higher education and their political issues are presented and analysed in depth in several recent OECD publications (2004a, 2004b, 2006, 2007, 2008b). Statistics regarding student mobility are published and updated regularly (OECD, 2009a). This chapter examines the future of cross-border higher education, notably *via* three prospective scenarios, after underlining a few evolutions in the major cross-border higher education trends and highlighting four main internationalisation strategies. It maintains that the increasing success of cross-border higher education should continue and examines the possible evolution of the different internationalisation strategies, in particular in terms of convergence.

2.2. Trends in cross-border higher education

The major trends in cross-border higher education can be summed up in two words, growth and diversification: *growth* in the number of foreign students enrolled in foreign education programmes (or abroad); *diversification* of the cross-border education offer with the emergence of new forms of cross-border mobility. This section describes these major trends while highlighting a few recent changes.

Trends in international student mobility

International student mobility constitutes the main form of cross-border higher education. In 2007, there were 3 million foreign students in the world, *i.e.* nearly three times more than thirty years ago (see Box 2.1 for definitions).[1] OECD countries host approximately 85% of the world's foreign students, *i.e.* 2.5 million students; however, in 2007, two-thirds (67%) of the foreign students located in the OECD area were from a non-OECD member country. These two proportions have remained stable in the past decade. The percentage of mobile higher education students in the world also remained stable between 1998 and 2007, at around 1.8% of the worldwide number of higher education students (Unesco, 2009). Nevertheless, as mobile students mostly study in a OECD country, where the expansion of higher education has been slower than in the rest of the world, over the past few years the proportion of international and foreign students in the education systems of OECD countries has sharply increased, almost doubling over this period, from 4.5% to 8.7% on average for an OECD country (Figure 2.1 and Figure 2.2).

Generally speaking, the less a country receives foreign students, the more these students tend to come from neighbouring countries or countries from the same continent. Thus, 99% of the foreign students hosted by Sub-Saharan African countries are themselves from Sub-Saharan Africa, and the percentages are approximately 80% for Latin America, southern Asia and Pacific countries and nearly 70% for Arab and Central Asian countries – compared with only 27% for western Europe and North America taken together (Unesco, 2006).

Europe was the main host region of the OECD area in 2007, catering for 1.3 million foreign students, *i.e.* 52% of the foreign students listed and 95% more than in 1998. This is the number one host region for European and African students and an attractive region for students from North and South America and Asia. At the beginning of

> **Box 2.1. Foreign and international students in international statistics**
>
> International statistics on student mobility have improved in recent years. In 2006 for the first time, the OECD published data on mobile international students in addition to the data on foreign students. While foreign students are identified by their nationality, international students are identified by their previous country of study or their residence. In certain countries, national data on foreign students include both resident and non-resident higher education students (levels 5A, 5B and 6 of the International Standard Classification of Education). Thus, "foreign" students are generally an overestimate of genuinely mobile international students. For the 18 countries in which the information is available, mobile students represented on average 74% of foreign students in 2007, even if the differences between the countries are sometimes considerable: 31% of Norway's foreign students are mobile; in Canada, Spain, Sweden and New Zealand, this figure is around 52% while this proportion exceeds 80% in 8 countries. There are more "international" or mobile students in Finland and Iceland than there are foreign students, as their definition is based on the previous country of education: part of their mobility concerns their nationals who have previously studied in other countries. Theoretically, the data only takes into account the foreign students enrolled in programmes for at least one full-time equivalent semester. Students sent abroad for shorter periods who remain enrolled in their institution of origin and/or who continue to pay tuition fees to this institution should not be listed as foreign students in the host country. Although foreign students may not be international students (mobile), this chapter focuses, for practical reasons, on the data regarding foreign students as an approximation of student mobility: it is available for a larger number of countries and is the only type of data enabling a longitudinal approach

Figure 2.1. **Number and percentage of foreign and international students in the OECD area, 2007**[1]

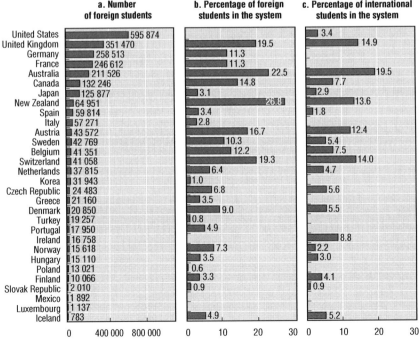

1. See Box 2.1 and OECD (2009a) for the definitions.

Figure 2.2. Number of national students abroad and mobility rate to foreign countries, 2007 (first countries of origin in terms of student numbers)

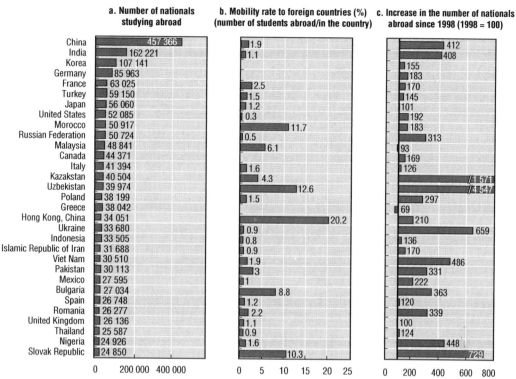

Sources: OECD and Unesco (UIS).

the Bologna Process in 1998, a time when European political decision-makers found European higher education unattractive to foreigners, Asian students were the only ones relatively reluctant to study in Europe: 49% of them opted for North America compared with only 28% for Europe. The situation was more balanced in 2007 (Table 2.1). OECD countries in North America welcomed 756 000 foreign students, *i.e.* 58% more than in 1998, but have slightly lost ground for Asian and North American students. Finally, member countries from Asia and the Pacific recruited 425 000 foreign students, *i.e.* 145% more than in 1998, notably by enhancing intra-regional mobility.

In terms of outgoing mobility, nearly half of the foreign students in the OECD area were from Asia, with 1.2 million students abroad in 2007, *i.e.* twice more than in 1998. Europe had 714 000 students abroad (63% more than in 1998); Africa had 283 000 (twice more than in 1998); South America 16 000 (3.7 times more); North America 97 000 (7% more) and Oceania 19 000 (40% more). The limited increase in the outgoing mobility in North America is perhaps related to mobility towards non-OECD member countries; however, as these destinations only represent 15% of the worldwide outgoing mobility, it more likely reflects a relative stagnation of its outgoing mobility.

The geographical breakdown of hosted foreign students varies depending on the major OECD regions (Table 2.2). North America attracts the largest number of Asian students. More than half (61%) of the total number of foreign students in North America is from Asia, compared with 14% from Europe, 12% from South America, 8% from Africa and 5% from North America. In the European OECD countries, students are primarily from Europe (44%), followed by Asia (29%), Africa (18%) and the Americas (8%) – while in Asia 85%

Table 2.1. **Destination of foreign students in the OECD area by region of origin (%) and changes between 1998 and 2007 (% points)[1]**

Destination	OECD area						Total OECD
	North America		Europe		Asia Pacific		
Origin	2007	98-07	2007	98-07	2007	98-07	
Africa	20	1	77	–2	3	1	100
North America	44	–12	43	4	13	8	100
South America	56	0	41	0	2	–1	100
Asia	40	–9	32	4	28	5	100
Europe	16	–1	81	2	3	–1	100
Oceania	27	–3	19	0	54	3	100
World	**31**	**–5**	**52**	**1**	**17**	**4**	**100**

1. The total percentage is not always 100% (and the sum of changes 0) due to rounding operations. Interpretation: 20% of the foreign students from Africa were located in North American OECD countries in 2007, i.e. 1 percentage point more than in 1998.

Table 2.2. **Breakdown of foreign students in the major OECD regions (%), 2007, and changes between 1998 and 2007 (% points)[1]**

Destination	OECD area							
	North America		Europe		Asia Pacific		Total OECD	
Origin	2007	98-07	2007	98-07	2007	98-07	2007	98-07
Africa	8	2	18	2	2	0	12	2
North America	5	–6	3	–2	3	0	4	–3
South America	12	7	5	2	1	0	7	4
Asia	61	–1	29	4	85	2	48	2
Europe	14	–1	44	–7	5	–2	29	–4
Oceania	1	0	0	0	3	–1	1	0
Total	100	0	100	0	100	0	100	0

1. See Table 2.1. Interpretation: in North American OECD countries, 8% of the foreign students came from Africa in 2007, compared with 6% in 1998 (plus 2 percentage points).

of students were from Asia. In terms of breakdown of foreign students by region, Europe boasts the most balanced profile even though most of European nationals remain in Europe (Table 2.2).

This regional analysis should not conceal the fact that foreign and international students remain concentrated in a limited number of countries (Figure 2.1). The eight countries hosting the most foreign students catered for 75% of the world's foreign students – Russia (2%) and South Africa (2%) being the only two countries that do not belong to the OECD. Five OECD countries host two thirds (66%) of the total. In 2007, 24% of the world's foreign students were located in the US, 14% in the UK, 10% in Germany, 10% in France, 8% in Australia. The top four English-speaking host countries (US, UK, Australia and Canada) hosted half (51%) of the total number of foreign students enrolled in the OECD area, a proportion which remains significant albeit down compared with 1998 (72%). In Europe, the UK and Germany hosted 68% of Asian students in Europe in 2007 (respectively 43% and 25%). France, for its part, hosted 52% of the African students in Europe (and 40% of all international African students enrolled in the OECD area).

The four countries hosting the most foreign and international students have remained the same in recent decades; however, since 1995, the UK has become the second host country and France the fourth (compared with fourth and second respectively). Several countries have experienced remarkable growth in student mobility, notably Australia, that has become the number five country for hosting international students (and number one in relative terms), but also the UK. Student mobility however has become more dispersed: international students have varied their destinations and the internationalisation process has been beneficial to a larger number of countries. The relative share of international students of the major hosting nations of the 1980s, i.e. the US and France, has progressively diminished while certain countries such as Australia and the UK have experienced remarkable growth.

In relative terms, i.e. if one looks at foreign students in percentage of total enrolments, the situation is somewhat different. Among the 63 countries for which the information was available in 2007, Liechtenstein (86%), Macao (China) (50%), Qatar (28%) and Cyprus (25%) were the top hosting countries for international or foreign students (Unesco, 2009). While Australia, the UK, Germany and France remain among the major hosting countries, the US drops from first to twenty ninth rank. In the OECD area, Australia, the UK, Austria, Switzerland and New Zealand have the largest proportion of international and foreign students in their higher education systems (Figure 2.1).

The main countries of origin of international and foreign students have remained the same in the past decade. China (including Hong Kong) is by far the country with the most student nationals abroad, with 17% of the foreign students of the OECD area in 2007. This represents five times more students abroad than in 1998, when Chinese students represented 7% of the foreign students of the OECD area. India jumped from eighth to second place among the countries of origin, with four times more students abroad in 2007 than in 1998, i.e. 6% of the total number of foreign students. South Korea (4%), Germany (3%) and France (2%) are the other main countries of origin (Figure 2.3). Outgoing mobility in OECD countries has also increased, albeit less so than incoming mobility (Figure 2.2).

In relative terms, the situation is once again somewhat different. The main countries of origin of foreign students (in absolute terms) have in fact relatively few students abroad in light of the size of their higher education system (Figure 2.3). The small countries are often those with the largest number of nationals studying abroad in relation to the size of their higher education system. These countries generally provide a limited offer, both in terms of quantity and discipline variety, which is why their nationals mostly study in neighbouring countries, under more or less tacit agreements. Thus, Luxembourg had more than twice as many students enrolled abroad than in its own territory. For many larger African countries, the significant student mobility is probably due to limited hosting capacity in their own territory (Figure 2.4).

The new forms of cross-border higher education

Student mobility is only one of the forms of cross-border higher education, even if it is the most significant in terms of volume. An increasingly large number of students are willing to explore new possibilities: following a higher education or post-secondary course provided by a foreign university without leaving their own country. In the past ten years, the international mobility of programmes and institutions has increased, notably towards Asia and the Middle East. These new forms of higher education only represent a limited proportion of cross-border higher education, but they constitute an innovation which may mark the beginning of an in-depth transformation of higher education in the long term.

Programme mobility is the second most common form of cross-border higher education after international student mobility. Even though it encompasses distance

Figure 2.3. **Increase in the number of national students abroad and foreign students in OECD countries, 1998-2007 (1998 = 100)**

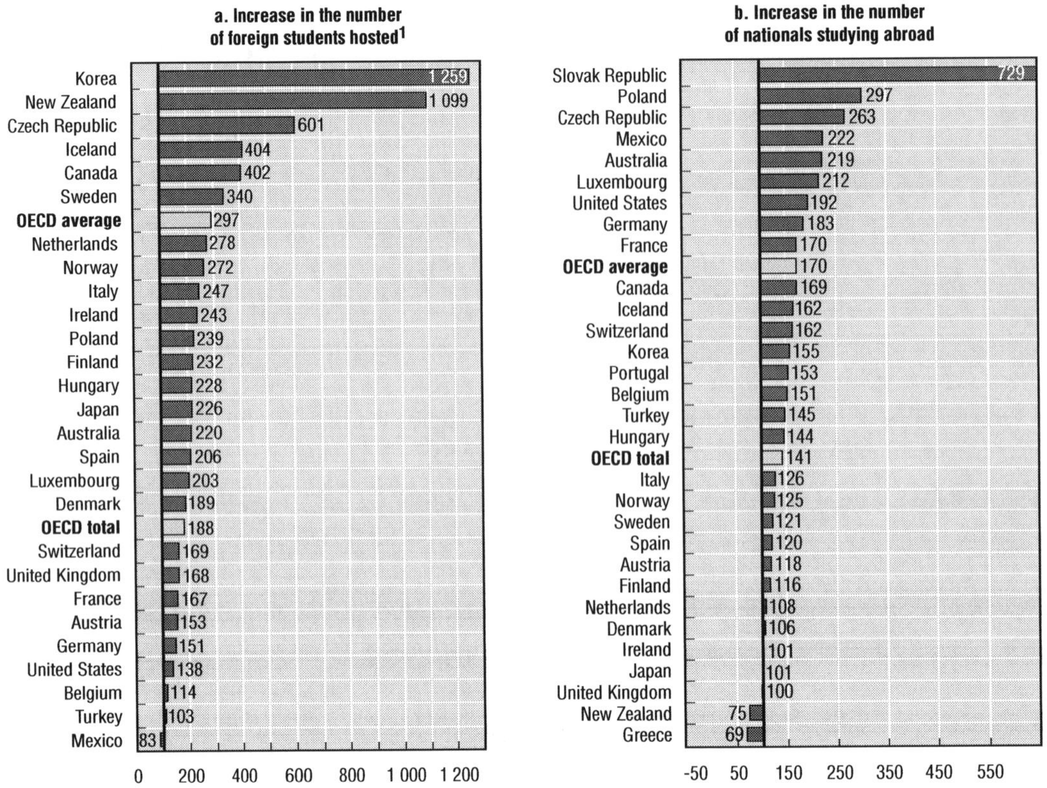

a. Increase in the number of foreign students hosted[1]

Country	Value
Korea	1 259
New Zealand	1 099
Czech Republic	601
Iceland	404
Canada	402
Sweden	340
OECD average	297
Netherlands	278
Norway	272
Italy	247
Ireland	243
Poland	239
Finland	232
Hungary	228
Japan	226
Australia	220
Spain	206
Luxembourg	203
Denmark	189
OECD total	188
Switzerland	169
United Kingdom	168
France	167
Austria	153
Germany	151
United States	138
Belgium	114
Turkey	103
Mexico	83

b. Increase in the number of nationals studying abroad

Country	Value
Slovak Republic	729
Poland	297
Czech Republic	263
Mexico	222
Australia	219
Luxembourg	212
United States	192
Germany	183
France	170
OECD average	170
Canada	169
Iceland	162
Switzerland	162
Korea	155
Portugal	153
Belgium	151
Turkey	145
Hungary	144
OECD total	141
Italy	126
Norway	125
Sweden	121
Spain	120
Austria	118
Finland	116
Netherlands	108
Denmark	106
Ireland	101
Japan	101
United Kingdom	100
New Zealand	75
Greece	69

1. Belgium, Mexico and Netherlands: 1999 instead of 1998.

Sources: OECD and Unesco (UIS).

education – which includes Internet training (or e-learning) (OECD, 2005a; Larsen and Vincent-Lancrin, 2006; OECD, 2009b), generally completed by face-to-face education in local partner institutions – it takes above all the form of traditional face-to-face education, provided in this case by a partner institution abroad. The relationships between the foreign and local institutions result in a variety of contractual arrangements ranging from development aid to market contracts.

University partnerships (exclusively based on the principle of non-profit collaboration) are the traditional and probably most common forms of international mobility of higher education programmes and institutions within the OECD area. This type of partnership often goes hand in hand with the mobility of students and academics. Sometimes, student mobility involves a certain mobility of the programmes, the purpose of which is either to facilitate the mutual recognition of the academic credits obtained in the partner institution as part of the qualification awarded by the institution of origin, or to enable the awarding of a joint qualification. More rarely, university partnerships can also include the joint development of programmes. For example, any institution participating in the Socrates-Erasmus programme had a bilateral convention with an average of 47 partner institutions in 2000 (Teichler, 2002).

Cross-border education of a commercial nature now plays an essential part in the Asia Pacific region where it mostly takes the form of franchising and twinning. Generally speaking, as part of a franchise, a local service provider is authorised by a foreign

Figure 2.4. **Mobility rate to foreign countries (countries with a percentage of over 20%), 2007**

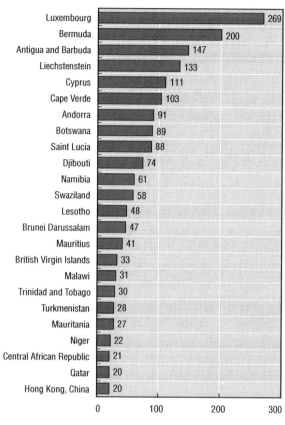

Source: Unesco.

institution to provide all or part of one of its education programmes under pre-determined contractual conditions. Most of the time, this education leads to a foreign qualification. In a twinning programme, students are enrolled with a foreign service provider and follow a foreign programme; part of the education is provided in their country of origin and completed in the country of origin of the foreign institution. This cross-border education method usually requires the mobility of both students and programmes.

It is difficult to estimate the number of cross-border educational programmes or the number of students enrolled in foreign programmes provided in their country. On an international scale, the two most active countries in this domain, the United Kingdom and Australia, boast approximately 300 000 students enrolled in their cross-border programmes, mostly in Asia (McBurnie and Ziguras, 2007). Each of the 38 public Australian universities currently offers programmes abroad, the number of which soared from a mere 25 in 1991 to 1 600 in 2003. More than 85% of them are located in China (including Hong Kong), Singapore and Malaysia, while the others are dispersed throughout the rest of the world, from India to Canada and from Indonesia to South Africa. The number of students enrolled in Australian programmes in their own country represented 30% of the total number of international students enrolled in Australian institutions in 2007, i.e. a 6% increase on 1996 (and a 6% drop since 2001) (IDP Australia).

Possibly due to the greater entrepreneurial risk involved, institution mobility remains limited; nevertheless, it has become an important part of cross-border higher education: it corresponds to the direct foreign investments made by higher education institutions or training companies. The most characteristic form of this type of mobility is the opening of campuses abroad by universities, and of training centres abroad by other educational service providers. According to the *Observatory on Borderless Higher Education*, there were approximately one hundred foreign higher education campuses worldwide in 2006, most of which were opened in the past 15 years and often after 2000 (Verbik and Merkley, 2006).[2]

For example, as of 2009 the University of Nottingham (England) had campuses abroad in China and Malaysia, the University of Liverpool (England) had created an institution in China with US and Chinese partners, the Monash University (Australia) had campuses in Malaysia and South Africa, the RMIT University (*Royal Melbourne Institute of Technology*) (Australia), in Viet Nam, and New York University (NYU) (United States) had ten campuses abroad.

Institution mobility however affects a larger number of countries than before, including those outside the OECD area. For example, the university of Paris 4-Sorbonne (France) opened a campus in Abu Dhabi in 2006, the Essec business school (France) opened a campus in Singapore in 2005, the German university of Cairo (2002) is operated by the universities of Ulm and Stuttgart, and the S.P. Jain Institute of Management and Research (India) opened campuses in Dubai (2004) and Singapore (2006).

Institution mobility also encompasses the creation of brand new education institutions (not affiliated to an institution of origin) as well as the partial or total acquisition of an institution abroad. This form for example is favoured by US listed group *Laureate International Universities*, which in 2009 owned approximately 40 campus universities in 18 countries, in South and North America (Brazil, Chile, Costa Rica, Ecuador, Honduras, Mexico, Panama, Peru, United States), in Asia Pacific (Australia, China, Malaysia) and Europe (Germany, Cyprus, Spain, France, Switzerland, Turkey).

With regard to the host countries, the information is also fragmented. Most of the offshore campuses are located in the Middle East, in the Gulf countries (United Arab Emirates and Qatar) and in Asia (notably Singapore, Malaysia and China) (Verbik and Merkley, 2006). In 2007, China re-approved 831 programmes or institutions operated in partnership with a foreign institution (705 programmes and 126 institutions). Conversely, only two *new* cross-border programmes and two new cross-border institutions were approved: the Chinese incentive policy for foreign programmes and campuses in its territory therefore seems to be at a halt (Dong, 2008).

Three recent evolutions in institution mobility should be underlined.

The first lies in the grouping of offshore campuses in regional clusters: the hosting of foreign institutions is an increasing part of a regional innovation or knowledge economy development strategy. An example of this model is the *Knowledge Village* (Dubai), the *Education City* (Qatar) as well as other educational areas currently being developed such as the *Kuala Lumpur Education City* supported by the Malaysian government and due to open in 2011. The development of cross-border education in Singapore is also part of this logic (Olds, 2007; McBurnie and Ziguras, 2009).

The second notable evolution is due to changes in the financing models of campuses abroad. While most of the initial offshore campuses self-financed their move abroad, they are currently increasingly funded by local partners (government or industrial companies) who provide them with a campus or even subsidise them. The Chinese campus of the University of Nottingham for example was funded by its industrial partner. Abu Dhabi, for example, also financed and subsidised the campuses abroad of the Sorbonne University and New York University. Cities or education cities rent out or lend premises and provide centralised logistical services (Verbik and Merkley, 2006). For the institutions, these funding methods significantly limit the risk associated with international mobility.

Finally, the mobility of programmes and institutions increasingly affects doctoral or research programmes, even though they only related to a minority of offshore campuses in 2006 (roughly 5% of the offshore campuses offered doctoral programmes, according to Verbik and Merkley [2006]). Since 2007, at the instigation of the Portuguese government, the Massachusetts Institute of Technology (MIT), the Carnegie Mellon University and the University of Texas in Austin have been offering Master and doctorate programmes in partnership with Portuguese institutions to reinforce the quality of training and research in certain disciplines, notably engineering. In 2008 a partnership was also established with the *Fraunhofer-Gesellschaft* (the German research centre company). In Singapore and Malaysia, the governments are also striving to attract foreign research organisations and get them to contribute to their national research, albeit not always successfully (McBurnie and Ziguras, 2009; Olds, 2007).

2.3. Principal current strategies for the internationalisation of higher education

Not all countries have an explicit policy for the internationalisation of their higher education, far from it. The increasingly structured and proactive nature of these public policies and institutional strategies for internationalisation however constitutes one of the outstanding changes of the past decade (OECD, 2008b, 2006). Current practices reveal four main strategies, reflecting the variety of political motivations and instruments implemented in this domain. These strategies are not always coordinated and even less so directly decided upon at government level, and their results vary considerably from one country to the next, even with similar political intentions or instruments. A tentative typology provides a rough outline of the current scene in terms of internationalisation policies. Although different, these major strategies pursue objectives which are not mutually exclusive. The traditional internationalisation strategy is based on mutual understanding while the other three – strategies based on *skilled migration, revenue generation, capacity building* – which emerged in the 1990s, are more focused on economic considerations.

Strategy based on mutual understanding

The strategy based on *mutual understanding* pursues above all political, cultural, academic and development aid objectives. It authorises and encourages the international mobility of national and foreign students and teacher-researchers, *via* grants and academic exchange programmes as well as partnerships between higher education institutions. This approach does not generally involve any vigorous campaign to recruit foreign students but targets a small elite of domestic and foreign students. Otherwise, the approach consists of an open door policy. Coordination efforts are primarily focused on development aid and national geostrategic choices. For this type of approach, grant programmes are often managed by the ministry of Foreign affairs. In terms of migration, foreign students are supposed to return to their country of origin for a relatively long period at the end of their studies.

This historic strategy in terms of internationalisation remains the main focus of countries like Mexico, Italy or Spain – and most developing countries. In the US, the programmes of the Fulbright commission are typical examples. The Socrates-Erasmus programme was also launched by the European Union as part of this logic, involving student and teacher exchanges, the networking of departments and universities across Europe and the joint development of study programmes, with the objective of creating a feeling of "European citizenship" among young Europeans, improving mutual understanding *via* the knowledge of several European languages. Although their knowledge of languages and neighbouring countries helped with subsequent student emigration and with the creation of a common labour market, study trips abroad remain short and continue to be part of the curriculum of the country of origin. The programme is therefore based on the student's return to his/her country of origin, and its very concept relies above all on long-term benefits: international students will keep special links with their host country, resulting in positive political, cultural and commercial consequences for this country.

Strategy based on excellence and competition for talent

The second strategy, based on *excellence and competition for talent*, pursues the same objectives as the previous strategy but also involves a more proactive and targeted approach to the recruitment of foreign students: this more intensive and proactive search for internationalisation constitutes a significant feature compared with the previous strategy.

In line with the logic of the knowledge economy, it aims at attracting talented students (and academics) likely to become knowledge workers for the host country's economy and to enhance the quality and competitiveness of the country's research and higher education sectors. The internationalisation of higher education allows the comparison of national institutions with foreign higher education institutions and often results in innovations and improvements to adapt to the demands and expectations of the foreign students or national students returning from a trip abroad. In addition, in the context of ageing societies and international competition based on knowledge and innovation, industrialised countries are increasingly in competition with one another to attract foreign talent to the host country and integrate international students into this strategy (OECD, 2008c). In this context, the studies of international students are subsidised by the host country in the same capacity as national students (and foreign residents).

Grant systems may remain a major action resource but they are often supplemented by other measures: the active promotion abroad of the country's higher education sector (advertising campaigns, participation in international exhibitions, etc.) combined with less restrictive visa or immigration regulations for the populations targeted (OECD, 2008b; Vincent-Lancrin, 2008; Suter and Jandl, 2006). Sometimes, specific services are designed to facilitate the studies and stay of foreigners in the host country. These services are often managed by national agencies such as the DAAD in Germany, CampusFrance in France, Nuffic in the Netherlands or the British Council in the United Kingdom. France, for example, created the EduFrance agency in 1998, which became CampusFrance in May 2007, to promote its higher education abroad and improve the way foreign students are received.

Furthermore, teaching in English can be developed and encouraged (in non-English speaking countries): the number of Anglophone programmes rose from 328 to 568 between 2005 and 2008 in France (CampusFrance, 2009); in Germany, the DAAD website listed 727 English-speaking study programmes in 2009; and there were about 1 300 of them in the Netherlands in 2007, according to Nuffic.

The populations targeted are varied: students from certain regions; post-graduate students or future researchers rather than undergraduate students, or students specialising in a specific field. This strategy generally results in an increase in the number of foreign students hosted in the country but has no real repercussions in terms of (commercial) mobility of programmes and institutions. Due to a lack of autonomy or incentives, this can be difficult if not impossible, and generally remains tied to a development aid policy or traditional academic partnerships.

Germany, one of the most active countries in this domain, Canada (in certain provinces), France, the United Kingdom (for European Union students) and the United States (for post-graduate students) are examples of this approach. While the internationalisation strategy of Japan and Korea was based on mutual understanding, this strategy has evolved in recent years, with significant efforts being made to attract talented foreign students and anglicise their most prestigious institutions. Generally speaking, perhaps driven by international rankings and excellence initiatives as well as by the mixed migratory results of these policies, the logic of improving the quality of national education and research has become predominant in this strategy.

Initiated in 1998, the Bologna Process marks a shift in the internationalisation policy adopted at European level and notably orients the European Union's Socrates-Erasmus programme towards this second strategy: the mobility of students and academics is now helping to create an area of higher education and research in Europe aimed at making European higher education more attractive (outside Europe, in particular in Asia) and transforming the economy of European countries into a knowledge-based economy (Huismans and van der Wende, 2004, 2005; Witte *et al.*, 2009; European Commission, 2008). The purpose of harmonising European systems is no longer only to promote mobility within Europe but also to make European higher education more attractive internationally, in particular compared with the United States. At the beginning of the process, the United States hosted 49% of the foreign students from Asia, compared with 40% in 2007 (Table 2.1). However, competition between European nations is just as fierce as co-operation.

Strategy based on revenue generation

The third strategy, based on *revenue generation*, pursues the objectives of the first two strategies, but also has directly commercial objectives: the idea is also to develop the exportation of education services.

One of the specific characteristics of this approach is to charge international students who (generally) receive no public subsidies for higher education services at market price. Compared with national students, international students therefore often generate additional income for the higher education institutions, which encourages them to become entrepreneurial on the international education market. Public authorities grant considerable autonomy to the institutions, seeking to establish the reputation of their higher education sector and protect foreign students *via* quality assurance mechanisms.

This strategy generally results in a substantial increase in the number of international students paying the full cost of their education and in the development of for-profit programme and institution mobility. It is sometimes accompanied by the reduction in the relative share of public financing in universities' resources, or even the reduction of public financing per student. It can also include an active trade negotiations policy aimed at lowering the obstacles to cross-border education activities, for example *via* bilateral agreements or as part of the negotiations of General Agreement on Trade in Services (GATS) in the World Trade Organisation (WTO) (see OECD, 2004a and 2007, for a presentation of the GATS and its consequences on education). It can also be accompanied by a brand policy, as is the case in the United Kingdom with the *Education UK* brand, or by a coordinated exporting policy as is the case in Australia (Marginson and McBurnie, 2004).

Migrating conditions are generally more flexible with regard to the paid employment of students during their studies; however, as with the first strategy, differentiated policies are often implemented to limit the subsequent permanent immigration of some students, while facilitating (as in the second strategy) the subsequent move of others. The authorities and institutions are therefore faced with the issue of geographical balance of international students not only in commercial terms (diversifying the countries of origin to achieve financial stability) but also in terms of immigration.

Examples of this approach can be found in Australia, New Zealand, the United States (for undergraduate students), Canada (in certain provinces), the United Kingdom, Denmark, the Netherlands and Ireland (for students from outside the European Union, as the European Union regulations oblige the countries to adopt the same enrolment fees for national students and those from other Union member countries). Education services in Australia represented the third export item in 2007 and the number one service export item, *i.e.* AUD 13.7 billion.

Strategy based on capacity development

The fourth strategy, based on *capacity development,* consists of encouraging studies abroad and the establishment of foreign courses and institutions in the country. It mostly concerns emerging countries. When a country lacks sufficient domestic capacity to meet all its demand for higher education, or does not have a national system of adequate quality, cross-border education can help reinforce its capacity in terms of educational offer and human resources for its economy and higher education system (Vincent-Lancrin, 2007). The objective is both quantitative and qualitative.

While the two above-mentioned strategies (competition for talent and revenue generation) are primarily geared towards exporting education services, the capacity development strategy focuses on importing education services.

Grant programmes supporting the international mobility of civil servants, teachers, academics and students constitute significant action resources in this respect, as are the measures taken to encourage foreign institutions, programmes and academics to provide their education services on a commercial basis, possibly in partnership with a local service provider. Countries can use the trade negotiations of the GATS to demonstrate their interest in this type of cross-border services (OECD, 2004a, 2004b, 2007). Programme and institution mobility is generally achieved under a government regulation which ensures that these activities are compatible with the country's academic and economic development strategy. Twinning agreements and partnerships developed with local providers are encouraged (and sometimes imposed) to facilitate the transfer of knowledge between foreign and local education institutions.

In the short term, this approach results in a considerable increase in the number of outgoing national students and in that of foreign profit-making education programmes and institutions coming into the country to meet local demand. Once the country's capacity has been developed, this strategy is no longer needed as such, and its success should theoretically lead to a change in strategy – but a higher education sector fairly different from that in past years. With this strategy, the coordination of the education policy with the economic and commercial policy plays an important role. In particular, countries must ensure that their quality assurance system covers foreign programmes and institutions and that these programmes and institutions actually contribute to the achievement of their national objectives. Their migrating policy must promote the temporary mobility of professionals and often includes measures encouraging the return of their nationals who left to study or complete their education abroad, in order to prevent a massive brain drain.

This strategy is mostly implemented in the Middle East and South East as well as northern Asia – Malaysia, Hong Kong (China) and China, Singapore, Indonesia, Viet Nam, Dubai, Qatar, Abu Dhabi, etc. As noted above, Portugal has also adopted this strategy to reinforce its research capacity in certain fields.

2.4. Student mobility growth perspectives

This section examines the growth potential of student mobility, which remains the most common form of cross-border higher education and notably of student mobility. McBurnie and Ziguras (2009) offer an additional analysis focused on programme and institution mobility. What are the growth perspectives for student mobility? Is it likely to be replaced by new forms of cross-border higher education?

Growth potential of cross-border higher education

Several factors indicate that student mobility will continue to increase in the upcoming decades. The number of international students depends on the number of people eligible to study abroad, on the number of positions open to international students, and on individual decisions to study abroad. This choice can be perceived as the result of a subjective evaluation of the monetary and non monetary costs associated with studies abroad and of the immediate and future monetary and non monetary benefits that the students (and their families) hope to derive from them.

Firstly, the increase in student mobility partly results from the worldwide expansion of higher education. The number of higher education students worldwide should continue to rise, at a fast rate outside the OECD area and at a moderate rate within this area (OECD, 2008a; Altbach *et al.*, 2009; Teixeira, 2009). Consequently, the number of potentially mobile higher education students should continue to increase. Major countries like China, India and soon Indonesia will probably continue to drive student mobility growth in the next few years. Insofar as it is the main destination of international students, the OECD area should experience a rapid increase in the number of international students, even if this number remains stable on an international scale. The declining appeal of the OECD area seems unlikely in the short term, if only because international rankings are becoming increasingly predominant in the students' decisions.

Secondly, the demand is unlikely to be rapidly rationed by the institutions and governments. As mentioned above, institutions and governments have invested heavily in internationalisation and created a context designed to encourage mobility. Although there is still work to be done, the infrastructures supporting student mobility have improved, both in the countries of origin and host countries with regard to administrative and social issues. In Europe, a survey carried out by the association of student unions shows that the majority of its members reported major or minor improvements relating to nine aspects of intra-European mobility assistance policies, the only exception being the language preparation which precedes a trip abroad (ESU, 2009). The information for foreigners on the countries' education offer has improved, including that on mobility grants. Progress in the recognition of foreign diplomas and qualifications should increasingly facilitate short-term mobility as well as the return to the country of origin (OECD, 2004b) – even though the absence of recognition also constitutes, to a certain extent, a mobility driver for those seeking to emigrate or having emigrated (Vincent-Lancrin, 2008).

Thirdly, student mobility is becoming a predominant part of the institutions' educational policy as they try to extend mobility options for their students *via* agreements between institutions. Thus, mobility is often compulsory or strongly encouraged in the programmes of the most prestigious institutions. By imitation, this could lead less prestigious institutions to encourage student mobility. The strategies adopted by institutions and governments to create world famous institutions or simply to improve their position at national level are effectively based on the internationalisation of their studies and on international mobility, with all the associated prestige and knowledge opportunities (Marginson and van der Wende, 2009a, 2009b; Salmi, 2009).

Fourthly, student mobility should continue to increase simply because new technologies will continue to make it increasingly easy to travel and stay in touch with family and friends at an acceptable cost, as will the drop in air transport and tourism costs and media globalisation, which makes certain parts of the world more visible and accessible to everyone. The Internet and the focus on foreign languages in educational policies should help increase the skills of foreign language students (in English in particular). These skills are already substantial in many countries and facilitate student mobility (HIS, 2008). Japan and Korea have also implemented vigorous English teaching campaigns and internationalisation (or Anglicisation) campaigns of their universities (*e.g.* Yonezawa *et al.*, 2009; Kim, 2007).

Finally, individual incentives to study abroad should continue to play an important part. In 2005, a mobility period during studies was associated with a higher salary, relatively significant depending on the country, for graduates at the beginning of their career – on average 8 to 10% more than non mobile students (Table 2.3). In Europe, Schomburg and Teichler (2007) and Teichler (2007) have observed a reduction in the impact and the subjective perception of the impact of student mobility on the beginning of a professional career. In a study of Swiss students who participated in international exchange programmes, Messer and Wolter (2007) show the existence of a wage premium in Switzerland which is attributable to the (pre-mobility) characteristics of the students rather than to the mobility period. Even if the mobility premium did not really exist or diminished over time for intra-European mobility, which is not certain, it is likely to continue to exist for people from poor or emerging countries. The possibilities of subsequent emigration to a wealthy country should continue to be perceived as a potentially significant individual incentive (Marmolejo *et al.*, 2008).

The high financial cost of student mobility is a significant obstacle. Despite growing public aid, this cost limits the mobility of students from underprivileged backgrounds within the European Union (HIS, 2008). This being said, the majority of student mobility is financed by the families, which has not limited the growth of this mobility (OECD, 2004a). The social consequences of the economic crisis (2008-09) could therefore limit the desire of

Table 2.3. **Difference in salary between mobile and non-mobile higher education graduates, five years after the end of their studies (2005) (%)**

	Men	Women
Germany	17	16
Austria	3	11
Belgium	2	4
Spain	7	12
Estonia	–1	3
Finland	4	7
France	23	27
Italy	20	10
Norway	13	13
Netherlands	5	6
Czech Republic	12	14
United Kingdom	–3	10
Switzerland	–1	–1
Country average	**7.8**	**10.2**

Interpretation: In Germany, the male students who had a mobility period abroad earn, on average, 17% more than non mobile male students, and mobile female students 16% more than non mobile female students.

Sources: Schomburg and Teichler (2007) (REFLEX data).

public authorities and families to invest in studies abroad, although the effects of this crisis are complex: for example, the impact of the crisis on the exchange rates can make certain study destinations more accessible to the students of certain countries. The fluctuations of the oil price and air transport also play a part. However, even global crises are never truly global: although the economic growth of certain countries of origin of the students such as China or India has slowed down due to the crisis, they have not been hit by a recession in 2008 and 2009. Australia, which recruits a lot of Asian students, in particular Chinese, registered a record 20% growth in international students in 2008.[3] Finally, the implementation of student grant and loan systems could reduce the objective and subjective difference in cost between domestic and international studies, especially if student grants and loans can be transferred abroad (OECD, 2008b).

Internationalisation could however reach a natural ceiling due to political considerations. The proportion of international students amounted to nearly 20% of the total number of students in Australia in 2007. Independently of the countries' hosting capacity, a point might be reached beyond which the populations will become hostile to the hosting of a larger number of foreign students. Although this may already happen at institution level, would it be politically acceptable if a higher education system, especially if it remains public, hosted 50% to 70% of foreign students? It all depends on the context but student mobility is part of the bigger issue of migration and of public opinion sometimes adverse to migration and foreigners. The examples of Belgium and Austria with regard to French and German students using international mobility to bypass the *numerus clausus* in the medical disciplines in their own country attest to these limitations, as do the recurring public interrogations in Australia or Canada on the potentially negative impact of large numbers of international students on the quality of higher education. In addition, not all countries are equally equipped to host foreign students, and not only for linguistic reasons: the size of the labour market, climate, international visibility and other factors are taken into account when deciding which country to study in.

Nevertheless, even in light of these limitations, the progress margin of student mobility remains significant in the upcoming decades. Even by setting a natural ceiling for the hosting of international students at an average of 15% of the total number of students in the OECD area, this would mean 8.2 million international students in 2025 (on weighted average and using the projections of OECD, 2008a), which leaves substantial room for growth.

Student mobility or programme and institution mobility?

Can student mobility be replaced by programme and institution mobility, which is less costly for students? This seems unlikely in the medium term.

Programmes and institutions abroad are an alternative to mobility for students. They enable them to benefit from a foreign diploma at a lesser cost than a trip abroad. Many students effectively enrolled in foreign Australian campuses perceive these campuses as a way to combine family life and work with international studies and to develop an international identity (Chapman and Pyvis, 2006). However, these programmes do not so much compete with mobility as complement it, and they stimulate student mobility between the institutions' domestic and foreign campuses. In Australia, most of the providers have adopted a three-year study model, starting abroad and finishing in Australia (as per a 2 + 1 or 1 + 2 model). The obtaining of a foreign or international diploma also facilitates subsequent mobility.

The growth potential of institution mobility is limited by the risk and cost for the foreign institution. This form of cross-border higher education has so far yielded little profit: the (identified) benefits of foreign campuses have been limited, and the losses, substantial. As suggested by McBurnie and Ziguras (2009), the opening of foreign campuses still corresponds more to a race for prestige than for profit. The increasingly frequent funding of campuses by investors or governments of the host country could facilitate the development of this form of cross-border education. However, this emerging trend is not yet sufficiently established.

Programme mobility is easier and less costly but, when in the form of a franchise, the quality of the cross-border services provided by the local partner is difficult to control by the institution of origin. Consequently, their development may be more limited than anticipated or supplemented by trips to the foreign institution, therefore involving physical mobility.

Finally, it is now clearly apparent that student mobility has a greater economic impact on the students' host country than the international mobility of its programmes and institutions. International students generate an economic activity far beyond enrolment fees, which only represented 48% of their expenditure in Australia in 2008 and 44% in the United Kingdom in 2004. The presence of international students in the territory has an indirect impact as it results in living expenditure but also the visit of their parents and families to the country in which they are studying, or subsequent qualified migration (ACPET, 2009; Lenton, 2007). In the United Kingdom, the revenue generated by international students studying in their own country in campuses or programmes abroad only represented 4% of the revenue associated with cross-border higher education in 2004 (Lenton, 2007). Similarly, a New Zealand survey estimated the contribution of international students to New Zealand's Gross Domestic Product at NZD 884 million compared with NZD 23 million for higher education programme and institution mobility activities (Education New Zealand and Ministry of Education, 2008). Therefore it is likely that governments will see no interest in encouraging the replacement of student mobility by the international mobility of programmes and institutions.

Student number projections

According to a study by Böhm *et al.* (2002), the number of international students could rise at a compound rate of 5.8% per year worldwide to reach 7.2 million by 2025. More or less optimistic, the different scenarios proposed in terms of worldwide economic and demographic growth estimate the number of international students at between 5.8 and 9 million in 2025. Five years later, using a revised methodology and new data, Banks *et al.* (2007) revised these projections down, banking on 3.7 million international students in 2025, *i.e.* an annual compound growth rate of 2.7%.

A less sophisticated way to forecast student numbers consists of extrapolating past trends. The growth in student mobility was relatively stable from 1975 to 2001, with a compound annual rate of 3.3%, and accelerated significantly from 2001 to 2007, with a compound annual rate of 8.1%. By using simple extrapolation techniques (least squares method), several scenarios relating to student mobility evolution can be envisaged. Depending on these scenarios, the projections regarding the number of foreign students would range from 3.7 to 6.4 million students in 2025.

Figure 2.5 presents the number of foreign students collected by Unesco and the OECD during the past decades, as well as four types of projection: a logistic extrapolation based on the past five years, leading to 3.7 million foreign students (compound annual growth rate of 1.07% between 2007 and 2025); a linear extrapolation based on the past 15 years, *i.e.* 4.5 million in 2025 (2.21% per year); a polynomial extrapolation based on 32 years of observations, *i.e.* 5.6 million in 2025 (3.55% per year); finally, an extrapolation assuming a compound growth identical to that of the 1975-2007 period, *i.e.* 6.4 million in 2025 (4.22% per year).

Figure 2.5. **Increase in the number of foreign students worldwide (1975-2007) and projections looking forward to 2030**

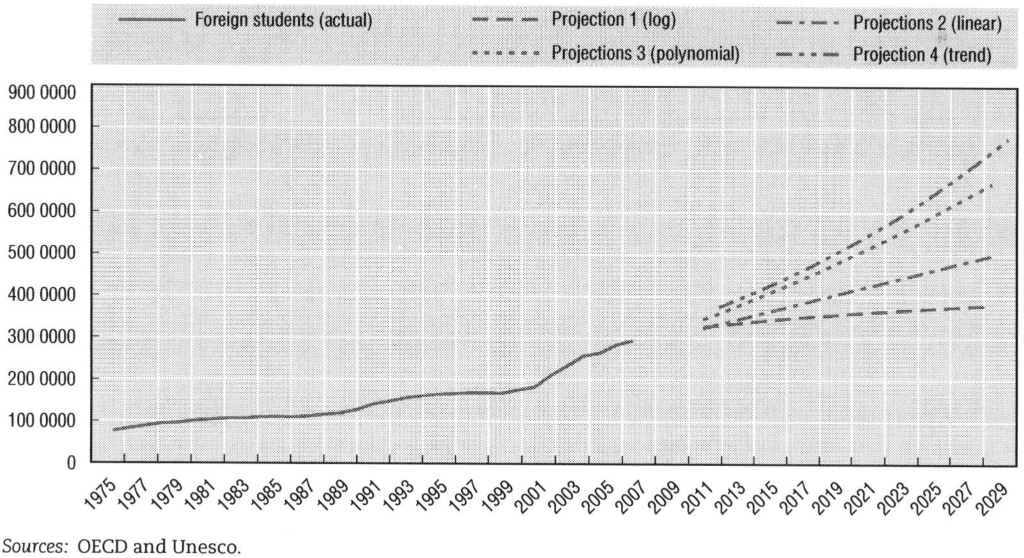

Sources: OECD and Unesco.

All scenarios are based on a long-term growth in the number of students, albeit more or less significant. The first quantitative scenario assumes that the growth experienced in the 2000s is exceptional and bound to slow down, but would be in line with the previous decades: over the years, the growth of the 1975-2000 period would have led to approximately 4 million foreign students in 2025. The second scenario (linear) represents a combination of the two contrasted growth rates of the 1990s and 2000s. The third scenario takes into account the entire past evolution while giving more importance to the latest period; finally, the last scenario corresponds with a constant compound annual growth rate over the entire period. All these quantitative scenarios are conservative: they are far below the recent growth rate but take into account the fact that it is easier to rise rapidly when the initial level is low. All these scenarios are positioned at a lower level than that mentioned above for a mobility ceiling.

It should be noted however that these scenarios are not based on an explanatory model of the growth and extrapolate the trends without claiming to be forecasts.

2.5. Three future scenarios for cross-border higher education

There are many possible implications of the growth in student mobility and cross-border higher education, for national higher education systems (OECD, 2004a, 2007) as well as for migration-related (Vincent-Lancrin, 2008) and quality issues (OECD, 2005b). This section does not examine these issues but offers a qualitative, forward-looking reflection on the evolution of cross-border higher education. Based on our analysis, three futures scenarios can be envisaged for cross-border higher education, all three based on the growth in internationalisation.

First scenario: sustained diversified internationalisation

In this first scenario, internationalisation continues while preserving the diversity of higher education systems both in terms of institution autonomy, foreign students hosting conditions, funding, quality assurance, educational offer and internationalisation strategy. Higher education institutions continue to have very different incentives for engaging (or not) in cross-border activities. The growth in higher education would probably continue with growing polarisation between the three exportation models described above.

The revenue-generating strategy concerns above all English-speaking and Asian countries such as Singapore, Malaysia or Hong Kong (China): these countries' institutions sell their higher education programmes by setting their enrolment fees at the international market price, by franchising their education programmes throughout the world, by validating those of other institutions abroad and finally by opening campuses abroad or providing their services for the management of private institutions abroad. This type of offer is attractive to countries with sufficiently sizeable wealth to finance it. Higher education is clearly becoming a service industry in these countries, partly based on the English language.

Higher education institutions in other countries continue to participate in internationalisation in different ways. Higher education institutions in continental Europe and Japan seek to actively recruit international students by continuing to subsidise their studies, in the same way as with their national and resident students. At institution level, this strategy pursues national and international prestige, while governments use it as a way to reinforce their knowledge-based economy by remaining integrated into international knowledge networks and, in some cases, as a way to deal with a shortage of qualified labour in certain sectors (for example science or engineering).

Finally, the mutual understanding strategy is still favoured by the countries lacking the desire or resources necessary to engage in international competition but wishing to keep an open-minded attitude in order to promote academic and cultural exchanges, sometimes similar to a "wait-and-see" strategy.

In this scenario, national quality assurance systems are established in almost all countries and play a key role in the coordination of the international mobility of students and highly qualified personnel. Countries continue to use mostly national quality assurance and qualification recognition criteria, with marked specific national characteristics in terms of content and structure of the programmes and qualifications, except perhaps within the European Union. The recognition of diplomas and qualifications remains a relatively complex process, examined on a case-by-case basis with the exception of certain regulated professions (such as engineering, medicine, nursing, etc.) for which international terms of reference define the minimum qualifications needed to exercise these professions on an international scale.

Second scenario: convergence towards a liberal model

In this scenario, higher education becomes a service industry based on commercial trade. The competition to attract foreign students paying their tuition fees at market price has become fiercer and most of the OECD countries and emerging economies have liberalised their market for international students by granting higher education institutions the liberty to determine the level of enrolment fees for foreign students. All forms of cross-border higher education continue to increase significantly insofar as developing countries have failed to meet their domestic demand or perceive cross-border higher education as a way to stimulate their national higher education and improve its quality – this notion has gained ground in wealthy countries. A large number of new service providers, including private companies, have therefore entered the cross-border higher education market, often in partnership with traditional universities.

Despite a growth in their international activities, English-speaking countries have lost market share compared to the other OECD countries on the international higher education market. In countries where universities have managed to gain new revenue on the international stage, public funds have decreased. Students and their families as well as employers are increasingly accepting the need for increased private investments in higher education, which triggers a heated debate on access to higher education for the students from less privileged backgrounds, as many consider that the implementation of a scholarship and loan system is insufficient to cover all their requirements. Finally, certain higher education institutions experience financial difficulties, as they are unable to recruit enough students because of this new competition.

In this scenario, national quality assurance as well as diploma and qualification recognition systems have been implemented in almost all countries. These systems increasingly coordinate their quality assessment references and recognition procedures on an international scale. In some cases, agencies or professional bodies may have the authority to recognise higher education diplomas and professional qualifications at a supranational level, notably for regulated professions such as medicine, engineering or accounting. There are more and more international rankings and some institutions sometimes receive negative publicity for providing international students with an education of dubious quality. To protect themselves against these reputation effects, institutions seek certifications and increasingly try to join one of the three competing "quality circles" with the most reputable cross-border higher education institutions, which represents a definite competitive advantage.

The GATS and regional trade agreements are commonly used to regulate trade in educational services. Many countries consider their higher education sector as export industries and have made binding commitments regarding market access and national treatment in the educational services sector. There is therefore growing tension between the traditional not-for-profit higher education offer and for-profit cross-border higher education. One can imagine a situation in which the World Trade Organisation is asked by a member to arbitrate a trade dispute on educational services on the grounds that, in certain countries, public funds would be used to reduce the price of higher education on the international market: these public funds would therefore represent hidden forms of subsidies distorting the competition in the trade of educational services.

Third scenario: the triumph of the (former) emerging economies

With sensible capacity development strategies aimed at developing their human resources and competences, including in cross-border higher education, the former "emerging economies" have become developed economies and their higher education systems are extremely competitive, both in terms of quality and price. Many higher education institutions and service providers from emerging nations have established partnerships with institutions and companies from developed English-speaking countries to develop their own competence. These nations initially established flexible but rigorous quality assurance and accreditation regulations to guarantee a minimum level of quality and local pertinence of cross-border and domestic educational programmes. As a result, the quality of higher education in these countries considerably improved, which enabled them to retain more of their students after their studies abroad and, above all, to attract a large number of students from emerging and developing countries. In this scenario, English-speaking India would probably become the world's number one higher education exporting country, with a strong capacity to attract foreign students to its institutions, both in its territory and in the countries where they have progressively provided their services.

International students continue to mainly study in the OECD area, albeit less so in light of the competition from emerging economies' institutions, and mostly for short-term periods and post-graduate programmes. This leads to difficulties in certain economically advanced countries. First of all, higher education institutions are lacking the financial resources previously obtained from international students, so much so that several governments have had to grant them extra public funding. Secondly, most developed countries are facing an ageing population and a greater need for skilled migration – a need that the drop in the number of international students does not help fulfil. Several countries are launching scholarship programmes for the brightest foreign students, allowing them to become residents after they graduate. The mobility between OECD countries of course continues and elite western universities remain very attractive to international students, despite extremely high enrolment fees. Like today, these very selective institutions are limiting their cross-border activities to the hosting of the brightest students and academics.

Programme and institution mobility continues to involve many institutions from developed countries but mostly the universities and private companies with long-time presence abroad, notably in the form of offshore physical campuses. However, the institutions and programmes of former emerging nations are also very active and it has been predicted that they will soon dominate the market of cross-border higher education in the form of programme and institution mobility. These programmes mostly operate almost exclusively using local teaching staff.

2.6. Closing remarks

To conclude, cross-border higher education has increased significantly in the past decade and has diversified beyond the traditional form of student mobility. All signs indicate that this growth will continue in the upcoming decades – unless there is a sudden halt in globalisation due to a major political crisis. Even the economic crisis seems to slow down rather than stop this trend. As suggested by the tentative scenarios, this continuation can take several forms. The first internationalisation scenario *via* diversity remains the most likely; it is in fact the actual scenario of the past decade. However, the ongoing debate in many western European countries on the funding of higher education and, in certain countries, on the autonomy of the institutions, indicates the possibility of a switch to the second scenario. Signs of this are already apparent in England, Australia, New Zealand and certain parts of Asia. This scenario already corresponds, to a certain extent, with the competitive environment of business and management schools, with their international rankings, quality labels and advertising campaigns in internationally published magazines. Finally, certain signs indicate that the third scenario is somewhat plausible: many Indian higher education institutions are present in Africa, although a genuine revolution of the mentalities would be needed in India for its higher education institutions to open up to cross-border education.

Several elements however indicate that the OECD area will continue to be the number one hosting area for international students, and therefore that the expansion of higher education throughout the world will result in an expansion of the number of international students. Major countries such as China, India and soon Indonesia will probably continue to drive the internationalisation growth in the years to come. In the long term however, this growth could be limited by the expansion of their domestic higher education capacities and by the growth in other forms of cross-border higher education, less costly for students. As noted above, if capacity development strategies actually work, the reinforcement of the enrolment capacity and quality of emerging countries' higher education systems should effectively reduce the appeal of studying abroad or at least following entire courses for the students from these countries: student mobility would then become shorter and probably more focused on postgraduate or even doctoral levels, as is often the case with student mobility between European and American OECD countries. Conversely, student mobility at international level would continue to grow insofar as these countries will become increasingly attractive as host countries as they continue to develop, initially for the students from developing and emerging countries and ultimately for those from industrialised countries. The OECD area's "market share" of international students could therefore decrease in the long term.

Notes

1. The figures used in this chapter are, unless otherwise mentioned, those of the OECD Education Database for all member and non-member countries covered by this database (OECD, 2009a), and those of Unesco for all other countries (Unesco, 2009). When the 2007 data is missing, the last available year is used as an estimate.

2. The report lists 82 foreign campuses (defined as an entity operated by the foreign institution or a partnership on behalf of the foreign institution) which award qualifications from the foreign

institution and exclude a number of forms of campus abroad. This figure mostly concerns the English-speaking world and probably underestimates the actual number of campuses abroad.

3. Press release of 26 February 2009 from Minister Julia Gillard, "Record Growth in International Students in 2008", *www.deewr.gov.au/Ministers/Gillard/Media/Releases/Pages/Article_090226_151822.aspx*.

Bibliography

Altbach, P., L. Resiberg and L. Rumbley (2009), *Trends in Global Higher Education. Tracking an Academic Revolution*, CIHE, Boston.

Australian Council for Private Education and Training (ACPET) (2009), *The Australian Education Sector and the Economic Contribution of International Students*, Access Economics.

Banks, M., A. Olsen and D. Pearce (2007), *Global Student Mobility: An Australian Perspective Five Years On*, IDP Education, Sydney, Australia.

Böhm, A., D. Davis, D. Meares, and D. Pearce (2002), *Global Student Mobility 2025*, IDP Education, Sydney, Australia.

CampusFrance (2009), Courrier CampusFrance No. 9, *http://editions.campusfrance.org/lettre_adherents/n8_janv_fev2009.pdf*.

Chapman, A. and D. Pyvis (2006), "Quality, Identity and Practice in Offshore University Programmes: Issues in the Internationalisation of Australian Higher Education", *Teaching in Higher Education*, Vol. 11, No. 2, pp. 233-45.

European Commission (2008), *The Impact of ERASMUS on European Higher Education: Quality, Openness and Internationalisation*, Bruxelles, *http://ec.europa.eu/education/erasmus/doc/publ/impact08.pdf*.

Dong, X. (2008), "Development of Transnational Education in P. R. China", presentation at APEC Capacity Building Seminar on Transnational Education Services, 24-26 September 2008, Manilla, Philippines.

Education New Zealand and New Zealand Ministry of Education (2008), "The Economic Impact of Export Education", *www.international.ac.uk/resources/EconomicImpactReport08.pdf*.

ESU (European Students' Union) (2009), *Bologna with student eyes 2009*, Louvain.

Harfi, M. and C. Mathieu (2006), "Classement de Shangai et image internationale des universités : quels enjeux pour la France ?", *Horizons stratégiques*, Vol. 2, pp. 1-16.

Hazelkorn, E. (2007), "The Impact of League Tables and Ranking Systems on Higher Education Decision Making", *Higher Education Management and Policy*, Vol. 19, No. 2.

Higher Education Information System (HIS) (2008), *Social and Economic Conditions of Student Life in Europe*, Bertelsmann, Bielefeld.

Huisman, J. and M.C. van der Wende (eds.) (2004), *On Cooperation and Competition, National and European Policies for the Internationalisation of Higher Education*, Lemmens Verlag, Bonn.

Huisman, J. and M.C. van der Wende (eds.) (2005), *On Cooperation and Competition II, Institutional Responses to Internationalisation, Europeanisation and Globalisation*, Lemmens Verlag, Bonn.

Institute for International Education (IIE) (2008), *Open Doors 2008. Report on International Educational Exchange*, Sewickley, PA, United States.

Kim, K.-S. (2007), "The Making of a World-class Research University at the Periphery: Seoul National University, 1994-2005", in P. Altbach and J. Balan (eds.), *World Class Worldwide: Transforming Research Universities in Asia and Latin America*, Johns Hopkins University Press, Baltimore.

Knight, J. (2004), "Internationalization Remodelled: Definition, Approaches, and Rationales", *Journal of Studies in International Education*, Vol. 8, No. 1, pp. 5-31.

Larsen, K. and S. Vincent-Lancrin (2006), "The Impact of the ICT on Tertiary Education: Advances and Promises", in B. Kahin and D. Foray (eds.), *Advancing Knowledge and the Knowledge Economy*, MIT Press, Cambridge.

Lenton, P. (2007), *Global value. The Value of UK Education and Training Exports: An Update*, British Council, *www.britishcouncil.org/global_value_-_the_value_of_uk_education_and_training_exports_-_an_update.pdf*.

Marginson, S. and G. McBurnie (2004), "Cross-border Post-secondary Education in the Asia-Pacific Region", in *Internationalisation and Trade in Higher Education: Opportunities and Challenges*, OECD Publishing, Paris.

Marginson, S. and M. van der Wende (2009a), "The New Global Landscape of Nations and Institutions", in *Higher Education to 2030, Volume 2: Globalisation*, OECD Publishing, Paris.

Marginson, S. and M. van der Wende (2009b), "Europeanisation, International Rankings and Faculty Mobility: Three Cases in Higher Education Globalisation", in *Higher Education to 2030, Volume 2: Globalisation*, OECD Publishing, Paris.

Marmolejo, F., S. Manley-Casimir and S. Vincent-Lancrin (2008), "Immigration and Access to Higher Education: Integration or Marginalisation?", in *Higher Education to 2030, Volume 1: Demography*, OECD Publishing, Paris.

McBurnie, G. and C. Ziguras (2007), *Transnational Education: Issues and Trends in Offshore Education*, Routledge Falmer, London.

McBurnie, G. and C. Ziguras (2009), "Trends and Future Scenarios in Programme and Institution Mobility Across Borders", in *Higher Education to 2030, Volume 2: Globalisation*, OECD Publishing, Paris.

Messer, D. and S. Wolter (2007), "Are Student Exchange Programs Worth it?", *Higher Education*, Vol. 54, No. 5, pp. 647-63.

Organisation for Economic Co-operation and Development (OECD) (2004a), *Internationalisation and Trade in Higher Education: Opportunities and Challenges*, OECD Publishing, Paris.

OECD (2004b), *Quality and Recognition in Higher Education: The Cross-border Challenge*, OECD Publishing, Paris.

OECD (2005a), *E-learning in Tertiary Education: Where Do We Stand?*, OECD Publishing, Paris.

OECD (2005b), *Guidelines for Quality Provision in Cross-Border Higher Education*, www.oecd.org/dataoecd/27/51/35779480.pdf.

OECD (2006), "The Internationalisation of Higher Education: Towards an Explicit Policy", in *Education Policy Analysis: Focus on Higher Education – 2005-2006 Edition*, OECD Publishing, Paris.

OECD (2007), *Cross-border Tertiary Education: A Way towards Capacity Development*, OECD Publishing, Paris.

OECD (2008a), *Higher Education to 2030, Volume 1: Demography*, OECD Publishing, Paris.

OECD (2008b), *Tertiary Education for the Knowledge Society*, OECD Publishing, Paris.

OECD (2008c), *The Global Competition for Talent: Mobility of the Highly Skilled* , OECD Publishing, Paris.

OECD (2009a), *Education at a Glance 2009*, OECD Publishing, Paris.

OECD (2009b), *Higher Education to 2030, Volume 3: Technology*, forthcoming, OECD Publishing, Paris.

Olds, K. (2007), "Global Assemblage: Singapore, Foreign Universities, and the Construction of a 'Global Education Hub'", World Development, Vol. 35, No. 6, pp. 959-75.

Sadlak, J. and L. N. Cai, *The World-Class University and Ranking: Aiming Beyond Status*, Unesco-CEPES, Bucharest.

Salmi, J. (2009), *The Challenges of Establishing World-class Universities*, World Bank, Washington, DC.

Salmi, J. and A. Saroyan (2007), "League Tables as Policy Instruments: Uses and Misuses", *Higher Education Management and Policy*, Vol. 19, No. 2.

Schomburg, H. and U. Teichler (2009), "International Mobility of Students and Early Career", in U. Teichler, *Higher Education and the World of Work*, Sense Publishers, Rotterdam, pp. 269-83.

Suter B. and M. Jandl (2006), *Comparative Study on Policies towards Foreign Graduates: Study on Admission and Retention Policies towards Foreign Students in Industrialised Countries*. International Centre for Migration Policy Development (ICMPD), Vienne, *www.thehagueprocess.org/News/news/documenten/ComparativeStudyonGraduatedStudents_Final.pdf*.

Teichler, U. (2007), "Higher Education and the European Labour Market", in U. Teichler, *Higher Education and the World of Work*, Sense Publishers, Rotterdam, pp. 253-68.

Teichler, U. (ed.) (2002), *Erasmus in the Socrates Programme: Findings of an Evaluation Study*, ACA Papers on International Cooperation in Education, Bonn, Lemmens Verlags.

Teixeira, P. (2009), "Mass Higher Education and Private Institutions", in *Higher Education to 2030, Volume 2: Globalisation*, OECD Publishing, Paris.

UNESCO (2006), *Global Education Digest 2006: Comparing Education Statistics across the World*, Paris.

UNESCO (2009), *Global Education Digest 2009: Comparing Education Statistics across the World*, Paris.

Verbik, L. and C. Merkley (2006), "The International Branch Campus – Models and Trends", *The Observatory on Borderless Higher Education*, October.

Vincent-Lancrin, S. (2008), "Student Mobility, Internationalisation of Higher Education and Skilled Migration", in *International Organisation for Migrations, World Migration 2008: Managing Labour Mobility in the Evolving Global Economy*, Geneva.

Vincent-Lancrin, S. (2009), "What is Changing in Academic Research? Trends and prospects" in *Higher Education to 2030, Volume 2: Globalisation*, OECD Publishing, Paris.

Witte, J., J. Juisman and L. Purser (2009), "European Higher Education Reforms in the Context of the Bologna Process : Where are we and Where are we Going ?", in *Higher Education to 2030, Volume 2: Globalisation*, OECD Publishing, Paris.

Yonezawa, A., K. Akiba and D. Hirouchi (2009), "Japanese University Leaders' Perceptions of Internationalization: The Role of Government in Review and Support", *Journal of Studies in International Education*, Vol. 13, No. 2, pp. 125-42.

Higher Education to 2030
Volume 2: Globalisation
© OECD 2009

Chapter 3

Trends and Future Scenarios in Programme and Institution Mobility across Borders

by

Grant McBurnie and Christopher Ziguras*

This chapter examines the future prospects for cross-border mobility of higher education institutions and programmes. The chapter develops four alternative future scenarios, by taking into account elements such as the state of economic development and domestic higher education provision in host countries. The scenarios draw on current trends in student demand, programme delivery and government policies, with a specific focus on Australia and South-East Asia.

* Royal Melbourne Institute of Technology.

3.1. Introduction

Writing about the future of transnational higher education would be much easier if more was known about what is happening now. By transnational higher education, we refer to the mobility of educational programmes and institutions across borders. Data collected by the OECD and UNESCO tell us a great deal about the patterns of international student mobility, and historical trends are clearly evident. But when it comes to moving programmes and institutions – rather than learners – across borders, there is a remarkable paucity of hard data.

The overall picture that can be gleaned is that: transnational education is a growing phenomenon that has existed in one form or another since the earliest days of education, but whose modern commercial incarnation has taken off largely since the late 1980s with a sharp rise in the last decade; that hundreds of thousands of students (Bashir, 2007, p. 34; McBurnie and Ziguras, 2007, p. 24-25) are enrolled in foreign programmes in their home country, with the largest numbers currently in Asia; that the chief foreign providers abroad are institutions from the United Kingdom, Australia and the United States of America. For some countries, transnational education represents a significant proportion of student enrolments. After 20 years of continued growth, more than one third of the higher education students in Singapore were enrolled in transnational programs in 2004 according to government statistics (Lee, 2005; Ministry of Education, 2006). Offshore enrolments in Australian universities have grown from around 20 000 in 1996 to 66 363 in 2008, representing nearly one-third of the international enrolments in Australian universities, while another 30 958 offshore students were enrolled in Australian public technical and vocational education institutions in 2006 (IDP Education Australia, 2008; National Centre for Vocational Education Research, 2008).

In this chapter, we first briefly discuss some limitations relating to quantitative forecasting of future trends in transnational higher education. We then draw on current trends in student demand, programme delivery and government policies to develop four scenarios for the future of transnational higher education. Our focus is on degree-level higher education, rather than vocational education and training. We concentrate on Australia and South-East Asia as these regions have to date been at the forefront of developments in transnational higher education.

In the first scenario, we see the world of higher education becoming "more foreign" in many countries, if optimistic forecasts of continued rapid growth in demand for transnational education prove correct. This growth will become more broad-based, as patterns of delivery pioneered in South-East Asia are rolled out across the globe and institutions outside the United Kingdom, Australia and the United States adopt transnational delivery. In scenario 2, "The world churns", we explore the possibility that mass transnational education may be a relatively short-lived phase in importing countries, who may "outgrow" their demand for transnational education by developing their preferred domestic education providers. In Scenario 3, "Branch campuses clusters", we postulate the development of clusters of branch campus of prestigious universities located in cities that act as regional hubs for international business services, education and research. In the fourth scenario, "Raising the bar", we explore the implications of a backlash against transnational programmes that are perceived to be of low quality.

These scenarios are not mutually exclusive. They may overlap and aspects may take place simultaneously in different parts of the world. The cluster trend, for example, could take place in both growth and decline scenarios for transnational education enrolments. The scenarios are not intended to encompass all possibilities, but they do allow us to envisage some of the broad, long-term implications of the trends which we see emerging today.

3.2. Limitations in forecasting growth

There is little data available on transnational higher education. Very few governments collect statistics on that, and to date no such figures are published by OECD or UNESCO. Some countries keep track of foreign programmes and transnational enrolments in their own country (notably Singapore and Hong Kong), but national figures are kept by only one major exporting country, Australia. Other scattered sources of information include "breaking news" and commissioned reports issued by the London-based Observatory on Borderless Higher Education, reports in the higher education press, institutional websites, occasional government audit reports, and a smattering of academic publications.

The most common assumption presented by critics and proponents of transnational education is that of continued growth in the number and size of internationally mobile programmes and institutions. This is based on the hypothesis that the past decade's rapid growth (OECD, 2004) will continue into the future. We explore some of the difficulties related to this assumption in the light of the Australian example below.

One of the most detailed estimate of future demand for transnational higher education is IDP Education Australia's study of global student mobility from 2000 to 2025 (Böhm et al., 2002). The forecasts (see Table 3.1) are based on an estimate of how economic growth and population growth affect participation rates in higher education and demand for international education. The most difficult part of the forecasting is estimating transnational student numbers, because there is a paucity of data on which to base predictive models. Australia is the only major exporting country with detailed data on transnational students but volatility of Australia's transnational experience coupled with the small numbers of students in most countries makes even this data unreliable.

One difficulty is in estimating what IDP calls the "transnational ratio", which is ratio of transnational to onshore international students from a particular country. This ratio is difficult to ascertain, since in the five years prior to 2000 the proportion of international students in Australian universities enrolled offshore increased from a quarter to over a third of all international students. Clearly, if this trend were to be simply extrapolated, all international students would be enrolled offshore by around 2030.

Böhm et al. (2002) found no relationship between a country's per capita income and the transnational ratio. With little to work with, the authors developed a formula that begins with the 2000 ratios and assumes that the proportion of transnational students would increase with per capita incomes of the host countries. Using this model, they predicted that by 2025, 44% of all international students enrolled in Australian universities would be offshore, and their distribution would be very similar to the picture in 2000 (Böhm et al., 2002, p. viii).

Table 3.1. **Enrolments of students in transnational Australian higher education from 2000 to 2025 by region (actual and forecasted numbers)**

Importing region	2000 Actual	2005 Forecast	2005 Actual	2010 Forecast	2015 Forecast	2020 Forecast	2025 Forecast	2000-25 Forecast compound annual growth rate
Africa	520	669	1 951	1 037	1 612	2 428	3 752	8.2%
Sub-Saharan Africa	520	669	1 951	1 037	1 612	2 428	3 752	8.2%
North Africa	0	0	0	0	0	0	0	0%
Middle East	160	239	1 025	420	674	939	1 241	8.5%
Asia	31 530	49 696	47 315	87 318	151 896	252 448	423 653	11.0%
East Asia	11 361	19 065	18 017	33 106	60 490	109 867	207 867	12.3%
South-East Asia	20 010	30 117	26 442	52 510	87 839	136 140	204 708	9.7%
South Asia	159	514	2 856	1 702	3 567	6 441	11 078	18.5%
Central Asian Republics	0	0	0	0	0	0	0	0%
America	682	1 023	899	1 433	1 983	2 493	3 022	6.1%
North	665	996	899	1 391	1 918	2 400	2 897	6.1%
Central	0	0	0	0	0	0	0	0%
South	17	27	0	42	65	92	125	8.3%
Europe	515	787	846	1 089	1 475	1 828	2 259	6.1%
West	453	664	846	880	1 148	1 366	1 604	5.2%
East	62	123	0	209	327	462	654	9.9%
Oceania	144	187	739	254	354	459	569	5.7%
Other	m	m	1 685	m	m	m	m	m
World Total	**33 551**	52 601	**54 460**	91 551	157 993	260 595	434 496	10.8%

m = missing data

Sources: Böhm et al. (2002); 2005 actual numbers from IDP (2005).

Böhm et al.'s bold formula-driven predictions may prove to be accurate for the aggregate numbers of Australian transnational students, but they are unlikely to be accurate for individual importing countries, as they do not take account of the local conditions that enhance or retard the growth of transnational education. In particular, Böhm et al.'s global market approach is unable to consider the degree to which local government policies impact on the extent of foreign provision, especially recognition of transnational qualifications, openness to foreign investment, and the ability of non-government institutions to operate in a higher education market. The forecast does not take into account the possibility of Australian higher education institutions spreading their services to completely new regions in the future.

Table 3.1 shows Böhm et al.'s forecast of transnational student numbers in Australian higher education institutions in their moderate income growth scenario. Under these conditions Böhm et al. predict that, in 2025, there would be more than 430 000 transnational students enrolled in Australian higher education institutions, of which almost all are in the Asian continent. This would represent roughly a 13-fold increase compared to 2000.

We have included 2005 actual data from the same data set as that used to develop the forecast. This allows us to see that the overall growth of the transnational students between 2000 and 2005 was more than initially predicted by Böhm et al. (54 460 actual transnational students worldwide against 52 601 forecasted). We can see that smaller markets grew more rapidly than larger ones so while the two largest regions continued to grow substantially (South-East Asia up by 32%, East Asia up 59%), the biggest percentage growth occurred in newer markets for Australian providers, most of which was in countries with lower incomes than the traditional transnational markets (Sub-Saharan Africa up 275%, Middle East up 540%, South Asia up 1 696%, Oceania 413%). The proportion of Australia's transnational students in East and South-East Asia was 93% of all transnational students in 2000 and, even though Böhm *et al.* had predicted this concentration to continue, it had dropped to 82% by 2005.

In the framework of our four scenarios, we will discuss under what conditions the growth of transnational higher education would or would not continue in the future.

3.3. Scenario one: the world of higher education becomes more foreign

Under what conditions can the growth scenario come to fruition? We suggest that the driver will be four sets of key actors embracing transnational education due to its perceived benefits for them: 1) importing governments will continue to use transnational education to rapidly absorb higher education demand; 2) exporting governments and 3) institutions will pursue transnational education for financial and reputational reasons; and 4) students will enrol in transnational education due to lack of domestic opportunity, the perceived prestige of foreign education, and because it is cheaper than studying abroad. We explore these in turn.

Figure 3.1. **Growth of transnational higher education – Scenario 1**

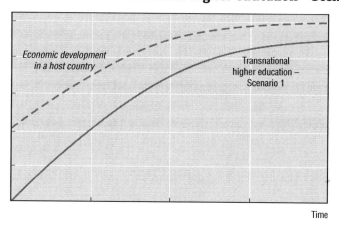

Transnational education can help importing governments to meet local student demand through the provision of additional places more rapidly and cheaply than by expanding local infrastructure (OECD/World Bank, 2007). Under this scenario, local private providers that are not empowered to grant degrees in their own right are permitted to partner with recognised foreign universities in order to offer the latter's credentials. The cost of such education expansion is therefore shifted from the public purse to the private – the fee-paying student and the non-government provider. The importing government recognises various other advantages. By reducing the outflow of funds that accompany students studying abroad, transnational education can assist importer countries with their balance of payments. Further, the user-pays approach to meeting student-demand frees up public funds that can be spent on other government priorities. The presence of foreign providers can create local employment opportunities for academic and managerial staff. In the case of full branch campuses, there is an expansion of local infrastructure (libraries, laboratories, IT facilities, classroom space), as well as expanded curriculum material, and administrative systems. The effect of competition and collegiality with foreign providers may have beneficial impacts on local academic and managerial practices. While host governments are eager to meet heavy demand, the regulatory requirements on foreign providers are relatively light. As the bulk of demand is met, the importing government in turn becomes more selective about which providers are admitted, the conditions of entry and the ongoing regulatory and quality assurance requirements.

There is a well-established trend in recent years for some governments in developed countries to reduce the state component of funding for higher education (see for example OECD, 2008). Where there is not an absolute decrease in public funding, there is likely to be a proportional decrease due to a policy consensus toward increasing the non-government/ student share of contributions to education costs. This is likely to spread and accelerate, as the demographic profile of developed countries may imply that those governments will be focussing on meeting the expenses for pensions and health care of the ageing population. In the first scenario, universities will variously be allowed, encouraged or obliged to generate external earnings through such activities as commissioned research and the provision of fee-charging courses to international students. To date, the chief exporters of transnational education have been Anglophone countries. As developed and many transitional countries around the world are increasingly pressured by a decline in the local traditional student-aged numbers, and sundry funding pressures, the entrepreneurial university approach will spread more widely, shaped by local conditions and approaches. Already, we can see such developments in various European, Middle-eastern and Asian countries.

Governments sometimes also see themselves as deriving reputational benefits from the export of higher education. In the case of Australia, for example, the international export of its higher education is already consonant with the national goal of being a "clever country" (focusing on the value-added tertiary sector of the economy) and reducing its reliance on the export of raw materials. The frequently cited example of success in this endeavour is the fact that education had become Australia's third largest export industry in 2007 – having grown six-fold as a percentage since 1982 – surpassed only by coal and iron ore (Hall and Hooper, 2008, p. 12). In this scenario, the export of higher education is a mark of a nation's international success in the knowledge economy.

Some governments and industry bodies already maintain detailed statistics on international student numbers and characteristics, and carry out econometric modelling of the economic benefits to the nation and the associated impact on employment. For example, an Australian study reported that in the year 2002 there were 253 780 international students in Australia (including higher education, English-language courses, vocational and pre-tertiary education), spending a total of AUD 5.18 billion (USD 2.82 billion), with just over half spent on tuition fees and just under half spent on other expenditure in Australia – with an employment impact of some 42 650 jobs (Kenyon and Koshy, 2003, p. 6). By 2007, official estimates of the value of international education had grown to AUD 12.5 billion (USD 10.45 billion) (AEI 2008)[1]. A complementary report (see Giesecke, 2004) with detailed data on the economic effects of international students in Australia modelled the potential impacts of changes in international student numbers and economic behaviour across a number of scenarios.

Similar detailed economic data are not presently available for offshore education, partly due to the difficulty of capturing the information, and partly because less attention has been paid to mobile programmes than to mobile students. In the future, as transnational enrolments grow, and programme mobility becomes increasingly attractive to governments with an exporting capacity, data will be gathered and analysed closely by governments and international organisations. One would not expect similar wide economic benefits for the exporter of offshore education, as most of the student non-tuition expenditure remains in the country where the program is undertaken.

Higher education providers undertake transnational education for financial, reputational and academic reasons. As discussed above, in response to reductions in government funding (be it proportional or absolute), institutions pursue external earnings through fee paying international students. While offshore activities are generally less profitable than onshore (McBurnie and Ziguras, 2007, Chapter 3), under this first scenario transnational education is still attractive as it allows institutions to increase their international student numbers by reaching those for whom study abroad is not practical or affordable, and by enrolling greater numbers than can be accommodated on the home campus.

Perceived reputational benefits are another key factor in the institution's decision to establish offshore. The International Association of Universities (IAU) recently conducted a survey (2006) of more than 500 universities across 95 countries, concerning their rationales for internationalisation. The most frequently cited rationale (by 28% of the respondents) was "competitiveness", with "international development co-operation" ranking fourth. The IAU noted that this signified "a major shift over the past few years" (IAU, 2006; Lane 2006). A concern with prestige, profile, and being competitive or "world class" is certainly reflected in the rhetoric of institutions and governments. In terms of transnational education, universities with an "international footprint" (as they sometimes call it) regard their presence abroad as enhancing their profile, demonstrating that they are not limited to their national boundary, that they are literally on the international map.

Universities profess a range of academic motivations for offshore activities. For example, Australian universities currently present the academic dimension of their offshore activities as a component of the broader internationalisation of the key institutional missions of teaching, research and community engagement. Benefits include enhanced opportunities for student and staff mobility, international collegial interaction, the development of new or expanded curriculum material (to meet local needs) and research opportunities. The academic rationale is perhaps most clearly illustrated by locally-focused research programmes conducted in the host country. For example, the Centre for Sustainable Energy Technologies of the UK-based University of Nottingham was opened in September 2008 in its offshore campus in Ningbo, China. The aim of the centre is to contribute to sustainable development by translating research into practical, energy efficient and affordable solutions for domestic and non-domestic construction in China.

The demand for transnational education is a subset of the overall student demand for foreign education. Reasons include:

- the difficulty of getting into the desired course domestically, due to a shortage of available places;
- the desired course or specialisation is not offered domestically;
- the perceived superior quality of foreign education;
- the belief that the foreign qualification confers greater prestige to the graduate;

● the benefit of improving foreign language skills (especially English, currently the international language of business);

● belief that there are relative employment advantages in terms of getting more highly-paid job, career advancement and greater international mobility of the foreign qualification; and

● there may be enhanced options for migration to the country that has awarded the degree.

These reasons can be seen as applicable both to student mobility and to programme and institution mobility. From the student perspective, the advantages of transnational education include:

● not having to pay international travel and living expenses (which are normally more costly than domestic expenses);

● tuition fees for the transnational course are frequently cheaper than those charged at the foreign provider's home campus;

● family life is not disrupted;

● work life (and hence earning capacity) does not have to be disrupted, whereas education abroad normally requires the student to be enrolled full-time in order to obtain a visa;

● the student does not have to grapple with such practical issues as finding accommodation and dealing with the health system in a foreign country; and

● one does not have to consider issues of safety and security in a foreign country.

In short, transnational education does not usually include the experience of living and studying in a foreign country, but for many students this is outweighed by financial considerations and the lack of disruption to lifestyle.

3.4. Scenario two: as the world churns

The growth scenario above assumes that the host governments in emerging economies will continue to support the creation and expansion of foreign higher education programmes and campuses. An alternative scenario emerges, if one considers transnational education to be a less desirable substitute for a local university place or overseas study. In countries where there is a pool of students who miss out on a local university place and cannot afford to study overseas, lower cost transnational programmes have grown to meet this demand. But over time, as the capacity of the local public and private institutions grows, and more students can afford to study abroad or access local institutions at lower cost, demand for transnational programmes may well peak and decline in mature markets. In this scenario, large-scale transnational education of the type that developed in South-East Asia in the 1990s may turn out to be a short-lived phase in any one country rather than a permanent feature. Transnational education is therefore a temporary strategy to address unmet demand, a phase in a longer-term trajectory of building domestic capacity.

This scenario is based on the shift we have seen within the last decade as various net importers of education expand domestic provision and (particularly in Asia and the Middle East) declare their ambition – and put strategies in place – to become net exporters. For example, Malaysia seeks to reduce the proportion of students studying in foreign programs by increasing the capacity and quality of domestic institutions and tightening the regulatory regime relating to foreign providers (McBurnie and Ziguras, 2007, Chapter 3). We

Figure 3.2. **Growth of transnational higher education – Scenario 2**

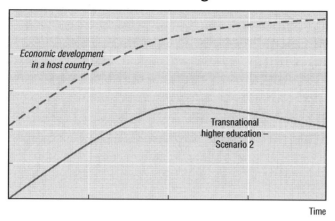

extrapolate that, as countries further develop economically, the size and quality of domestic provision will grow apace, reducing the desirability of foreign provision and, in some cases, spurring export strategies.

The trajectory of transnational education is best viewed within four broad phases of higher education development that can be discerned in many countries in the region of South-East Asia since the 1980s. With rapid economic development, demand for higher education quickly outpaced the capacity of local public universities to respond, particularly in those fields in demand in increasingly globalised economies, such as engineering. In this first phase, the number of students travelling abroad to study grows dramatically. Chinese Taipei, Singapore, Malaysia and Hong Kong experienced this growth of outward mobility in the 1980s and 1990s (OECD, 2004), Currently numbers of mobile students are growing from those countries whose economic growth has come later, such as China, India and Viet Nam: for example, in 2005, 250 068 Chinese, 129 172 Indian and 14 730 Vietnamese were studying in selected OECD countries (Australia, France, Germany, New Zealand, United Kingdom and United States), compared to 63 313, 43 349 and 5 567 mobile students in 1999, respectively (UIS, 2008).

Over time, the capacity of the local system to meet the education demands of its citizens is built up, leading to a second phase in which growth of outward student mobility slows. At this stage foreign universities are able to play important capacity-building and demand absorption roles, chiefly in partnership with local private providers and public institutions. In some countries, such as China, the growth of local institutions is funded primarily by governments through public universities; while in others, such as Korea, the growth has been largely in the non-government sector. In developing and middle-income countries the proportion of private funding for higher education is on average higher than in the economically advanced countries (UNESCO and OECD, 2003).

One route to foreign involvement in mass higher education is through the acquisition of local private institutions by global conglomerates. Since the late 1990s, for-profit education groups in the United States have begun to look to the rest of the world for further expansion opportunities. The largest of them – Laureate, Apollo, Kaplan and Career Education – compete to identify and enter the world's most promising higher education markets. Unlike public and not-for-profit institutions, who either work in collaboration with local institutions or establish a new campus, the foreign for-profits prefer to acquire an existing local institution. The advantages of this are that once foreign investment approval has been given, the for-profit exporting institutions have a functioning institution with staff, buildings, licensing and accreditation already in place. The parent company will expect to be able to boost the profitability of the acquired college or university by injecting capital to increase capacity, boosting marketing, overhauling administrative and management systems, and introducing programmes and curriculum that are able to be shared across their institutions in different countries (Garrett, 2005). These big companies may be based in Chicago, New York or Phoenix, but they are global actors by investing the capital raised from global financial markets worldwide.

In many countries, foreign higher education institutions have significant competitive advantages over their local competitors that explain why transnational programmes were able to take market share away from local institutions. Historically, foreign providers have been less regulated than their domestic counterparts, as it has taken host governments time to develop regulatory measures for the relatively recent phenomenon of transnational education. The growth of new, domestic private providers has been slowed by accreditation requirements, which require that institutions grow incrementally in order to demonstrate effective functioning at a certain level before being granted more autonomy and the ability to offer higher qualifications. By contrast, foreign providers can arrive with their home-country *bona-fides* (such as accreditation) already established. Finally, foreign Anglophone universities are able to meet a demand for vocationally-oriented programmes taught in English, whereas local institutions often have difficulty recruiting suitably qualified and experienced staff to teach in English.

A third phase is reached when domestic providers are able to respond to student demand and the number of students seeking degrees abroad flattens out. The most economically developed countries in Asia have now reached this phase. As local institutions become more competitive and governments become concerned with quality over quantity, lower-status transnational programmes get squeezed out. In Singapore and Malaysia, many longstanding transnational programmes are being challenged by local private institutions, which are now being accredited to award their own degrees after years of partnering with foreign universities.

Compared to other sectors of the economy, governments may not be as content to import education or attract overseas-based producers to make up for local supply shortages. Skilled labour is a key component of the knowledge economy, including innovation. The human capital that is developed through education, however, is impermanent and mobile, and students educated by foreign universities would have highly-enhanced opportunities to work for foreign corporations and to emigrate given the opportunity. While many governments tend to be attracted to the idea of a small number of high quality foreign universities enriching the local education system (and in some cases perhaps becoming part of the domestic landscape), few are attracted to the vision of mass foreign institutions constituting a significant proportion of their higher education sector.

A fourth phase involves a country shifting from being a net importer to a net exporter of education services. When domestic capacity and quality is sufficiently established, governments are able to encourage higher education, primarily by attracting foreign students. In recent years Singapore, Malaysia, the United Arab Emirates and Qatar have all sought to establish themselves as education hubs, drawing students from their regions and beyond. In this phase, governments work to attract branch campuses of highly prestigious foreign universities to be a major draw card. For the host country, the anticipated benefits are financial and reputational, as well as academic, potentially generating more research and development. This phenomenon will be considered in detail as a separate scenario on branch campus clusters below.

The implications of this second scenario are that transnational student numbers may not necessarily keep growing as Böhm *et al.* (2002) forecast. Instead numbers will grow, peak and decline but at different rates in each country, leaving global growth slower.

3.5. Scenario three: branch campus clusters

In line with the trajectory of some countries shifting from being net importers to net providers of education services, transnational education will mature in the form of a limited number of dense "branch campus clusters" of high prestige institutions located in leading cities acting as regional hubs in Asia, the Middle East, Africa and Latin America. They will be primarily focussed on attracting international students, as well as providing options for domestic students. This phenomenon combines transnational education with student mobility. The scenario is grounded in, and extrapolated from, the recent growth of branch campuses together with the declared strategies of some countries/cities to become education "hubs", attracting international students regionally and globally.

Figure 3.3. **Growth of transnational higher education – Scenario 3**

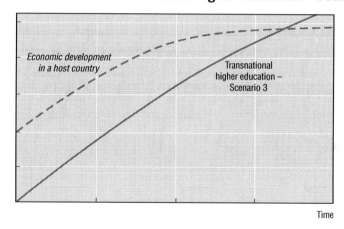

The number of international branch campuses has grown substantially since 2000, according to the Observatory on Borderless Higher Education's recent survey (Verbik and Merkley, 2006) that lists 82 campuses dotted around the globe in 2006, against 24 in 2002. Here we refer, like the Observatory, to a substantial bricks-and-mortar presence[2]. A growing number of cities both in developed and developing countries now host a foreign branch campus: Adelaide has Carnegie Mellon (United States) as its sole foreign university; Bologna has the Johns Hopkins School of Advanced International Studies (United States); Ho Chi Minh City (Saigon) has a campus of the Royal Melbourne Institute of Technology (Australia); and Johannesburg has a campus of Monash University (Australia).

The most striking feature of the branch campus distribution lies in the clusters of campuses that have developed in Dubai's Knowledge Village in the United Arab Emirates, Qatar's Education City and Singapore, which together accounted for 36% of the world's international branch campuses in 2006 (Verbik and Merkley, 2006). As of 2009, Dubai

Knowledge Village now constituted the world's largest cluster of branch campuses with 15 foreign universities from Europe, Canada, Australia, India and the Middle East. These institutions include Heriot Watt University, Middlesex University, Shaheed Zulfikar Ali Bhutto Institute of Science and Technology, Mahatma Gandhi University, Islamic Azad University, SP Jain Centre of Management, Manipal Academy of Higher Education, EHSAL European University College Brussels, University of Wollongong, and University of New Brunswick. Knowledge Village has grown rapidly since its commencement in 2002 and aims to have 30 foreign universities by 2015. Neighbouring Qatar has adopted a similar strategy, with mostly American, international branch campuses, including Carnegie Mellon, Cornell, Georgetown University School of Foreign Service, Texas A&M University and Virginia Commonwealth University.

The leading example is arguably Singapore, whose Global Schoolhouse programme aims to increase the number of international students from 70 000 in 2005 to 150 000 by 2015. This is to be done by attracting foreign universities to increase the capacity of the system and focus primarily on international students. This shift in international activity from partner-supported transnational programmes to branch campuses is consistent with Singapore's efforts to move up the value chain. In 1998, Singapore's Economic Development Board launched its World Class Universities programme, aiming to attract at least ten foreign universities to establish a significant presence in Singapore within ten years. After five years, an impressive list of leading international universities had been enticed to establish operations in Singapore, including Massachusetts Institute of Technology, Johns Hopkins University, the Georgia Institute of Technology, the Wharton School of the University of Pennsylvania and Stanford University (United States), Technische Universiteit Eindhoven and Technische Universität München (Germany) Shanghai Jiao Tong University (China) (Ministry of Education, 2003). In 2008, Singapore boasted branch campuses of several foreign universities, including INSEAD (France), S P Jain Institute of Management and Research (India) as well as University of Chicago Graduate School of Business and Harrah Hotel College of The University of Nevada, Las Vegas (United States). In addition, Singapore has its domestic universities serving mainly local students: the National University of Singapore, Nanyang Technological University, Singapore Management University and SIM University.

Are these clusters likely to be isolated and temporary phenomena, or are these the beginnings of a significant trend? This question can be explored in the light of dynamics taking place in other industries. Specialised clusters, involving an agglomeration of companies and organisations from related industries, have long been a common feature of industrial geography. Manufacturing industries have always tended to cluster together, primarily around proximity to physical inputs, suppliers and transportation networks. Agglomeration resulted from companies collocating to take advantage of a large labour force, reduced transaction costs, specialised suppliers and concentration of potential customers.

Service industries would seem to have less reason to cluster in particular sites than manufacturing industries, but they have proved just as "sticky" despite the apparently "slippery" environment in which place should matter less as communications and transportation pose less restrictions on business location. More recently, specialised clusters focused on research and development have emerged, especially in the information technology industry, such as Silicon Valley and Bangalore. This is surprising as computer-based and knowledge-intensive work was assumed to be less location-sensitive than manufacturing industries for whom the transportation of physical inputs and outputs is a major cost (Porter, 1998, 2000). There are also clearly concentrated clusters of internationally-oriented firms in the finance sector (including London, Tokyo, Hong Kong, Singapore, New York), film production (Hollywood, Mumbai, Hong Kong), publishing (New York and London), air travel (Atlanta, London, Frankfurt, Singapore), and even clusters of intergovernmental organisations (Paris, Geneva, Brussels, New York).

Why have universities chosen to locate branch campuses in these Asian and Middle-eastern locations in particular? After all, these locations are not long-standing centres of internationally celebrated academic excellence (compared with the lands of the Ivy League, Oxbridge, the Sorbonne and so forth), but relatively recent entrants into the global higher education industry, and so the choice of location is by no means an obvious one.

The answer is perhaps that education is but one part of a larger picture. Dubai, Qatar and Singapore are all seeking to be the pre-eminent international business hubs for their regions, attracting and developing branches of multinational corporations by developing attractive clusters of specialised services in finance, accounting, advertising, property development, and law. It is increasingly common for headquarters, research and development, marketing, production and customer service to be geographically dispersed and these cities are positioning themselves to attract the most knowledge-intensive aspects of companies' operations. These require high quality, internationalised higher education providers, especially in business, IT and law. There is clearly a proximity-based synergy from the co-location of corporate headquarters, business services firms, research and development infrastructure, publishers and education providers. In many ways, the same features of a city are attractive to universities as to any other international organisation, and for example Singapore displays its honours proudly: ranked the world's most cost-competitive place for business by KPMG, world's easiest place to do business by the World Bank, world's sixth best business environment by the Economist Intelligence Unit, and the world's second most "network ready" country by the World Economic Forum (EDB 2007). In this environment it is notable that one of the Singapore strategy's aims is to attract top international student graduates to remain on in the country as skilled immigrants.

The sustainability of Singapore's branch campus cluster will depend upon being able to generate synergies among educational institutions (both local and international) and related businesses and government. One of the features of clusters is that the presence of competition, as well as suppliers and consumers, is attractive to new entrants in higher education and related industries. The National University of Singapore is a major drawing card, but so too is the presence of the other universities, as well as publishers who have located their regional headquarters in Singapore, including educational publishers Sage, Cambridge, McGraw-Hill, Thomson and Pearson, and news and information publishers Reuters, Lexis-Nexis and Dow Jones (Ko, 2007). Singapore's concentration of educational, research, publishing and business organisations is enticing to students from the region, coupled with the obvious advantages of proximity, and the less visible but increasingly important access to employment and residence after graduation (Gribble and McBurnie, 2007).

3.6. Scenario four: raising the bar

In this fourth scenario, there is an overall marked reduction in the number of mobile programmes and institutions, and the number of students enrolled in such programmes. The recent growth of transnational education is seen as a phase which runs its course. It

Figure 3.4. **Growth of transnational higher education – Scenario 4**

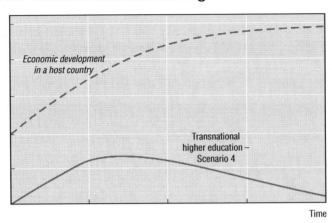

declines under pressure from the same key actors responsible for its growth, who now see it as less beneficial and indeed carrying negative consequences.

Under this scenario, transnational education provided through partner-supported delivery is increasingly regarded by students and host governments as a low quality alternative to the traditional, domestic campus experience. After years of transnational education growth in response to high student demand for foreign education in the context of inadequate domestic provision, there is a local backlash against transnational education. It is seen to be overly commercialised, more oriented toward market expansion and reaping profits rather than having a primary commitment to academic values or any genuine concern about the needs of the student. Students are disenchanted with the level of service that is provided. The pre-packaged and mass-produced curriculum materials without regard to the cultural context, social traditions, subtleties and specific requirements of the host country. At the same time, while the technologically mediated transnational education may be increasingly high-tech, it is low-touch, with a relatively minor face-to-face component and little time for discussion. The academic staff teaching the course are usually a combination of part-time locals teaching evening classes and the fly-in fly-out ("FIFO") teachers – jet-lagged foreign staff who have flown in for a weekend or week's worth of eight-hour teaching days, during which they try to cram in a semester's worth of content. The qualifications from transnational education are not highly prestigious in the eyes of students and their prospective employers.

Following several well-publicised collapses or "strategic withdrawals" of transnational education operations, students, voting with their feet, are wary of committing their money, time and educational future to such courses. Market-savvy students realise that transnational education is inherently less stable than its domestic counterpart, due to geographical (and perhaps organisational, financial and managerial) distance from the home base. In some cases, operations cease, or hitherto partner-supported offerings become fully online with no local face-to-face component, or students may transfer to the home campus at a reduced cost, or can be relocated with another provider. Even where providers make every effort to cater to student needs, students may be left stranded or at least disrupted, needing to pick up the threads elsewhere, with a disjointed study career, having to repeat some content already completed, and other forms of inconvenience. In some cases, students engage in public protests, and aggrieved clients pursue legal action against the foreign provider.

At the same time, students find that the local system has expanded with offerings that are of comparable (or better) quality than much of the transnational education on offer, and which are cheaper than paying foreign fees. Mainstream demand can be well met by the domestic system. In this scenario, prestigious foreign programmes are simply icing on the cake, providing enhanced choice for risk averse students in niche areas. In some countries, students who have met the high academic requirements to gain entry into the free public system protest against foreign providers, taking the view that such institutions allow academically inferior students to "buy" their way into a degree, and thus unfairly compete for scarce graduate jobs.

Under the "raising the bar" scenario, host government policies aim to deter lesser quality private and foreign providers, protect local institutions from competition and deter the over-commercialisation of the sector. They raise quality assurance requirements, and demand greater (and more costly) commitment from foreign providers. National, international and disciplinary rankings/ratings and other measures ("key performance indicators") are used to filter out less prestigious providers. Providers are required to maintain a substantial research profile that requires well-qualified staff, time allowance for research, and increased outlay for staff travel costs, library holdings and equipment.

Some host governments pursue a more directly protectionist path. They may express concern about low quality, misleading of students, negative effects on local system due to cherry-picking, and lessening of government prerogatives. These arguments are already expressed in the context of critiques of the General Agreement on Trade in Services (GATS) and other Free Trade Agreements. Some people are concerned that commercially-oriented transnational education exacerbates socio-economic inequities of student access by further favouring the privileged who can pay fees. They claim detrimental effects on the nation-building role of education, due to the influence of foreign curriculum and pedagogy (sometimes referred to as "cultural imperialism"), and undermining of the local system by foreign providers cherry-picking popular disciplines (such as business and information technology), thereby reducing the state's ability to cross-subsidise less popular or high-cost courses. The additional academic employment provided by transnational education may be geared only to a limited range of teaching programmes, and without provision of time and resources for staff to carry out research – staff would be treated as semi-skilled workers in a "teaching factory".

As governments and institutions in exporting countries go further down the path of combining education with entrepreneurial roles, there is a domestic backlash in the provider's home country. When transnational programmes are profitable and the surplus is directed back into the domestic education system, or for other nation-building government priorities, there can be a fruitful synergy between commercial and public good aspects. However, there are grounds for public dissatisfaction when transnational education activities are seen to lose money – or when it is perceived that domestic students fail to gain university entry, or there is local overcrowding or substandard facilities, because money is being diverted to foreign ventures.

The "raising the bar" scenario envisages that publicity is given to the large travel budgets of entrepreneurial universities, and concern is expressed in the press about the amount of time staff spend overseas rather than at the home institution. There are allegations that commercial operations are more prone to an undue lack of transparency (with sins of omission and commission masked by appeals to "commercial in confidence" protections), and are open to various forms of academic corruption including lower entry standards, soft-marking, grade inflation and leniency toward instances of student plagiarism. A recent example of an exporter dealing with such allegations is the investigation by the NSW Independent Commission Against Corruption (ICAC) into "the handling by certain present and former staff of the University of Newcastle of plagiarism by students at an offshore campus" (ICAC 2005). The report recommended that the University take disciplinary action against named staff, and in a chapter on "corruption prevention issues" made recommendations concerning "assessment policy, policy compliance, administrative capacity, internal investigative capacity and risk management" (ICAC, 2005, report summary).

In this scenario, responding to negative publicity and public pressures, exporting governments introduce increasingly strict guidelines for the conduct of universities' entrepreneurial activities, particularly transnational education operations. These would include combinations of the following measures:

- institutions must submit plans to the government for approval;
- the institution must demonstrate that public resources will not be diverted from domestic programmes to foreign programmes;
- business plans and financial performance must be vetted by external auditors at the institution's expense;
- annual reports on foreign ventures are made available for public scrutiny;
- transnational programmes must show an agreed rate of return in order to be continued; and
- the institution must demonstrate that it has appropriate measures in place to deal with exigencies in the case of failed programmes.

These measures give less leeway to institutions pursuing entrepreneurial activities. We are not aware of any country so far adopting all of these measures, but several countries have introduced some similar steps. In the case of leading exporters Australia and the United Kingdom, for example, the quality assurance agencies (Australian Universities Quality Agency (AUQA) and the Quality Assurance Agency for Higher Education (QAA), respectively) scrutinise offshore programs and publicise their findings on their websites and elsewhere. Several traditional importer countries have ratcheted up their regulatory requirements. For example, China now vets the financial and organisational aspects of transnational providers on its soil, as well as examining their academic performance (Feng and Gong, 2006; Helms, 2008).

From a financial perspective, the attractiveness of transnational education to exporting institutions is severely diminished: costs of provision are going up, and demand is going down. There is less student demand for the reasons discussed above and hence there is less fee income available. Reduced numbers also means that per capita costs rise, in contrast to the low marginal costs per additional student as set out in the growth scenario. As the host government ratchets up quality requirements and the home government makes more stringent demands on exporters, it is increasingly expensive and onerous for foreign institutions to comply with regulatory demands. In financial terms, universities operating abroad experience mixed results, ranging from modest returns to massive losses. In part, this is because public institutions are not fundamentally entrepreneurs; they are not solely focused on the bottom line, and it can be argued that they are not all automatically well-equipped with the qualities employed by successful corporations in the commercial world.

Heavy involvement in transnational education diminishes the reputation of the university. It is seen as being too commercially oriented at the expense of more traditional activities such as research and academic co-operation (rather than market competition), and transnational education is seen as a form of "knowledge recycling" rather than "knowledge creation". The growth of national and, more recently, international rankings systems cause large transnational education engagement to be a reputational liability. Subjected to the widely-used indicators of institutional quality – such as research output, student selectivity, and resources – transnational programmes do not fare well. Transnational education is seen as negative in terms of:

- entry score (students are likely to have insufficient marks to gain entry into prestigious local institutions);

- staff/student ratio (where transnational education is delivered as substantially stand-alone curriculum material supported by discussion in large groups, the measure will be unfavourable);

- physical and financial resources (transnational operations would have less resourced than mainstream university campuses);

- graduation and retention rates (part-time and distance education students – compared to their full-time, classroom based counterparts – suggest that this is probably another measure disadvantageous for transnational programmes); and

- research measures including published output, citations, institutional research funding and research awards won by staff. Most transnational operations would rate "zero" on any research measure. With the exception of some branch campuses, research is simply not part of the transnational education mission.

In short, under the "raising the bar" scenario, transnational education is a costly undertaking that returns reputation benefits only for those higher education institutions able to make a major commitment, including significant research operations offshore.

3.7. Conclusion

Transnational education will continue to underscore a number of key questions – and conflicts – concerning the role of higher education institutions in the international marketplace. What is the relationship between the domestic and international mandates of the public university in this scenario: will the interests of the home public take second place as the university's resources are diverted to international ventures? The university's traditional tasks are teaching, research and community service. It can be argued that in most cases transnational higher education only addresses the first of these. Will the growth of transnational education be at the expense of the other two roles of the university? Historically the international relationship between universities has primarily been one of co-operation, through shared and joint research and scholarship, student and staff exchange, and working together in aid/development projects.

For exporters, the current phase of transnational education involves a shift away from co-operation in favour of competition, as institutions vie against each other for the fee paying international student dollar. In the future, this may be paralleled by an alternative trend, as we could also see the rise of transnational provision organised on lines of linguistic, diasporic and religious affiliation. Such entities could include, for example, a World Islamic University, the University of Chinese Diaspora, and the International Francophone University. These institutions might be formed by consortia of institutions from several countries, producing curricula and providing teaching staff for mobile programmes. They could be focused on international co-operation rather than competition, and the academic and community service aspects of higher education rather than the financial aspects of transnational education.

It seems likely in most of our scenarios that there will be an expansion of provider types and a greater geographical spread. There will be a variety of provider types, including traditional public universities, private for-profit and not-for-profit providers, conglomerates and consortia, and various combinations of the aforementioned. There will also be a greater number of countries participating in transnational higher education both as exporters and as importers.

For example, Australia is typically considered as an education exporter. Consistent with its GATS and other Free Trade Agreement commitments, in mid-2006 the federal government (in co-operation with its states) liberalised and made more transparent the requirements for foreign education providers to operate on its territory. Following the opening of the US Carnegie Mellon campus in Australia in 2006, (which enjoys an AUD 20 million grant from the South Australian government), there has been discussion of interest from providers variously from the United States, England, Scotland and China (Maslen and Slattery, 2006). Australia is now also an importer of transnational education, a phenomenon that seems likely to grow, as providers see the opportunity to service Australian students *and* to use Australia as a geographically congenial base to attract students from the Asia-Pacific region and elsewhere. At the same time, major transnational education host countries such as Singapore and Malaysia – also driven by reputational, academic and financial goals – are strengthening their domestic provision whilst seeking to attract prestigious foreign providers, with a view to achieving education-hub status and becoming net exporters of education in their own right. This phenomenon could spread to include more countries from Europe, Asia, the Americas, the Middle East and Africa.

Most of the current transnational education appears to be Anglophone, and studying in the international business language is one of the attractions of foreign study. However, this does pose problems: learning a foreign language is a hindrance for many students (and limitations in their English-language ability may lower the academic performance of otherwise excellent students); the quality of classroom interaction (be it face-to-face or virtual) may be impoverished where students are obliged to express themselves in a language that is not their first; and there are concerns that the dominance of English as an imported language of education functions as a form of "cultural imperialism". For transnational education to significantly expand in the future, we anticipate that English cannot continue its dominance. The potential growth of higher education markets in the regions such as the Middle East, Africa and Latin America may increase demand for transnational higher education provision in French, Arabic or Spanish. Anglophone and other providers are also likely to offer an increasing number of courses in the local languages, both in response to student demand, and to meet host governments' requirements.

Regardless of the scenario, transnational education will inevitably include a variety of standards of offering, from the highest quality state-of-the-art online and campus environment, to poorly written curriculum material quickly cobbled together in response to short-term money-making opportunities. The transnational education developed will also affect the way that quality assurance is carried out domestically both in the host and exporting countries. The need for effective quality assurance will be underlined and further guidelines refined in the shared interests of students, importing and exporting governments, reputable providers, and international organisations.

Notes

1. The larger increase in US dollar (USD) equivalents is caused by considerable appreciation of the Australian dollar (AUD) between 2002 and 2007.

2. It is notable, that even a shingle on a shop front is called a campus by some operators.

Bibliography

AEI (2008), *Export Income to Australia from Education Services in 2007*, Canberra: Australian Education International, Department of Education, Employment and Workplace Relations.

Bashir, S. (2007), *Trends in International Trade in Higher Education: Implications and Options for Developing Countries*, Washington DC, The World Bank.

Böhm, A., D. Davis, D. Mearesand D. Pearce (2002), *Global Student Mobility 2025: Forecasts of the Global Demand for International Higher Education*, Canberra: IDP Education Australia.

EDB (2007), *Singapore Rankings*. Economic Development Board. Available online *www.edb.gov.sg/edb/sg/en_uk/index/why_singapore/singapore_rankings.html*.

Feng, G. and S. Gong (2006), *Sino-Foreign Joint Education Ventures: National, Regional and Institutional Analysis*, London, The Observatory on Borderless Higher Education.

Garrett, R. (2005), *The Global Education Index 2005 – Part 2: Public Companies Relationships with Non-Profit Higher Education*, London, Observatory for Borderless Higher Education.

Gribble, C. and G. McBurnie (2007), "Problems with Singapore's Global Schoolhouse", *International Higher Education*, 48.

Hall, G. and K. Hooper (2008), "Australia's Exports of Education Services", *Reserve Bank of Australia Bulletin* June 12-17.

Helms, R.M. (2008), *Transnational Education in China: Key Challenges, Critical Issues, and Strategies for Success*, London, The Observatory on Borderless Higher Education.

IAU (2006), *Internationalisation Survey: Preliminary Findings*, Paris, International Association of Universities.

ICAC (2005), Government of New South Wales, Independent Commission Against Corruption *Report on Investigation into the University of Newcastle's Handling of Plagiarism Allegations*. Available at: *www.icac.nsw.gov.au/files/pdf/Orion_pub2_97i3.pdf*.

IDP (2005), *International Students at Australian Universities, Sem 2, 2005*, National Overview Sydney, IDP Education Australia.

IDP Education Australia (2008), *International Students at Australian Universities, Sem 1, 2008*, National Overview, Sydney, IDP Education Australia.

Kenyon, P. and P. Koshy (2003), *The Economic Benefits to Australia from International Education*, Canberra, Commonwealth Department of Education, Science and Training.

Ko, K.H. (2007), *SAGE Builds Hub for Asia-Pacific Publishing in Singapore*, Economic Development Board, available online:
www.aspirations.com.sg/etc/medialib/downloads/media_release_2007.Par.72001.File.tmp/Speech%20by%20Mr%20Ko%20Kheng%20Hwa,%20EDB%20Managing%20Director,%20Singapore%20Economic%20Development%20Board,%20at%20the%20official%20opening%20ceremony%20of%20Sage%20Publications%20Asia-Pacific%20Pte%20Ltd.pdf.

Lane, B. (2006), "A Chance to Compete Globally", *The Australian*, 26 April.

Lee, S.J. (2005), "Educational Upgrading through Private Educational Institutions", *Singapore Statistics Newsletter*, September 15-17.

Maslen, G. and L. Slattery (2006), "Passport to Campus of the Future", *Australian Financial Review* Vol. 10, July 31.

McBurnie, G. and C. Ziguras (2007), *Transnational Education: Issues and Trends in Offshore Higher Education*, Routledge Falmer, London.

Ministry of Education (2003), *Restructuring the University Sector — More Opportunities, Better Quality: Report of the Committee to Review the University Sector and Graduate Manpower Planning*, Singapore, Higher Education Division, Ministry of Education.

Ministry of Education (2006), *Education Statistics Digest*, Singapore, Ministry of Education.

National Centre for Vocational Education Research (2008), *Delivery of VET Offshore by Public Providers, 2006*, Canberra: Department of Education, Employment and Workplace Relations.

OECD (2004), *Internationalisation and Trade in Higher Education, Opportunities and Challenges*, OECD Publishing, Paris.

OECD and the World Bank (2007), *Cross-border Tertiary Education: A Way towards Capacity Development*, OECD Publishing, Paris.

OECD (2008), *Tertiary Education for the Knowledge Society. Volume 1 Special Features: Governance, Funding, Quality*, OECD Publishing, Paris.

Porter, M.E. (1998), "Clusters and the New Economics of Competition", *Harvard Business Review* Vol. 76, No. 6, pp. 77-90.

OECD (2008), *Tertiary Education for the Knowledge Society. Volume 1 Special Features: Governance, Funding, Quality*, OECD Publishing, Paris.

UNESCO and OECD (2003), *Financing Education: Investment and Returns*, Paris: UNESCO Institute for Statistics and OECD.

UNESCO Institute of Statistics (UIS) (2008), Education Statistics, *http://stats.uis.unesco.org/unesco/ReportFolders/ReportFolders.aspx*

Verbik, L. and C. Merkley (2006), *The International Branch Campus: Models and Trends*, London: Observatory on Borderless Higher Education.

Higher Education to 2030
Volume 2: Globalisation
© OECD 2009

Chapter 4

Europeanisation, International Rankings and Faculty Mobility: Three Cases in Higher Education Globalisation

by

Simon Marginson* and Marijk van der Wende**

This chapter discusses three examples that are particularly relevant for reflecting on the future of globalisation in higher education. It first examines the future potential of the policy developments within Europe, after which it takes a critical look on global institutional rankings and cross-border faculty mobility worldwide.

* Centre for the Study of Higher Education, the University of Melbourne.
** Center for Higher Education Policy Studies (CHEPS), University of Twente, and the Vrije Universiteit Amsterdam.

4.1. Introduction

This chapter explores the implications of globalisation in higher education for national policy and for individual institutions. Nations, and institutions, have space in which to pilot their own global engagement. Yet this self-determination operates within limits that constrain some nations and institutions more than others. At the same time the perception that there is a rapidly developing global market for Higher Education is in which individual institutions compete globally and the influence of nation states is greatly reduced is both an overstatement and an oversimplification. This perception can be found both with some proponents and opponents of the World Trade Organisation (WTO) negotiations in the General Agreement on Trade in Services (WTO/GATS, 2005). Critical responses to WTO/GATS range from concerns about vulnerable systems in developing nations, to the effects of foreign competition in established systems, to opposition to globalisation as such. Proponents on the other hand see it as a driver of change and national benefit by governments that have an interest in educational trade or see the GATS agenda as potentially helpful in implementing reforms along new public management lines.

Though there is no doubt that in conjunction with the new public management, the WTO/GATS round has encouraged the interpretation of globalisation as the development of worldwide markets and global competitiveness. After a decade of WTO, it appears that the transformative potential of WTO/GATS within national systems has often been exaggerated (OECD 2004a, OECD/World Bank, 2007). The study by Vlk (2006) finds little evidence for loss of government control of the higher education sector as an effect of GATS. The failure of negotiations to bring the Doha round of trade liberalisation to completion suggests that in the foreseeable future, the liberalisation of trade in higher education will occur more on a bi-lateral or regional basis than through global multilateralism.

These findings do not negate the potential for multilateralism in higher education as such, but suggests multilateralism is unlikely to be limited to a deregulatory trade agenda in which the nation-state reduces its role in the sector. This chapter therefore focuses on certain key areas of policy that have a strong multilateral dimension and may have a more transformative potential: Europeanisation (Section 4.2), institutional rankings and typologies (Section 4.3) and cross-border faculty mobility (Section 4.4). A fourth area that might have been included is cross-border issues in accreditation and quality assurance, but these have been addressed separately in *Quality and Recognition in Higher Education: The Cross-border Challenge* (OECD, 2004b).

4.2. Europeanisation

In Europe, responses to globalisation are increasingly shaping policies and setting the agenda for the future of higher education. However, there is no single trend or strategy that can be readily identified. As well as different perceptions of globalisation and the related challenges there are also different levels (European, national, institutional) at which responses are formulated and implemented. For the European Union as a whole, with the European Commission (EC) being a major policy actor, we can distinguish different phases and approaches (Huisman and van der Wende, 2004). Yet the way in which individual countries respond to these policy initiatives can be quite diverse. After the European Commission of the then-European Economic Community became active in higher education, in the mid-1970s, its initiatives were for a long period restricted to stimulating co-operation and mobility between "closed" national systems in which the controlling power entirely lay with the member states (the "subsidiarity principle"). Such initiatives were successfully extended across levels and countries until the end of the 1990s. Beginning with an initiative to stimulate action at the level of individual academics and students, the first ERASMUS programme; gradually through the SOCRATES programme the curriculum and the institutional level were included. With the enlargement of the European Union, especially after 1992 with preparations for the adhesion of twelve new central and eastern European member states, the activities underwent a substantial geographic expansion. The rationales for these activities were seen as mainly academic and cultural, for example scholarly exchange, mutual learning processes and the role of foreign languages. The agenda was strongly focused on the European integration process, and consequently on intra-European co-operation (see for example Corbett, 2005).

Yet it is also undeniable that the process of European integration, cemented by the completion of the European internal market in 1992, was driven by an important economic agenda. Mindful of this, the European Commission launched in 1991 a Memorandum on Higher Education underlining the role of higher education in the economic and social cohesion of the European Union. The response of the higher education community was particularly negative and critical of this use of an economic rationale for higher education.[1] It was ten years before the European Commission was able to come back with another message on the role of higher education in economic growth and competitiveness.

Two major vehicles: the Bologna Process and the Lisbon Strategy

In the late 1990s in European higher education, awareness of global competition rose. It was realised that despite all the success that had been achieved in enhancing intra-European mobility the picture in relation to extra-European mobility was a less successful one. Once intra-European movement was taken out of the picture, Europe had lost its position as the number one destination for foreign students to the United States, was losing too many of its own graduates and researchers to R&D positions in the United States, and had substantially less efficient degree structures than the United States because its graduates entered the labour market at an older age than did American graduates. Awareness of these factors led to initiatives at various levels.

First, in 1998 the ministers of four countries (the United Kingdom, Germany, France and Italy), called for the harmonisation of degree structures. This was the initiative that triggered the "Bologna Process", launched in the signing of the Bologna Declaration by 29 countries one year later. This was an important bottom-up initiative towards system convergence with a view to enhancing the international competitiveness of European higher education. This bottom-up character of the Bologna Process should be understood in terms of the limited competencies of the European Commission, who joined the process only later, in the field of higher education policy.

The European Commission itself was able to become more active in higher education policy after 2000, which was the year that the heads of state and government declared in

Lisbon that the European Union should become by 2010 the most competitive and dynamic knowledge economy in the world. Shortly after that, education was defined as one of the key areas in achieving this goal. This provided the European Commission with an important political mandate in the area of education policy (though this mandate was not supported by any extended legal power). The European Commission quickly developed a wide range of initiatives under what became the "Lisbon Strategy".

The Bologna Process and the Lisbon Strategy are the main vehicles or frameworks guiding the European response to globalisation in higher education. Although they emerged in very different ways (bottom-up *versus* top-down) and could be characterised as intergovernmental (Bologna) versus supra-national (Lisbon), they seemed to converge slowly into one over-arching approach.

Patterns of convergence

The Bologna Process represents the totality of commitments freely taken by each signatory country (46 nations as of 2009)[2] to reform its own higher education system in order to create overall convergence at European level, as a way to enhance international/ global competitiveness. Its non-binding character was a crucial facilitator, given the need to overcome reluctance in Europe towards standardisation and harmonisation.

The achievements of the Bologna Process have been substantial and influential. The range of policy issues included in the Bologna Process was extended, throughout the medium of ministerial meetings that took place every two years to follow up on the implementation of the process. The initial focus on a change of degree structures into a two-cycle (undergraduate-graduate) system, and the wider implementation of ECTS (European Credit Transfer System) with the aim of enhancing the readability and recognition of degrees, extended into the development of a European Qualifications Framework, the description and "tuning" of competences and learning outcomes at curriculum level, and substantial initiatives in the areas of quality assurance and accreditation (Reinalda and Kulesza, 2005). Since the 2005 ministerial meeting in Bergen the work programme has been extended to the "third cycle" i.e. the reform of studies at the doctoral/PhD level. Reforms would focus on length and structure of these programmes, interdisciplinarity, supervision, assessment, etc. A series of biannual studies have demonstrated that the implementation of the two-cycle degree structure was established in almost all countries by 2005, although in various modes and at a varying speed of introduction (Reichert and Tauch, 2005). The London ministerial conference in 2007 aimed to further the establishment of a Register of European Quality Assurance Agencies as well as adopted a strategy for the external dimension of the Bologna Process aiming at promoting attractiveness and competitiveness of the European Higher Education Area. At the Leuven conference in 2009, lifelong learning, higher education access, and mobility were highlighted.

Despite such achievements as the convergence of degree structures and the introduction of common frameworks for quality assurance and qualifications, certain tensions between harmonisation and diversity have continued. In-depth studies and comparisons between countries show that the actual implementation of the new structures can vary significantly. Lub *et al.* (2003) find substantial differences between the Netherlands, where the new two-cycle system replaced the existing long first-cycle degree system, and Germany, where the new system was implemented in parallel to the existing system and despite quick growth in the number of new degree programmes, only a small fraction of the total student population actually participates in these programmes.[3] Alesi *et al.* (2005) find in a comparison between six countries that there is no unified logic of the system of new degree programmes. This point applies both to the breadth of the introduction – in each country different groups of subjects are excluded from the new structure, and different time-frames set for the introduction – and to the duration of the new programmes. The 3 + 2 year model, a bachelor degree followed by a master degree, is the basic model; but there are many variations from this model. For example, the United Kingdom is a notable exception: in that nation masters degrees mostly take one year.

Likewise Witte (2006), in a comparison of England, France, the Netherlands, and Germany, finds that there is variation in the degree of change following from the Bologna Process, especially if one looks at implementation. She concludes that the four countries under study weakly converged between 1998 and 2004, in the direction of the English system, but although the changes leading to that convergence all occurred within the framework of the Bologna Process, this does not necessarily mean that they have been caused by it. Rather, the Bologna Process has often served to enable, sustain and amplify developments that have been driven by deeper underlying forces or particular interests at the national level; for example to the pressures to reduce study length, the time within which a student must complete a degree or drop out. Sometimes the Bologna Process has simply provided a mental frame for developments that were unrelated to degree structures as such. This illustrates that actors align themselves with the international context and international perceptions only when those perceptions are consistent with nationally-grounded preferences. At the same time, international perceptions have a very high legitimating power when they support national preferences; even though those international perceptions may be selective and biased, sometimes even wrong, and are rarely questioned.

Diversification trends and policies

Apart from the fact that the Bologna Process is implemented quite differently *across* countries, weakening its harmonising or convergence effects, parallel to it, divergent trends can be observed. This is especially the case *within* countries. Examples are Germany and France, where there is increased diversity in each case. This is partly due to the parallel existence of different degree structures in the transition phase, but also derives from the increased curricular autonomy of Higher Education Institutions (Witte, 2006). In a number of countries, among the trends in governmental policies are increased autonomy and a push for more diversity in the system. This is especially the case in those national systems which aim to enhance participation in higher education; for example the United Kingdom, Sweden, Finland and the Netherlands, where participation targets of 50% have been formulated. More diversity is seen as a necessary condition to achieving these aims. The EC also advocates increased diversity, as a condition for excellence and greater access (European Commission, 2005).

At the same time, another process of convergence can be observed. As both academic and professionally oriented higher education institutions offer bachelor and master programmes, there are frequent and increasing instances of functional overlap. This convergence of the two main types of higher education may lead to a change in those nations with such binary systems. But again, in response to this situation, nations exhibit diversity and an overall trend towards a unitary system cannot be confirmed. In Hungary it has been decided to abolish the binary system and to replace it with a more varied range of programmes, especially at master's level. In contrast the Netherlands intends to maintain the binary system and wants more institutional types to emerge. In Finland and Austria, binary systems were established only over the last decade. The United Kingdom, which abolished its binary system in the early 1990s, is now looking to re-establish more diversity with the above-mentioned aim of thereby enhancing participation. These trends raise questions about the level at which diversity is defined and pursued, and whether it is systemic, institutional, or programmatic diversity (Birnbaum, 1983).

A more contemporary point is that "there has been a gradual shift in the meaning of 'diversity' – from diversity among national systems of higher education to a European-wide diversification in institutions and programmes with different profiles" (Hackl in Olsen, 2005, p. 20). In this scenario the questions are whether and how diversification can lead to an effective division of labour at European level; whether a co-operation or rather a competition-based process would be the most appropriate way to achieve this; and how individual countries will balance such a division of labour at European level with their national priorities. A Delphi-based study on the future European higher education and research landscape (CHEPS, 2005) shows a strong belief among actors in the field that the division of labour will imply research-intensive doctoral-granting institutions that will become concentrated in the north west of Europe. All scenarios presented in the study are consistent in this respect, which raises crucial questions on the involvement of countries in other parts of Europe. Although mobility and networking could engage individual researchers from these countries, consequences for national capacity and linguistic and cultural diversity could still be serious.

Here also, an important distinction needs to be made between changes at the undergraduate and the graduate levels. Increasing participation rates require diversity to be enhanced especially at the undergraduate level, thereby enabling non-traditional students to enrol. In terms of programmatic diversity, the introduction of the associate or foundation degree, awarded after two years of higher education, is important here, but often this is seen to contradict the spirit of the Bologna Declaration.[4] At the graduate level, where the patterns of activity are closely related to research strengths, there is a trend towards greater concentration and specialisation. As has been reported also from other parts of the world (Patterson, 2005) what is envisaged here is a concentration of academic strengths, collaboration and networking, with specific activities allocated to particular institutions, rather than the current, even frenetic, expansion of each institution's activities (p. 356).

These various trends indicate that the current dynamics in European higher education are at one and the same time characterised by trends of convergence, aiming for harmonisation; and divergence, searching for more diversity. In understanding this, the distinctions between different levels of education (undergraduate and graduate/research) and the different types of diversity (institutional and programmatic) are important. Ironically perhaps, both kinds of trend – convergence and diversification – have been instigated in order to enhance competitiveness in the global context. Higher participation rates among a larger number of domestic students, fostered by diversity of provision, are seen to enhance the potential of each country as a knowledge economy. Allowing more cross-border mobility within Europe, and attracting more students from other regions, objectives fostered by harmonisation and convergence, are seen to enhance the performance of the European knowledge economy as a whole. At the same time, this implies patterns that to an extent are confusing, and it raises questions about the further direction of the process of Europeanisation in higher education. Given that multi-level actions and interactions are involved, these questions are not easy to answer, and future directions are not easy to predict. The aforementioned study on the future of European higher education (CHEPS, 2005) indicates that more diversity is indeed expected, but presents quite different scenarios with respect to its consequences. They may range from a "centrally organised diversity", the transparency of which would be based on the "Bologna logic" and primarily ensured by a single European quality assurance (accreditation) system; through great variation existing in more hybrid and networked structures, but still ensured by European frameworks for quality assurance (accreditation); to a truly "anarchic or unclassifiable" diversity, leading to public concern regarding quality of provision.

As noted, though supranational frameworks may enable developments at national level, and perceptions of the international context may support national policy changes, actual national preferences and implementation modes and options may differ from nation to nation. Combined with the trends towards increasing institutional autonomy and diversity, this may be the reason why many actors are expecting an increase in vertical differentiation with respect to quality and reputation, despite efforts to achieve convergence and harmonisation. This expectation and the trends and policies in favour of autonomy and diversity, have prompted the initiatives to introduce systems for typologies and ranking within Europe, as discussed below.

Coordinating policies for a European knowledge economy

As noted, whereas the Bologna Process emerged bottom-up and the role of the European Commission in the process was initially limited but over time gradually developed into a leading one, the initiative for the Lisbon Strategy was taken by the European Commission at supra-national level, and in its implementation it exhibits a more top-down character. However, the strategy cannot be characterised completely as top-down, since the formal competences of the European Commission in the area of education policy have not been enlarged. This means that instruments used are not (legally binding) EU directives, but take the form of recommendations, communications, consultations, or other working documents. This "open method of coordination", based on common objectives, is translated into national action plans and implemented through sets of indicators, consultative follow-up and peer review (pressure) (see also Gornitzka, 2005).

For the implementation of the Lisbon Strategy, the European Commission published in 2001 a first report setting out the steps to be taken in response to the challenges of global competition in higher education (EC, 2001). The report explicitly referred to market-oriented approaches to internationalisation in the United Kingdom, Germany, France, and the Netherlands and stressed the need to attract more students from other regions to the European Union. This laid the foundation for the establishment of the ERASMUS MUNDUS programme in 2004. This programme includes a global scholarship scheme for third country nationals, linked to the creation of "European Union Masters Courses", based on inter-university co-operation networks. The programme enrolled almost 1 200 students and 211 scholars, about 40% from Asia, in master programmes in the academic year 2007-08,[5] and is expected to grow further. These figures can be compared to the 1 300 foreigners that enter the United States every year as fellows of the Fulbright programme, on which ERASMUS MUNDUS was largely modelled.

Following up the Lisbon summit of 2000, in 2002 the European Commission published a detailed work programme on the future objectives of education and training systems in the European Union (European Commission, 2002), emphasising the central role of those systems in achieving the aim of Europe becoming the world's most competitive and dynamic knowledge society by 2010. The general goals of improving quality, enhancing access and opening up the education and training systems to the wider world were worked through in a set of more specific objectives for the various education sectors. Those most relevant to higher education were the objective of increasing graduates in mathematics, science and technology by 15% while improving gender balance, to ensure that more than 85% of all 22-year-olds had achieved at least upper-secondary education level, and to ensure that 12.5% of the 25-64 year-old adult working population participated in lifelong learning.

In 2003, the European Commission launched a large-scale consultation on the role of higher education institutions in the European knowledge economy (EC, 2003a). It showed a particular concern about the funding of higher education. The increasing underfunding of European higher education institutions was seen to be jeopardising their capacity to attract and keep the best talent and to strengthen the excellence of their research and teaching activities. The consultation round took two years, and was paralleled by a series of critical messages on growth and innovation. Two important reports published in 2003 (EC, 2003b, 2003c) revealed that the objective of boosting EU spending on R&D from 1.9% to 3% of GDP – the principal target for research expressed in the Lisbon Strategy – was far from being met; that the R&D investment gap between the European Union and the United States increasingly favoured the United States;[6] and that brain drain out of Europe and notably to the United States remained on the rise. It was clear that the European Union was hindered in catching up with its main global competitors by a lack of investment in human resources,[7] by not producing enough higher education graduates,[8] and by attracting less talent than its competitors.[9] Furthermore the European Union had too few women in scientific and technological fields; rates of early school leaving were still too high and rates of completion of upper secondary education still too low(with nearly 20% of young people failing to acquire key competences); there were too few adults participating in lifelong learning; and there was a looming shortage of qualified teachers and trainers (EC, 2004).

Brain drain

Another common problem addressed by the European Union was net brain drain out of national systems; which is significant both in terms of loss of researchers to the English-speaking world (especially the United States), out of Europe altogether; and also the internal transfer of research capacity from eastern Europe to the north western European nations. These dimensions can also intersect in unpredictable and varying ways. Sometimes eastern European talent substitutes for west European talent, sometimes not. In the case of Germany, which is losing many doctoral graduates in the United States and the United Kingdom, its own standing as an attractor of foreign faculty and doctoral students has diminished. Berning (2004, p. 177) remarks that while German research universities are seen as uniformly good there is a lack of the highest prestige "centres of excellence" found in the United States, and

> German study courses and degrees have lost part of their former international reputation. This is mainly due to the worldwide expansion and adoption of the Anglo-American HE system, its courses and degrees, but not to a lack of scientific quality in

Germany. The consequence is a loss of foreign students from countries close to Germany but now following the Anglo-American mainstream (e.g. East Asia, Turkey). The loss of foreign students may cause a loss of young scientists from abroad too. Within the frame of the Bologna Process HE institutions in Germany try to gain back that intellectual power by introducing new study courses and degrees, sometimes by English as a teaching language, and by internationalising all academic activities (Berning, 2004, p. 177).

With a view to improve internationally visible, high-quality research in Germany, the German government agreed on the so-called "Excellence Initiative" in 2005. Within this framework, additional grants (in total worth of EUR 1.9 billion) will be allocated in particular to nine German universities[10] for their institutional strategies aimed at developing and expanding their international competitiveness in their areas of excellence. In addition, approximately 40 graduate schools and 30 clusters of excellence are supported through the Initiative, a process, which is envisaged to be continued with further rounds after the current funding period of 2006-11.

The problems similar to Germany are less immediate and severe in France. In France, as in Germany and the United Kingdom, the system is large enough to ensure that most of its needs for academic labour can be met from internal sources (Musselin, 2004a, p. 73) while at the same time France is less troubled than Germany by the loss of its talented researchers into the American institutions. There is a relatively low level of outward mobility (Martinelli, 2002, p. 126ff.) and high return rates. However there is greater brain drain in disciplines such as life sciences where foreign opportunities are much more favourable, especially in the United States (Musselin, 2004b, p. 151); that is, in the market sensitive areas. In this context, the European Commission took rapid initiatives to stem the brain drain, launching the European researcher's charter, and a code of conduct for the recruitment of researchers; initiating the European year of researchers launched in 2003; establishing a mobility portal and networks, and extending options in the Framework Programme for Research in order to encourage EU-born researchers to return home, and to attract non-EU scientists to the European Union (European Commission, 2003d).

Extension of the European policy agenda

Early in 2005 a new stage of the Lisbon Strategy was announced. Major EU conferences on higher education and research were organised, and in a follow-up communication on the contribution of universities to the Lisbon Strategy (2005), further and wider measures were announced. These initiatives were focused on achieving world-class quality,[11] improving governance, and increasing and diversifying funding. The European Commission stated that "while most of Europe sees higher education as a 'public good', tertiary enrolments have been stronger and faster in other parts of the world, mainly thanks to much higher private funding" (EC, 2005, p. 3). This contrasted with the strong emphasis that many in the higher education community have placed on "higher education as a public good" and on the role of universities with respect to social and cultural objectives rather than economic purposes, especially in the context of the Bologna Process (van Vught et al., 2002).

The European Commission identified the main bottlenecks retarding access and excellence as: uniformity in provision, due to a tendency to egalitarianism and a lack of differentiation; insularity, in that systems remained fragmented between and even within countries, and higher education as a whole remained insulated from industry; over-regulation, in that a strong dependence on the state inhibited reform, modernisation, efficiency; and underfunding.[12]

The pathways to more access and excellence were seen to be more diversity and enhanced flexibility. At this point the Lisbon Strategy absorbed the Bologna objectives of coherent structures, compatibility and transparency, designed to improve the readability and attractiveness of European higher education internationally. Likewise the Bologna instruments such as the European Credit Transfer System (ECTS), the International Diploma Supplement (IDS) and the European Qualification Framework (EQF) were taken into the Lisbon agenda.[13] The European Commission also spoke out for the first time on issues such as the governance and funding of higher education, arguing for greater institutional autonomy, deregulation and professionalised management, combined with competition-based funding in research and more output-related funding in education, supported by more contributions from industry and from students via tuition fees.

These statements related to what was seen as "good practice" in certain member states; notably the United Kingdom, where a risky political initiative to raise higher ("top-up") tuition fees in order to provide the university sector with sufficient capital to counteract global competition had succeeded by a narrow political margin; and also systems such as the Netherlands where deregulation and institutional autonomy had been advanced. At the same time there had been a more open debate in the Nordic countries about tuition fees for domestic students and differential fees for foreign (non-EU) students. These issues remained highly controversial in other parts of Europe, however.

As well as pushing for the more widespread adoption of these practices, the European Union added new instruments and initiatives to its own toolkit of policy mechanisms. A notable effort was made to enhance investments in research, innovation and excellence. In the context of the EU budget for 2007-13, major budget growth has taken place in order to enable investment in the new Framework Programme for R&D (FP7) and an integrated programme for education (the Lifelong Learning Programme). Furthermore, there was the establishment of the European Research Council (ERC), set up to fund innovative, ground-breaking basic research, not linked to any political priorities, with competitive funding awarded based on peer review (as with the National Science Foundation allocations in the United States). There has also been significant progress towards the establishment of a European Institute of Technology (EIT), to be located in Hungary and become a European equivalent of the US Massachusetts Institute of Technology (MIT) and extra funding for networks and centres of excellence for studies at the doctoral level.[14]

Mid-term concerns and challenges

In 2005 these ambitions were seriously constrained by severe obstacles in achieving a political agreement on the new EU Treaty (the so-called "European Constitution"), a process that was halted after French and Dutch referenda failed to gain a majority in favour of the new Treaty, and on the new EU budget. Furthermore, in 2008, the Irish voters rejected in a referendum the so-called Lisbon Treaty designed to replace the "European Constitution" that was rejected earlier. With this set back, it remains unclear how to go forward with the European Union reform process.

Despite these disappointments positive points for the European Commission can be reported. First, the role of the European Commission, especially in the higher education policy area, has expanded and become less controversial. This is a gain in terms of both legitimacy and coordinating capacity. The establishment of the European Research Council (launched in 2007) and of the European Institute of Technology, top technology institute (planned to be operational in 2009/10), are major examples. However, in the original form of a new single-site institution the European Institute of Technology was heavily criticised and it has been revised to a network of "knowledge communities" (teams put together by universities, research organisations and industry) headed by a governing board that would identify strategic scientific challenges in interdisciplinary areas. The knowledge communities will be selected on a competitive basis, set a medium to long-term (10-15 year) research, education and innovation agenda, and have a fair amount of flexibility to determine their own organisational structure. The European Institute of Technology will be able to award its own degrees (EC, 2006). The European Union asserts that the European Institute of Technology will be a high-quality "brand" and institutions will compete to join.

Second, individual countries have started to respond to the wider EU agenda on global competitiveness. Although the overall targets for investments in R&D and higher education have not been reached, many countries do not as yet reach their individual targets, and in some cases investments have even decreased, with the expected additional contributions from private sources proving especially problematic; as noted several nations have developed initiatives to strive for more excellence and to widen access, notably the Nordic countries, the United Kingdom, the Netherlands, Germany and, more recently, France. Comparable to the EU-level initiative of creating the European Institute of Technology, various countries are concentrating extra investments in selected institutions, for example the creation of a group of top universities in Germany and in Austria, the creation of centres of excellence and a new research funding agency (Agence Nationale de Recherche, ANR) in France, and the formation of a federation of the three technical universities in the Netherlands. Also in Denmark the government recently announced mergers between higher education institutions in order to achieve a better international position. The same can be observed in Finland (Aalto University) or Sweden. In an even more radical way, the Centre for European Reform stated in a pamphlet on university reform (Lambert and Butler, 2006) that "bad universities should be closed with resources spread too thinly around the European Union's 2 000 higher education establishments…". Network formations are also occurring across borders, supported by both national and European regional funding; for example the formation of a "top-technology region" through co-operation between the universities of Aachen (Germany), Eindhoven (Netherlands), and Leuven (Belgium) with commitments from major companies such as Philips.

Third, there is awareness of global competition, particularly from Asia:

Alarming for Europe is not only that China regards the United States and Japan, and not Europe, as its potential peers to be matched in research and higher education. As announced officially, China aims at matching the United States and Japan with respect to innovations by 2020. Given Europe's stagnation and the dynamics in East Asia, one can easily predict the day when East Asia – and not Europe – will possess "the world's leading knowledge-based economy" (EUA, 2006).

Institutions have also underlined weaknesses in their collective profile compared to the United States:

It is evident that the European university system needs to broaden access on a more equitable basis, that it has to reach out to increased excellence and that it must allow for more diversification within the system. The American university system is, as the President of the American Council of Education, David Ward, put it, "elitist at the top, and democratic at the base; the European university system seems to be neither (EUA, 2006).

At the same time there are constructive responses in relation to collaboration with industry, for example the EUA's Responsible Partnering Initiative, presented at the European Business Summit; and also elite-networks have been set up to pull excellence and research capacity together, for example the League of European Research Universities (LERU).

Reflections on higher education dynamics in Europe

Serious challenges remain to be addressed, however. Besides the complexity of parallel trends of convergence and divergence, conceptual and political confusion continues to exist over strategies for co-operation and competition. On the one hand the European Union is considered to be an "area" for higher education and research, as indicated in the European Research Area (ERA) and the European Higher Education Area (EHEA), in which co-operation is seen as the pathway towards stronger global competitiveness of the European Union as a whole. The European Commission's traditional role is to stimulate such co-operation. On the other hand the European Union is seen as an internal market subject to internal competition strategies, which were likewise introduced to achieve stronger global competitiveness, for example in the European Research Council and notably, the Services Directive.[15] When additional funding or prestige is concerned as in the case of the proposed European Institute of Technology, on one hand this may generate better performance, on the other hand it may result in the weakening of co-operation and concerted action. In the intellectual field this confusion emphasises the need for clearer concepts. In the political field it suggests the need for more coordinating power, as is proposed in the new EU Treaty. From the conceptual point of view, major efforts need to be made to better understand the dynamics of higher education systems in light of (global) competition.

Olsen (2005) underlines the existence of competing visions in Europe, between the university as a service enterprise in competitive markets, the university as an instrument for national political agendas, and the university as a public service model based on the argument that higher education cannot be solely market-driven because the logic of the market does not apply easily to education. He regards the situation as unsettled, given the multitude of partly inconsistent criteria of success and competing understandings of what forms of organisation and governance will contribute to good performance. Jacobs and van der Ploeg (2006) acknowledge that most European higher education institutions find it difficult to compete with the best universities in the Anglo-American world, but also argue that higher education cannot be left to the market alone and that government interference may be necessary to correct for market failures. In their view, the challenge for reform of the European system is to achieve the diversity and quality for which the US system is praised without throwing out the benefits of the European system. In other words, Europe would benefit from reforms that would move European higher education in the direction of the Anglo-American system with much more choice, differentiation and competition; but Europe should not throw away the baby with the bathwater. Europe should strive to provide the best possible access to the smartest students from less privileged backgrounds. At the same time, Europe should be careful not only to invest in top academic universities but maintain and cherish the high average quality of institutions.

Van Vught (2006) is also concerned about the potential for simplistic market-type strategies in relation to the social dimension of higher education. The introduction through public policy of increased competition does not necessarily lead to more responsiveness of higher education institutions to the needs of the knowledge society. Rather than being driven by a competition for consumer needs, higher education institutions may be driven by a competition for institutional reputation. In addition, the creation of more institutional autonomy in such a "reputation race" leads to costs explosions, related to hiring the best faculty and attracting the most talented students; institutional hierarchies; and social stratification of the student body.

Internal diversity and global competitiveness

Other problems concern internal differences in performance between countries and systems, differences that are large, deep-rooted and difficult to overcome. The European Union includes some of the top higher education systems in the world, performing on a par with and on some measures performing even higher than the United States and Japan, as well as a range of new member states that are arguably at a very different overall technological level to that of the EU15 group. Effective solutions to accommodating this diversity and lack of cohesion in terms of supra-national decision making have yet to be established, though these elements are also part of the new EU Treaty. As compared to other regions and economies undergoing the transformations associated with the knowledge economy, the European Union is engaged in major institutional changes as well. Finally, as discussed above, there is the continuing difficulty that the perceptions of global competitive pressure and the principle of competition vary substantially between countries and cultures; there is the complexity of parallel trends of both convergence and divergence and challenges related to effectively combining strategies for co-operation and competition.

Major policy questions and choices for national governments and higher education institutions are related to these strategic categories. Governments have to consider the best way to make their national higher education system more globally competitive: national-level co-operation or competition; European-level co-operation or competition; or (more likely) a mix of these four options? Overly simplistic or one-sided competitive models will enhance vertical differentiation by building strength in certain institutions or areas by weakening others and may in fact lead to a lack of diversity. Therefore these choices need to be guided by a vision on an effective division of labour and a good balance between global competitiveness, European excellence, and national priorities and interests (including issues of cultural and linguistic diversity). The development of such a vision is not bound to national-level actors. Also the European Union as a whole has been urged to better define its priorities and opportunities for co-operation and competition in a wider international context (EURAB, 2006). Various scenario studies indicate that specialisation and concentration in the research function of the university will increase (OECD, 2006a) and, as mentioned before, this may in Europe lead to a concentration of this function and related type of Higher Education Institutions in the North West of Europe (CHEPS, 2005). It is unclear as yet, whether the European Research Council and the European Institute of Technology will contribute to this effect or will turn out to be instruments to counterbalance it.

Conclusions on Europeanisation

National policies often demonstrate combinations of various strategic options. For example, measures to make national research funding more competitive through the national research council may be combined with policies that urge institutions to cooperate more closely within the national context, for example through mergers. At the same time, institutions are stimulated to cooperate at the European level by participating in EU R&D projects and the government supports the establishment of the European Research Council as it believes that competitive funding measures are even more effective at supra-national level. Similar examples could be given for the teaching function. This illustrates the complexity of the environment for institutions in terms of partners, competitors and strategic options. Consequently the outcome of the process at a meta-level is even more difficult to predict. Clearly, successful strategies depend on the right mix of competitive and cooperative options. It is a major challenge for governments to design such strategies in an effective and coherent way, conscious of the fact that in doing so and in resourcing institutions they define to a large extent the internationalisation opportunities for higher education institutions, while at the same time those governments work in the context of wider multilateral agreements that are designed to provide distinct frameworks for competition or co-operation.

4.3. University rankings and typologies

The emergence of global university rankings is another cause and effect of the globalisation of higher education. University rankings simplify the complex world of higher education in two areas of great public and private interest: institutional performance, and institutional status. They emphasise vertical differences between institutions and between nations; that is, differences of power and authority. They obscure horizontal differences, in the form of differences of purpose and type. Despite the attractions of diversity – a universal value in higher education – league tables seem to have a compelling popularity regardless of questions of validity, of the uses of the data and of the effects in system organisation and the quality of higher education. Rankings are easily recalled and quickly become part of common sense knowledge of the sector. It is not surprising that media companies are often in the forefront of rankings development. Institutional rankings have long been used in different national systems and in some cases guide allocations of public funds. In the United States the annual *US News and World Report (USNWR)* survey, which commenced in 1983, has been influential in determining institutional prestige and influencing flows of students, faculty and resources and shaped institutional strategies designed to maximise *US News* scores. In China several systems of rankings are in use (Liu and Liu, 2005). Now, the advent of world rankings has launched a new more globalised era. Worldwide rankings norm higher education as a single global market of essentially similar institutions able to be arranged in a "league table" for comparative purposes. Rankings have given a powerful impetus to intranational and international competitive pressures and have the potential to change policy objectives and institutional behaviours.

Outcomes of rankings

The first and most influential globally-oriented listing, the annual research university rankings prepared by the Shanghai Jiao Tong University Institute of Higher Education (SJTUIHE), commenced in 2003. The annual *Times Higher* world university rankings were launched in 2004. Both sets of rankings were immediately plausible because they locked into prior perceptions of the status of names such as Harvard, Stanford, Yale, Berkeley, MIT, Cambridge and Oxford. Table 4.1 lists the top 20 universities as determined by each ranking system. In outcome the *Times Higher* appears as the more nationally plural, with 13 American universities in the top 20 compared to 17 in the Shanghai Jiao Tong table, four UK universities not two, and universities from four other nations (Canada, Japan, Hong Kong [China] and Australia) rather than the one (Japan) in the Jiao Tong listing. One effect of this outcome is to broaden the circle of consent for the *Times* rankings.

Table 4.1. **The Global Super-league: the world's leading universities as measured by the Shanghai Jiao Tong University (2007), and *The Times Higher* (2007)**

Shanghai Jiao Tong research university rankings				The Times Higher university rankings			
	University	Points	Country		University	Points	Country
1	Harvard University	100	USA	1	Harvard University	100	USA
2	Stanford University	73.7	USA	2	University of Cambridge	97.6	UK
3	University of California - Berkeley	71.9	USA	2	University of Oxford	97.6	UK
4	University of Cambridge	71.6	UK	2	Yale University	97.6	USA
5	Massachusetts Institute of Technology (MIT)	70.0	USA	5	Imperial College London	97.5	UK
6	California Institute of Technology	66.4	USA	6	Princeton University	97.2	USA
7	Columbia University	63.2	USA	7	California Institute of Technology	96.5	USA
8	Princeton University	59.5	USA	7	University of Chicago	96.5	USA
9	University of Chicago	58.4	USA	9	University College London	95.3	UK
10	University of Oxford	56.4	UK	10	Massachusetts Institute of Technology	94.6	USA
11	Yale University	55.9	USA	11	Columbia University	94.5	USA
12	Cornell University	54.3	USA	12	McGill University	93.9	Canada
13	University of California - Los Angeles	52.6	USA	13	Duke University	93.4	USA
14	University of California - San Diego	50.4	USA	14	University of Pennsylvania	93.3	USA
15	University of Pennsylvania	49.0	USA	15	Johns Hopkins University	92.9	USA
16	University of Washington - Seattle	48.2	USA	16	Australian National University	91.6	Australia
17	University of Wisconsin - Madison	48.0	USA	17	University of Tokyo	91.1	Japan
18	University of California - San Francisco	46.8	USA	18	University of Hong Kong	90.7	Hong Kong
19	Johns Hopkins University	46.1	USA	19	Stanford University	90.6	USA
20	Tokyo University	45.9	Japan	20	Carnegie Mellon University and Cornell University	90	USA

Source: SJTUIHE (2007); *Times Higher* (2007).

While there has been disquiet in higher education about the impact of the rankings, and numerous instances of critique of the methods (especially in institutions and nations where performance was below self-expectation) it is notable that there have been few concerted efforts to discredit the process. It appears that global ranking has secured mainstream public and policy influence. Given this, research universities are impelled to succeed within the terms of the measures and will adopt institutional policies and strategies which optimise their position, especially their position in the Shanghai Jiao Tong rankings which are based on credible metrics of performance. Rankings have exacerbated competition for the leading researchers and best younger talents. Within national systems, the rankings have prompted the desire for higher ranked universities both as symbols of national achievement and prestige and as engines of knowledge economy growth. There has been a growing emphasis on institutional stratification and concentration of research resources. All these responses have cemented the role of the rankings themselves and intensified competitive pressures.

Shanghai Jiao Tong University rankings

The Shanghai Jiao Tong University (SJTU) rankings do not constitute a holistic comparison of universities, though despite the efforts of the SJTUIHE group they have been widely interpreted as such. The SJTUIHE group argues that the only data sufficiently reliable for the purpose of ranking are broadly available and internationally comparable data of measurable research performance (Liu and Cheng, 2005, p. 133). It is considered impossible to compare teaching and learning worldwide "owing to the huge differences between universities and the large variety of countries, and because of the technical difficulties inherent in obtaining internationally comparable data". Further, the SJTUIHE group did not want to employ subjective measures of opinion or data sourced from universities themselves as used in some rankings systems. An additional rationale for using research performance data is that arguably research is the most important single determinant of university reputation and widely accepted as merit-based. The SJTUIHE has consulted widely throughout the higher education world on the calculation of the index and compilation of the data. The successive measures have proven to be increasingly robust.

The major part of the SJTU index is determined by publication and citation performance in the sciences, social sciences and humanities: 20% citation in leading journals; 20% articles in *Science* and *Nature*; and 20% the number of Thomson/ISI Highly Cited researchers on the basis of citation performance (Section 4.5; ISI, 2008). Another 30% is determined by the winners of Nobel Prizes in the sciences and economics and Fields Medals in mathematics, in relation to their training (10%) and their current employment (20%). The remaining 10% is determined by dividing the total derived from the above data by the number of staff. The SJTU rankings favour universities large and comprehensive enough to amass strong research performance over a broad range of fields, while carrying few research inactive staff. They also favour universities particularly strong in the sciences, universities from English language nations because English is the language of research (non English language work is both published less and cited less) and universities from the large US system because Americans tend to cite Americans (Altbach, 2006). In 2008, 4 031of the Thomson/ISI "HighCi" researchers were located in the United States. Harvard and its affiliated institutes alone have 168 Highly Cited researchers, more than the whole of France or Canada. Stanford has 144 Highly Cited researchers, more than all the Swiss universities together; UC Berkeley 84 and MIT 76. There are 44 at the University of Cambridge in the United Kingdom (ISI, 2008).[16]

The Nobel Prize criterion is the most controversial as prizes are submission based and claims are made that scientific merit is not the only determining factor as politicking enters the decisions. David Bloom (2005, p. 35) notes that of the 736 Nobel Prizes awarded till January 2003 670 (91.0%) went to people from high-income countries as defined by the World Bank, the majority to the United States, with 3.8% from the Russia/Soviet Union and eastern Europe and 5.2% from emerging and developing nations. The last nations had their best prospect of winning a Nobel Prize for Literature (10.1%) or Peace (19.8%) but these are excluded from the SJTU index. Of the nine scientists from emerging or developing countries who won Nobels in Chemistry, Physics, Physiology or Medicine, four were working in the United States and two in the United Kingdom and Europe.

The Times Higher rankings of universities

The *Times Higher* aims to be "the best guide to the world's top universities" and a holistic ranking rather than one limited to research (*Times Higher*, 2007). A high value is placed on institutional reputation and on the level of "internationalisation": these rankings appear to have been designed to service the market in cross-border degrees in which UK universities are highly active. A total of 40% of the *Times* index is comprised by an international opinion survey of academics and another 10% by a survey of "global employers". There are two internationalisation indicators: the proportion of students who are international (5%) and the proportion of staff (5%). Another 20% is determined by the student-staff ratio, a proxy for teaching "quality". The remaining 20% is comprised by research citation performance. Compared to the Jiao Tong outcome the *Times* rankings boost the number of leading British universities and reduce the US universities in the world's top 100 from 54 to 31. However the *Times Higher* rankings are open to methodological criticisms. Reputational surveys indicate the market position of different institutions but not their merits, a distinction the *Times* fails to make. The surveys are non-transparent. It is not specified who was surveyed or what questions were asked. Further, the student internationalisation indicator rewards volume building not the quality of student demand or programmes; teaching quality cannot be adequately assessed using a resource quantity indicator such as student-staff ratios; and research plays a minor role in the index. The *Times Higher* rankings reward a university's marketing division better than its researchers. This does not square well with the way higher education is seen in many nations.[17]

Limitations of university rankings

Rankings are the subject of a burgeoning research literature. The comparison of ten rankings by van Dyke (2005) concludes that although the rankings share broad principles and approaches, they differ considerably in detail related to aims, systems, cultures and availability and reliability of data. A common problem is that most rankings systems purport to "evaluate universities as a whole" (Dyke, 2005, p. 106). As Rocki (2005, p. 180) notes in reflecting on the Polish experience: "The variety of methodologies, and thus of criteria used, suggest that any single, objective ranking could not exist." Dill and Soo (2005) compare five rankings system. They find that the tables vary in their validity, comprehensiveness, comprehensibility, relevance, and functionality. Usher and Savino (2006) cover 19 league tables and university rankings systems from around the world. Like van Dyke (2005) they make the point that the different rankings systems are driven by different purposes and are associated with different notions of what constitutes university quality. Usher and Savino also note the arbitrary character of the weightings used to construct composite indexes covering different aspects of quality or performance. "The fact that there may be other legitimate indicators or combinations of indicators is usually passed over in silence. To the reader, the author's judgment is in effect final" (Usher and Savino, 2006, p. 3; Dalsheimer and Despréaux, 2008).

Regardless of the particular methods, most rankings systems share common limitations. First, institution rankings norm one kind of higher education institution with one set of institutional qualities and purposes, and in doing so strengthen its authority at the expense of all other kinds of institution and all other qualities and purposes. It might be argued that the comprehensive research university is the only kind of institution sufficiently widespread throughout the world to underpin a single comparison, and the science disciplines are common to these institutions. However the Jiao Tong rankings not only take comprehensive research universities as the norm, their blueprint is a particular kind of science-strong university in the Anglo-American tradition. Around the world there is considerable variation in the size, scope and functions of leading research universities. The 200 000-300 000 student national universities in Mexico City and Buenos Aires combine national research leadership with professional preparation and broad-based social access and necessarily carry a large group of non-researching staff, disadvantaging them in Jiao Tong index. Further, there are no cross-national measures of the performance of vocational education systems or institutions equivalent to the SJTUIHE measures in research universities. While in most nations vocational education commands lesser status than research-based universities the German *Fachhochschulen* (vocational technical universities), relatively well resourced and with equivalent status to academic universities plus links to industry, are in high international standing. Similar comments can be made about vocational provision in Finland, Switzerland and France. Another model in high regard is the Indian Institutes of Technology (IITs).

Second, holistic institutional rankings are a chimera: no ranking system can cover all of the attributes and purposes of institutions, and all rankings are particular and limited. Thus the desire for holistic rankings, or at least the appearance of completion, leads to methodological anomalies. It is dubious to combine different purposes and the corresponding data using arbitrary weightings. Composite approaches muddy the waters and undermine validity. The links between purpose, data and numbers are lost. While reputational survey data might be an indicator of competitive position it is invalid to mix these subjective data with objective data such as resources or research outputs.

Third, rankings readily become an end in themselves without regard to exactly what they measure or whether they contribute to institutional and system improvement. Rankings foster holistic judgments about institutions that are not strictly mandated by the data used to compile the rankings and the methods used to standardise and weight the data. "League tables" become highly simplistic when treated as summative but this is *normally* the case. The desire for rank ordering overrules all other considerations. For example a common problem is that in rankings systems institutions are rank ordered even where differences in the data are not statistically significant.

Fourth, no ranking or quality assessment system has been able to generate comparative data based on measures of the "value added" during the educational process, and few comparisons focus on teaching and learning at all (Dill and Soo, 2005, pp. 503 and 505) though such data might be useful for prospective students.[18] Instead there are various proxies for teaching "quality" such as quantity resource indicators, student selectivity and research performance. But "empirical research... suggests that the correlation between research productivity and undergraduate instruction is very small and teaching and research appear to be more or less independent activities" (Dill and Soo, 2005, p. 507); and student selectivity is simply a measure of reputation. When holistic rankings of institutions become centred on measuring and/or forming reputation, and the measures derive from selectivity of entry and research status, the terms of inter-institutional competition are being defined by credentialism rather than by the formative outcomes of higher education. The implication is that students' only concern is the status of their degrees, not what they learn.[19]

Problems of reputation-based rankings

Fifth, reputational surveys not only favour universities already well known regardless of merit, degenerating into "popularity contests" (Altbach, 2006); they are open to the charge that they simply recycle and augment existing reputation (Guarino *et al.*, 2005,

p. 149) regardless of whether it is grounded in the real work of institutions or not. "Raters have been found to be largely unfamiliar with as many as one-third of the programmes they are asked to rate" (Brooks, 2005, p. 7). Well known university brands generate "halo" effects. For example one American survey of students ranked Princeton in the top 10 Law schools in the country, but Princeton did not have a Law school (Frank and Cook, 1995, p. 149). Moreover, regardless of the particular selection of qualities measured, any system of holistic national global rankings tends to function as a reputation maker that entrenches competition for prestige as a principal aspect of the sector and generates circular reputational effects that tend to reproduce the pre-given hierarchy.

Responses of institutions to global rankings

The incentives triggered by global rankings are likely to have powerful effects, and there may be downsides. American higher education institutions have learned to shape their organisational trajectories and behaviours so as to maximise the US News position. Failing to respond collectively to US News the sector acquiesced at the definition and norming of its purposes and values by a media company and lost partial control over its agendas. There have been perverse effects from the public interest viewpoint, for example the manipulation of student entry to maximise student scores and refusal rates, and the growth of merit-based student aid at the expense of needs-based aid (Kirp, 2004). The logical strategic response to the Times Higher rankings is to step up reputational marketing and international recruitment while lowering student-staff ratios, possibly at the expense of research which commands only 20% of the Times index. On the other hand the logical response of research universities to the Jiao Tong rankings is to concentrate more effort on research at the expense of other functions so as to step up research outputs across the range of disciplines and attract more Highly Cited researchers, if necessary with inflated salaries, and to discard faculty that do not contribute to the SJTUIHE-measured outputs. However, this might be at the expense of teaching, the volume of student places, professional training and community service functions, and research not published as high science. While no hard data are yet available, it does appear likely that the Jiao Tong rankings have triggered a broad-based move to increased concentration on high science outputs so as to lift ranking positions. It seems certain that intensified competition on the basis of research performance will exacerbate the global demand for high quality scientific labour with likely effects also on mobility and price. In turn this is likely to increase the stratification of research labour and the academic profession(s) both within national labour markets and between global and national labour markets.

Responses of national systems to global rankings

In some systems the emergence of national rankings systems has been accompanied by a new emphasis on competition and vertical differences among research universities, and between research universities and other types of institution, for example in China (Yang, 2005, p. 186). Likewise, given that the logical response to Jiao Tong is to focus on research performance, in some nations the advent of global rankings has been associated with a new policy emphasis on greater concentration of research effort and stratification between different grades of university. Various nations are talking about developing a small segment of higher quality research universities. For example Germany, in the framework of its "Excellence initiative", has selected a top nine group, and Australian policy makers have floated the possibility of a designated "world class" group of two to five institutions. If this becomes a zero-sum game in which there is little or no total increase in the investment in basic research and building the research strength of some institutions occurs by weakening others, it would seem to constitute little gain in national capacity overall, unless improved Jiao Tong rankings for particular universities opens up a broader set of global strategic options and/or generates economies of scale and scope at the national level.

Another possible development is that in the absence of policy moves to shore up diversity by other means, attention to global research rankings may weaken the standing of non-research institutions and trigger the evolution of more unitary but vertically differentiated systems. There is no reason to assume that intensified competition will generate specialisation unless the incentive structure concurs. In addition, conjunctural developments could favour a drift towards homogeneity: the trend to corporate autonomy provides institutions with greater freedom in determining their mission according to a market logic, while in Europe some polytechnics might seek to reshape themselves as universities to fit the new common programme structure secure. This draws attention to the importance of policy measures to sustain existing typologies or to develop new ones as required.

European higher education does not have a long standing tradition of league tables as in the United States. Global rankings have met with some scepticism and critique. But these rankings are also potent in Europe and the level of representation of European institutions (just ten in the Jiao Tong top 51 and 12 in the *Times Higher* top 50) have prompted media criticism, and reflection and action in both EU and national government circles. To policy makers it is clear a global higher education market is emerging, consistent with the introduction of market-type steering models at national level. University rankings are often cited when proposals for greater investment in the European higher education and research area are formulated, and also in relation to proposals for the further concentration of funding in networks and centres of excellence. The European Union's proposed European Institute of Technology would draw together existing research bases in a mega-university or network capable of challenging the rankings of the US universities. Another widely recognised policy implication of rankings is the importance of transparent consumer information and measures to secure consumer protection. Further, there will be strong policy pressure to ensure the additional investments in higher education and R&D provided as part of the Lisbon Strategy are located in successful institutions that have demonstrated the capacity to generate high dividends: this favours the continued systematic use of rankings and other kinds of comparison as a guide to policy.

A better approach to university rankings

All rankings are purpose-driven and rankings tailored to specific and transparent purposes. Therefore, only rankings interpreted in the light of those purposes can provide useful data for the purposes of students, university self-reflection and public accountability. If policy-useful rankings are to emerge, problems of methodology and issues of ownership remain to be dealt with, issues largely avoided until recently. In this respect the following minimum design requirements are suggested (van der Wende, 2006). Rather than seeking to construct spurious holistic measures, policy-related research should facilitate a broad range of comparative measures, corresponding to the different purposes, enabling a horizontal approach to diversity and choice. Institutions should not be ranked as a whole but on their various functions taken separately including the different aspects of research and teaching, and the different disciplines, locations and discrete service functions. The system of rankings should be based on a transparent balance of facts about performance, and perceptions of performance based on peer review. Ranking methods should generate information relevant for different stakeholders and provide data and information that are internationally accessible and comparative. Because "quality is in the eye of the beholder", ranking should be interactive for users, particularly students. Users should be able to interrogate the data on institutional performance using their own chosen criteria. In terms of ownership, it is important that institutions are involved themselves and committed to maximum openness. Institutions operating on a broad basis (preferably not just national but regional) should establish an independent agent to collect, process and analyse data, and undertake publication with a designated media partner that operates as the agent of communication rather than the arbiter of values and methodologies.

As of 2008, the system of rankings which most nearly meets these requirements is that developed by the Centre for Higher Education Development (CHE) in Germany (www.che.de) and issued in conjunction with the publisher Die Zeit (Ischinger, 2006). This system includes data on all higher education institutions in Germany and now also encompasses Switzerland and Austria. The Netherlands and Belgium (Flanders) are preparing to join. Some Nordic institutions are also showing interest. The CHE ranking system is thus well positioned to develop into a European-wide system. It has also received positive responses from parts of the English-speaking world (Usher and Savino, 2006; van Dyke, 2005). The chief virtue of the CHE rankings, which has far-reaching implications for the form of competition in higher education, is that it dispenses with a spurious holistic (summative) rank ordering of institutions and instead provides a range of data in specific areas, including single disciplines. CHE notes that there is no "one best university" across all areas and "minimal differences produced by random fluctuations may be misinterpreted as real differences" in holistic rankings systems. Further, the CHE data provided an interactive web-enabled Database permitting each student to examine and rank identified programmes and/or institutional services based on their chosen criteria (CHE, 2006) and to decide how the different objectives ought to be weighed (see also IHEP, 2006). The Commission on the Future of Higher Education in the United States has recommended a comparable concept enabling consumers to rank colleges based on variables of their choosing, in contrast with the approach of US News (Field, 2006).

In June 2009, the European Commission launched a new project of multi-dimensional global university ranking, carried out by a consortium of Dutch, German, French and Belgian institutions.

Institutional typologies

In the face of the normalising effects of holistic rankings another policy means of sustaining diversity is to systematise or strengthen institutional typologies. Moves of this kind to encourage horizontal institutional diversity have recently emerged in both the United States and Europe. In the United States the 2005 revision of the Carnegie Classification of institutions replaced the old single classification system with multiple parallel classifications. The aim was to optimise the information-producing advantages of classification while minimising the downside, its potential to be used as a ranking mechanism (Sapp and McCormick, 2006). In Europe there is early discussion about a European typology that would employ a multi-classification approach while making the heterogeneous higher education landscape more transparent. The European Commission states that:

> European universities have for long modelled themselves along the lines of some major models, particularly the ideal model of the university envisaged nearly two centuries ago by Alexander von Humboldt, in his reform of the German university, which sets research at the heart of the university and indeed makes it the basis of teaching. Today the trend is away from these models and towards greater differentiation (EC, 2003a, pp. 5-6).

The European Commission sees more diversity at the level of institutions and programmes as a condition for achieving wider access and greater excellence. The European Higher Education Area in size is comparable to the US system and is even more complex. It is organised at both national and regional levels and each unit has distinctive legislative conditions, cultural and historical frames, and a vast array of different languages in which the various forms, types and missions of higher education institutions can be expressed. It is generally agreed that this diversity should be conserved and even increased, while rendering it coherent (van Vught *et al.*, 2005). A European typology of institutions should weaken vertical stratification by making a larger range of diverse institutional profiles attractive, and facilitate alternatives to one-size fits all policies (van Vught *et al.*, 2005).[20]

Conclusions on university rankings

Global university rankings are a potent device for framing higher education on a global scale. It would seem better to take stock of them on a multilateral basis than solely to respond to them individually. There is a danger national governments will focus only on moves within the market competitive game, such as research concentration policies and self-investment, without regard for the terms of competition and its purposes and effects including better ranking systems in the student interest, typologies and other global public goods. Any system of rankings is purpose-driven and contains in-built biases so that the outcomes are shaped by the assumptions and values built into the comparisons and calculations. "The fact is that essentially all of the measures used to assess quality and construct rankings enhance the stature of the large universities in the major English-speaking centres of science and scholarship and especially the United States and the United Kingdom" (Altbach, 2006). It is important to work for "clean" rankings which are transparent, free of self interest, and methodologically coherent. For example, reputational data and outcomes data should not be combined in one scale. All rankings systems are incomplete in describing the reality of higher education. For example, the performance of a nation's research-intensive universities says nothing about its specialist business schools or technical training institutes. As institutions have different goals and missions and are internally differentiated, it is invalid to measure and compare individual institutions on a holistic basis and to compare individual institutions and whole systems in this manner across national borders. Policy should strive to correct the perverse effects arising from league tables, and to advance horizontal institutional diversity and informed student choice using typologies and customised rankings.

4.4. Global faculty mobility

There is a strong discursive bias in favour of academic mobility in governmental, public and higher education circles. The virtues of cross-border passage are "largely diffused and taken for granted in many higher education and research public policies, so that specific measures and devices are developed by many countries in order to promote academic mobility" (Musselin, 2004a, p. 56). The near universal enthusiasm for mobility is nested in long-standing assumptions about the internationalised character of universities, the freewheeling transferability of intellectual capacity and the contribution of knowledge transfer to national innovation and competitiveness. More recently these values have been fed also by notions of globalisation as inevitable and the concept of "borderlessness" in faculty work (Gibbons *et al.*, 1994; Nowotny *et al.*, 2001). The Bologna Declaration commits nations to "promotion of mobility by overcoming obstacles to the effective exercise of free movement with particular attention to... for students, access to study and training opportunities and to related services; [and]... for teachers, researchers and administrative staff, recognition and valorisation of periods spent in a European context researching, teaching and training, without prejudicing their statutory rights". The European Commission's (European Union's) policy on a European Research Area stresses the need for research co-operation and more abundant and more mobile human resources. Repeatedly, mobility is presented as the solution to capacity weaknesses in the developing world; and indeed it is always significant for small nations unable to support large concentrations in all research fields, and migration-based nations such as the United States, Canada, Australia and New Zealand for which migration has always been a major source of labour and ideas.

In an increasingly international professional labour market, qualifications should be recognised internationally with as few difficulties as possible. Given the national and cultural embedding of education, national control over qualifications will remain necessary, making systems of recognition of foreign qualifications indispensable. Recognition procedures should be transparent, coherent, fair and reliable and impose as little burden as possible to mobile professionals (OECD, 2004a, p. 24).

In practice mobility is not universal, and its freedoms and extensions are not unproblematic goods. From the viewpoint of both national and global goods, there are two heterogeneous policy objectives: the objective of free academic movement in and out of all national higher education systems, and the objective of strengthening the academic capacity of each national system. In a world where nation-states are the site of policy and institutional disembedding is only partial, and a world also characterised by vertical diversity and unequally directed cross-border flows of researchers, in few national situations outside the United States are these two objectives always compatible.

Policy responses to uneven people flows

An increasing number of nations are focused on the provision of scholarships, salaries and conditions of work capable of attracting foreign doctoral students and post-doctoral researchers and scholars into the national research system, and also the repatriation of their own nationals working abroad; and some are following programmes of selective investments designed to elevate individual research universities as concentrations of research talent and output. Chinese Taipei is an example of economy that have succeeded in partly reversing an historical pattern of brain drain, partly via policies to draw back expatriate PhD graduates and researcher nationals (*e.g.* Luo and Wang, 2002). Korea might be another one in the sense that he high stays rates of its graduates in the United States has diminished, but there is some recent evidence of an upward trend since the 1990s (to moderate stay rates) (Jin, 2007). Singapore is building research cadre in its universities by policies designed to attract foreign talent through globally competitive salaries and research infrastructure. In many nations, the highly mobile character of research labour and the importance of cross-border experience and partnerships in knowledge transfers mean that the national research diaspora is no less strategically significant than nationally-based researchers.

This suggests that there is scope for more inventive cross-border strategies. Many foreign researchers working in the United States lack ways and means to contribute back to higher education in their countries of origin. It is not always recognised that in a world of plural identities (Sen, 1999), when researchers cross borders to secure a more fecund intellectual setting or better career prospects, national commitments often survive. One possibility is the creation of dual academic appointments, with the American-based foreign researcher working in the country of origin during the American summer term. Another is the formation of cross-national research groups initiated from outside the United States and involving personnel working in the United States, reversing the more common pattern of American initiation of collaborative projects. Precisely because research is highly mobile the national research diaspora working in the United States provides all nations and their universities with additional people resources and opportunities to better position themselves within the global knowledge system. These can be tapped by means such as repatriation programmes, funding short-term movements, joint appointments and joint projects. Such opportunities are more readily accessed by those nations with domestic research capability.

National and global career structures

Kaulisch and Enders (2005, pp. 131-32) note that faculty work is shaped by three overlapping sets of institutions: 1) the generic science system, and systems in each discipline which to a varying extent are cross-national, emphasise the autonomy and mobility of researchers, and foster competition based on scholarly merit and prestige; 2) rules about work, competition and careers, where academic work is embedded in national policy and cultural settings; and 3) the organisational operations of universities, which both reflect national and local traditions and are touched by common trends such as massification, growing expectations about social relevance and the nationally-parallel global transformations (discussed in Marginson and Van Der Wende, 2009). A fourth element in the mix that might be of growing importance is the impact of internationalisation and globalisation on academic careers.

Faculty mobility has long been a positive professional norm though varying by nation and field (El-Khawas, 2002, pp. 242-43), and also varying somewhat in motive. A small number of researchers have expertise and reputations that confer superior opportunities in many countries. Though their salaries and career structures vary in the different locations, they constitute a global labour force that in the context of research rankings and global competition is increasingly important to national systems. Governmental or institutional efforts to attract and retain them have transformative potential in those systems. However, most faculty have primarily national careers and use cross-border experience to advance their position at home, travelling mostly at the doctoral or post-doctoral stages and for short visits. "BtA – Been to America – still plays a dominant role" (Enders and de Weert, 2004a, pp. 146-47). A third group consists of faculty with lesser opportunities at home compared to abroad, due to remuneration or conditions of work, the denial of national careers due to social or cultural closure, or an economic freeze on hiring. This group has less transformative potential than elite researchers because it does not constitute a sellers' market or leave a gap that undermines national education systems.[21]

As these three categories illustrate, faculty career structures remain primarily national in form. (Perhaps this is why cross-border academic mobility is associated universally with freedom.) There remain many formal and informal differences between nations in the mechanisms of training, appointment, tenure and promotion, in levels of remuneration and in conditions of work; and some systems are more open to foreign scholar appointments and careers than are others. Even within western Europe with the commitment to a common research area and roughly comparable levels of remuneration in research-intensive institutions, cross-border academic employment is still inhibited to a surprising degree (Guellec and Cervantes, 2002, p. 85). Musselin finds that "one of the most striking national patterns of each system is its academic labour market, salaries, status, recruitment procedures, workloads, career patterns, promotion rules being very different from one country to another" (Musselin, 2005, p. 135). There are continuing differences in relation to the legal status of faculty, remuneration and its regulation, language, and procedures for appointment and promotion (Musselin, 2004a, pp. 56-62). And again, "the proportion of staff with and without tenure is highly variable... each country defines its own career requirements for the profession... the various stages of a career do not obey the same rules" (Musselin, 2003; Enders and Musselin, 2008).

An emerging global labour market?

Despite the largely national patterning of career structures, it is often argued both that global mobility is increasing and the global element in faculty careers is becoming more significant. For example, Altbach finds that "the most visible impact of globalisation is the emergence of a worldwide market for academic talent, stimulated in part by the large numbers of students who study abroad". He also remarks that the global faculty labour market and doctoral student flows "are overwhelmingly a South-to-North phenomenon" (Altbach, 2002, pp. 7-9). The OECD's *Science, Technology and Industry Scoreboard* (2004) concludes that intensified global competition for scientific labour feeds the evolution of a distinctively global market that in some research fields is beginning to subsume national labour markets (OECD, 2004b, p. 39. See also p. 22; Gayathri, 2002, p. 201). But has cross-border academic mobility of all kinds *increased* and has it *also* reached a "tipping point" that constitutes a qualitative increase in the role of global elements, that is, an integrationist global transformation (Marginson and Van Der Wende, 2009)? Perhaps assumptions that mobility is desirable tend to readily generate perceptions that mobility is increasing. The evidence is more uneven.

Up to 2001 the American data indicate that foreign faculty mobility into the United States was increasing at all levels from doctoral training to mid career short visits and longer term migration and since 2001 doctoral numbers and faculty exchange have continued to grow though more unevenly and at a slower rate. These flows have not changed the character of the American faculty labour market itself except to increase the foreign element in its composition; and elsewhere the picture is different. The outward flow of researchers to the United States is common to most nations, developed and developing. While western Europe and the English-speaking nations benefit from brain gain from developing nations, in net terms they lose researchers to the United States. In other words the global flows are not simply a "North-South phenomenon".

The pattern of internal change in national markets outside the United States is not uniform or clear-cut. The evidence is fragmented, particularly longitudinal data (Mahroum, 2001, p. 220); and the trends are mixed, with few obvious changes taking place in the rules governing national labour markets. On one hand there is a general increase in cross-border mobility at doctoral stage, facilitated by a partial convergence of structures for doctoral training. For example, many higher education systems across Europe have shifted their paradigms for doctoral training towards the "professional model" (Enders, 2005, p. 120). This type of nationally-convergent global transformation (Marginson and Van Der Wende, 2009) may be the first step toward worldwide convergence in faculty labour markets. Its implications extend beyond the standardisation of doctoral training itself to the standardisation of career structures at the point of entry, while facilitating cross-border recognition of qualifications and broadening employability.[22] Data from many nations record a pattern of increase in cross-border research collaborations and in travel for conferences and short exchange visits. In relation to China, Guochu and Wenjun (2002, p. 198) note that the number of foreign experts working in China's institutions of higher education rose from 1 255 in 1980 to 14 020 in 1999. Within Europe, between 1997 and 2000 intra-European mobility under the Socrates programme grew by 71% (Vincent-Lancrin, 2009; see also Smeby and Trondal, 2005, pp. 456-57).[23] On the other hand it is less clear that postdoctoral mobility and longer term academic migration are increasing except for one way movement into the United States (for a more detailed review of the evidence see Marginson, forthcoming).

Within the OECD there is considerable variation in the extent to which those holding higher education are foreign-born (OECD, 2006b, p. 29). This exceeds 10% only in Switzerland, Australia, New Zealand, Ireland and Canada. Typically faculty ranks are more internationalised than the population as a whole but again there is much national variation. In a European collection on the international aspects of faculty careers Enders and de Weert (2004b, pp. 25-26) note "there is much agreement" in surveys of staff "on the proposition that recruitment and selection procedures which recognise international and intercultural experience is growing"; and that "particularly in the top scientific fields, international experience especially on the post-doc level is increasingly becoming an important factor in recruitment and selection of staff".

On the other hand there is doubt about whether the composition of entrants into national professions has changed, or the career arrangements themselves have loosened or are converging between nations. The authors of several national chapters find that survey respondents are sceptical about the positive effects of long stays abroad on one's career, noting it is difficult to re-enter European nations with closed career systems (Enders and de Weert, 2004b, p. 26). In Spain, university to university movement is blocked and the cessation of growth in the academic workforce has compounded barriers to foreigners and foreign-trained Spanish seeking to re-enter. "The internationalisation of academic staff in Spanish universities is extremely limited" (Mora, 2004, p. 413). Musselin (2004a, 2005) finds no sign of a process of Europeanisation in academic recruitment and careers paralleling the common higher education space (Musselin, 2004a, p. 72). There is also continued variation in the degree of academic globalisation by field of study with researchers in science, engineering and technology more prone to cross-border movement than those in other fields.

Nevertheless, there are signs of cross-field convergence in the degree of international movement in some but not all nations;[24] and in Europe the broadening recognition of professional qualifications and the European Research Area encourage convergence in academic labour markets. These effects will take time to show. Specific measures such as the coordinated EC approach to the brain drain towards the United States and recruiting non-European researchers also have integrative potentials.

Global competition for mobile researchers

Stratification of personnel in higher education has many roots; epistemic, economic, social and regulatory. It is affected by market competition within systems, funding regimes, performance management and the growth of commercial science. It is not determined solely by globalisation, and global factors interact with the other elements. But in the wake of global rankings, high performing researchers find themselves in a stronger bargaining position. It is significant that the main driver of elite researcher mobility is the large open American system characterised by a relatively high degree of labour deregulation, individual bargaining and variation in salaries and remuneration. In some countries governments, institutions and faculty unions will find themselves under pressure to facilitate the differentiation of salaries previously held in a roughly equal position across fields and between individuals at the same level regardless of merit. Global competition will increase the impetus for the introduction or enhancement of techniques enabling greater flexibility in reward structures such as performance-related pay. If so, one option will be to differentiate the national system along American lines between research-intensive universities and the others, facilitating the differentiation of status and rewards within systems, without creating a major increase in the fiscal cost of higher education. Another option will be to deregulate or regulate faculty salaries and conditions of work sufficiently so as to enable a more pronounced differentiation within individual universities (see Enders and Musselin, 2008). Where such moves tend to undermine national egalitarianism and professional traditions there is likely to be policy conflict.

In 2003-04, the average salary at American doctoral universities for full professors for 9-10 months of the year was USD 100 682, and average total compensation was USD 125 644, rising to USD 152 540 in the independent private universities. US academic faculty also have earning opportunities during the summer break. There are greater rewards at the peak of the American system: 6% of full professors earned more than USD 200 000 in salary alone in 2003-04 (Academe, 2006). By comparison Enders and de Weert (2004b, p. 18) note that the annual income of European professors typically ranged from EUR 55 000-60 000 in the Netherlands and Germany to EUR 40 000-50 000 in France, Finland, Spain and Italy, down to EUR 13 000-20 000 in Greece and eastern Europe.[25] A number of Asian nations approach or exceed European salary levels. In relation to Singapore, Lee (2002a) remarks that "the recently revised salary scales are internationally competitive and rank among the highest in the region". Professors earn from USD 82 800 to USD 117 000 per annum and are on par with the United States except at the top end of the American profession. Singapore has set out to create a cosmopolitan globally competitive higher education system. Almost half of its faculty are expatriates from other nations. In Korea the gap with American salaries has narrowed. In Korea in 2000 the average annual salary for a full professor in a public university was USD 39 037; in a private university USD 42 628 (Lee, 2002b, p. 182). After PPP conversion Korea is on par with OECD Europe. By contrast, in Argentina in 2001, the annual salary of the small minority of full professors paid full-time varied from USD 12 492 to USD 27 084 depending on seniority (Marquis, 2002, p. 69). In many emerging nations salaries are lower than this and a full-time academic salary cannot support a middle class standard of living. Working in two jobs is common, reducing the time for original research (Altbach, 2002, pp. 18-19).

While salaries, opportunities for non-salary earnings, good research infrastructure and American career opportunities are not the only factors that determine work satisfaction[26] all else being equal they constitute a significant set of incentives particularly for younger researchers. Eventually, perhaps, all national systems that aspire to front rank research performance will have little choice but to offer competitive salaries and conditions of work or face the loss of too many personnel to institutions in the United States and in other systems such as Singapore that are prepared to offer quasi-American salaries and research infrastructure. The growing role of the global pool of researchers centred primarily on American higher education and privileged *vis-à-vis* both other national systems and the majority of faculty whose work is centred on teaching, may also encourage fragmentation of the teaching-research nexus and the relative expansion of research-only positions. There are signs of this already, for example in the United Kingdom (Enders and de Weert, 2004b, p. 24).

Conclusions on global faculty mobility

In the last 15 years there has been a significant increase in shorter-term movement across borders for academic purposes, varying by nation and academic field; but except in the United States, there is as yet no clear-cut evidence of a generalised increase in foreign entry into national academic labour markets that would suggest the broad substitution of non-national labour for national labour. Research rankings and the formation of global higher education markets have intensified competition for globally mobile scientists, and increased the salience of global salary standards (quasi-US salaries) for that group. Though such effects are playing out on a relatively small scale at the top end of the academic labour markets they are strategically significant for national governments, which need to monitor "brain circulation" closely and ensure sufficient flexibility in reward structures. In the absence of a policy-driven convergence of career structures, which at this stage seems to be a possibility only in Europe, an increase in the mobility of the highest calibre researchers, instead of transforming national labour markets and career structures holistically, is more likely to generate segmentation effects. In other words the global labour market may both grow and tend to become further decoupled from national labour markets. This could only square with a universal trend to globalisation of the sector if within national systems there is an increase in the vertical stratification of career structures and of resource distribution between research-intensive and other institutions.

For the foreseeable future, developments in academic labour will be determined primarily by the large national systems. There are significant obstacles to the development of a fully integrated labour market across the whole of the European Union given the degree of material inequality between the national higher education systems of western Europe on one hand and those in Greece, eastern Europe (and Turkey) on the other. An integrated labour market common to western European nations could be viable. Given the pulling power of the American academic labour market, a robust European market could develop only if it was bounded by coherent regulatory structures broadly consistent across the European region in the framing of careers (permitting some local and national idiosyncrasies), and economically viable. In other words there would need to be a progressive convergence towards a common approach to the main career markers such as procedures for initial selection and the granting of tenure and promotion; the customary time spans and the scope for variation of career norms. If no such regional convergence emerges, then it is likely that in the long run the different national labour markets will become more stratified within the global environment. Within and beyond Europe, unless corrective action is taken, national systems operating at lower than OECD average resource levels are likely to experience a worsened brain drain to resource strong nations.

From the national point of view mobility ceases to be a universal good when it is associated with largely one-way movement out of the country. The global public good requires expansion of higher education capacity throughout the world. Education is a crucial element in the building of democratic agency and economy (Sen, 2000; Taskforce, 2000). Given the vertical differences between national systems, including the inability of poorer nations to pay globally competitive salaries, an unregulated global free market in academic labour does not optimise the global public good. One possibility is that aid policies could be targeted to the subsidisation of academic salary structures and retention in developing and transition nations. There are a number of issues at stake: the future of academic independence which is affected by the tenure and security of work as well as whether governments or managers intervene directly; the degree to which national systems facilitate cross-border careers; the extent to which a common labour pool of high calibre researchers becomes translated into a common set of conditions of work across different national systems; and the evolution of the teaching-research nexus. Given the growth of global research competition, the pressures to divide teaching and research functions are likely to intensify but whether this will translate into a new norm of faculty work is less clear.

4.5. Conclusions

In all three policy areas – Europeanisation, institutional rankings and cross-border faculty mobility – developments are moving quickly.

In relation to Europeanisation, coming close to 2010, Europe is evaluating its achievements in the Bologna Process and the Lisbon Strategy and is considering next steps. These European-level strategies are necessary, and their success is increasingly acknowledged outside Europe (see for instance Adelman, 2008). Discussions in Europe suggest that the complexities of convergence and divergence have become better understood, and that agendas should focus even more on transparency, for example measures and instruments such as multidimensional rankings and classifications in higher education (Van Den Broucke, 2008). In developing robust higher education and R&D systems, political and strategic questions on the right mix of co-operation and competition and the level at which they work out most effectively (i.e. national, regional, supranational) will continue to be important. These systems should not only aim at being globally competitive, but also globally attractive and engaged. Europe's ability to engage with diversity and pluriformity can serve as a strong basis for policies designed to foster creativity and innovation.

In relation to international comparisons in the form of rankings and associated metrics of publication and citation, global rankings will likely continue, gain more policy importance and become more sophisticated. Despite reservations about their impact they will play a greater rather than lesser role in shaping the horizon of thought and triggering policies and behaviours. Rankings are likely to strengthen the role of external comparison itself, and encourage convergent and imitative practices in institutional organisation and research. They may generate powerful tendencies to the conflation of diversity unless corrective action is taken. Classification systems serve a number of policy objectives, including the maintenance of structured diversity from above, and are also likely to continue to develop. It seems that some nations and institutions will become particularly active in designing systems of comparison and a wider professional culture of comparison and comparative metrics will become apparent. In this context, metrics based on questionable social science, such as the *Times Higher Education Supplement* that rests on a peer survey with a 1% response rate (Marginson, 2007), are likely to lose ground. Comparative indicators may emerge linking graduate output to national, regional and global labour markets. Global patterns in doctoral education would be also open to calculation and cross-border comparison; as would the relative attractiveness of national systems, institutions and cities to foreign personnel (rankings of the "liveability" of cities are already used for this purpose). Social equity in student entry, institutional engagement and impact, and the contribution of institutions to the global public good in key areas such as climate change and health, are among other areas that may be open to comparison in the future.

In relation to academic labour markets, though these labour markets are nationally embedded and career structures remain heterogeneous, it appears that the specifically global element in labour markets has gained weight, especially since the advent of global university rankings. It is likely that global academic mobility will increase (see also Marginson and Van Der Wende, 2009), especially at the top end of the research labour force. National innovation systems would come under increasing pressure to offer high salaries and special packages of conditions and infrastructure support to leading researchers, enhancing tendencies to the bifurcation or differentiation of national career structures. Nations unable to compete for high value academic labour could become, or remain, partly decoupled from the global research system. Some nations may focus on drawing doctoral graduate nationals back from the USA and elsewhere, whether permanently or *via* oscillating employment. "Bring them back" policies have already been relatively successful in a small number of rising economies including Chinese Taipei. The global element in academic labour markets could be dominated by the cross-border movements of the diasporas of India and China because of their demographic weight, coupled with the growing levels of educational participation, and national investments in innovation, in those countries and elsewhere. Future global competition for research talent may in part focus on Chinese-born nationals who have an important role in the national innovation systems of both the USA and China, especially in Engineering and technologies.

Notes

1. On a larger international scale (including notably developing countries) and later in time, the same type of response emerged from the 1998 UNESCO World Conference on Higher Education, which also strongly rejected the competitive, market-driven model and stressed that appropriate [national] planning must be based on co-operation and coordination between institutions of higher education and responsible state authorities.

2. Membership of the EU is not required for joining the process, which explains the fact that the number of Bologna signatory countries exceeds the number of EU member countries (27).

3. In 2001, 10% of the total number of study programmes was structured in bachelor-master, with 1% of the student population enrolled in them. In 2003, this had increased to 23% of programmes, catering for 3.5% of the student population.

4. Because the Bologna Declaration required a minimum of three years for the first degree. This has been solved by considering this type of "short cycle higher education" as integrated into or linked to the first degree (MSTI, 2005).

5. See: *http://europa.eu.int/comm/education/programmes/mundus/index_en.html*.

6. Eighty percent of this comes from the difference in domestic business R&D expenditure between the EU and the United States. Further analysis showed that the United States attract one-third

more R&D expenditure from EU companies than US companies allocate to the EU (a net outflow of EUR 5 billion in 2000) (EC, 2003b).

7. Especially private investments in education in the EU (0.6% of GDP) lag behind the United States (2.2%) and Japan (1.2%). The biggest difference is in higher education: the United States spends between two and five times more per student than EU countries (EC, 2004).

8. On average in the EU, 21% of the EU working-age population holds a higher education qualification, compared to 38% in the US, 43% in Canada, 36% in Japan and 32% in Korea (EC 2005).

9. The EU produces more higher education graduates and doctors in science and technology (25.7%) than the United States (17.2%) and Japan (21.9%) but the percentage of them at work as researchers is much lower in the EU (5.4 per 1 000 population in 1999), than in the United States (8.7) and Japan (9.7). This is due to career changes, a limited European labour market for researchers, and better opportunities and working conditions in the United States (EC, 2004).

10. Technical University of Aachen, Free University of Berlin, University of Freiburg, University of Göttingen, University of Karlsruhe, University of Konstanz, University of Heidelberg, University of Munich, and the Technical University of Munich.

11. It was explicitly stated as a problem that apart from some British universities there were no European universities in the top 20 of the world and relatively few in the top 50 as ranked by the Shanghai Jiao Tong University.

12. EU spending on research (1.9% of GDP) compared badly with the United States, Japan and Korea (all close to 3% thanks to much higher investments from industry). Higher education spending in the EU (1.1% of GDP) also compared badly with the United States and Korea (both 2.7%, again related to differences in private investments). It was calculated that in order to match the US figure, the EU would need to spend an additional EUR 150 billion a year on higher education. It was suggested to set a 2% of GDP aim for funding of higher education (EC, 2005).

13. The EC stated even that: "The Education and Training 2010 work programme, recognising the extreme importance of modernisation of higher education, *over and above* the reforms called for in the Bologna Process which, *a fortiori*, are also important for achieving the Lisbon objectives" (EC, 2005, p. 11).

14. Called "the third cycle" in the context of the Bologna Process. This is an important area where the European Higher Education Area (EHEA) and the European Research Area (ERA) effectively intersect.

15. The proposed EU directive on services in the internal market seeks to remove barriers to the freedom of establishment for service providers in member States and barriers to the freedom to provide services as between member States. Higher education (as a sector providing services) is not excluded, although it is not clear yet what exactly the impact of the new directive will be on cross-border activities in higher education. This directive was developed by the EC's directorate for internal market and can be seen as an example of wider EU policy interfering with higher education policies and as an EU equivalent to GATS, a trade framework which also intervened with higher education, but which was dealt with by yet another EC directorate (for trade).

16. A limitation is that the citation data are often a decade old or more, measuring past research rather than present research capacity. However, it is difficult to see how a reliable metric of present capacity could be created.

17. Arguably, by focusing on criteria relevant to the cross-border degree market, the *Times* rankings created anomalies. For example it appears that the *Times* inflated the performance of Australian universities, which achieved a massive 12 universities in the world's top 100, compared to Canada which has a similar system in many respects but with stronger research performance and a higher participation level. Canada had only three universities in the *Times* top 100. This kind of outcome feeds into perceptions that the *Times* rankings are a rigged game.

18. Altbach states "there are, in fact, no widely accepted methods for measuring teaching quality, and assessing the impact of education on students is so far an unexplored area as well" (Altbach, 2006; see also Guarino *et al.*, 2005, p. 149).

19. Research in the United States and UK research suggest that only some potential students are interested primarily in the prestige ranking of HEIs; and interestingly, these students tend to be drawn disproportionately from high achieving and socially advantaged groups (Dill and Soo, 2005, p. 513), as if these students more than others take for granted the educational benefits of participation and focus rather on the status and networking benefits of prestigious institutions. This area would benefit from further research.

20. In China the classification of institutions is being reconsidered using the original framework of the Carnegie Classification, now known as the "basic classification", in conjunction with the indicators developed by the SJTU to define a "world class university" (Liu, 2006).

21. Another factor encouraging mobility is cross-national differences in academic autonomy, which may be especially important in the social sciences and humanities. Historically the code of academic freedom has made the United States attractive to doctoral students and faculty from many developing nations (Altbach, 2002, p. 16).

22. Note, however, that the social and economic role of PhD training varies among nations at the high end of educational spending and participation (Enders and de Weert 2004a, p. 139). In the OECD group the average rate of PhD graduation relative to total population is 1.3%. It ranges from 2.8% in Sweden to 0.1% in Iceland and Mexico. In France and the United States the rate is 1.2%, in Germany 2.0% (OECD, 2005, p. 55).

23. In Italy data on participation in the two European mobility programmes, Socrates and Erasmus, show a rapid increase, with growth of 48% between 1998-99 and 2001-02 (Boffo *et al.*, 2004, pp. 260-261).

24. In relation to France Musselin (2003) emphasises that "the academic system developed around individual disciplines" with distinctive cultures. Fields such as medicine, law and some humanities remain partly *sui generis* in many nations, more so when the national language is not shared beyond the border. But Smeby and Trondal (2005, pp. 459ff) note in relation to Sweden that between 1981 and 2000 there was a tendency towards convergence between disciplines in relation to indicators such as cross-border collaboration and publication in English.

25. Note that these are not Purchasing Power Parity (PPP) comparisons. Accounting for differences in the cost of living in the respective nations narrows the cross-border differentials.

26. "The perspective of obtaining a tenured position early, may be decisive for a young foreign academic to apply in a foreign country" (Musselin, 2004a, p. 58). Here both American and German tenure tracks are prolonged, especially the latter. France and Australia offer shorter routes to permanency.

Bibliography

Academe (2006), "Annual Report on the Economic Status of the Profession, 2003-2004", accessed on 22 June 2007, *www.aaup.org/AAUP/comm/rep/Z/ecstatreport2003-04/default.htm*.

Adelman, C. (2008), *The Bologna Club: What U.S. Higher Education Can Learn from a Decade of European Reconstruction*. Washington: Institute for Higher Education Policy. Retrieved 21 September 2008 at: *www.ihep.org/assets/files/TheBolognaClub.pdf*.

Altbach, P. (2002), "Centers and Peripheries in the Academic Profession: The Special Challenges of Developing Countries", in P. Altbach (ed.), *The Decline of the Guru: The Academic Profession in Developing and Middle-income Countries*, Boston College, Chestnut Hill, pp. 1-22.

Altbach, P. (2006), The Dilemmas of Ranking, *International Higher Education*, Vol. 42.

Berning, E. (2004), "Petrified Structures and Still Little Autonomy and Flexibility: Country Report Germany", in J. Enders and E. de Weert (eds.), *The International Attractiveness of the Academic Workplace in Europe*, Herausgeber und Bestelladresse, Frankfurt, pp. 160-82.

Birnbaum, R. (1983), *Maintaining Diversity in Higher Education*, Jossey-Bass Publishers, Washington.

Bloom, D. (2005), "Raising the Pressure: Globalization and the Need for Higher Education Reform", in G. Jones, P. McCarney and M. Skolnik (eds.), *Creating Knowledge: Strengthening Nations: The Changing Role of Higher Education*, University of Toronto Press, Toronto, pp. 21-41.

Boffo, S., R. Moscati and M. Vaira (2004), "The Academic Workplace: Country Report to Italy", in J. Enders and E. de Weert (eds.), *The International Attractiveness of the Academic Workplace in Europe*, Herausgeber und Bestelladresse, Frankfurt, pp. 243-63.

Brooks, R. (2005), "Measuring University Quality", *The Review of Higher Education*, Vol. 29, No. 1, pp. 1-21.

Van Den Broucke, F. van (2008), Closing address at the Seminar: Bologna 2020: Unlocking Europe's potential – Contributing to a better world. Ghent, 19-20 May 2008. Retrieved 21 September 2008, *www.vlaanderen.be/servlet/ Satellite?c=MIN_Publicatie&cid=1205995932155&lyt=1141721285950&p=1100806249017&pagename=mi nister_frank_vandenbroucke%2FMIN_Publicatie%2FPublicatie_met_relatiesMIN&ppid=1142511947285&sit e=minister_frank_vandenbroucke&subtype=Toespraak.*

Alesi, B., S. Burger, B. Kehm and U. Teichler (2005), *Bachelor and Master Courses in Selected Countries Compared with Germany*, Federal Ministry of Education and Research, Bonn/Berlin.

A Center for Higher Education Development (CHE) (2006), *Study and Research in Germany*, University rankings, published in association with *Die Zeit*, accessed on 16 March 2006, *www.daad.de/ deutschland/studium/hochschulranking/04708.en.html*.

Centre for Higher Education Policy Studies (CHEPS) (2005), "The European Higher Education and Research Landscape 2020. Scenarios and Strategic Debates".

Corbett, A. (2005), *Universities and the Europe of Knowledge. Ideas, Institutions and Policy Entrepreneurship in European Union Higher Education Policy, 1955-2005*, Houndsmill, Palgrave Macmillan.

Dalsheimer N. and D. Despréaux (2008), "Les classements internationaux des établissements d'enseignement supérieur ", Éducation et formations, Paris, France.

Dill, D. and M. Soo (2005), "Academic Quality, League Tables, and Public Policy: A Cross-national Analysis of University Rankings", *Higher Education*, Vol. 49, pp. 495-533.

van Dyke, N. (2005), "Twenty Years of University Reports Cards", *Higher Education in Europe*, Vol. 30(2), pp. 103-24.

El-Khawas, E. (2002), "Developing an Academic Career in a Globalizing World", in J. Enders and O. Fulton (eds.), *Higher Education in a Globalizing World: International Trends and Mutual Observations, A Festschrift in Honour of Ulrich Teichler*, Kluwer, Dordrecht, pp. 242-54.

Enders, J. (2005), "Border Crossings: Research Training, Knowledge, Dissemination and the Transformation of Academic Work", *Higher Education*, Vol. 49, pp. 119-33.

Enders, J. and E. de Weert (2004a), "Science, Training and Career: Changing Modes of Knowledge Production and Labour Markets", *Higher Education Policy*, Vol. 17, pp. 135-52.

Enders, J. and E. de Weert (eds.) (2004b), "The International Attractiveness of the Academic Workplace in Europe – Synopsis Report", in J. Enders and E. de Weert (eds.), *The International Attractiveness of the Academic Workplace in Europe*, Herausgeber und Bestelladresse, Frankfurt, pp. 11-31.

Enders, J. and C. Musselin (2008), "Back to the Future? The Academic Professions in the 21st Century", in *Higher Education 2030, Volume 1: Demography*, OECD Publishing, Paris.

EUA (2006), *The Contribution of Universities to Europe's Competitiveness*, Speech of EUA President Prof. Georg Winckler to the Conference of the European Ministers of Education, Vienna, 16-17 March 2006, *www.eua.be/eua/jsp/en/upload/EUA_Winckler_Handout_160306.1142503397992.pdf*.

European Commission (2001), *Communication of the European Commission to the European Parliament and the Council on Strengthening Co-operation with Third Countries in the Field of Higher Education*, EC, Brussels.

European Commission (2002), *The Concrete Future Objectives of Education Systems*, Report from the Commission, EC, Brussels.

European Commission (2003a), *Communication from the Commission: The Role of Universities in the Europe of Knowledge*, COM(2003) 58 final, EC, Brussels.

European Commission (2003b), *Key Figures 2003-2004: Towards a European Research Area*. Science, Technology and Innovation, EC, Brussels.

European Commission (2003c), *Brain drain Study – Emigration Flows of Qualified Scientist*, Study carried out by Merit, *http://ec.europa.eu/research/era/pdf/indicators/merit_exsum.pdf*

European Commission (2003d), *Communication of the European Commission to the European Parliament and the Council*, Researchers in the European Research Area: One Profession Multiple-careers, COM(2003)436 final.

European Commission (2004), *Education and Training 2010. The Success of the Lisbon Strategy Hinges on Urgent Reforms*, COM(2004)685 final.

European Commission (2005), *Communication from the Commission. Mobilising the Brainpower of Europe: Enabling Universities to Make their Full Contribution to the Lisbon Strategy*, COM(2005)152 final.

European Commission (2006), *Communication of the European Commission to the European Council. The European Institute of Technology: Further Steps towards it Creation*, COM(2006)276 final.

European Research Advisory Board (2006), *International Research Co-operation*, Final Report EURAB.

Field, K. (2006), Another Accountability Idea: A New Database that would Customize College Rankings, *Chronicle of Higher Education*, 31 March.

Frank, R. and P. Cook (1995), *The Winner-take-all Society*, The Free Press, New York.

Gayathri, V. (2002), "Rethinking High-skilled International Migration: Research and Policy Issues for India's Information Economy", *International Mobility of the Highly Skilled*, OECD Publishing, Paris, pp. 201-12.

Gibbons, M., C. Limoges, H. Nowotny, S. Schwartzman, P. Scott and M. Trow (1994), *The New Production of Knowledge: The Dynamics of Science and Research in Contemporary Societies*, Sage, London.

Gornitzka, A. (2005), "Coordinating Policies for a 'Europe of Knowledge'. Emerging Practices of the 'Open Method of Coordination' in Education and Research", Arena Working Paper No. 16, Oslo. *www.arena.uio.no*

Guarino, C., G. Ridgeway, M. Chun and R. Buddin (2005), "Latent Variable Analysis: A New Approach to University Ranking", *Higher Education in Europe*, Vol. 30, No. 2, pp. 147-65.

Guellec, D. and M. Cervantes (2002), "International Mobility of Highly Skilled Workers: From Statistical Analysis to Policy Formulation", *International Mobility of the Highly Skilled*, OECD Publishing, Paris, pp. 71-98.

Guochu, Z. and L. Wenjun (2002), "International Mobility of China's Resources in Science and Technology and its Impact", *International Mobility of the Highly Skilled*, OECD Publishing, Paris, pp. 189-200.

Huisman, J. and M.C. van der Wende (eds.) (2004), "On Co-operation and Competition. National and European Policies for Internationalisation of Higher Education", ACA Papers on International Co-operation, Lemmens, Bonn.

Institute for Higher Education Policy (IHEP), in conjunction with UNESCO-CEPES (2006), *Berlin Principles on Ranking of Higher Education Institutions*, 30 May, accessed on 30 June 2006, *www.ihep.org*.

Institute for Scientific Information, Thomson-ISI (2008), Data on highly cited researchers, ISIHighlyCited.com, accessed July 2008, *http://isihighlycited.com/*.

Ischinger, B. (2006), "Higher Education for a Changing World", *OECD Observer*, June.

Jacobs, B. and R. van der Ploeg (2006), "Guide to Reform of Higher Education: A European Perspective", *Economic Policy*, Vol. 21, Issue 47, pp. 535-92.

Jin, M. (2007), "Understanding Korean Brain Drain by a Comparison of the Employment Situation between Returned PhDs and Non-returned PhDs with US Higher Education Degree in Science and Engineering", *Journal of Educational Administration*, 25(3), 271-93.

Kaulisch, M. and J. Enders (2005), "Careers in Overlapping Institutional Contexts: The Case of Academe", *Career Development International*, Vol. 10(2), pp. 130-44.

Kirp, D. (2004), *Shakespeare, Einstein and the Bottom-line: The Marketing of Higher Education*, Harvard University Press, Cambridge MA.

Lambert, R. and N. Butler (2006), *The Future of European Universities: Renaissance or Decay?*, Centre for European Reform, London.

Lee, M. (2002a), "The Academic Profession in Malaysia and Singapore: Between Bureaucratic and Corporate Cultures", in P. Altbach (ed.), *The Decline of the Guru: The Academic Profession in Developing and Middle-income Countries*, Boston College, Chestnut Hill, pp. 141-72.

Lee, S.H. (2002b), "The Changing Academic Workplace in Korea", in P. Altbach (ed.), *The Decline of the Guru: The Academic Profession in Developing and Middle-income Countries*", Boston College, Chestnut Hill, pp. 173-206.

Liu, N. (2006), "The Differentiation and Classification of Chinese Universities and the Building of World-Class Universities in China", Presentation at the seminar at Leiden University, 16 February, Dream of Chinese for WCU, *www.leidenslatest.leidenuniv.nl/content_docs/ presentation_prof._liu.ppt#364,4*.

Liu, N. and Y. Cheng (2005), "The Academic Ranking of World Universities", *Higher Education in Europe*, Vol. 30(2), pp. 127-36.

Liu, N. and L. Liu (2005), "University Rankings in China", *Higher Education in Europe*, Vol. 30(2), pp. 217-27.

Lub, A., M.C. van der Wende and J. Witte (2003), "The Implementation of the Bachelor-Master System in Germany and the Netherlands", *TEAM*, Vol. 9, pp. 249-66.

Luo, Y.-L. and W.-J. Wang (2002), "High Skill Migration and Chinese Taipei's Industrial Development", *International Mobility of the Highly Skilled*, OECD Publishing, Paris, pp. 253-70.

Mahroum, S. (2001), "Foreign Scientific Researchers in Selected OECD EU Countries: Data Sources and Analysis", *Innovative People: Mobility of Skilled Personnel in National Innovation Systems*, OECD Publishing, Paris, pp. 219-28.

Marginson, S. (2007), "Global University rankings", paper for symposium, *Comparing Colleges: The Implications of Classification, Ranking and Peer Analysis for Research and Practice*, annual conference of the Association for Studies in Higher Education, Louisville, Kentucky, United States, 6-10 November 2007, *www.cshe.unimelb.edu.au/people/staff_pages/Marginson/ASHE%202007% 20PRESENT%20global%20university%20rankings.pdf*.

Marginson S. and M. Van Der Wende (2009), "The New Global Landscape of Nations and Institutions", in *Higher Education 2030, Volume 2: Globalisation*, OECD Publishing, Paris.

Marginson, S. (forthcoming), "The Academic Profession(s) in the Global Era", chapter prepared for J. Enders and E. de Weert (eds.), *The Academic Profession and the Modernization of Higher Education: Analytical and Comparative Perspectives*.

Marquis, C. (2002), "Universities and Professors in Argentina: Changes and Challenges", in P. Altbach (ed.), *The Decline of the Guru: The Academic Profession in Developing and Middle-income Countries*, Boston College, Chestnut Hill, pp. 53-76.

Martinelli, D. (2002), "A Brain Drain among Young PhDs: Mirage or Reality?", *International Mobility of the Highly Skilled*, OECD Publishing, Paris, pp. 125-32.

Ministry of Science, Technology and Innovation (MSTI) (2005), *A Framework for Qualifications of the European Higher Education Area*, Bologna Working Group on Qualifications Frameworks, Copenhagen.

Mora, J. (2004), "Academic Staff in Spanish Universities: Country Report Spain", in J. Enders and E. de Weert (eds.), *The International Attractiveness of the Academic Workplace in Europe*, Herausgeber und Bestelladresse, Frankfurt, pp. 395-414.

Musselin, C. (2003), "Internal versus External Labour Markets", *Higher Education Management and Policy*, Vol. 15(3), pp. 9-23.

Musselin, C. (2004a), "Towards a European Academic Labour Market? Some Lessons Drawn from Empirical Studies on Academic Mobility", *Higher Education*, Vol. 48, pp. 55-78.

Musselin, C. (2004b), "The Academic Workplace: Up to Now it is not as Bad... But! Country Report France", in J. Enders and E. de Weert (eds.), *The International Attractiveness of the Academic Workplace in Europe*, Herausgeber und Bestelladresse, Frankfurt, pp. 141-59.

Musselin, C. (2005), "European Academic Labour Markets in Transition", *Higher Education*, Vol. 49, pp. 135-54.

Nowotny, H., P. Scott and M. Gibbons (2001), *Rethinking Science: Knowledge and the Public in an Age of Uncertainty*, Polity, Cambridge.

OECD (2004a), *Internationalization and Trade in Higher Education: Opportunities and Challenges*, OECD Publishing, Paris.

OECD (2004b), *Quality and Recognition in Higher Education: The Cross-border Challenge*, OECD Publishing, Paris.

OECD (2004c), *OECD Science, Technology and Industry Outlook*, OECD Publishing, Paris.

OECD (2005), *Education at a Glance: OECD Indicators*, OECD Publishing, Paris.

OECD (2006a), "Four Futures Scenarios for Higher Education", OECD Publishing, Paris.

OECD (2006b), "Background Report. Higher Education: Quality, Equity and Efficiency", prepared for the meeting of OECD Education Ministers, 27-28 June, Athens.

OECD/World Bank (2007), *Cross-border Tertiary Education: A Way towards Capacity Development*, OECD and the World Bank, Paris and Washington DC.

Olsen, J.P. (2005), "The Institutional Dynamics of the European University", Arena Working Paper, accessed on 22 June 2007 at: *www.arena.uio.no/publications/working-papers2005/papers/wp05_15.pdf*.

Patterson, G. (2005), "Collaboration/competition Crossroads: National/supranational Tertiary Education Policies on a Collision Course", *Tertiary Education and Management*, Vol. 11, pp. 355-68.

Reichert, S. and C. Tauch (2005), *Trends IV: European Universities Implementing Bologna*, EUA, Brussels.

Reinalda, B. and E. Kulesza (2005), *The Bologna Process: Harmonizing Europe's Higher Education*, Barbara Budrich Publishers.

Rocki, M. (2005), "Statistical and Mathematical Aspects of Ranking: Lessons from Poland", *Higher Education in Europe*, Vol. 30, No. 2, pp. 173-81.

Sapp, M. and A. McCormick (2006), "Revision of the Carnegie Classifications", *Special Issue – AIR Alert #25*, Update 1.

Sen, A. (1999), "Global Justice: Beyond International Equity", in I. Kaul, I. Grunberg and M. Stern (eds.), *Global Public Goods: International Co-operation in the 21st century*, Oxford University Press, New York, pp. 116-25.

Sen, A. (2000), *Development as Freedom*, Anchor Books, New York.

Shanghai Jiao Tong University Institute of Higher Education (SJTUIHE) (2007), *Academic Ranking of World Universities*, accessed July 2008 at *http://ed.sjtu.edu.cn/ranking.htm*

Singh, M. (2001), *Re-inserting the "Public Good" into Higher Education Transformation*, paper to conference on "Globalisation and Higher Education – Views from the South", University of Cape town, March, South African Council on Higher Education, Pretoria.

Smeby, J. and J. Trondal (2005), "Globalization or Europeanization? International Contact among University Staff", *Higher Education*, Vol. 49, pp. 449-66.

Taskforce on Higher Education and the Developing World (2000), *Peril or Promise*, World Bank, Washington.

The Times Higher (2007), World University Rankings, *The Times Higher Education Supplement*, Originally published on 9 November 2007, accessed July 2008, *www.timeshighereducation.co.uk/*.

Usher, A. and M. Savino (2006), "A World of Difference: A Global Survey of University League Tables", accessed on 2 April 2006 at *www.educationalpolicy.org*.

Vincent-Lancrin, S. (2009), "What is Changing in Academic Research? Trends and Prospects", in *Higher Education 2030, Volume 2: Globalisation*, OECD Publishing, Paris.

Vlk, A. (2006), "Higher Education and GATS: Regulatory Consequences and Stakeholders' Responses", CHEPS/Universiteit Twente, accessed 22 June 2007, *www.utwente.nl/cheps/documenten/thesisvlk.pdf*.

Vught, F.A. van (2006), "Higher Education System Dynamics and Useful Knowledge Creation", in J. Duderstadt and L. Weber (eds.), *Universities and Business: Towards a Better Society*, Economica, New York.

Vught, F.A. van, J. Bartelse, D. Bohmert, N. Burquel, J. Divis, J. Huisman and M.C. van der Wende (2005), *Institutional Profiles. Towards a Typology of Higher Education Institutions in Europe*, Report to the European Commission, *http://doc.utwente.nl/53776/1/engreport05institutionalprofiles.pdf*.

Vught, F.A van, M.C. van der Wende and D.F. Westerheijden (2002), "Globalisation and Internationalisation. Policy Agendas Compared", in J. Enders and O. Fulton (eds.), *Higher Education in a Globalizing World. International Trends and Mutual Observations*, Kluwer, Dordrecht, pp.103-121.

Wende, M.C. van der (2006), The Challenges of University Ranking, Presentation at the seminar at Leiden University, 16 February 2006, *www.leidenslatest.leidenuniv.nl/content_docs/presentation_prof._van_der_wende.ppt*

Witte, J. (2006), "Change of Degrees and Degrees of Change", Comparing Adaptations of European Higher Education Systems in the Context of the Bologna Process, Dissertation, CHEPS.

WTO/GATS (2005), World Trade Organization website on negotiations on the General Agreement on Trade in Services (GATS) in relation to educational services, accessed 11 September 2005, *www.wto.org/english/tratop_e/serv_e/education_e/education_e.htm*

Yang, R. (2005), "The Chinese Professoriate in Comparative Perspective: Self-perceptions, Academic Life, Gender Differences and Internal Differentiation", in A. Welch (ed.), *The Professoriate: Portrait of a Profession*, Springer, Dordrecht, pp. 193-204.

Higher Education to 2030
Volume 2: Globalisation
© OECD 2009

Chapter 5

What is Changing in Academic Research? Trends and Prospects

by

Stéphan Vincent-Lancrin*

This chapter analyses the trends and driving forces that can be observed in academic research over the past two decades in the OECD area. It gives an outlook of the main current characteristics of academic research at a macro level in terms of funding and activities in comparison with research performed by other sectors. It also highlights future challenges and sketches in appendix a few possible future scenarios for academic research in a 20-year time frame.

* OECD, Directorate for Education, Centre for Educational Research and Innovation (CERI). The author gratefully acknowledges Sharon Standish (OECD, Directorate for Science, Technology and Industry) and Kiira Kärkkäinen (OECD/CERI) for their help with the data.

5.1. Introduction

What is changing in academic research? What has changed over the past decades and what might change in the coming ones? Could the research mission of universities be carried out in slightly or radically different ways in the medium term? This chapter aims to cast light on the trends and driving forces that can be observed in academic research over the past two decades in the OECD area. It gives an outlook of the main current characteristics of academic research at a macro level in terms of funding and activities in comparison with research performed by other sectors. It also highlights future challenges and sketches a few possible future scenarios for academic research in a 20-year time frame.

In this chapter, academic research is understood as research and development (R&D) undertaken in the higher education sector, including universities, polytechnics, etc., and research centres that have close links with higher education institutions.[1] The trend analysis mainly draws on quantitative data from the OECD R&D, Patent and Main Science and Technology Indicators (MSTI) Databases, from the latest editions of *Science and Engineering Indicators* by the US National Science Board (NSB) (NSB, 2004, 2006, 2008) and from the OECD Education Database. All unreferenced data come from the OECD Databases.

Before focusing on academic research, one should bear in mind a few facts about and trends in the overall R&D efforts of OECD countries.

First, R&D has grown significantly during the two past decades within the OECD area, which accounted for about 80% of all R&D expenditures in the world (OECD, 2005a). Gross domestic expenditure on R&D amounted on average to 2.3% of GDP (Gross Domestic Product) in 2006, against 1.9% in 1981. In real terms (that is, controlling for inflation[2]), R&D expenditures have more than doubled between 1981 and 2005.

Second, with some variations across countries, the business sector carries out and funds the bulk of R&D in the OECD area.[3] In 2006, Turkey and Greece were the only countries reporting more R&D expenditures in the higher education than in the business sector. The prominence of the business sector has sharpened over the past decades. Between 1981 and 2006, the share of R&D performed by the business sector has risen from 65.4% to 68.8% of the total R&D effort in the OECD area. Business expenditures on the performance of R&D have risen from 1.3 to 1.6% of GDP, that is by 170% in real terms. The business enterprise sector has also increased its financing of R&D from 1% to 1.44% of GDP between 1981 and 2006. This increasing performance and funding of R&D by businesses is one of the most significant trends of the past decades – explaining to some extent why OECD economies are often described as increasingly knowledge-based economies (Foray, 2004; Boyer, 2002).

Finally, another major trend lies in the relative decline of government as a performing sector and as a funding source of R&D. The share of R&D performed by the government sector (*e.g.* military research, agronomy, academies of science, ministries, etc.) has (almost continuously) decreased from 17.9% to 11.4% between 1981 and 2006. The government-funded R&D also decreased from 0.84% to 0.66% of GDP between 1981 and 2005, and the percentage of total R&D financed by government, from 44.0% to 29.5%. This funding decline is relative though: in real terms, government expenditures have actually increased by 60% since 1981. The share of government military R&D has decreased significantly between 1986 and 2001 (from 46 to 28%), but has increased again after the events of 11 September 2001 and amounted to 33% of government R&D spending in 2006.[4]

The remainder of the paper will focus on academic research, where parallel trends can be observed.[5] The first section documents the growth in funding and output. The second section shows that academic research can be characterised by its large proportion of basic research and government funding, although the mode of allocation of public funding has changed in the past twenty years (Section 5.3). A noteworthy trend has been the rise of the private funding of higher education and performance of basic research by the non-academic sectors (Section 5.4). Internationalisation of academic research has grown significantly (Section 5.5), while a new attitude of civil society towards research (Section 5.6) and new computing and networking opportunities offered by information and communication technology (ICT) are emerging as new driving forces for the future of academic research (Section 5.7). The last section concludes (Section 5.8) while an annex brings all these trends together in four future scenarios (Annex 5.A1).

5.2. The massification of academic research

Following general trends in R&D, except for government research, higher education research has gained ground during the past twenty years. Between 1981 and 2006, the share of R&D performed by the higher education sector has increased from 14.5% to 17.1% of the total R&D effort within the OECD area (Table 5.1). While higher education's share of R&D remains much smaller than within the business sector, the former has increased more quickly. Expenditures on R&D in the higher education sector amounted to 0.39% of GDP in 2006 in the OECD area, against 0.28% in 1981. This increase represents almost a three-fold increase in R&D expenditures in real terms during this time period (while R&D expenditures in businesses "only" doubled).

Two other pieces of evidence of this massive increase of academic research lie in the number of higher education researchers and the output of scientific articles.

Between 1981 and 1999, the number of higher education researchers has increased by 127% (full time equivalent) – that is by 7% a year on average.[6] Although this increase reflects a general growth of R&D personnel in the OECD area (research personnel in the business sector has grown by 118% in the same period), the percentage of higher education researchers has slightly increased and amounted to 26% of all researchers in the OECD area in 2003, up from 24% in 1981 (and from 22% in 1985). Here again, variations across countries are significant: while this share is low in the United States (14.8% in 1999) and weights much in the aggregated mean, higher education researchers represented on average 39% of all researchers in an OECD country in 2006 (and 35% at the EU-15 aggregated level).

The growth of the research output is another major trend in academic research during the past two decades (Figure 5.1). It is highly correlated with (and probably well explained by) the growth of R&D expenditures and of researchers in the higher education sector. About 709 500 new scientific articles have been published in 2005, a 52% increase compared to the 466 000 published in 1988 (NSB, 2008).[7] About 80% of them were produced by OECD countries. Most of these articles result from research carried out in the academic sector. In the United States, the higher education sector authored 75% of all the US scientific articles in 2005 (NSB, 2008). The share is probably higher in other countries where the non-academic sector is smaller.

Table 5.1. **Share of gross domestic expenditure on R&D (GERD) performed by sector, 1981, 2006 (%)**

		Business enterprise	Government	Higher education	Private non-profit
Australia	1981	25.02	45.11	28.55	1.32
	2004	54.14	15.97	26.81	3.09
Austria	1981	55.85	9.03	32.80	2.33
	2006	67.75	5.14	26.70	0.41
Canada	1981	48.11	24.42	26.66	0.82
	2006	52.37	8.78	38.40	0.45
Czech Republic	1981	m	m	m	m
	2006	66.18	17.55	15.87	0.41
Denmark	1981	49.70	22.67	26.74	0.88
	2006	66.56	6.73	26.10	0.60
Finland	1981	54.66	22.55	22.24	0.56
	2006	71.30	9.35	18.73	0.62
France	1981	58.92	23.59	16.42	1.07
	2006	63.40	17.24	18.10	1.26
Germany	1981	68.97	13.44	17.06	0.53
	2006	69.60	13.91	16.49	m
Greece	1981	22.46	63.08	14.46	x
	2006	30.04	20.81	47.81	1.34
Hungary	1981	m	m	m	m
	2006	48.28	25.37	24.35	m
Iceland	1981	9.61	60.74	25.97	3.68
	2005	51.51	23.53	21.96	2.99
Ireland	1981	43.58	39.31	16.03	1.08
	2006	67.66	6.29	26.05	m
Italy	1981	56.37	25.72	17.91	x
	2005	50.36	17.32	30.21	2.12
Japan	1981	65.96	12.02	17.56	4.46
	2005	76.45	8.29	13.40	1.86
Korea	1981	m	m	m	m
	2006	77.26	11.56	9.95	1.23
Netherlands	1981	53.26	20.77	23.18	2.78
	2006	59.2	13.61	27.18	n
Norway	1981	52.87	17.65	28.95	0.52
	2006	53.03	16.04	30.93	m
Poland	1981	m	m	m	m
	2006	31.54	37.03	31.00	0.43
Slovak Republic	1981	m	m	m	m
	2006	43.06	32.76	24.10	0.07
Spain	1981	45.49	31.57	22.95	x
	2005	53.79	17.04	29.03	0.14
Sweden	1981	63.65	6.09	29.99	0.26
	2006	74.88	4.49	20.42	0.21
Switzerland	1981	74.20	5.92	19.88	x
	2004	73.74	1.07	22.90	2.29
Turkey	1981	m	m	m	m
	2005	33.83	11.55	54.61	m
United Kingdom	1981	62.96	20.64	13.55	2.85
	2005	61.62	10.56	25.59	2.24
United States	1981	69.31	18.50	9.74	2.45
	2006	70.34	11.13	14.28	4.25
Total OECD	1981	**65.4**	**17.9**	**14.5**	**2.3**
	2006[1]	**68.6**	**11.4**	**17.1**	**2.5**
European Union	1981	62.03	18.80	17.81	1.36
	2006[1]	63.25	13.98	20.75	0.84
Russian Federation	1981	m	m	m	m
	2006	66.60	27.03	6.12	0.25
Slovenia	1981	m	m	m	m
	2006	60.38	24.42	15.04	0.17

1. Most recent available year used in case of a missing value. "x": included in another column; "n": negligible; "m": missing.

Figure 5.1. **Science and engineering article output by major publishing region/country (1988-2005) (thousands)**

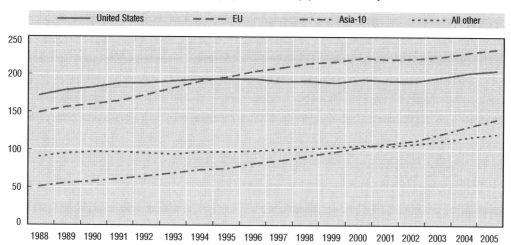

Note: Article counts from set of journals covered by Science Citation Index (SCI) and Social Sciences Citation Index (SSCI). Articles classified by year of publication and assigned to region/country/economy on basis of institutional address(es) listed on article. Articles on fractional-count basis, *i.e.* for articles with collaborating institutions from multiple countries/economies, each country/economy receives fractional credit on basis of proportion of its participating institutions. Asia-10 includes: China (including Hong Kong), India, Indonesia, Japan, Malaysia, Philippines, Singapore, Korea, Chinese Taipei, Thailand.
Source: NSB (2008).

Similarly, the number of new academic books published has increased – and probably the number of books published by academics. For example, books published by US university presses have increased by 32% between 1993 and 2007; and academics have probably been responsible for a larger amount of the significant increase in books published in the United States over the same period (*www.bookwire.com* and *www.bowker.com*).

An interesting and puzzling recent trend has been the flattening of the scientific article output of the United States between 1992 and the early 2000s, and of Canada, the United Kingdom and the Netherlands from the late 1990s, although real expenditures and the number of researchers continued to grow (NSB, 2004). The article output has recently grown again. The reasons might relate to the age structure of the research workforce (does a researcher produce less when close to retirement?), a change in professional practices (for example a change of attitude towards the widespread practice of slicing research outputs in minimal publishable pieces), more time needed for integrating increasingly collaborative and interdisciplinary research, but also to the increasing time spent to raise funding under new governance models (Bell *et al.*, 2007).

The massification of higher education has been an important driver of this growth. Enrolments and participation rates in higher education have increased dramatically since the Second World War, and higher education systems have adjusted by creating new institutions and hiring new staff who generally teach and carry out research. For example, in the United States enrolments in higher education have doubled from 8.5 to 17.3 million full and part-time students between 1970 and 2005; in Japan they increased by 85%; in France they doubled (according to national statistics) (see also OECD, 2008a). Between 1985 and 2005, the number of higher education students enrolled (full time) within the OECD area has increased by 91%, from about 20 to 38.2 million students – that is a pace of 4.6% a year on average.[8] As a result of this growth, the academic workforce has risen, and given that academics typically teach and carry out research, albeit to a greater or lesser extent according to their status, so have the research workforce (full time equivalent) and research output. However, it is noteworthy that in the United States (the only country for which this piece of information is available), the recent growth of the academic workforce has concerned academics whose primary activity has been research rather than teaching – which may be one reason for the more rapid growth of research personnel compared to the student population.

Other drivers of this growth lay in the "professionalisation" of the academic profession (including specialisation and standardisation of the trade), the importance of the quantitative research output in academic career paths and the emergence of strong external incentives to publish following the introduction of research assessment exercises in several countries (OECD, 2008b; Enders and Musselin, 2008). The well-known "publish or perish" rule is actually rather recent. By comparison, a very influential and respected scholar like Ludwig Wittgenstein has published one book in his life time. While the quantity of scientific literature has increased, we have no compelling information about the evolution of its overall quality over time.

Whether this growth of academic research will continue in the future depends on at least two factors, assuming that the massification of higher education and the emergence of a "knowledge economy" (and thus the growing importance granted to research) have really been the main drivers of this growth. Albeit likely to continue in most OECD countries over the next decades (OECD, 2009a), the expansion of higher education systems will slow down in many OECD countries: entry rates are above 45% in 16 OECD countries, which are close to universal higher education; between 35 and 45% in seven others, which can still increase their participation; and below 35% in only three countries. Enrolments have been flat for years in some OECD countries, and countries like Japan and Korea are actually already facing a slight decline in enrolments. In this context, massification might become less of a driver of growth for academic research. The drive of the knowledge economy will probably continue. But given that growth in the knowledge economy relies on innovation and R&D in general, and not necessarily on R&D carried out in the higher education sector, academic research will probably be under pressure to demonstrate its value added compared to other sectors in order to continue growing.

5.3. Basic research: the main mission of academic research?

What is special about academic research then? Basic research is clearly part of the answer. In 2006, basic research accounted for about 15% of the gross domestic expenditures on R&D in the OECD area, like in 1981. The higher education sector represents less than one fifth of all R&D expenditures in the OECD area, but it carries out the bulk of basic research in most OECD countries. In 2005, an OECD country had on average 55% of its basic research performed in the higher education sector. And the government and higher education sectors accounted together for 80% of the whole basic research (Table 5.2).

In 2005, the higher education sector devoted about 63% of its R&D activities (expenditures) on basic research in the OECD area, against 5% for businesses, 26% for government, and 46% for the private non-profit sector. Korea is the sole country where the business sector consistently spends more on basic research than any other sector (including the higher education sector), probably because of the weight of the business enterprise sector (it spends only 12% of its budget on basic research, but this amounts to 91% of the higher education's R&D budget). In eastern Europe (Czech Republic, Hungary,

Table 5.2. **Distribution of domestic basic research expenditures across sectors of performance (%)**

	Higher education			Government			Business enterprise			Private non-profit		
	1981	1992	2005	1981	1992	2005	1981	1992	2005	1981	1992	2005
Australia	55	59	60[9]	40	28	24[9]	3	9	10[9]	2	4	6[9]
Austria	m	m	75[9]	m	m	6[9]	m	m	18[9]	m	m	1[9]
Czech Republic	m	21[8]	34	m	75[8]	49	m	4[8]	16	m	m	0
Denmark	78[1]	74	73	19	22	6	2	3	19	m	m	2
France	m	65	67	m	19	16	m	13	14	m	3	3
Germany	59	56[2]	m	22	25[2]	m	18	19[2]	m	m	m	m
Hungary	m	37	42	m	56	53	m	7	4	1	m	m
Iceland	62	57	63	33	35	28	0	8	m	4	m	9
Ireland	65	64	59	20	5	8	15	30	33	1	1	m
Italy	63	55	62	30	38	25	7	7	10	m	m	3
Japan	59	47	41	12	10	16	26	37	40	3	5	3
Korea	m	31[5]	22	m	21[5]	18	m	45[5]	59	m	2[5]	1
Mexico	m	64[6]	49[4]	m	m	46[4]	m	3[6]	5[4]	m	0	0
New Zealand	m	m	52	m	33[6]	34	m	m	14	m	m	m
Norway	79	80	76	15	14	14	6	6	10	1	m	m
Poland	m	36[7]	47[3]	m	54[7]	47[3]	m	10[7]	6[3]	m	0[7]	0[3]
Portugal	m	78	63	m	7	4	m	1	14	m	15	19
Slovak Republic	m	16[7]	35	m	66[7]	50	m	17[7]	15	m	m	0
Spain	50	70	59[3]	37	17	13[3]	12	13	28[3]	m	1	0[3]
Sweden	90	92	m	4	3	m	7	5	m	0	0	m
United Kingdom	m	m	m	m	m	m	m	m	m	m	m	m
United States	49	47	57	29	21	17	15	24	14	7	8	12
Comparable mean	**64**	**64**	**61**	**24**	**20**	**17**	**10**	**15**	**21**	**2**	**3**	**7**
Country mean (for each year)	**64**	**55**	**55**	**24**	**29**	**25**	**10**	**14**	**18**	**2**	**4**	**3**

m = missing data
1. 1982 instead of 1981;
2. 1991 instead of 1992;
3. 2003 instead of 2005;
4. 2001 instead of 2005;
5. 1996 instead of 1992;
6. 1993 instead of 1992;
7. 1994 instead of 1992;
8. 1995 instead of 1992;
9. 2004 instead of 2005.

Slovak republic), the government sector undertakes more basic research than the higher education sector – although decreasingly so (in Poland the share of government sector and the higher education sector is already equal). Before the 1990s, eastern European countries followed the Soviet tripartite model according to which universities focused on teaching, Academies of science conducted basic research, and Academies and Ministries, applied research (Geuna and Martin, 2003): the distribution of national basic research between the higher education and government sectors still reflects this history (path dependency).

How has this distribution of basic research between sectors evolved over the past 20 years? The average shares of national basic research performed by the higher education and government sectors in the OECD country for which data are available for both 1981 and 2005 have decreased from 64 to 61%, and from 24 to 17%, respectively. And conversely, the shares of the national basic research performed in the business enterprise and private non-profit sectors have increased, from 10 to 21%, and 2 to 7%, respectively (Table 5.2). Should this growth continue at the same pace in the future, government and higher education would carry out about 70% of a country's basic research on average in 2025.

While the relative share of academia in overall basic research expenditures has decreased, the higher education sector is the only sector mainly devoted to basic research. At the OECD aggregated level, the percentage of basic research performed in total R&D has increased between 1981 and 2005 within all performing sectors: by 19% points in the private non-profit sector, whose share of basic research expenditures were just below 50% in 2005; by 6% points in the higher education and 5% points in the government sectors; and by 1% point only in businesses (Table 5.3). The capitalisation of the business sector explains that a seemingly insignificant growth has significant effects in the distribution of knowledge between sectors. The business enterprise sector actually spends only 5% of its R&D expenditures on basic research, which remains a marginal activity in its R&D

Table 5.3. **Basic research as a percentage of R&D performed by each sector (% of expenditure)**

	Higher education			Government			Business enterprise			Private non-profit		
	1981	1992	2005	1981	1992	2005	1981	1992	2005	1981	1992	2005
Australia	67	64	52^{12}	31	28	35^{12}	5	6	4^{12}	53	79	47^{12}
Austria	48^1	48^6	49^{12}	25^1	21^6	22^{12}	6^1	4^6	5^{12}	27^1	28^6	27^{12}
Czech Republic	m	41^7	59	m	48^7	75	m	1^7	7	m	3^{10}	18
Denmark	60^2	60	56	17^2	22	18	m	m	5	55^2	56	46
France	89^3	89	85	12^5	19	22	3	4	5	48^3	40	47
Germany	78	73^8	m	38	39^8	m	6	6^8	4^{14}	22	31^{11}	m
Hungary	33^4	44	45	34^4	55	51	2^4	5	3	m	m	m
Iceland	70	47	54	15	20	22	1	m	m	33	49	59
Ireland	46	33	52	5	4	27	5	6	12	6	8	m
Italy	52	52	57	25	36	40	2	3	6	m	m	43
Japan	30	33	36	13	16	24	5	7	6	9	15	19
Korea	m	m	35	m	m	23	m	m	12	m	m	8
Mexico	m	34^6	40^{14}	m	24^6	28^{14}	m	8^6	7^{14}	m	14^6	45^{14}
New Zealand	m	m	48	m	m	40	m	m	10	m	m	m
Norway	48	48^6	49	14	12^6	17	2	2^6	4	16	m	m
Poland	m	50^9	60^{14}	m	50^9	43^{14}	m	8^9	8^{14}	m	33^9	45^{14}
Portugal	54^2	43	45	10^2	7	6	1^3	1	9	35^2	26	41
Slovak Republic	m	84^9	80	m	40^9	78	m	8^9	14	m	m	0
Spain	50	51	48^{14}	21	18	21^{14}	5	5	12^{14}	12^3	31	42^{14}
Sweden	70	67^8	m	15	13^8	80^{13}	3	2^8	m	0	38^8	m
United Kingdom	m	m	m	m	16^6	42^{12}	m	5^6	6^{12}	m	m	m
United States	67	67	75	21	24	26	3	6	4	38	47	52
Total OECD	**57**	**66**	**63**	**21**	**24**	**26**	**4**	**6**	**5**	**27**	**47**	**46**
Comparable mean	55	52	54	19	21	29	*3*	4	6	31	38	42
Country mean (for each year)	58	54	54	20	26	35	3	5	7	27	33	36

Notes: "Total OECD" corresponds to the weighted mean; the "country mean" says for each year what is on average the percentage in an OECD country, Iceland and the United States having the same weight; "comparable mean" is a country mean that is comparable over time (i.e. calculated for countries available for all years).
m = missing data
1. 1985 instead of 1981;
2. 1982 instead of 1981;
3. 1986 instead of 1981;
4. 1987 instead of 1981;
5. 1983 instead of 1981;
6. 1993 instead of 1992;
7. 1995 instead of 1992;
8. 1991 instead of 1992;
9. 1994 instead of 1992;
10. 1996 instead of 1992;
11. 1989 instead of 1992;
12. 2004 instead of 2005;
13. 2001 instead of 2005; and
14. 2003 instead of 2005.

activities. At country level, the average share of basic research undertaken in the higher education sector remained stable at about 54%, while it followed the trends of the OECD aggregated level in the other sectors. This can be explained by the significant growth of academic basic research in the United States, which has offset the decline of the share of basic research performed by academia in smaller countries like Iceland or Australia.

In conclusion, basic research does indeed represent a special feature of academic research. But this might become decreasingly the case because of the rise of basic research within the private non-profit sector and, to a lesser extent, the government sector. A possible response would be for academic research to specialise even more in basic research to keep its specificity (or competitive advantage), as it has been the case from the 1990s in the United States. As we will see below, other forces might push academic research in other directions. It is noteworthy that this specialisation is partly beyond its control: should the business sector decide to carry out more basic research than it does, it would rapidly increase its share of the total basic research carried out on average in OECD countries. But this does not seem very likely in the near future: the low propensity for the business sector to carry out basic research shows that there is still a strong case for continued research in the public and non-profit sectors.

5.4. Academic research and new public management

Research performed by the higher education sector is largely government-funded in the OECD area (Table 5.4). In 2006, the government sector funded directly or indirectly 72% of the total academic research. Governments fund academic research through "general university funds", that is block grants directly given to higher education institutions (and then allocated by them to research and teaching), as well as through direct research grants and contracts given to particular academic research projects. In 2006, government funding amounted to more than 80% of academic research in 15 out of the 28 OECD countries for which information is available. The share of the government funding tends to be lower in countries with large private higher education sectors (as universities have then more private resources), where the level of tuition fees or private endowments is high, and where there is a tradition (or friendly fiscal policy) for donations and foundations. With 51% of government-funded academic research in 2005, Japan was by far the country with the lowest government-funded academic research in the OECD area. Probably due to the large size of its private component, the Japanese higher education sector funded on its own funds 45% of the country's academic research.

While the prevalence of public funding remains a major characteristic of academic research, a significant trend lies in the growing use of competitive or quasi-market forces for the allocation of this funding, both at governmental and institutional levels.

One hard piece of evidence of this shift lies in the evolution of the distribution of public funding for academic research between general university funds and grants awarded to separately budgeted research projects (Table 5.5). Between 1981 and 2006, the percentage of research funding through general university funds has dropped from 78% to 64% in the 12 OECD countries for which information is available for the three years analysed. While general university funds still funded over 70% of academic research in 2006 in ten OECD countries, they have decreased by 13% or more in New Zealand, Ireland, the United Kingdom, Canada, Finland, Turkey and Mexico since the beginning of 1990s as well as in Australia, Denmark, Norway, Sweden, Greece and Spain since the beginning of

Table 5.4. **Funding sources of higher education R&D (%)**

	Government			Business enterprise			Higher education			Private non-profit			Funds from abroad		
	1981	1992	2006	1981	1992	2006	1981	1992	2006	1981	1992	2006	1981	1992	2006
Australia	95	93	90[7]	1	2	6[7]	0	m	0[7]	3	4	1[7]	1	1	m
Austria	98	97[3]	89[7]	1	2[3]	4[7]	m	m[3]	2[7]	0	0	1[7]	0	0[3]	5[7]
Belgium	86[1]	71[3]	69[6]	9[1]	12[3]	11[6]	3[1]	7[3]	12[6]	0[1]	1[2]	2[6]	2[1]	8[3]	6[5]
Canada	79	71	62	4	8	8	10	15	21	7	6	8	1	1	1
Czech Republic	m	97	90	m	m	1	m	m	4	m	m	0	m	m	4
Denmark	96	88	83[6]	1	2	2[6]	m	m	m	2	5	8[6]	1	5	6[6]
Finland	95	88[3]	81	2	5[3]	7	m	4[3]	1	2	2[3]	2	1	2[3]	9
France	98	93	91[6]	1	4	2[6]	1	2	5[6]	0	0	0[6]	0	1	2[6]
Germany	98	92	82[6]	2	8	14[6]	m	m	m	x	x	m	m	1	4[6]
Greece	100	59[3]	66[6]	0	4[3]	9[5]	0	6[3]	3[6]	0	0[3]	1[6]	0	31[3]	21[6]
Hungary	m	83	77	m	11	13	m	m	m	m	m	2	m	2	8
Iceland	79	91	78[6]	1	5	11[6]	8	m	0[6]	0	0	1[6]	12	4	10[6]
Ireland	83	67	86	7	7	3	0	4	1	3	2	4	7	20	6
Italy	96	93	95[6]	3	5	1[6]	0	m	1[6]	m	m	m	1	2	m
Japan	58	50	51[6]	1	3	3[6]	41	48	45[6]	0	0	1[6]	0	0	0[6]
Korea	m	44[4]	77	m	22[4]	14	m	32[4]	8	m	2[4]	1	m	0	0
Luxembourg	m	m	99[6]	m	m	1[6]	m	m	m	m	m	m	m	m	m
Mexico	m	m	75[6]	m	m	1[6]	m	m	23[6]	m	m	0[6]	m	m	0[6]
Netherlands	97	96	87[7]	0	1	7[8]	0	0	2[8]	2	2	m	0	0	4[8]
New Zealand	m	66	58[6]	m	4	8[6]	m	20	26[6]	m	6	4[6]	m	4	3[6]
Norway	94	89[3]	87[6]	3	6[3]	5[6]	1	1[3]	2[6]	2	3[3]	3[6]	0	1[3]	3[6]
Poland	m	81[5]	79	m	11[5]	5	m	6[5]	7	m	1[5]	0	m	1[5]	8
Portugal	94[2]	80	91[6]	0[2]	0	1[6]	2[2]	2	3[6]	3[2]	1	1[6]	2[2]	17	4[6]
Slovak Republic	m	99	87	m	1	5	m	m	1	m	m	0	m	m	7
Spain	100	89	72[6]	0	7	7[6]	0	m	14[6]	x	0	1[6]	0	3	5[6]
Sweden	93	84[3]	76[6]	2	5[3]	5[6]	1	2[3]	2[6]	4	7[3]	11[6]	1	2[3]	6[6]
Switzerland	90	92	84[7]	10	2	9[7]	m	4	7[7]	m	3	0[7]	m	m	m
Turkey	m	83	68[6]	m	15	23[6]	m	m	m	m	3	9[6]	m	m	0[6]
United Kingdom	81	70	69[6]	3	8	5[6]	9	5	4[6]	5	12	14[6]	2	6	8[6]
United States	74	67	70	4	7	5	15	18	18	7	7	7	m	m	0
Total OECD	**78**	**73**	**72**	**3**	**6**	**6**	**16**	**17**	**15**	**4**	**4**	**5**	**1**	**1**	**2**
Comparable mean	**90**	**82**	**79**	**3**	**7**	**6**	**7**	**9**	**10**	**2**	**3**	**4**	**2**	**7**	**6**
Country mean (for each year)	**90**	**81**	**79**	**3**	**8**	**7**	**6**	**10**	**9**	**3**	**3**	**3**	**2**	**5**	**5**

Notes: Korea: excluding R&D in the social sciences and humanities; United States: excludes most or all of capital expenditure.
m = missing data
1. 1983 instead of 1981;
2. 1982 instead of 1981;
3. 1993 instead of 1992;
4. 1995 instead of 1992;
5. 1994 instead of 1992;
6. 2005 instead of 2006;
7. 2004 instead of 2006; and
8. 2003 instead of 2006.

1980s. Moreover, the allocation of these general university funds has been increasingly (partially) performance-related in many countries, generally based on university research evaluation that was introduced in several countries in the late 1980s and 1990s (Geuna and Martin, 2003).

General university funds give universities (and other higher education institutions carrying out research) full freedom to allocate these funds within their institution.[9] However, the management of these funds within universities has also become increasingly

Table 5.5. **Percentage of government funding of academic research, by mode of funding (% of public funds)**

	Direct government			General university funds		
	1981	1992	2006	1981	1992	2006
Australia	11	m	33[9]	89	m	67[9]
Austria	m	15[4]	21[9]	m	85[4]	79[9]
Belgium	46[1]	m	62[8]	54[1]	m	38[8]
Canada	51	46	60	49	54	40
Czech Republic	m	100	m	m	0.	m
Denmark	11	24	28[8]	89	76	72[8]
Finland	14	37[4]	45	86	63[4]	55
France	46	51	37[8]	54	49	63[8]
Germany	m	m	29[8]	m	m	71[8]
Greece	10	27[4]	29[8]	90	73[4]	71[8]
Hungary	100[2]	m	100	0	m	m
Iceland	m	95	78[8]	m	5	22[8]
Ireland	18	41	52	82	59	48
Italy	m	m	16[8]	m	m	84[8]
Japan	39	28	24[8]	61	72	76[8]
Korea	m	m	m	m	m	m
Luxembourg	m	m	26[8]	m	m	74[8]
Mexico	m	m	29[7]	m	100[8]	71[7]
Netherlands	6	5	14	94	95	86
New Zealand	m	21	70[8]	m	79	30[8]
Norway	16	25[4]	27[8]	84	75[4]	73[8]
Poland	m	100[5]	100	m	0[5]	0
Portugal	m	m	m	m	m	m
Slovak Republic	m	m	6	m	m	94
Spain	13	23	29[8]	87	77	71[8]
Sweden	26	35[4]	38[8]	74	65[4]	62[8]
Switzerland	m	19[3]	21[9, 10]	m	81	79[9]
Turkey	m	46	58[6]	m	54	42[6]
United Kingdom	19	35	50[8]	81	65	50[8]
United States	100	100	100	0	0	0
Comparable mean	**27**	**31**	**36**	**78**	**69**	**64**
Country mean (for each year)	**28**	**41**	**44**	**77**	**65**	**56**

m = missing data.
Notes: United States: excludes most or all capital expenditure.
1. 1983 instead of 1981;
2. 1987 instead of 1981;
3. 1982 instead of 1981;
4. 1993 instead of 1992;
5. 1994 instead of 1992;
6. 2002 instead of 2006;
7. 2001 instead of 2006;
8. 2005 instead of 2006;
9. 2004 instead of 2006; and
10. Federal or central government only.

competitive and based on departmental research evaluation (Hazelkorn, 2005). Direct government funding to separately budgeted research projects gives governments more control to choose the type of research they want to support. It is generally awarded by research councils following a competitive process: either a tender or following a competitive application process generally based on peer review.

This reflects recent trends in public management and in the governance of higher education institutions (OECD, 2008b), using to a greater extent than in the past competition and quasi-market forces to foster efficiency and accountability. In a context of mass tertiary education and ageing society, the best way to fund and deliver both research and teaching components of higher education is under debate in many OECD countries. Concerning levels as well as sources of funding, the debates include consideration of, among other factors, national budgetary priorities and the desire to increase the resources available; questions about the efficiency of resource use; ensuring that public policy objectives (*e.g.* high-quality education and research) are met; and determining what government should provide and how costs should be shared among different groups in society (taxpayers, students and families, companies). Moreover, there is a strong social demand for better public management. Accountability, transparency, efficiency and effectiveness, responsiveness and forward vision are now considered the principal components of good public governance, which universities are being (and will most likely) increasingly be asked to implement (Braun and Merrien, 1999). The shift towards more autonomy and entrepreneurship is a common trend in higher education management in most OECD countries (Etzkowitz *et al.*, 2000; Marginson and Considine, 2000; Martin, 2002; OECD, 2003a; OECD, 2008b).

One of the interesting effects of these new practices is the creation of a more concentrated academic research. This challenges the Humboldtian idea and the academic professional ethos according to which teaching and research should go together in higher education. In practice, as research funding becomes more concentrated in a few institutions, the ability of some higher education institutions and academics to carry out research becomes more limited (Enders and Musselin, 2008). Some countries already have differentiated types of academic research. In France, some academics employed by the National Centre for Scientific Research (CNRS) are full researchers – while being considered part of (and in practice very active in) the higher education sector. In many eastern European countries, academies of science (government sector) carry out much more research than university academics, who carry out mainly applied research. But even when such a dichotomy does not exist, the allocation of research funding can differentiate institutions and academics. In the United Kingdom, 19 of the 170 higher education institutions representing 21% of all enrolments (and 29% of all post-graduate enrolments) received 66% of the public funding for research in 2007; and the top 4 universities received 27% of this funding and represented 4% of tertiary education enrolments (and 6% of all postgraduate enrolments) (HESA, 2008a and 2008b). In the United States, academic R&D has been historically concentrated in few of the US higher education institutions: the share of all academic R&D expenditures received by the top 100 academic institutions decreased from 83% to 80% between 1986 and 1993 and has remained at that level through 2006 (NSB, 2008). Many other countries are developing "centres of excellence", regional "poles" or "clusters" of excellence, or are trying to establish world class higher education institutions (Salmi, 2008). This is the case in Germany with the *Excellenzinitiativ*, in Canada with networks of centres of excellence, in France with regional poles of excellence or the establishment of new institutions such as the Paris School of Economics, in Austria with the creation of the Institute of Science of Technology (Hackl, 2007), in Finland with the Aalto University, or in Korea with several initiatives to strengthen research excellence (Kim, 2007a, 2007b). While some institutions have always been implicitly privileged, this explicit shift towards excellence and a concentration of excellence within institutions is new to many European countries.

The possible future disconnection of academic research and teaching in higher education has already started. Will countries where research is spread relatively evenly across the whole system take a more concentrated approach in the future? This is to some extent where recent trends in public management seem to lead: academic research might just become concentrated in a relatively small share of the system while the largest number of institutions will carry out only little research, if any. The same could happen within higher education institutions as the role and status of academic staff become increasingly differentiated. Some experts view this concentration as a way to resurrect the elitist mission of higher education (*e.g.* Mittlestraß, 2002) or to foster competitiveness through research and innovation (Aghion *et al.*, 2008)

5.5. The rise of private funding

In spite of government's prominence in the funding of academic research, higher education research has increasingly relied on private sources of financing during the two past decades. Between 1981and 2006, the percentage of government-funded academic research has decreased by 6%, from 78% to 72%. In 1981, only Japan, the United States (and probably Korea) had less than 79% of government-funded academic research; in 2006, it was the case for thirteen OECD countries. Meanwhile, the share of the business sector in the financing of higher education research has doubled to reach 6% in 2006; similarly, the private non-profit sector has also funded a larger share of higher education research activities (Table 5.4). Some changes in the structure of funding are more significant at the country level (country mean): in an OECD country, the shares of academic research funding coming from the private for-profit sector, the non-profit sector and from abroad have all doubled (though remaining relatively small).

The first private source of funding of academic research lies in the higher education sector's own private funds. These "internal" expenditures for academic research have increased threefold in real terms between 1981 and 2006. While their relative share remained fairly stable over the years at the aggregate level (about 15% of academic research funding in 2006), they have typically increased at country level. This increase is not a mere adjustment for a decrease of governmental funding given that governmental funding has actually also risen in real terms. It might rather be explained by the expansion of the private higher education sector, the increase of tuition fees in many countries, by new entrepreneurial activities of higher education institutions, like commercial cross-border higher education or commercial courses for adult learners, commercial e-learning, etc. (Ruch, 2001 ; Larsen and Vincent-Lancrin, 2002; OECD, 2004a; OBHE, 2004; Newman *et al.*, 2004). Higher education institutions have had more private resources that they could invest in their academic research, although variations across OECD countries are significant.

On the research side, the growth of academic patenting and licensing highlights the growing "commercialisation" of higher education. In the United States, the Bayh-Dole act of 1980 allowed universities to retain title to inventions resulting from federally supported R&D, giving an incentive to universities to patent and license such inventions. From the mid-1990s, following the United States example, a number of OECD countries have tried to encourage the commercialisation of technology developed at academic research institutions by granting the ownership of intellectual property rights to universities and public research organisations (OECD, 2003b). Independently of these policy efforts, new opportunities in the bio-medical fields have been a strong driver of increased patenting (Geuna and Nesta, 2003).

Between 1994 and 2006, the number of patent applications filed under the Patent Co-operation Treaty (PCT) by universities has doubled in the United States, more than tripled in the OECD area and in the world, and increase more than fivefold in the European Union. The share of patents owned by universities has also significantly increased over the period (Table 5.6 and Figure 5.2).

The United States is the country where this trend is best documented.[10] The number of patents received by US universities has increased significantly over the past 30 years from about 250-350 patents in the 1970s to more than 2700 patents in 2005. During this time period, the number of institutions that were awarded patents in a year has doubled to reach 160 institutions in 2005. The top 25 recipients consistently received over 60% of all academic patents. Revenues from these intellectual property rights have increased sharply during the past decades and net royalties from academic patenting and licensing activities amounted to more than USD 925 million in 2004 for the 164 reporting institutions (NSB, 2008). That being said, the income generated by licenses represents less than 4% of overall academic research expenditures in the United States, where this type of income is the highest within the OECD area, and much less of the overall higher education expenditures. In 2005 the Massachusetts Institute of Technology *alone*, that is the top patenting private US university, had operating revenues of USD 2030 million and spent USD 997 million on sponsored research (that is, more or less the same as the royalties earned by *all* US institutions). In 2000, the university licenses have generated a gross income of USD 80 million in Australia, USD 1 million in Korea, and EUR 3 million in Switzerland. Here again, this is modest compared of the overall budgets for research and higher education in these countries

The financing of academic research by businesses remains small in absolute terms and amounted to more than 10% of the funding of academic research in only six countries for which information was available in 2006 (Turkey, Korea, Germany, Belgium, Ireland and Hungary). However, its growth highlights increasing links between business and higher education research. In the United States, the share of the business sector's cross-sectoral (co-authored) articles with higher education has increased from 20% to 51% between 1988 and 2005, and continued to have the fastest increase in cross-sectoral collaborations between 1995 and 2005; the share of the higher education sector's cross-sectoral articles with the business sector has remained stable around 6% (NSB, 2004, 2008). However, academic researchers collaborate (or rather, co-author) more with the private non-profit sector: the share of collaborative articles of academia with the non-profit sector amounted to 10% of the cross-sectoral output of academic institutions in the United States in 2005, up from 8% in 1995 (NSB, 2008).

This growing collaboration might reflect the willingness of many countries to see higher education institutions play a role in regional development and participate in regional and national innovation systems, following success stories like the Silicon Valley, as well as an increased business interest in these collaborations (OECD, 2007b; OECD, 2001; Storper and Salais, 1997). This might also come from the willingness of the academic sector to value its applied research and its experimental development (that is the 45% of expenditures not spent on basic research at country level).

Table 5.6. **Number, growth and share of patent applications filed under the Patent Co-operation Treaty, owned by universities (1994-2006)**[1]

Applicant's country	Number		Growth	Share of patents owned by universities (%) – countries with more than 250 PCT filings	
	1994-96	2004-06	1994-96 = 100	1994-96	2004-06
Australia	140	293	209	5.71	5.00
Austria	2	124	8 278	0.14	4.42
Belgium	36	175	484	4.43	6.16
Canada	181	398	220	6.43	5.63
Czech Republic	1	13	944	m	3.76
Denmark	3	129	4 300	0.18	4.01
Finland	16	12	73	0.76	0.22
France	155	709	458	2.50	4.09
Germany	44	927	2 108	0.24	1.93
Greece	1	2	248	m	m
Hungary	0	4	1 711	m	1.02
Iceland	0	0		m	m
Ireland	10	125	1 215	2.93	11.39
Italy	15	277	1 806	0.79	3.72
Japan	8	2520	31 497	0.08	3.27
Korea	2	511	25 541	0.30	3.22
Luxembourg	0	1		m	0.11
Mexico	7	18	250	m	3.98
Netherlands	72	199	277	1.57	1.53
New Zealand	6	15	242	1.39	1.50
Norway	2	30	1517	0.20	1.79
Poland	2	6	367	m	2.02
Portugal	0	46	13 861	m	m
Slovak Republic	0	2		m	m
Spain	37	322	871	5.13	9.89
Sweden	1	2	208	0.02	0.02
Switzerland	30	202	677	0.97	2.05
Turkey	0	3		m	0.37
United Kingdom	429	944	220	4.89	6.38
United States	3 799	8 479	223	6.49	5.99
OECD	**4 999**	**16 486**	**330**	**3.81**	**4.22**
EU27	**826**	**4 036**	**488**	**1.57**	**3.09**
World	**5 157**	**17 603**	**341**	**3.83**	**4.21**
Brazil	3	66	2 211	m	7.06
Chile	1	12	2 402	m	m
China	10	416	4 377	2.94	4.03
Estonia	2	14	683	m	m
India	0	12		m	0.50
Israel	123	385	313	12.58	8.59
Russian Federation	4	7	176	0.58	0.44
Singapore	4	128	3 195	m	9.38
Slovenia	0	2		m	m
South Africa	4	44	1 245	m	4.04

m = missing data.

1. Patent counts are based on the priority date, the applicant's country of residence, using fractional counts of patents filed under the Patent Co-operation Treaty, at international phase (EPO designations). Sectoral allocation of patents is based on an algorithm developed by Eurostat.

To sum up, the rise of private funding in academic research still rests less on funding from the private sector than on the private resources earned by higher education themselves. While government funding has continued to increase in real terms and

Figure 5.2. **Number of patent applications filed under the Patent Co-operation Treaty, owned by universities in selected regions/countries (1994-2006)**

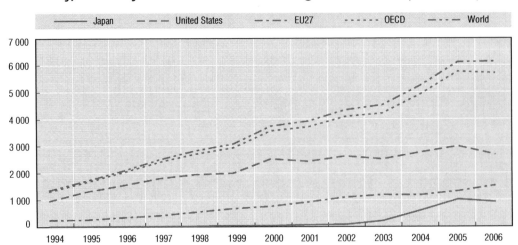

remains prominent, other sources of funding have increased more rapidly and led to a more diversified system. Should these trends continue in the future, mainly thanks to the higher education and non-profit sectors, one can imagine academic research half privately and publicly funded in the OECD area: this balanced funding would represent a gradual evolution of academic research and of higher education systems towards a more private system, most likely within a non-profit framework.

5.6. The internationalisation of academic research

Reflecting the internationalisation of higher education (OECD, 2004a, 2007, 2008b, 2008c), and, more generally, the globalisation of economies and societies, academic research has become more internationalised in many respects over the two past decades. International academic mobility, international collaboration, international influence of science, and funding from abroad have all increased, while new poles of research are gradually emerging in the world. Finally, international competition and international rankings set a new context for countries and institutions.

The growing international mobility of academics and of doctoral students highlights the internationalisation of academic research. Flows of academics into the United States increased by 77% between 1994 and 2007, to reach about 106 000 persons in 2007(IIE, 2008). In Korea and Japan, while the number of foreign scholars is still relatively small, it has increased significantly over the past decade. The number of international visiting scholars has almost tripled from 1993 to 2005, from 13 000 to 35 000. The number of foreign academic staff has doubled between 1992 and 2008, from 7 200 to 17 500 (MEXT, 1993, 2008).[11] Similarly, the number of foreign academic staff has doubled in Korea between 2000 and 2008, from 1 300 to 3 200 people and from 2.3% to 4.8% of all academic staff (KEDI). While covering only a small part of academic flows in Europe, the intra-European mobility of academics under the Socrates programme of the European Commission more than tripled between 1997 and 2007, to 28 500 persons in 2007 (European Commission). The same pattern can be observed for doctoral and postdoctoral students (OECD, 2008c). In the United States, the number of foreign (non-resident) postdocs has tripled between 1985 and 2005, to 27 000, and the share of foreigners in all postdocs at US institutions has increased from 40 to 55%. At the German Max Planck Institutes, 55% of junior and guest researchers were *not* German (NSB, 2008). Some emerging countries, like Malaysia, are trying to build capacity in higher education by attracting foreign research institutions and by moving away from the import of foreign educational programmes through franchising. This growing cross-border mobility of academic researchers shows the internationalisation of the academic workforce and research, partly driven by an increasing competition between countries to attract foreign talents in their country (OECD, 2004a, 2005b, 2006, 2008c).

Partly related to this mobility,[12] international collaboration has grown significantly in academic research. This is reflected in the growth of internationally co-authored (or collaborative) scientific articles, that is articles with at least one international co-author (in terms of institutional affiliation). Between 1988 and 2005, the total number of international articles more than doubled, increasing from 8 to 18% of all scientific articles. Apart from Turkey, all countries have increased their national share of internationally co-authored articles. In an OECD country, the average share of internationally co-authored articles in the domestic scientific article output has increased from 26 to 46% between 1988 and 2005 (Table 5.7). Moreover, the breadth of countries with which each country collaborates for scientific research has increased. Between 1996 and 2003, all countries (for which information is available) have raised the number of countries with which they have jointly authored articles: for an OECD country, the average number of collaborating countries in scientific activities has risen from 96 to 117 countries (Table 5.7).

This trend goes beyond the OECD area. The internationalisation of academic research does indeed correspond to the emergence of new poles of science in the world. Non-OECD countries (for which there is information) have accounted for a larger share of total R&D expenditures over the past decades, China alone representing half of the R&D expenditures of non-OECD countries (OECD, 2005a). The trends described above can be observed in emerging and developing countries, which have for example expanded more the number of countries they collaborate with than developed countries (NSB, 2004).

Citation of foreign scientific articles provides an index of accessibility, visibility and acknowledged influence and productivity of scientific literature across borders, and also, if one takes into account the practice of courtesy citations, a measure of the insertion of a country's researchers in international networks of scientists and academics. Foreign scientific articles are increasingly cited in the scientific literature worldwide: in 1992, foreign articles accounted for 55% of all citations, against 62% in 2001 (NSB, 2004). The number of cited articles is highly correlated with the country's output of scientific articles and financial input in research. The United States produced 29% of the world output of scientific articles in 2005, and its scientific literature accounted for 41% of citations in the world scientific literature.[13] US articles remain the most cited, but the share of US scientific output in world citations has declined over time, including in the articles from the top 1% most cited journals (Figures 5.3 and 5.4). Other countries and regions, notably in Asia, are becoming important poles of science and have expanded their scientific output and their worldwide visibility in terms of citation and "relative prominence"[14] over the last decade.

The growing international nature of research can also be observed through the rise of foreign funding of R&D. Data are rather patchy for the early 1980s. However, the fact that data have become more systematically collected is in itself a piece of evidence of the increasing importance of funding coming from abroad for the performance of academic

Table 5.7. **Share and breadth of international scientific collaboration over time, by country/economy**

	Share of international collaboration in national output (%)			Number of collaborating countries	
	1988	1996	2005	1996	2003
Australia	18	27	41	101	114
Austria	29	45	57	78	101
Belgium	32	46	58	111	121
Canada	20	31	43	110	130
Czech Republic	m	48	52	65	72
Denmark	27	44	54	89	112
Finland	23	36	48	m	m
France	23	35	49	126	146
Germany	22	34	47	123	136
Greece	30	38	40	68	82
Hungary	34	51	56	71	77
Iceland	47	52	65	m	m
Ireland	30	42	52	53	77
Italy	24	34	43	110	126
Japan	9	15	23	97	128
Korea	27	27	28	54	91
Mexico	30	41	46	77	98
Netherlands	22	36	49	110	131
New Zealand	21	33	48	55	66
Norway	27	40	52	64	87
Poland	26	46	47	70	90
Portugal	37	52	54	51	86
Spain	21	32	42	88	115
Slovak Republic	m	42	60	51	54
Sweden	25	39	50	100	116
Switzerland	37	48	59	112	116
Turkey	22	23	19	57	94
United Kingdom	18	29	44	144	158
United States	10	18	27	155	172
OECD Country mean	**26**	**37**	**46**	**96**	**117**
EU-15	**17**	**27**	**36**	**136**	**143**
Brazil	30	42	35	83	106
Chile	30	47	55	63	78
China	22	28	25	83	102
India	10	16	22	82	107
Indonesia	76	82	85	37	60
Israel	29	38	44	70	91
Russia	2	27	43	82	94
Singapore	24	31	41	50	64
South Africa	14	30	49	76	104
Slovenia	m	46	49	m	m
Estonia	m	58	54	29	47

m = missing data.

Note: For the share of national scientific output with international co-authors, 2003 instead of 2005 for Iceland, Slovak republic, EU-15, Chile, Indonesia, Slovenia, Estonia; in 1988, former USSR instead of Russia. For the number of countries, 1994 and 2001 instead of 1996 and 2003 for Czech Republic, Greece, New-Zealand, Norway, Portugal, Slovak Republic, Switzerland, Indonesia, Estonia (italicised numbers, excluded in the mean calculation). Calculations are based on data from the Institute for Scientific Information, Science Citation Index and Social Sciences Citation Index; CHI Research, Inc.; and National Science Foundation, Division of Science Resources Statistics, special tabulations.

Source: Calculations based on NSB, 2006 and 2008.

Figure 5.3. **Share of world citations of science and engineering (S&E) articles, by major region/country (1995, 2000, 2005)**

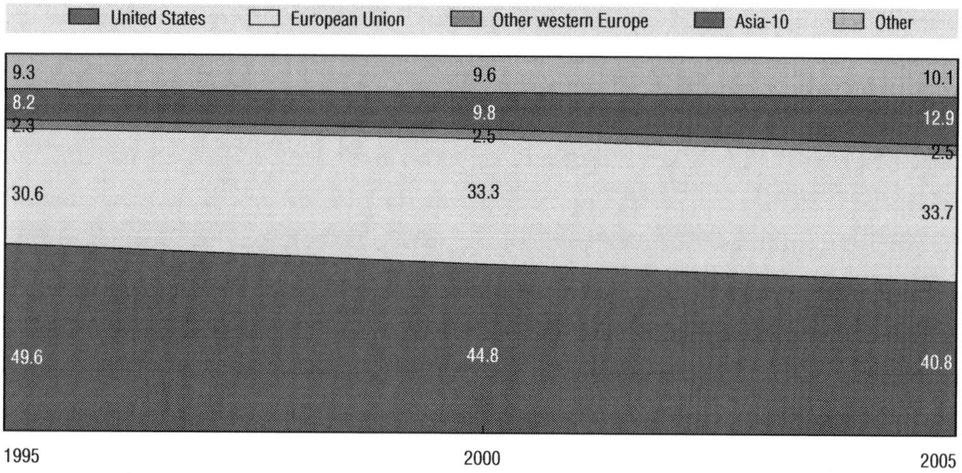

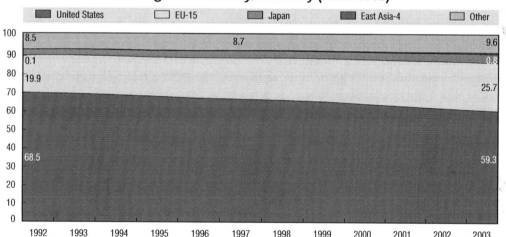

Note: Data cover journals in the *Institute for Scientific Information Database*. Asia-10 includes: China (including Hong Kong), India, Indonesia, Japan, Malaysia, Philippines, Singapore, Korea, Chinese Taipei, Thailand.
Source: NSB, 2008.

Figure 5.4. **Share of citations in top 1% cited S&E journals, by frequency of citation and region or country/economy (1992-2003)**

Note: Journals covered in the *Institute for Scientific Information Database*. East Asia-4 includes China, Korea, Singapore and Chinese Taipei.
Source: NSB, 2006.

research. On average, in the 15 countries for which data are available for both years, the share of funding coming from abroad for the performance of academic research has tripled over the past two decades, representing 6% in 2006 versus 2% in 1981 (Table 5.4). This can partly be traced back to the strategies and policies of several countries to promote and fund international collaboration in science. The European Union has funded ambitious programmes geared towards intra-European collaborative research, such as its "Framework programmes". In the United States, federal agencies such as the National Science Foundation, the US Department of Energy (DOE), and the National Institutes of Health (NIH), have (or had) programmes helping fund internationally collaborative research.

The inclusion of R&D in the General Agreement on Trade in Services (GATS) in the World Trade Organisation (WTO) as part of the business services sector might also represent a future transformative force for a further internationalisation of academic research, should it become more privatised.[15] While the inclusion of education services under the GATS has received much attention (OECD, 2004a, 2004b, 2007c; Larsen and Vincent-Lancrin, 2002; Knight, 2002, 2003), the inclusion of research services in the GATS has been relatively unnoticed, although research represents a significant part of academic activities. While they still have to be analysed, the issues are probably similar to those for education services, albeit to some extent easier as they do not involve the same quality issues.

Finally, regardless of the GATS, the growing importance of worldwide or international rankings of higher education institutions, generally according to research criteria, changes the scope of the competition between higher education institutions. Two examples are the worldwide rankings of the Shangai Jiaotong University and of the *Times Higher Education Supplement* (Altbach, 2006). These rankings are setting an international competition between countries and institutions for attracting international scholars and students and for receiving international funding, which is becoming more available. One of its policy implications, related to the movements of concentration described in Section 5.3, lies in the political willingness to create "world class" research universities in several countries, from China through to Nordic countries such as Denmark or Finland (Salmi and Saroyan, 2007; Salmi, 2009; Marginson and van der Wende, 2009; Hazelkorn, 2007; Harfi and Mathieu, 2006; Sadlak and Nian, 2007).

All this emphasises the double nature of internationalisation in higher education, leading at the same time to more collaboration *and* more competition between countries and higher education institutions (Huismans and van der Wende, 2004, 2005). Unless a war, return to nationalism or international pandemy stops it, possibly as a development of a severe economic and social crisis, the internationalisation of higher education and of academic research is likely to continue in the foreseeable future, with more international collaboration, mobility and worldwide competition for internationally available funding. With the emergence of new poles of science, might governments and businesses be tempted to outsource their basic research in countries where labour costs for research are lower? A stronger worldwide division of labour according to specialties and competitive advantages may then appear.

5.7. A new social contract for research

Higher education institutions have not only become more accountable to governments concerning the efficient and effective use of their research funding, as evoked in Section 5.3, they have also become more accountable to society at large. As Callon (2003) has emphasised, the rise in the number of "socio-technical controversies" on issues regarding the environment (global warming, pollution), health (therapeutic cloning, AIDS, muscular dystrophy), food (bovine spongiform encephalopathy, genetically modified organisms), or the patentability of genetic materials represent evidence of a change in the social contract between research and society. Discussion of research is no longer confined to scientists and policy makers: "concerned groups" (or "lay people") have become much more involved in the design, implementation and constructive critique of research, when not in research itself.

Even though they might always have had an influence, concerned groups (patients, families of patients, etc.) were generally not acknowledged as legitimate in positing research problems or making decisions about them. The first power lay with the scientists, while the second was delegated to policy-makers. While this is still to some extent the case, for understandable reasons, concerned people have increasingly managed over the past decades to raise research questions, to voice critiques about the research outcomes or methodology, to challenge research protocols on ethical grounds, to contribute to research by providing researchers with evidence from their personal experience, etc. Callon (2003) gives several examples from different countries. Several studies have been published about the involvement of patients' associations in France in clinical research, from muscular dystrophy to AIDS or to cancer (Callon *et al.*, 2001; Rabeharisoa and Callon, 1999, 2002).

There are several ways to influence or to be involved in research. One way consists in hiring experts or researchers to challenge and monitor the "official" outcomes. Another lies in funding academic research. Part of the small increase in the share of research funding from the private non-profit sector described in Section 5.4 highlights this trend. In France, a survey on the funding of research by patients' associations estimated that their research funding amounted to 36% of all research funding from charitable and philanthropic association or foundations. This funding obviously gives them some control and decision power about the undertaken research, and forces academic researchers and policy makers to be more transparent in their research and scientific policy decisions.

Hippel (2005) shows that this opening to society cannot only be observed in academic research but also in innovation more generally: innovation is no longer supply-driven but increasingly user-centred. End users are increasingly involved in innovation and contribute to the design and improvement of many, if not most, new industrial and consumer products, according to their actual needs (rather than what manufacturers believe their needs are). For example, the industrial boards and equipment used for windsurfing incorporate user-developed innovations designed by the pioneers of windsurfing for the high-performance sport. Many other examples can be found in software development or in innovation more generally (Lundvall, 1988).

The reasons for this opening of science to public society can be traced back to many factors. The increasing educational attainment of the population in all OECD countries may have led to a blurring of the boundaries between the so-called experts and the lay people, facilitating the emergence of "lay experts". The emergence of a new history, sociology and philosophy of science challenging the ivory tower model of science may have contributed to a better acknowledgement of the role of concerned groups, as well as the rise of new forms of political activism in the 1960s. But given that these concerned groups generally build themselves by creating a community of people with the same experience or needs, which previously went unnoticed because they were scattered, the easy access to information thanks to information and communication technologies, from radio, TV, Internet and instant messaging, have allowed them to reach a critical mass more rapidly and to more easily share their information and experience.

This involvement of concerned groups and civil society in science and technology issues, including academic research, might continue to grow and reshape social and governmental demands towards science. Callon (2003) proposes to institutionalise the role of civil society by facilitating the explicit recognition of new concerned groups as well as by encouraging, developing and funding more collaborative research involving these groups. Even without public action, one can imagine that these groups will increasingly voice their concerns, participate in research and be recognised. This might be one aspect of a "knowledge society".

5.8. Technology

Information and communication technology (ICT) also represents a driver of change in academic research. Because ICT has not revolutionised university teaching and access as quickly as was too optimistically expected in the early 2000s, its past influence and future promises now tend to be downplayed. ICT has not yet revolutionised teaching and learning and represents in most cases an add-on to traditional face-to-face teaching rather than a substitute or a catalyst for new pedagogies. This is partly due to the immaturity of e-learning tools but also to the cultural resistance of students and academics to use existing tools, because of some scepticism about its quality (OECD, 2005c; OECD, 2009). However, ICT continues to gain ground in higher education and has already enhanced the on-campus student experience, through student portals, the use of the Internet, digital libraries, etc. (Larsen and Vincent-Lancrin, 2006).

ICT has arguably already had a much stronger impact on academic research. It has significantly contributed to some of the trends identified in the above sections: internationalisation, growth (and possibly quality) of the research output, and opening to civil society. Internationalisation of research has been facilitated by cyberinfrastructure, which allows researchers to collaborate and share ideas and expertise across the world without travel, through e-mails. While the increase of international collaboration has been the strongest trend, domestic collaboration has also increased in the past decades, from 31 to 41% of all articles between 1988 and 2005 (Figure 5.5). The growth of research output can also partly be derived from the easier and quicker access to information, to digital datasets and to recent research that are often online and remotely accessible (digital libraries, etc.). Similarly, the emergence of concerned groups relies on a critical mass of isolated individuals sharing the same needs or experience. Their emergence has been facilitated by the Internet; and their influence of research, by the easier access to information allowed by digital libraries and other knowledge repositories.

Figure 5.5. **Percentage of worldwide S&E articles co-authored domestically and internationally (1988-2005)**

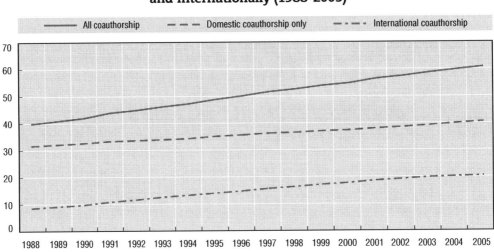

Source: NSB (2008).

Computers, digital data, and networks have indeed revolutionised the research environment (as much as society at large). As Atkins *et al.* (2003) put it, "new technology-mediated, distributed work environments are emerging to relax constraints of distance and time. These new research environments are linking together research teams, digital data and information libraries, high-performance computational services, scientific instruments, and arrays of sensors." This new distributed environment has been referred to as "cyberinfrastructure" (Atkins *et al.*, 2003; Atkins, 2005).

In some fields, ways of researching have been transformed dramatically by ICT thanks to rapid acceleration of computer and network performance, which have allowed researchers to simulate, model and visualise more complex systems and to democratise advance computing. Atkins *et al.* (2003) give examples in all fields of science and engineering. Interestingly, the digitisation of data also enables more interdisciplinary work, and sometimes the emergence of new fields, thanks to the reuse of data sets in unexpected ways or the linking of several data sets.

The exponential growth of computing and storage capacity will continue in the foreseeable future and many experiments that are still impossible because they would involve too massive data collection and computation will soon become possible, for example in sky modelling (astronomy) or climate modelling (atmospheric science). While high end technologies could be seen as widening the digital divide between the poor and the rich, the lead universities and the others, it is now possible to share (sometimes expensive) research instruments remotely and to have more academics and students participating in cutting edge research, thanks to simulation and visualisation techniques. While issues of intellectual property rights can somewhat hinder collaboration and open repositories of knowledge, this is a growing phenomenon. One aspect of revolutionising cyberinfrastructure lies in the democratisation of research and research instruments and tools, allowing less endowed researchers to follow and contribute to their field more than they could in the past, if not to the same extent as leading researchers.

5.9. Concluding remarks

What is changing in academic research? In brief, academic research is growing in scale, becoming more international, more collaborative, both between sectors and with lay people, and also more competitive.

First, academic research has expanded considerably over the past decades, partly because of the expansion of tertiary education. In addition to the productivity of researchers, scientific output depends on the available stock of academic researchers, so that its continued growth will be linked to the continued expansion of higher education systems and to the balance between teaching and research in the academic profession (OECD, 2008a).

Second, basic research continues to be, but to a decreasing extent, a speciality of the higher education sector. While the share of basic research has slightly increased in its research output, the higher education sector has somewhat less contributed to the total amount of basic research over the past decades. The private non-profit sector has considerably increased the share of its research activities devoted to basic research. While the business sector has only slightly increased the share of basic research in its research activities, this had an observable impact on its share of all basic research performed. Given its R&D expenditures compared to other sectors, a small increase of the share of basic research in its R&D expenditures could turn the business sector into a major player in basic research.

Third, the sources of finance for academic research and the methods of allocating funds have evolved over the past decades. Academic research is still largely publicly financed, but has overall relied more on private funding. This increase is mainly attributable to the private resources that universities have raised through increased tuition and commercial activities rather than from increased funding from the business sector. This reflects changes in the governance of public higher education and public research with more funding competitively allocated directly to researchers rather than through university funding. These governance changes are often accompanied by an increasing importance given to excellence and quantitative measures of research output.

Fourth, academic research has become more international and more collaborative. International and inter-sectoral collaboration has increased, facilitated by ICT decreases in travel costs and by an increasingly specialised division of labour in science. The collaboration with civil society has also increased. Factors behind these changes include increased competition between scientists (linked to increased productivity requirements) as well as between institutions and countries (linked to international rankings). One driver of this competition has been the emergence of Asia as a new scientific centre.

Globalisation and the international visibility of the research output of institutions has led many countries to concentrate their academic research in centres of excellence or in a few research teams. While this concentrated model has long been in place in the United States and in the United Kingdom, it is relatively new in other countries, where excellent research used to be more spread across institutions (and within countries). Concentration improves brand image and an institution's position in rankings, which is particularly important in attracting international funding. However, as long as international funding remains a small share of the funding of research in higher education, a key challenge for higher education policy will be to strike a good balance between concentration and dispersion of excellence. Excellence is important to create emulation and knowledge accumulation and sharing. However, there is no clear evidence that a system with very few excellent universities gathering all top research departments in the country leads to higher average quality at the system level than a system of good universities with a small number of excellent departments (creating some emulation for other local departments).

Another question for policy-makers is related to the trend for more competitive allocation of research funding. At the same time as emphasising the accountability and efficiency of public spending, how can funding systems accommodate and encourage risk-taking in research activities (and tolerate failure)?

The future scenarios presented in Annex 5.A1. explore some of the different models that could come out of these trends.

Notes

1. This is the definition adopted by the *Frascati Manual* (OECD, 2002). Higher education includes: "all universities, colleges of technology and other institutions of post-secondary education, whatever their source of finance or legal status; all research institutes, experimental stations and clinics operating under the direct control of or administered by or associated with higher education

institutions." Public research organisations with strong links with universities – such as the CNRS (National Centre for Scientific Research) in France – are thus included, while academies of science are not. For student enrolments data, higher education refers to general and vocational tertiary education, that is levels 5A, 5B and 6 of the International Standard Classification of Education (ISCED).

2. Throughout the paper, "real term" comparisons are based on deflated data expressed in constant prices (US dollars [USD] of 2000) and power purchasing parities (PPP).

3. The performance of R&D by each sector is measured by their share of gross domestic expenditures on R&D. Another indicator lies in their respective research personnel.

4. The patterns of military R&D vary significantly in the European Union and the United States. The share of military research has indeed decreased and levelled off in the European Union since 2001: military R&D accounted for 13% of government R&D expenditures in 2006, against 58% in the United States.

5. More on general trends in R&D can be found in OECD (2007a).

6. Data for large countries like the United States are missing after 1999.

7. These figures exclude the output in humanities, but include social sciences and psychology.

8. OECD Education Database. My estimate for 1985.

9. In some countries, academic research is not financed through general university funds. For example, in the United States, general university funds are conceptually considered as exclusively devoted to instruction. Although these funds probably support some departmental research at US public universities, the corresponding data are generally not collected (and would only appear as funds spent by the universities themselves).

10. The information is from the US Patent and Trademark Office.

11. Full-time foreign academic staff rose from 2 700 to 5 900 over the period, that is 2 to 3.5% of all academic staff.

12. The US National Science Foundation notes a moderately high correlation between the number of US PhDs awarded by country to foreign-born students in 1992-96 and the volume of papers co-authored by the United States and those countries in 1997-2001 (NSB, 2004).

13. Relative to its population, the United States ranked 13th in terms of article production in 2003: see Indicator D.5 in OECD (2007a).

14. One calculates a "relative citation index" for a country or a region by adjusting the frequency of citation of its scientific literature for its world share of scientific articles (NSF, 2005).

15. In the GATS services sectoral classification list, "research and development services" are included in the business services, with three sub-categories: R&D services on natural sciences; R&D services on social sciences and humanities; interdisciplinary R&D services.

Bibliography

Aghion, P., M. Dewatripont, C. Hoxby, A. Mas-Colell and A. Sapir (2008), *Higher Aspirations: An Agenda for Reforming European Universities*, Bruegel, Brussels.

Altbach, P. (2006), "The Dilemmas of Ranking", International Higher Education, Vol. 42, pp. 2-3.

Atkins, D.E., K.K. Droegemeier, S. I. Feldman, H. Garcia-Molina, M.L. Klein, D.G. Messerschmitt, P. Messina, J.P. Ostriker, M.H. Wright (2003), *Revolutionizing Science and Engineering through Cyberinfrastructure* (Washington, NSF), *www.cise.nsf.gov/sci/reports/toc.cfm*.

Atkins, D.E. (2005), "University Futures and New Technologies: Possibilities and Issues", Unpublished discussion paper for an OECD expert meeting.

Bell, R. K., D. Hill and R. F. Lehming (2007), *The Changing Research and Publication Environment in American Research Universities*, National Science Foundation, Working Paper SRS 07-204, Arlington, VA.

Boyer, R. (2002). *La croissance, début de siècle. De l'octet au gène* (Paris, Albin Michel). English translation: *The Future of Economic Growth: As New Becomes Old* (Cheltenham, UK, Edward Elgar) 2004.

Braun, D. and F-X Merrien (1999) *Towards a New Model of Governance for Universities? A Comparative View.* (London, Jessica Kingsley).

Callon, M. (2003), "The Increasing Involvement of Concerned Groups in R&D Policies: What Lessons for Public Powers?", in A. Geuna, A. J Salter and W. E. Steinmueller (eds), *Science and Innovation. Rethinking the Rationales for Funding and Governance*, pp. 30-68, (Cheltenham, UK Edward Elgar).

Callon, M., P. Lascoumes and Y. Barthes (2001), *Agir dans un monde incertain : Essai sur la démocratie technique* (Paris, Le Seuil).

Enders, J. and C. Musselin (2008), "Back to the Future: The Academic Profession of the 21st Century", in OECD, *Higher Education to 2030, Volume 1: Demography*, OECD Publishing, Paris.

European Commission (2003), *Towards a European Research Area: Key Figures 2003-2004*, Brussels, EC.

Etzkowitz, H., Webster, A., Gebhardt, C. and B.R.C. Terra (2000) "The Future of the University and the University of the Future: Evolution of Ivory Tower to Entrepreneurial Paradigm", *Research Policy*, Vol. 29, pp. 313-30.

Foray, D. (2004). *The Economics of Knowledge*, Cambridge, MA, MIT Press.

Geuna A. and B. R. Martin (2003), "University Research Evaluation and Funding: An International Comparison", *Minerva*, Vol. 41, 277-304.

Geuna, A. and L. Nesta (2003), "University Patenting and its Effects on Academic Research", SPRU Electronic Working Paper Series No. 99.

Hackl, E. (2007), "The Creation of a Centre of Excellence: The Austrian Example: The Idea of an Elite University, Networks and Policy", Paper presented at the Consortium of Higher Education Researchers, Dublin.

Harfi, M. and C. Mathieu (2006), "Classement de Shangai et image internationale des universités : quels enjeux pour la France ?", *Horizons stratégiques*, Vol. 2, pp. 1-16.

Hazelkorn, E. (2007), "The Impact of League Tables and Ranking Systems on Higher Education Decision Making", *Higher Education Management and Policy*, Vol. 19, No. 2.

Hazelkorn, E. (2005), *University Research Management. Developing Research in New Institutions*, OECD Publishing, Paris.

Higher Education Statistics Agency (HESA) (2008a), *Students in Higher Education Institutions 2006-2007*, London.

Higher Education Statistics Agency (HESA) (2008b), *Resources of Higher Education Institutions 2006-2007*, London.

Huisman, J. and M.C. van der Wende (eds.) (2004), *On Co-operation and Competition, National and European Policies for the Internationalisation of Higher Education*, Lemmens Verlag, Bonn.

Huisman, J. and M.C. van der Wende (eds.) (2005), *On Co-operation and Competition II, Institutional Responses to Internationalisation, Europeanisation and Globalisation*, Lemmens Verlag, Bonn.

Hippel (von), E. (2005), *Democratizing Innovation* (Cambridge, MA, MIT Press), *http://web.mit.edu/evhippel/www/democ.htm*.

Institute for International Education (IIE) (2008), *Open Doors 2008. Report on International Educational Exchange*, Sewickley, PA, United States.

Kim, K.-S. (2007a), "The Making of a World-class Research University at the Periphery: Seoul National University, 1994-2005", in P. Altbach and J. Balan (eds.), *World Class Worldwide: Transforming Research Universities in Asia & Latin America*, Johns Hopkins University Press, Baltimore.

Kim, K.-S. (2007b), "A Great Leap Forward to Excellence in Research at Seoul National University, 1994-2006" *Asia Pacific Education Review*, Vol. 8, pp. 1-11.

Knight.J. (2002) "Trade in Higher Education Services: The Implications of GATS" Observatory on Borderless Higher Education (London, OBHE).

Knight, J. (2003), "GATS, Trade and Higher Education. Perspective 2003: Where are We?", *Observatory Report*, May, *www.obhe.ac.uk/products/*.

Larsen, K., Momii, K. and Vincent-Lancrin, S. (2004), *Cross-Border Higher Education: An Analysis of Current Trends, Policy Strategies and Future Scenarios*, Observatory on Borderless Higher Education, *www.obhe.ac.uk/products/reports/pdf/November2004_1.pdf*.

Larsen, K. and S. Vincent-Lancrin (2002), "International Trade in Educational Services: Good or Bad?", *Higher Education Management and Policy*, Vol. 14, No. 3, pp. 9-45, OECD Publishing, Paris.

Larsen, K. and S. Vincent-Lancrin (2006), "The Impact of ICT on Tertiary Education: Advances and Promises", in Foray, D. and B. Kahin (eds.), *Advancing Knowledge and the Knowledge Economy* (Cambridge, MA, MIT Press), forthcoming.

Lundvall, B.-A. (1988), "Innovation as an Interactive Process: From User-Producer Interaction to National Systems of Innovation", in G. Dosi, C. Freeman, R. Nelson, G. Silvenberg and L. Soete (eds), *Technology and Economic Theory*, London: Pinter, pp. 349-69.

Marginson, S. and Considine, M. (2000) *The Enterprise University: Power, Governance and Reinvention in Australia*, Cambridge, Cambridge University Press.

Marginson, S. and M. van der Wende (2009), "The New Global Landscape of Nations and Institutions", in OECD, *Higher Education to 2030, Volume 2: Globalisation*, OECD Publishing, Paris.

Martin, B.R. (2002) The Changing Social Contract for Science and the Evolution of the University, in A. Geuna, A.J. Salter and W.E. Steinmueller (Eds) *Science and Innovation: Rethinking the Rationales for Funding and Governance*, Aldershot, Edward Elgar.

MEXT (1993), *School Basic Survey*, Tokyo.

MEXT (2008), *School Basic Survey*, Tokyo.

Mittelstraß, J. (2002), "Die Modernität der klassischen Universität", *www.uni-konstanz.de/FuF/Philo/Philosophie/Mitarbeiter/mittelstrass/Marburg-2002.htm*.

National Science Board (NSB) (2004), *Science and Engineering Indicators 2004*. Two volumes, Arlington, VA, National Science Foundation, *www.nsf.gov/statistics/seind04/pdfstart.htm*.

NSB (2006), *Science and Engineering Indicators 2006, www.nsf.gov/statistics/seind06/toc.htm*.

NSB (2008), *Science and Engineering Indicators 2008, www.nsf.gov/statistics/seind08/toc.htm*.

Newman, F., L. Couturier and J. Scurrie (2004), *The Future of Higher Education. Rhetoric, Reality, and the Risks of the Market*, San Francisco, Wiley & Sons.

OBHE (Observatory on Borderless Higher Education) (2004), *Mapping Borderless Higher Education: Policy, Markets and Competition* (London, OBHE).

OECD (2001), *Cities and Regions in the New Learning Economy*, OECD Publishing, Paris.

OECD (2002), *Frascati Manual. Proposed Standard Practice for Surveys on Research and Experimental Development*, OECD Publishing, Paris.

OECD (2003a), "Changing Patterns of Governance in Higher Education", *Education Policy Analysis*, OECD Publishing Paris.

OECD (2003b), *Turning Science into Business. Patenting and Licensing at Public Research Organisations*, OECD Publishing, Paris.

OECD (2004a), *Internationalisation and Trade in Higher Education. Opportunities and Challenges*, OECD Publishing, Paris.

OECD (2004b), *Quality and Recognition in Higher Education: The Cross-border Challenge*, OECD Publishing, Paris.

OECD (2005b), *Trends in International Migration - 2004 Edition*, OECD Publishing, Paris.

OECD (2005c), *E-learning in Tertiary Education: Where do we Stand?*, OECD Publishing, Paris.

OECD (2006), "The Internationalisation of Higher Education: Towards an Explicit Policy", *Education Policy Analysis 2005*, OECD Publishing, Paris.

OECD (2007a), *OECD Science, Technology and Industry Scoreboard*, OECD Publishing, Paris.

OECD (2007b), *Higher Education and Regions: Globally Competitive, Locally Engaged*, OECD Publishing, Paris.

OECD (2007c), *Cross-Border Tertiary Education: A Way Towards Development*, OECD Publishing, Paris.

OECD (2008a), *Higher Education to 2030, Volume 1: Demography*, OECD Publishing, Paris.

OECD (2008b), *Tertiary Education for the Knowledge Society*, 2 volumes, OECD Publishing, Paris.

OECD (2008c), *The Global Competition for Talent*, OECD Publishing, Paris.

OECD (2009), *Higher Education to 2030, Volume 3: Technology*, OECD Publishing, Paris.

Rabeharisoa, V. and M. Callon (1999), *Le pouvoir des malades : L'Association française contre les myopathies et la recherche*, Presses de l'École des Mines, Paris.

Rabeharisoa, V. and M. Callon (2002), "The Involvement of Patients' Associations in Research", *International Social Science Journal*, Vol. 171, p. 57-65 (Paris, Unesco).

Ruch, R.S. (2001), *Higher Ed, Inc. The Rise of the For-Profit University* (Baltimore, John Hopkins University Press).

Sadlak, J. and L. N. Cai, *The World-Class University and Ranking: Aiming Beyond Status*, Unesco-CEPES, Bucarest.

Salmi, J. (2009), *The Challenges of Establishing World-Class Universities*, World Bank, Washington DC.

Salmi, J. and A. Saroyan (2007), "League Tables as Policy Instruments: Uses and Misuses", *Higher Education Management and Policy*, Vol. 19, No. 2.

Storper, M. and M. Salais (1997), *Worlds of Production* (Cambridge, MA, Harvard University Press).

Tremblay, K. (2005), "Academic Mobility and Immigration", *Journal of Studies in International Education*, Vol. 9, No. 3, pp. 1-34.

Vincent-Lancrin, S. (2004), "Building Future Scenarios for Universities and Higher Education: An International Approach", *Policy Futures in Education*, Vol. 2, No. 2, 245-63.

Von Hippel, E. (2005), *Democratizing Innovation*, MIT Press, 2005, *http://web.mit.edu/evhippel/*.

ANNEX 5.A1

Future Scenarios for Academic Research

Drawing on the trends depicted in the chapter, as well as on other trends in higher education and society, this annex proposes a set of scenarios for higher education research in a 20-year time frame. The scenarios build on the scenarios and methodology described in Vincent-Lancrin (2004) but with a focus on academic research.

Future scenarios do not aim to predict the future, or to picture what a desirable future would be like, but merely aim to provide stakeholders with tools for thinking strategically about the uncertain future before them, which will be partly shaped by their actions and partly by factors beyond their control. The use of scenarios enables complex trends to be combined, tensions between people's actions to be highlighted, emerging trends to be brought into the picture, and what trend reversal or radical innovation might entail. Scenarios are just possible futures, they do not have (or mean) to be likely or desirable. The challenge of scenario building is to strike a good balance between relevance (continuity with dominant and emerging trends) and imagination (discontinuity). This is why they often magnify trends or features that can already be observed at a small scale in some part of the world. Given that they try to help stakeholders better understand where they are and where they want (or do not want) to go, they do not really need to be realistic, but they must try to be interesting.

The four scenarios presented in this section build on the trends presented above: the increasing importance of knowledge; the growth of private funding and decline of government funding; the rise of competition from other sectors in basic research; the growing collaboration and competition at the national and international levels; the growing demand for accountability and transparency from governments and civil society; the new opportunities offered by technology progress; and the persistence of mass higher education systems (or continuing massification where it has not reached its peak).

A simple way to present scenarios is to select two key dimensions that would design a possibility space and emphasise some strategic directions. As shown in Figure 5.3, the possibility space has been designed around two dimensions: administration versus market forces; international focus versus national focus. The horizontal axis emphasises the governance pattern of the whole system: is it governed by administrative rules, which are more supply-driven, or does it become demand-driven, like on a market? It is noteworthy that a demand-driven system with market forces does not necessarily involve private for-profit higher education institutions. The vertical axis emphasises the depth of international integration in higher education. While participating and responding to globalisation is and will continue to be a challenge and opportunity for higher education, leading to both collaboration and competition, the national (or even

Figure 5.A1. **Four scenarios for academic research**

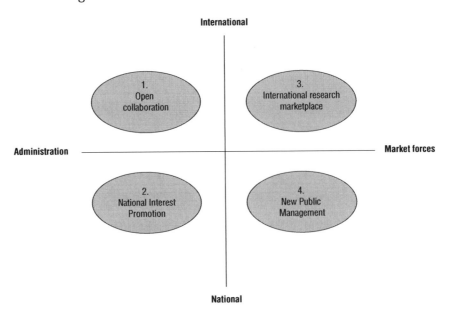

regional) missions of higher education systems are still important and may become increasingly important in the future. Although we tend to take globalisation and internationalisation for granted, we should also consider the possibility of a backlash against globalisation, following a war, a pandemy, or citizens' hesitations to go beyond a certain level of international integration.

While these two dimensions somehow shape the scenario stories, one should bear in mind that they are multidimensional. This means that the combination of some of their features is to some extent arbitrary. Technology is, for example, a cross-cutting force that could have a role in all scenarios, although it is mainly emphasised in the first scenario (where it could be a real driver). Scenarios must indeed be different enough to generate interesting discussion, which implies making choices. Nothing prevents stakeholders from making different choices, though, and combining the details differently into new scenarios of their own.

To help understand how they have been built, it might help to explicit how they relate to the previous sections of the paper. Scenario 1 mainly emphasises the trends depicted in Sections 5.1, 5.5, 5.6 and 5.7. Scenario 2 draws on the current state of the art (the dominance of government funding through general university funds, growing importance of research), on the rise of geopolitical concerns reflected in the recent growth of military research, and finally on a reversal of the trends of Section 5.5. Scenario 3 amplifies the trends pictured in Sections 5.3, 5.4 and 5.5. And Scenario 4 combines the trends highlighted in Sections 5.2 and 5.3, keeping at their current level the trends of Section 5.4.

The four scenarios are the following

Scenario 1: Open collaboration

In this scenario, one can imagine academic research remaining mainly publicly funded and very internationalised in a way that involves more collaboration than competition. This scenario is very much driven by technology and by the ideal of free and open knowledge – an ideal that civil society could increasingly impose on the grounds that academic research is largely paid for by taxpayers and should thus be freely available and following the lobbying of some patients' associations. There could also have been a backlash against patenting and intellectual property rights, regarded as an inefficient means of supporting innovation, not the least because of the existence of international networks of repositories of knowledge and research available through the web. In this scenario, global networking is important and goes beyond higher education institutions, involving industries as well as individuals and concerned groups. Governments across the world can easily share their large research investments since they can be remotely operated, benefiting research teams scattered across the globe. While there is still a strong stratification of higher education institutions, or, in some countries, of research departments, some attracting much more funds and others and having different working conditions, this technology-driven networking induces much quicker spill-over in the lower ends of higher educations systems as well as in developing countries. The hierarchy between higher education institutions is more relevant for the recruitment of academic researchers than for students. Indeed, academics and students in less prestigious higher education institutions could now access research tools and recent knowledge that were difficult to access before: recent research is indeed available on the web in real time, as well as new data sets on which can be used for new research and new simulation, computing and visualisation tools, and virtual "collaboratories" are open to everyone. Cutting edge academic research requiring heavy investments has thus democratised and crosses national borders. The media sometimes question the model when a foreign company develops a new product thanks to this open sharing, stressing the tension with the traditional economic logic, but its defenders argue that the reverse has also been true in the past and that the knowledge has actually been produced internationally. Although sensitive research is classified, some people also fear that this proliferation of knowledge facilitates terrorism. Finally, there are still some debates about the digital and knowledge divide between developing and developed countries, but everybody acknowledges some improvement compared to 20 years ago.

Scenario 2: National interest promotion

In this scenario, higher education would remain mainly publicly funded and administered, academics keeping their control over the research process as trusted professionals. Governments have put a strong emphasis on the national missions of higher education. Higher education institutions have become more embedded in their local communities and regional economy. A growing scepticism about internationalisation has indeed grown in the population, for a variety of reasons including recent terror attacks and wars, concerns about the rising number of immigrants, and the feeling that national identity was becoming threatened by globalisation and foreign influence. For geo-strategic reasons, governments have launched ambitious new military research programmes and have classified an increasing number of research topics in natural sciences, life sciences and engineering. International collaborative research continues, but with a more limited number of "friendly" countries. As many research outcomes have been increasingly regarded as strategic for the country, for economic or military reasons, the scope of academic research has somewhat diminished (while government research has regained ground). Albeit a small number of elite higher education institutions and research departments continue to be very internationalised, and to keep their top ranks nationally, the average higher education institution has research interests that are more related to their immediate neighbouring cities and regions. And in the public, academic research is associated with humanities and social sciences, two fields valued for maintaining national culture alive. Other fields of academic research have become more integrated with local economies, but thus less visible nationally. Academics continue to teach and to research, but teaching has become more clearly their first objective, and research, a welcome by-product – an arrangement that was found to match students' and policymakers' expectations.

Scenario 3: International research marketplace

In this scenario, one could imagine that higher education institutions compete globally to provide research services to governments, businesses and civil society as for-profit institutions. The liberalisation process at the WTO now encompasses research services supplied by higher education institutions, be they public or private. Academic research had become very close to a great deal of research carried out in the business sector, which undertakes a good share of basic research now; and it was equally funded by public and private sources, with the dramatic increase of revenues from their licensed discoveries, and their growing involvement in the business sector. Most people agreed that there was thus no longer any reason not to expose research services from the higher education sector to worldwide competition – or at least most of it, as most countries refused to make any commitment in the GATS for some research sub-sectors that they considered "vital" to their national security. Research and teaching are currently viewed as distinct services, as they have always been in the GATS, and higher education institutions have increasingly disintegrated their activities, concentrating on what they considered to be their core business (either teaching or research). So-called "research universities" thus hardly teach (when they continue to do so), while average higher education institutions carry out some supply-driven research but with small budgets. There is a fierce competition for academic researchers worldwide and between institutions to attract research super-stars. While cross-subsidisation of commercial research is strictly forbidden, academics are encouraged to carry out some disinterested research as a remedy to possible market failures. Basic research projects are still funded by governments, but following a tender to which all research centres in the world can – and do increasingly – apply. International rankings have first helped governments and private organisations and foundations to sort out the best institutions and research departments, but the research business has become so concentrated that these rankings are now useless. Outsourcing research to countries where research labour costs are still much lower than in the OECD area has proved to be very cost-efficient, and has been duly celebrated by taxpayers. Social scientists and journalists sometimes complain about the lack of relevance of some research, as foreign providers tend to downplay some cultural and historical features of the country, but the internationalisation of research teams should solve the problem. Although formerly "emerging countries" have gradually imposed their competitive advantage in some fields (technology in India, agronomics in China, etc.), some former developing countries are now "emerging". However, the United States is still the top exporter of research services, specialising in high-tech and capital intensive research.

Scenario 4: New Public Management

In this scenario, academic research remains mainly publicly funded but with a public management that makes extensive use of quasi-market forces. Higher education institutions are now autonomous. They still depend on the public purse for a significant share of their budget but have managed to diversify their funding sources, thanks to foreign education markets, the deregulation of tuition fees, the patenting of their academic research and their growing financial links with the business sector. The distinction between the higher education sector and the private non-profit sector does actually no longer make much sense, as most resources of university are now private, coming from students' households, business and private foundations. The division of labour between institutions has become stronger, most of them specialising in different missions regarding teaching as well as research – a differentiation that has not prevented most of them from continuing to carry out both research and teaching. Most higher education institutions have continued to allocate some research funding internally on their own funds. But the bulk of the allocation of public funds for academic research is generally indirect, financing separately budgeted research projects according to peer-reviewed selections. As a result, there is more competition nationally between higher education institutions and research money has been concentrated in a small share of them. (Only a small amount of research funding does actually cross national borders, except within the European Union where the recently created European Research Council funds an increasing share of European academic research.) Institutions are now much more accountable to the state and to their other financing sources. Higher education institutions still benefit from their research prestige to attract the best students and set their level of tuition fees. Some people recurrently voice their concern about the widening gap between elite and average institutions in terms of funding and quality, whereas others argue that concentration is the most efficient way to use a limited public budget, especially as advances made by the research institutions are then democratised by teaching institutions.

Scenarios aim at engaging stakeholders in discussion about strategic choices. So where are we and where could we go? What future do we want? What can and should we do to achieve it? Where are we probably going? While the paper proposes some possible answers to the first question, the subsequent questions are beyond its scope.

Here are just two comments for the discussion.

First, the chosen scenarios show that internationalisation and particular modes of provision (public or private) are conceptually disconnected. Internationalisation does not necessarily involve trade or liberalisation (Scenario 1), although it can (Scenario 3). Conversely, market mechanisms are not necessarily related to private provision or to internationalisation: they could be used in a public management framework (Scenario 4), with public higher education institutions responding to market incentives. However, an important question to discuss is under what conditions a scenario would be sustainable (or stable). For example, the level of public funding seems to be an important factor for the "new public management" scenario to be sustainable: if this level diminishes beyond a certain point (to be determined), one would probably rapidly end up in the "international research marketplace" scenario.

Second, the question of the concentration or even distribution of academic research across higher education systems features in all scenarios, and ranks high in the policy debates. As shown in Section 5.3, concentration of research already exists to a lesser or greater extent. And the strength of the link between academic research and teaching also varies accordingly across and between systems. To what extent should a country concentrate its academic research (or let it concentrate)? And if this concentration is desirable, what would be the best means? Linking academic research and teaching from the postgraduate level only? Separating academic research and teaching to a greater extent, as it is already the case in some countries? Redirecting incentives towards teaching (as the higher education economy is currently almost exclusively based on research)? What kind of effects would have these different types of differentiation? Finding the right balance at system level for higher education systems to both produce high level research and meet social and educational objectives at a reasonable social price will indeed continue to be one of the challenges of the next decades.

Higher Education to 2030
Volume 2: Globalisation
© OECD 2009

Chapter 6

The Giants Awake: The Present and Future of Higher Education Systems in China and India

by

Philip G. Altbach*

This chapter first presents historical developments and current characteristics of Chinese and Indian higher education systems. It then examines the respective roles of China and India in increasingly globalised higher education sphere by looking into cross-border mobility and international research competitiveness. The chapter finally explores the internal challenges related to higher education access, equity and emergence of private provision in China and India. It shows that while China and India are two of the world's largest academic systems, it is less clear that these systems will be globally competitive in the near future.

* Center for International Higher Education, Boston College. The author gratefully acknowledges Liu Nian Cai and Wu Yan of Shanghai Jiao Tong University, China, and Pawan Agarwal of the Government of West Bengal, Kolkata, India, and N. Jayaram of the Tata Institute of Social Sciences, Mumbai, India.

China and India, which together have a third of the world's population and are two of the most rapidly growing economies, are awakening to the significance of higher education for technological development and for the global knowledge economy. The economic realities of China and India's rapid growth are affecting the world, from increased demand for natural resources to their roles as exporters of products of all kinds, a pattern that will continue regardless of the current economic slowdown. A growing impact of these countries is in higher education; their higher education systems are already among the world's largest; and they are major exporters of students to other countries. This trend is likely to grow in the future, as these countries expand and improve their higher education systems. Although the booms of China and India have been fuelled in the main by cheap labour and inexpensive low-end manufacturing, the situation is changing, and the economic future of both countries depends on a better-educated workforce. Universities are central in the race to provide respective workforces with skills to make them competitive in the global knowledge system.

Both countries realise that higher education is key to development and recognise the necessity to expand their higher education systems and to build some world-class research universities at the top of a differentiated system. In 2006, India educated approximately 12% of its university-age population, while China enrolled about 22% (UIS, 2009). China is now number one in enrolments, with more than 25 million. India's 13 million enrolment ranks third. Both countries have been expanding rapidly in recent years. Since the early 1990s, China's postsecondary enrolments have grown from 5 million to 25 million in 2006, while India has expanded from 5 million to 13 million by 2006 (Agarwal, 2009; OECD, 2007b). Perhaps one-third of the world's 140 million postsecondary students are in Chinese and Indian institutions of higher education.

Significant quality problems exist in less-selective colleges and universities in both countries. Many of India's impressive number of engineering graduates, up to 75% according to a McKinsey report, are too poorly educated to function effectively in the economy without additional on-the-job training (Jha, 2009; Surowiecki, 2007). Part of China's growing problem of graduate unemployment is related to the qualifications of some students.

Higher education comprises a policy priority in both countries. China has for almost two decades been engaged in a significant upgrade in the quality of its top universities as well as in a major expansion of enrolments in all higher education sectors. While India has for decades recognised the importance of expanding higher education access and improving quality, only quite recently have significant resources been allocated, with the Knowledge Commission's higher education recommendations of 2006 and more recent government commitments (Tilak, 2007). Current plans, for example, call for expanding the number of top-tier higher education institutions (Agarwal, 2009).

Envisioning higher education prospects for China and India for two decades or more is highly problematical (Li, Whalley, Zhang, and Zhao, 2008). Current data, for example, often

Figure 6.1. **Number of higher education students (in millions) in the early 1990s and 2006**

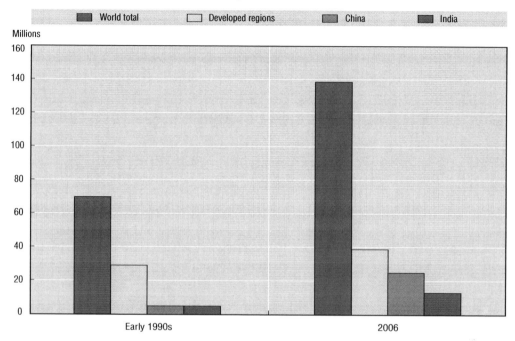

Sources: UNESCO Institute for Statistics (2009); Agarwal (2009); OECD (2007b).

lack accuracy or availability, making generalisations about the contemporary situation difficult. Future developments depend on the macroeconomic, social, and political trends, and these are less easy to envisage than is the case for most OECD countries.

Basic stability and consistent policy orientations for higher education, while reasonably clear as seen from today's perspective, cannot be predicted with great certainty into the coming decades for either country. In a way, China today may be seen as too stable while India as perhaps overly unstable. India's relatively open political system may permit it more flexibility in coping with adversity, but it could fail to produce practical solutions or imaginative plans to improve higher education. China's state planning apparatus has developed higher education impressively, especially at the top of the system, but may lack flexibility. Both may be buffeted by internal forces or regional and global changes more profoundly than many parts of the world. The past shows that China is capable of dramatic and sometimes unpredictable policy shifts. India, constantly debating new directions, changes gradually and often without clear planning.

The future of higher education policy in both countries depends to a significant degree on several factors. Demand relates to the continuing expansion of the middle class that has the resources to pay tuition and other fees and educational qualifications for admission. Other population groups have an interest in higher education access as well, but the middle class is the largest force, has dramatically expanded in recent years, and is likely to continue to grow. While estimates vary considerably, many experts agree that the Indian middle class now numbers more than 50 million, and China's is similarly large. Some estimates (for example by McKinsey Global Institute[1]) predict that by 2025, each country will have a middle class of perhaps 500 million. A significant number of these large groups will demand access to higher education, creating huge strains on the system. Government policy regarding funding higher education and supporting research universities and the elite sector of the system is a key factor shaping higher education prospects. As both countries join the ranks of the world's major economies, they will recognise the importance of world-class universities so as to compete globally. China has already moved to create and sustain an elite academic sector. India is beginning to grapple with this issue.

6.1. A difficult history

For higher education systems, history plays a role in the present. For both China and India, the academic past has created difficult and problematical results for the present – and likely the future. In common with all of the world's higher education systems, both inherited the western academic model (Ben-David and Zloczower, 1962). Both countries have largely not taken advantage of their extraordinarily rich indigenous intellectual and academic traditions. China, after all, invented national examinations with the Confucian examinations used for several millennia to choose civil servants and advanced institutions to train people for these tests. India had some of the world's oldest universities, such as Nalanada in Bihar. These academic traditions predated western universities by more than a thousand years. However, these ancient academic institutions and traditions have little salience today.

In the 19th century, forward-looking Chinese recognised the need to modernise so as to compete with the West and develop economically. Western academic models were chosen – through a small number of European-style universities established in the late 19th century along China's east coast in areas controlled by European powers (Hayhoe, 1999). Peking University was established with American assistance and the support of the waning imperial government. Christian religious organisations worked actively in China at the time and established several universities. Thus, by the time that the imperial system was overthrown in 1911, a small number of western-style universities existed, and many Chinese had been educated in the West and in Japan.

While the new republic moved to strengthen the existing universities and establish more institutions, civil war, economic disruption, and Japanese invasion prevented much progress from being made. At the time of the establishment of the People's Republic of China, in 1949, the higher education system was small and weak. The entire higher education system in China had only 205 universities, mostly concentrated on the east coast and in Beijing and a few other large cities, and a total of 116 504 students (Hayhoe, 1999). The new Communist regime looked to the Soviet Union for academic leadership and reorganised higher education in the Soviet model, by splitting up many of the existing universities into smaller specialised and vocationally oriented institutions in most cases linked to operational ministries. Research academies were established separate from the universities. Normal academic development was frequently disrupted. Academic freedom was limited and the emergence of an effective academic profession hindered. Few Chinese students or scholars gained an opportunity to study abroad, and those who had a chance were limited to the Soviet Union and the eastern European socialist countries.

The most severe disruption came with the Cultural Revolution, of 1966 to 1976, which closed the entire higher education system, sent many professors and students to rural areas to work, and destroyed a generation of academics. Few countries have suffered such a dramatic academic cataclysm. With the end of the Cultural Revolution in 1976 and the subsequent opening of China to the world, the universities were reopened and efforts were made to look to the West for academic guidance. Chinese students were able to study abroad. Universities were permitted to look abroad for new academic ideas and were given funds to re-establish themselves. The Soviet pattern of highly specialised vocational institutions was in part dismantled. Political control was loosened as well. By the 1990s, as China's economic boom began, the university system was poised to expand.

India was a British colony for more than two centuries, ending with independence in 1947, and this experience shaped higher education and continues to influence it. The British did not give much support to higher education in their colonies. Higher education first expanded mainly due to the initiative of the growing middle class in the mid-19th century and recognition by the British that an educated civil service was needed to administer India. In 1857, the first universities were founded in Calcutta, Bombay, and Madras. The Indian colleges and universities were British in organisation. These institutions, teaching exclusively in English, displaced the few traditional schools left, which simply withered and died. Higher education was based on an organisational pattern where the universities constituted examining bodies more than teaching institutions. Most of the teaching took place in undergraduate colleges affiliated to the universities; examinations and curriculum were by and large controlled by the universities. This structure enabled centralised control over the colleges. A small number of British academics were recruited to teach and lead the universities and colleges. Indians had an opportunity to study in Britain, and most returned home to serve in the administration, including in the colleges and universities. Moreover, many became involved in nationalist organisations that eventually played a leading role in bringing independence to India (Basu, 1974).

From the early 19th century, almost all higher education in India was entirely in English; no Indian language was used for instruction or examination. The curriculum was largely limited to fields useful to the administration and to India's emerging professional classes – such as law, the social sciences, and related fields. While the academic system remained quite small – at the time of independence with 369 000 students studying in 27 universities and 695 colleges (Agarwal, 2009) – it succeeded in educating a cadre of graduates who provided the leadership of India, Pakistan, Sri Lanka, and, later, Bangladesh. As late as 1961, only 1.5% of the relevant age group participated in postsecondary education (Agarwal, 2009). There was little research capacity at India's colleges and universities at the time of independence, as there had not been interest in spending money on research there; and since higher education was in English, more than 90% of the Indian population was excluded from access (Agarwal, 2009). India's higher education system at the time of independence was small, highly bureaucratised, restrictive on academic freedom, provided in a language most Indians did not understand, and had a restricted curriculum.

Despite many reports and much criticism, higher education expanded between independence and the end of the 20th century although there were few structural changes. Enrolments expanded from little more than 100 000 in 1950 to 9 million by the end of the century (Agarwal, 2009). Annual growth sometimes was 10%. Most observers agree that overall quality declined and that the basic structure of the system remained quite similar to the colonial period (Kaul, 1974).

The university arrangements inherited by both countries in the mid-20th century were not helpful for the development of an effective higher education system. In the following years, China made many changes in its universities, most followed Soviet patterns, but the actions were not effective in building universities that could compete internationally or serve the needs of China's modernisation. India, on the other hand, expanded higher education slowly in the years of independence and more rapidly later but made few structural changes. As a result, universities were less than effective in meeting the needs of Indian society.

6.2. Contemporary characteristics

Governance

Both countries emerged into the mid-20th century with somewhat dysfunctional academic organisations and continue to be characterised by little self-governance and strong, often governmental, bureaucratic controls. Both countries have yet to establish academic governance arrangements for their universities that maximise the decision-making input of the professoriate.

The model, which China followed after 1950, dismantled many of the comprehensive universities into smaller specialised institutions attached to the relevant operational ministries rather than the Ministry of Education. These smaller institutions were, for the most part, narrowly vocational and did not do much research. Research was mainly in the hands of the institutes of the academies of science that were divided by discipline or field and were not part of the university system. It was only after the Cultural Revolution that the specialised institutions were slowly reintegrated into universities. The dual Chinese administrative structure that continues to the present time has been questioned in terms of its academic effectiveness. China's unique combination of academic and political governance arrangements, with an academically selected president and an executive vice president chosen by the Communist Party, sometimes creates administrative tension and reduces self-governance by the academic community. In recent years China has however been looking toward an American-style academic leadership model. Some universities have been strengthening academic leadership, especially in the office of the president, and have been trying to give more authority to department chairs and other senior administrators and to implement a faculty responsibility system that includes accountability for research and teaching (Min, 2004).

India's post-independence academic system was inherited from the British. The universities, to which almost all of the 700 undergraduate colleges were affiliated, were mainly examining bodies, with small post-baccalaureate programs. These colleges, generally small with around 500 students, were affiliated to universities that determined the curriculum, set and administered examinations, guided admissions, and awarded degrees. The undergraduate colleges possessed little autonomy. This affiliating system continues to the present. There are not more than 18 000 undergraduate colleges. A few of the universities were single-campus "unitary" institutions without affiliated colleges, and these resembled academic institutions in the West with undergraduate and graduate as well as professional degree programs. A few research organisations in specialised fields do advanced basic research in some scientific disciplines. While much has been added to the Indian higher education establishment, little has changed in the basic structure of the universities (Jayaram, 2004).

Differentiation

Effective mass higher education systems are generally differentiated by function and often by funding sources and other variables. Most include a private sector as well.

Typically, differentiated academic systems are characterised by a hierarchy of institutions, with highly selective elite research-intensive universities at the top, comprehensive universities in the middle, and an array of less-selective and often non-baccalaureate colleges at the bottom. An array of specialised institutions also compose part of the system. The elite sector typically enrols only a small proportion of the students and is, disproportionately, generously funded. Except in the United States and Japan, almost all elite universities are public.

China has moved consciously toward a differentiated academic system, having so far paid special attention to the top of the system, especially to the 150 or so research universities that are the responsibility of the central government. Most of China's approximately 1 700 universities are funded by and responsible to the provincial governments and in some instances to municipal authorities. These universities tend to be in the middle and toward the bottom of the academic hierarchy. There is currently a move to expand the non-baccalaureate sector in ways fairly similar to American community colleges. The emerging private sector tends to be at the bottom of the hierarchy. While China has not formally developed a coherent and articulated academic system with clearly defined missions and variable patterns of funding, it seems that such a system is emerging. It is likely in the coming decades that a clearly articulated and differentiated academic system will develop with input from both the central government and the provinces.

While the Indian higher education system can overall be characterised as differentiated, it is noteworthy that this differentiation is neither coherent nor conscious at a system level and there is less differentiation within higher education sub-sectors. Indian academe has grown without planning in response to massification and the need for new kinds of institutions to serve an expanding economy. Responsibility for higher education is divided among several agencies in the central government, the states (which have different policies and perspectives), an increasingly powerful private sector, and occasionally the courts. There is no formal division of responsibility for access or research (Jayaram, 2004). Over the years, efforts to reform higher education have sidestepped the traditional universities and rather have added new institutions alongside them.

India has a widely respected small elite sector of specialised academic institutions, most notably the Indian Institutes of Technology, now numbering 13. There are 380 universities, mostly under the jurisdiction of Indian states, which have primary responsibility for education in India's federal system. These universities are, however, largely undifferentiated from each other. The 24 universities under the control of the central government tend to be somewhat better funded, and of higher quality than the rest, but there is no clear differentiation among the universities. India has a total of more than 18 000 postsecondary institutions – more than 17 000 of these are colleges offering mainly undergraduate degrees (Agarwal, 2009), but there is no differentiation among the colleges, although a few have taken advantage of legislation that permits high-quality colleges to separate from their sponsoring universities and offer their own autonomous degrees. These colleges are recognised as more prestigious than the rest. There are also a variety of other kinds of postsecondary institutions. So called "deemed" universities are university-level institutions, mostly specialised, recognised by the University Grants Commission, a central government agency, and thus have degree-granting authority. Additional technical institutions are recognised and evaluated by the All-India Council of Technical Education, another central government agency.

As of 2009, India has not as yet attempted to define a strategy for moving toward a coherently differentiated academic system. The variety of institutions, sponsorship, and jurisdiction make the emergence of such a system very unlikely under current circumstances. The government recently announced that it will establish an additional 8 Indian Institutes of Technology and 7 Indian Institutes of Management, along with 30 new research-oriented central universities, 10 National Institutes of Technology, 2 Indian Institutes of Science, and 1 000 new polytechnics (*Hindu*, 2008).

Funding

Both countries face significant challenges in funding their rapidly expanding higher education systems (Agarwal, 2009; OECD, 2007b). While the two have experienced rapid economic growth in recent years – 10% or higher GDP expansion – they remain developing economies. China, in 2008 had a per capita purchasing power parity income of USD 5 370, while India's was USD 2 740 (World Bank, 2008b). Overall, India spent 0.8% of GDP on tertiary education in 2005, against 0.8% in 2000 (UIS, 2009). China spent 0.4% of GDP on higher education in 1999 (UIS, 2009, later internationally comparable figure is not available). These figures are under expenditures for other emerging economies and well under the 1% or more spent by developed countries. In both countries, increasing tuition costs in both public and private sector institutions has shifted a growing burden for funding higher education to students and their families. Neither country contains an adequate system of grants or loans to ensure equal access to higher education, although both have some financial aid programs in place and have made efforts to provide access for poor students and students from disadvantaged populations.

The funding provided by public sources for higher education in China and India is inadequate in meeting demands for both quality and access. Public funding for higher education comes from a variety of sources and there seems to be relatively little coordination among them. In both countries, the bulk of funding emerges from the state and provincial governments, which have a large measure of autonomy relating to the amounts spent on higher education and how allocations are made. Some states and provinces prioritise higher education, while others do not. The central authorities in China and India are mainly concerned with funding the top tier of universities and ensuring that research is appropriately supported. China provided much more funding to the research universities in part through the 985 and 211 central-government-funded support programs – approximately 150 universities have participated in these key projects. The top universities also receive funding from local and provincial authorities. For example, the Shanghai government has provided resources to its research universities, as have other cities and provinces. The Indian government, largely through the University Grants Commission, sponsors 20 universities and provides funding for innovative programs university-based research, and to some other institutions.

Calculating private funding for higher education in China and India is quite difficult. Both countries have growing private higher education sectors, and public universities all charge tuition fees to students. Tuition fees for first degrees, in purchasing power parities, varied between USD 1 640 and USD 3 820 in China in 2004 and between USD 20 and USD 37 in India in 2001 (Marcucci and Johnstone, 2005). In India the large majority of students study in private colleges, some of which have public support from the state governments and a growing number that are "unaided" and have no public support. There are also 11, as of 2007, fully private universities that receive no government funding. Tuition levels vary in the private sector and are in some cases regulated by government authorities. The situation in China is similarly complicated. The *min ban* private universities and colleges are quite diverse in purpose and role. A small number are recognised by government authorities to grant degrees. All are dependent on tuition, and costs vary. Many Chinese public universities sponsor affiliated semi-private branches or other degree-offering programs that are not state funded and charge higher tuition. These programs are intended, in part, to provide needed revenues for their sponsoring universities as well as to increase access. Some critics have accused them for having low academic standards and a controversy has risen relating to the degrees offered.

6.3. China and India as international higher education players

Cross-border mobility

In very significant ways, both countries loom large on the international higher education scene and will become much more central in the future. Currently, their importance is largely unrelated to their own policies but results from the exodus of students and professionals to the West and elsewhere since the 1970s. China and India are the top two exporters of students and have been so for the past two decades. In 2008, approximately 200 000 Indians and 892 000 Chinese were studying abroad; these numbers constituted close to half of the world's total of international students (Agarwal, 2008). Regardless of enrolment expansion, the two countries are likely to remain at the top of the export lists in the coming decades for several reasons. The main reasons, in India particularly but also in China, consist of the insufficient number of places in elite universities for the brightest students. The prestige of a foreign degree from a top western university has considerable cachet. An insufficient number of places in the academic systems exist for the expanding numbers of students seeking entry, and an unknown number of young people will seek foreign education as a first step toward emigration (Agarwal, 2008; Altbach, 2006). For students who do not score at the top of the university entrance or other examinations, obtaining a degree abroad may often be seen as preferable to studying in a less-prestigious local university. The growing middle class in both countries can increasingly afford to send their children abroad. Growing numbers of Chinese and Indians will continue to go abroad for study.

Large numbers – statistics are unavailable – of Chinese and Indian scholars and researchers are working abroad. Probably a majority of these expatriates obtained their doctorates abroad and did not return to their home countries. From 1992 up to 2001, the average stay rate for Chinese and Indians who obtained their doctorates in the United States rose from 65% to 96% and from 72% to 86%, respectively (OECD, 2007a), although many have academic and other relationships with their home countries. According to the Chinese ministry of education, 815 000 students went abroad to study between 1978 and 2004, and 198 000 returned. Statistics for other western countries are likely similar in terms of non-return rates. Since the 1990s, more graduates appear to be returning home due to the improved economic and academic conditions in China and India, and there are deeper relationships between the diasporas and the home country. Both countries have worried about their "brain drains" and have sought, with very limited success, to attract their nationals home.

China has implemented an international education policy since 2000, and India is debating its approach to international higher education. China's multifaceted policy includes aggressive plans to attract international students to China. More than 200 000 international students were studying in China in 2007, with three-quarters of them from Asian countries (Figure 6.2). China awards more than 10 000 scholarships as well (China Scholarship Council, 2007). Many Chinese universities have expanded their campus facilities for international students. Chinese universities see hosting international students partly as a way of earning income as well as adding a valuable international dimension to the institution. Government-sponsored Confucius Institutes, now numbering more than 292 with plans for 1 000 by 2025, provide Chinese-language instruction and cultural programs, mainly on university campuses worldwide.

Figure 6.2. **Distribution of international students in China's higher education (2005)**

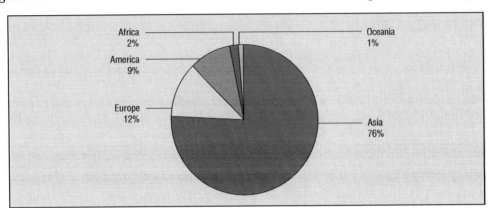

Source: Data from the China Scholarship Council, 2005, *http://en.csc.edu.cn/*.

India's international efforts lag behind those of China. In 2008, approximately 20 000 international students studied in India, most from South Asia, Africa, and from the Indian diaspora. Few Indian universities have either facilities or staff for international students. Some policymakers see a significant potential for India because much of the higher education system teaches in English. However, without significant investment in infrastructure, as well as a more coherent policy, Indian initiatives are unlikely to succeed (Agarwal, 2006).

Of special significance are the respective roles of China and India as regional higher education powers. China is already a key partner with its neighbours in northeast Asia – hosting, for example, 35 000 students from Korea. India, with South Asia's largest academic system, hosts students and has exchanges with Sri Lanka, Nepal, Bangladesh, and Bhutan. Political differences have so far prevented collaboration with Pakistan.

Other countries see China and India as major markets for their higher education initiatives. Foreign involvement is already significant in both countries, and considerable potential for expansion can be envisaged. For example, 11 000 students are studying in China for British academic degrees through various kinds of collaborative arrangements, and 200 British institutions have programs in China. American academic institutions, such as Johns Hopkins University, the University of Michigan, and many others including numerous small colleges, are also active in China. It is estimated that well over 1 000 foreign academic institutions have some kind of collaborative arrangement in China, including two full-fledged branch campuses of British universities (Fazackerley, 2007). At least 150 foreign academic institutions had various kinds of joint-degree or other collaborative arrangements in India, with the largest number (66) from the United States, second largest (59) from Britain (Helms, 2008). Most collaborations offer professional programs. News reports indicate strong international interest in India, and once legislation is in place the pace of collaboration and involvement is likely to increase significantly.

While China has had legislation in place that regulates foreign collaboration since 2003, India is still in the process of implementing rules. The role of independent branch campuses, ownership of institutions, the role of the private and the for-profit sectors, quality assurance for foreign institutions, the role of franchised overseas degree programs, and other complex issues have proved controversial. A complication in rule making and implementation for both countries are the varying jurisdictions of the central and provincial governments, as well as changing perspectives among policymakers. They seek to maintain control over foreign institutions and programs on their territories while welcoming international involvement (Helms, 2008; Agarwal, 2008).

Both countries, because of their size, the scope of the higher education market, the rise of the middle class, and academic potential, are of great interest to the international academic community. China and India are to play a key international role in higher education – mainly as a source of students and academics and as a place to do higher education "business". This would require both countries to implement transparent policies and regulations concerning foreign collaboration and involvement, in order to protect their own national interests and ensure quality as well as to clarify arrangements for potential overseas partners.

Research universities

At the pinnacle of any academic system are research universities (Altbach and Balán, 2007), which tend to be the link to the international network of science and scholarship, producers of much of the research in the academic system, and educators of the elites for key positions in society. Countries like China and India, with large academic systems and complex economies that are increasingly knowledge based, would tend to benefit from having a number of research universities that can compete with the top universities worldwide and serve the national academic system and rapidly growing economies. Both countries recognise the need for research universities at the top of the academic systems.

In 2008, neither country constituted an academic powerhouse, although China is moving in that direction. Neither country has a single university in the top 100 of the 2008 Shanghai Jiao Tong University's academic ranking of world universities, which mainly measures research productivity (SJTUIHE, 2008). China has two (Peking University and Tsinghua University) and India none in the top 100 of the 2008 *Times Higher Education*/QS ranking, which measures academic reputation as well as performance (*Times Higher Education*, 2008). Hong Kong, which is part of China but not integrated into the Chinese academic system, has several universities in the top ranks of these league tables. However, both systems have ambitions to join the top ranks of research superpowers.

For historical reasons, China and India have specialised research institutions that are separate from the universities. In the Chinese case, the research academies are part of the Soviet legacy of academic organisation. Most of India's research institutes stem from the pre-independence period. The institutes of the academies of science in China have excellent working conditions and generally higher prestige than the universities, and often attract the best talent. The number of research institutes in India is smaller, and their role is not quite so central. Some of the institutions sponsored by the Chinese Academy of

Science (CAS) and the Chinese Academy of Social Sciences offer Master's and doctoral degrees. For example, 30 000 graduate students are enrolled in CAS institutions. Similar institutes in India in some cases offer advanced degrees as well. It is viewed as better to have research and teaching in the same institutions, and some efforts have been initiated in China to integrate the institutes with neighbouring universities.

China has a multifaceted program to build world-class research universities, and well over USD 20 billion in purchasing power parity have been spent on building an elite sector in Chinese higher education since 1990s. At the core are several strategies. A series of mergers of more specialised universities were implemented in the 1990s to form the basis of some institutions, essentially re-establishing the comprehensive universities that existed prior to the Soviet-style changes in the 1950s. The most important effort included two major initiatives supported by the central government: the 1993 211 Higher Education Project that identified 100 universities for upgrading and establishing them as research-intensive institutions; in 1998, at the time of Peking University's centenary, the 985 project was inaugurated, aimed at creating 40 "world-class" universities in China (Liu, 2007; Ma, 2007). The 985 project built on China's existing research-oriented universities in all parts of the country but with the predominance in the coastal provinces and in Beijing. Central government funds were provided for infrastructure, including a number of impressive new campuses, and for a range of interdisciplinary centres and other upgrades. Provincial and other authorities gave additional support. For example, the Shanghai government has supported its four 985 project universities, adding resources to those of the central authorities. In some cases, neighbouring universities were merged, new campuses built, and emphasis placed on the research mission. A few additional universities, supported by provincial governments, have also attempted to join the ranks of the research universities.

China's research universities identify with the top world research universities and especially seek to emulate the top American research universities. In this respect, the Academic Ranking of World University – the Shanghai Jiao Tong ranking – emerged from a benchmarking effort of a prominent Chinese university. The 985 project emphasises graduate programs, interdisciplinary centres, and teaching courses and in some cases entire degree programs in English, publication in recognised international academic journals, and hiring faculty with international qualifications. The current Ministry of Education policy will not expand the number of 985 universities but will rather further strengthen the existing institutions. These reforms have had a profound impact on the top level of Chinese higher education. The infusion of funds has permitted impressive new facilities, including some entirely new campuses, to be built. Re-organisation has emphasised interdisciplinary work. Mergers have in some cases created centres of excellence. New organisational structures have strengthened academic productivity and a more effective career structure. The reforms have also diversified the academic system in general and created much greater inequalities between institutions and sectors. The variations in quality, funding, mission, and other factors between the top and the middle and bottom of the academic system are much greater than prior to the reforms.

India has no world-class research universities (Jayaram, 2007). The global higher education rankings include just a few Indian institutions, mainly the Indian Institutes of Technology, which are not universities but rather small high-quality technology institutions. While a small number of India's 431 universities have excellent research-focused departments and institutes, it is fair to say that few if any can claim overall excellence as research universities. The 25 universities sponsored by the central government tend to be of higher quality than the 230 state universities. Six of the central and 114 of the state universities have affiliated colleges – some 20 667 in all (Ministry of Human Resource Development, 2009). The highly regarded Indian Institutes of Technology and Indian Institutes of Management and a handful of other specialised institutions are recognised as internationally competitive. The Indian Institutes of Technology, for example, have a total enrolment of around 30 000 combined – more than half at the undergraduate level. But they are all small specialised institutions. Their research productivity, while impressive, is limited by the size and mission of the institutions (Indiresan, 2007).

The Achilles' heel of Indian higher education indeed represents the traditional universities. The state universities, particularly, are characterised by endemic underfunding, political interference, often a significant degree of corruption in academic appointments and sometimes admissions and examinations, and inadequate and ill-maintained facilities (Indiresan, 2007). The tremendous burden of supervising the affiliated colleges saps the energy and creativity of most universities. The University of Mumbai, for example, has 364 affiliated colleges, while the University of Calcutta has 170 and Delhi University 83. Although most of the students are located in the undergraduate colleges, the universities are responsible for examinations of huge numbers – for Mumbai, Calcutta, and Delhi, respectively. It is hardly surprising that the few successful reform efforts in the past half-century have bypassed the traditional universities and have established entirely new institutions, such as the Indian Institutes of Technology. The fact is that unless the traditional universities can be reformed and improved, Indian higher education will not be able to progress beyond the excellent periphery of the Indian Institutes of Technology and related mainly specialised institutions.

While many official reports have called for the reform of university and college affiliation, almost nothing has been accomplished in a half-century. Starting with the University Education Commission (Radhakrishnan Commission) in 1948-49 and proceeding to the 1964–66 Education Commission (Kothari Commission), numerous thoughtful recommendations for higher education reform were made, including proposals to foster research universities, "decouple" the colleges from the universities, and many others. Yet, the reforms have been targeted in establishing, for example, the Indian Institutes of Technology, the Indian Institutes of Management, and other innovations all, while ignoring the traditional universities. A combination of the lack of political will, entrenched academic and at times political interests, a divided political system, and resource constraints have contributed to this gridlock (Jayaram, 2007, pp. 74-6).

Current government plans to build new universities do not address the perplexing problems of reform. Initiatives to establish new Indian Institutes of Technology, central universities, technological institutes, and other institutions also do not grapple with the problems of the existing universities, nor do they indicate how these new universities will improve upon the existing organisation or other practices of the existing institutions. Indeed, the beacons of excellence in Indian higher education are likely to continue to be outside the traditional universities.

China is well on the way to creating world-class research universities and has devoted major resources and considerable planning to them. Significant challenges remain – including building an effective academic culture, academic freedom and other issues – but a very promising start has been made. India remains far from creating globally competitive research universities.

The Academic profession and academic culture

At the centre of any postsecondary institution stands the academic profession. Without well-educated and committed professors, no academic institutions can be academically successful. China and India, in part because of the scale of their academic systems, face major challenges in developing and sustaining a professoriate capable of providing instruction and leadership. The large number of academics needed for these expanding systems of higher education is unprecedented. Providing training at the doctoral level for a substantial proportion of the academic staff will be difficult to accomplish. Creating and sustaining conditions for academics to do their best work and to retain the "best and brightest" in the profession is also a concern. Finally, establishing an "academic culture" that promotes meritocracy, honesty, and academic freedom is mandatory for a successful academic system.

More than 550 000 full-time academics are teaching in Indian colleges and universities and 1 200 000 in China. An additional 350 000 part-time instructors work in Chinese higher education and a small but growing number in India. The large majority of academics are teachers of undergraduate students and do little, if any, research. Most academics in both countries do not have a doctorate and some have earned only a bachelor's degree; only 9% have doctorates in China, although 70% hold doctorates in the research universities, and around 35% in India, again with a higher proportion of PhDs in research-oriented university departments. Teaching loads tend to be quite high for those exclusively teaching undergraduates. Conditions for academics in colleges and universities located in rural areas and less-developed regions compare unfavourably with urban institutions. On the other hand, the small minority of academics, probably under 3% of the total, who teach graduate (postgraduate) students and are appointed to research-oriented departments in the better universities, are much better off in terms of remuneration and working conditions. In India, only academics holding positions in university departments and in specialised research institutions are expected to do research. Most, if not all, of these academics have doctoral degrees, often from distinguished universities in the West (Chen, 2003).

China and India face special problems because of the size, diversity, and organisation of their academic professions (Chen, 2003; Jayaram, 2003). Both academic systems have a long tradition of highly bureaucratic university management and major constraints on academic freedom. In the case of India, there was limited academic freedom and great deal of bureaucracy aimed at keeping academics, and students, under control prior to independence (Basu, 1974). China has seen a great deal of societal disruption, including the decade-long Cultural Revolution that closed the entire academic system, and frequent policy changes that have affected the academic profession.

Academic freedom is a central issue in both countries, although India can claim a better environment in this area. In India, academic freedom is official policy throughout the academic system. The problem concerns local adherence to its norms. A combination of overweening administrative power, sensitivity to religious and ethnic sensibilities, and some political inference in academic matters affects academic freedom. Despite these constraints, scholars can in general publish without restriction in academic journals or in newspapers or other publications. Violations of academic freedom are more the exception than the rule.

The situation in China differs considerably, although conditions are improving (He, 2002). Informal yet widely acknowledged restrictions on academic freedom exist in some fields. Academics, especially in the social sciences and some humanities fields, understand that some areas of research and interpretation are "off limits" and certain kinds of criticism may result in sanctions, including dismissal and on rare occasions prosecution. Academic journals, while providing more leeway than the popular media, exercise some controls over what can be published, and self-censorship is common. As Chinese universities seek to compete globally, academic freedom is becoming more recognised as a necessary part of a world-class university.

An effective academic culture must be free of corruption. Yet, some problems of corruption exist in both countries. In China, the most visible aspects of academic corruption are in the occasional reports of plagiarism and the misuse and at times falsification of data. In some less prestigious universities, there have been reports of bribery for admission or grades. When discovered, offenders are often humiliated and punished. Yet such corruption seems embedded in academe at least to some extent if one can judge from newspaper and Internet reports. The problem in India is much more widespread and generic, involving some plagiarism and related misconduct. In addition, academic administrators and sometimes professors may practice bribery in the admission of students, falsifying examination results, selling exam questions and answers, and other kinds of malfeasance. Academic corruption is more serious in some parts of India and in some institutions than it is in others. For example, the elite Indian Institutes of Technology, Indian Institutes of Management, and other top institutions have seen very few cases.

In order to build an effective academic system, the academic profession must be adequately paid and enjoy adequate campus working conditions. In a recent international survey of academic salaries, China and India were at the bottom of a group of 15 countries (Rumbley, Pacheco, and Altbach, 2008). At an average of USD 1 182 for China and USD 1 547 for India, salaries were about 25% of US averages and about 30%-35% most western European salaries yet permitting academics in both countries to live in the middle class of their countries. These comparisons are made on the basis of 2008 purchasing power parity. Further, unlike in many countries, most Chinese and Indian academics acquire full-time appointments. Many were able to earn more income through additional allowances. It is noteworthy that Indian salaries are on average higher than those in China, despite India's lower GDP. Moreover, the Indian government has recently announced plans for a significant salary increase. However, the fact that academic salaries do not compare favourably with the remuneration of similarly educated professionals at home or with academics in the developed countries may mean that many of the best-qualified people choose not to work in universities (see for example Marginson and Van Der Wende, 2009). The profession may not be able to retain the "best and brightest" in many cases.

Building an academic culture and providing adequate salary and working conditions for the professoriate are crucial for the entire profession, especially important for the top of the academic hierarchy. Indeed, building competitive research universities requires a reasonably well-paid professoriate with working conditions at least somewhat comparable to global standards, since top academics are part of a global labour market (Pacheco, Rumbley, and Altbach, 2008). China's top universities, such as Peking University and Shanghai Jiao Tong University, have a flexible remuneration policy that can pay top Chinese academics salaries significantly above local norms and in some cases permitting "star" professors to hold part-time appointments abroad. India has no such policies and, as a result, is unable in most cases to attract its best scholars to return home.

Figure 6.3. **Average academic salaries, selected countries**
USD, 2008 PPP

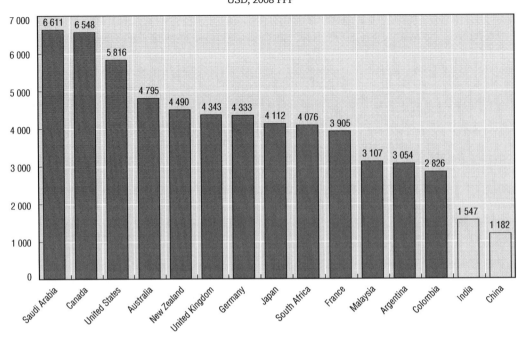

Source: Rumbley, Pacheco, and Altbach (2008).

The common practice in both countries of hiring one's own graduates for teaching positions, while common in many countries, can create problems for building a productive and independent academic culture. The university's own graduates may not be the best possible candidates for positions, and they have been socialised into the culture of the institution and can find it difficult to do their best creative work. They fit too easily into existing departmental and faculty hierarchies. China's top universities have recognised "inbreeding" as a challenge and have put rules into place to stop the practice, but most of the Chinese academic system still uses this hiring practice. Inbreeding is also frequent in India (Jayaram, 2003). Undergraduate colleges affiliated to a university generally hire graduates of that university. In some colleges, applicants for academic jobs can be expected to provide payment to persons hiring them or to the hiring institution – clearly a corrupt practice.

Both countries have elements of an effective academic culture in some of their top institutions as well as in other parts of the academic system. But the challenge remains to embed a transparent and competitive academic culture to reward merit in hiring and promoting academics up the ranks. Petty corruption persists at some institutions, as do overly bureaucratic controls, formal and informal limitations on academic freedom, the practice of inbreeding, and other problems. These issues hinder creating a world-class academic culture.

6.4. Societal challenges

Access and equity

The population of China exceeded 1.3 billion and that of India 1.1 billion in 2007 (World Bank, 2008b). One of the greatest challenges to higher education in both countries consists of providing access to the growing segments of the population demanding postsecondary education. A related issue is providing equity to population groups underrepresented in the student population. At present, India is still at the "elite" stage of access, with 12% higher education gross enrolment ratio in 2006, up from 6% in 1991 (World Bank, 2008a). The government has recognised the need to expand access to from 10% (Trow, 2006) to 15% of the age cohort during the 11th Five-Year Plan (2007-12) and to 21% by the end of the following plan, in 2017. This expansion would be the largest in India's history and will require a dramatic growth in institutions as well as expenditure. China, already at a 22% participation level in 2006 against 3% in 1991 (World Bank, 2008a), is approaching mass access. It builds from a higher base, but significant expansion will take place as well. In 2005, the minister of education indicated that the participation rate would be 40% by 2020. Indeed, the majority of the world's enrolment growth in the coming two decades will take place in just these two countries (Kapur and Crowley, 2008).

Figure 6.4. **Higher education participation in China and India (gross enrolment ratio 1991-2006, official targets for 2017 and 2020)**

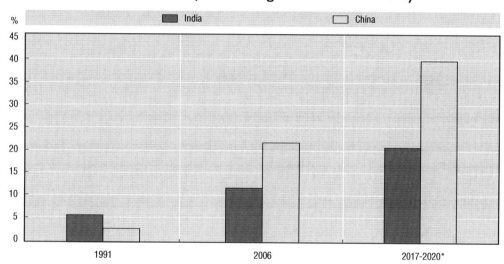

* Official targets

Sources: World Bank (2008a); Kapur and Crowley (2008); Trow (2006).

Both countries recognise the need to focus more on postsecondary education, and they have seen dramatic expansion in the past decade and plan on continued growth in the coming decades. A variety of strategies are evident, and they are similar in both countries. The private sector is a major source of "demand absorption". The countries have permitted the continuing expansion of private institutions, although both are ambivalent about the conditions under which the private sector should function, the role of for-profit institutions, and other topics (see the following section).

Not the same issue as access, equity involves higher education for population groups that may be underrepresented in the system and includes, depending on the country or region, gender and socio-economic inequalities, rural and urban disparities, and ethnic or other minority groups. The urban and rural divide, both in China and India is immense, with implications for access and equity. In common with many developing countries, a majority of the population lives in rural areas. Even with the dramatic urbanisation in both countries, a substantial majority of the population is still rural, where income, literacy, access to education at all levels, life expectancy, and quality of life measures are all lower than for the urban areas. Access to higher education is dramatically lower, and quality tends to be lower as well.

Equity is in many ways a more difficult challenge than higher education access. Historically, equity has been a major concern of Chinese and Indian government planners. Many of the top universities have regional quotas so that applicants from all over China can get access. In the past few decades, equity has become a less important priority than access. In higher education as in other aspects of the society and economy, the disparity between the affluent coastal areas and the vast interior is significant. Rates of access to higher education in western China are significantly lower than in the coastal provinces and the large cities, as is the overall quality of the universities (OECD, 2007b). Fewer data are available concerning access rates for China's minority groups and disparities according to gender or social class. From the beginning of the People's Republic, China has devoted considerable attention to these inequalities by encouraging expansion of access in western China. In the 1980s, loan programs were implemented to permit students from poor backgrounds to participate in higher education. However, major inequalities persist. It is possible that the continued prosperity in the high growth regions of the country may raise inequalities, although data are unavailable.

The most controversial issues in Indian higher education include the array of policies aimed at improving access and equity for tribal groups, lower castes, and *dalits* (a self-designation of the traditional "untouchable" or lower groups in the Hindu caste system). Policies relating to what in India is called "positive discrimination" are politically charged and often the subject of acrimonious debate, legal acrimony, and litigation. Since independence in 1947, positive discrimination, also called reservations, throughout the public employment system and in higher education in India has meant that *dalits* and some additional lower castes (known as Other Backward Castes) and tribal groups have proportions of seats in colleges and universities, positions in the civil service, and some other sectors reserved for them. This means that postsecondary institutions are required to hire, and enrol, a fixed percentage of these groups – almost half of the total. While positive discrimination has been a policy of the Indian government for decades, a considerable debate is still under way about both the justification and the effectiveness of the policy. Positive discrimination has been claimed as largely ineffective in raising the status of the groups it is intended to help and a mistaken social policy in a meritocratic society (Mahajan, 2007). At the same time, court orders have expanded the scope of the "reservation" system to institutions, such as the Indian Institutes of Technology, where it was not fully in place before. A 2008 government decision mandating that the Indian Institutes of Technology, seen as bastions of meritocracy, must hire professors according to the strictures of the positive discrimination laws has renewed debate about the policy in general.

In many parts of the world, despite years of policy innovation, equity remains a key dilemma and access still of concern for some social groups. For China and India, as well as other countries, access is in some ways the easiest problem to solve. Permitting the expansion of the private sector, various kinds of affirmative action programs, building postsecondary institutions in remote areas, providing financial incentives to students from disadvantaged groups, and other policies have helped to varying degrees. But inequality remains a characteristic of higher education systems, and China and India are no exceptions. Their challenges are greater in scale than those facing other countries only because of the large populations and the combination of disadvantages endemic in their societies.

Private provision

Worldwide, private higher education is the fastest-growing segment of postsecondary education (Altbach, 2005). China and India both have significant private higher education sectors, even though China's private higher education sector remains a relatively small part of total enrolments and number of institutions. About 4 300 000 students attend private postsecondary institutions – 1 600 000 in private universities, 1 800 000 in second-tier colleges of public universities, and 870 000 in other kinds of institutions (China, Ministry of Education, 2007). In addition, there is a large private vocational sector, and many of the private institutions are not authorised to grant degrees. A small number call themselves universities, and a smaller proportion has been awarded the right by the Ministry of Education to offer university degrees. Some of the new private schools are nonprofit entities, while others are owned by business enterprises, families, or other arrangements. While accurate statistics concerning the total number of private institutions in all categories – including many that are not authorised to offer degrees – are unavailable, the number is well over 1 000. Permission to establish private higher education institutions has occurred relatively recently, between 1982 and 1986, and most private institutions have been in existence for only a decade or two.

Semiprivate colleges have also been established. Some Chinese universities, to earn extra income and meet local demand for access, have established private affiliated colleges that have a relationship with the sponsoring university. Classes are taught by regular university staff for the most part. Some problems involve the degrees offered by these affiliated institutions. Many students expected that regular university degrees would be offered, although the actual degrees were not from the sponsoring institution. Conditions of study vary in these affiliated colleges. In some cases, students sit in the same classrooms with regular students, while in others they attend in the evening. In still other cases, the affiliated colleges are entirely different buildings.

In general, the private sector has grown in response to the demand for access to higher education and an interest in some vocational courses that cannot be met by the existing universities. The regulations concerning earning profits from higher education institutions are not entirely clear, and many different arrangements, often far from transparent, seem to be in place. Government agencies try to maintain some quality and fiscal control over the private sector. However, regulations change, and the numbers of institutions have been growing rapidly, problems of management, financial transparency, and quality assurance exist (OECD, 2007b). Nonetheless, the private sector is expanding and is becoming more diversified as a few private universities seek to compete with some of the better Chinese universities. For the present, however, if a student has a choice of enrolling in a public or a private institution, he or she will consistently choose the public institution, not only because of the cost of tuition (ranging between RMB 2000 and RMB 6 000 in public institutions, against RMB 8 000 and RMB 13 000 in private ones [OECD, 2007b]) but because of prestige as well. A few private universities have partnerships with overseas institutions. This may change in the coming decades as the private sector develops and perhaps partners with overseas universities, but the future is far from clear for the private sector. It is now a visible part of the Chinese higher education landscape and will likely expand to meet growing enrolment demand.

The situation in India is immensely more complicated (Gupta, Levy, and Powar, 2008). Technically speaking, most Indian undergraduate students study in private colleges;

perhaps 95% of these institutions are managed by private agencies such as religious organisations, cultural agencies, philanthropic groups, and others. Many, however, receive significant funds from government sources. These colleges are called "aided" institutions. Other colleges may receive no funding from government. These include many medical colleges (medicine is an undergraduate subject in India). Almost all are affiliated to universities.

A small number of private universities have been approved by state or central government authorities to offer degrees. These institutions do not receive any government funding and rely on tuition and in some cases philanthropic donations for funding. In addition, there are private specialised post-secondary institutions, mainly business schools. Some have degree-awarding authority while others offer only certificates because they lack government degree-granting approval. Almost all are financed by tuition payments.

Several of the older private universities have achieved considerable respect. The Birla Institute of Technology and Science, established in the 1900s and upgraded to "deemed university" status in 1964, is one of the top institutions in the country. Manipal University, founded in 1953 as a medical school, now has 24 colleges and 80 000 students in many disciplines and branches in Nepal, Malaysia, Dubai, and the Caribbean. Several of India's large corporations are in the process of starting universities, among them Reliance Industries, Mahindra and Mahindra, and the Vedanta Group. They are stimulated, among other things, by a recognition that many of India's existing universities are of low quality.

The growth of the private sector in India has been dramatic. Currently, 43% of the institutions and 30% of student enrolments are in private unaided institutions (Agarwal, 2009, p. 70). While accurate statistics are unavailable, the large majority of these institutions are for-profit or quasi for-profit, and many are family owned.

The expansion of the private sector has been facilitated by the complex and often dysfunctional regulatory framework for higher education in India. The state governments, along with central authorities, have the power to recognise colleges and universities. For example, in 2002, the state of Chhattisgarh, in a less-developed part of India, suddenly passed legislation for the recognition of private universities; 134 quickly applied and 97 were approved. Most of these were not located within the state but were in all parts of India. Some other states also recognised new private institutions. The University Grants Commission, seeing this anarchic situation, stepped in with new regulations, and after considerable dispute, the Indian Supreme Court recognised the authority of the University Grants Commission over the state governments in 2004. This example illustrates the complexity and the lack of overall direction relating to aspects of higher education policy making in India.

Financial and ethical lapses can be seen in some of the new private institutions. Enforcement of standards is lax and regulatory frameworks inadequate – leaving room for such problems as charging high fees for admission, a practice called "capitation fees" (substantial fees charged at the time of matriculation), tuition fees higher than those allowed by regulations, corrupt practices in admissions, hiring, and the award of degrees, and others. These issues have tarnished the reputation of the private sector (Gupta, 2008).

Private higher education in China and India is expanding. It is already a significant part of the higher education system, and its expansion will continue for a simple reason: the public sector is simply unable to provide the financial resources needed to provide the access demanded by growing populations. It is likely that the private sector will continue to function mainly at the bottom of the academic hierarchy, will be largely vocational in nature, and, as the economists say, will be mainly "demand absorbing". Both countries face a significant challenge to create a stable and transparent regulatory framework that provides both ground rules for the private sector and procedures for quality assurance and financial accountability. Questions such as the role of the for-profit sector and whether foreign private providers can link with local private universities and colleges remain mainly unanswered. While a few relatively high-quality private institutions now exist in both countries, fully comprehensive private research universities in the American or Japanese models are unlikely in China or India. The cost of starting and sustaining such universities is just too high.

6.5. The future

China and India are already major global forces in higher education (Altbach, 2007). As they move toward international norms of access to higher education, China and India could together be expected to account for over half of the global increase in student numbers. This will mean a dramatic expansion in the academic profession, as well as the need for more laboratory equipment and facilities, advanced computers, and other infrastructure. Some of the demand can be met internally, but it is likely that China and India will look abroad as well. Part of the expansion will be at the level of advanced graduate training. Both countries now have inadequate capacity for producing master's and doctoral degrees. The cost of adding facilities is high. Both countries will be required to provide significant additional financial support for higher education over the coming decades.

Part of the expansion will depend on the continued growth of the private sector and on distance education. The countries have yet to fully integrate the private higher education sector into the higher education system or to create appropriate regulatory and quality assurance frameworks for the private sector. Some ambivalence about the private sector continues. In the coming years the private sector must be integrated into the mainstream if expansion is to be fully accomplished.

China and India will play a major role in global higher education. These two countries are likely to continue to send large numbers of students abroad for advanced study and are likely to account for more than one-third of the total worldwide overseas student population. It is quite likely that large numbers of Chinese and Indian graduates will remain abroad although the proportions returning home will probably increase substantially given better opportunities for positions at home. Over the past several decades, about 80% of graduates from the two countries have not returned home (Agarwal, 2009). That percentage is likely to drop substantially although the proportion of returning will depend on salaries and working conditions at home. China, especially, has been creating opportunities in its universities for foreign-trained graduates.

Both countries could increasingly become hosts for students from abroad. To attract international students, China is already initiating plans and achieving considerable success. Providing that higher education institutions are upgraded, the Chinese and Indian economies rise in the world economy and these countries are seen as academic centres, students from abroad will be attracted. The largest numbers could be expected come from East and South-East Asia in the case of China, and South Asia in the case of India.

China and India may turn into major markets for higher education initiatives from abroad. As of 2009, both countries are considering a philosophy concerning foreign educational providers and are implementing regulatory frameworks to permit foreign involvement. Expansion requirements and efforts to improve quality can both benefit from international participation, although each country would need to develop a nationally beneficial policy framework for working with foreign providers. The issues are complex (see also McBurnie and Ziguras, 2009; Knight, 2008), and it is as yet unclear how a possible implementation of the General Agreement on Trade in Services (GATS) might impact on national policies (OECD, 2007a).

Will China and India emerge as "research superpowers" and develop world-class research universities in the coming decades? It is quite likely that China will have considerable success in building internationally competitive research universities. The universities developed with assistance from the 985 and 211 projects are making major progress. Continued development requires sustained support. A few globally competitive research universities do not prove that China will become a research superpower, but it will likely join the ranks of the major research-producing countries. Its top universities are likely to be among the key research institutions in the world in the coming two decades if current trends continue. It is much less likely that India will achieve this level of success. Its current top institutions, the Indian Institutes of Technology, and a few others, are too small and specialised to become world-class research universities, and current plans do not show that India is developing a realistic strategy. Despite the use of English as the main academic language and the existence in India of many extraordinarily well-trained and bright scholars and scientists, it seems unlikely that India will have internationally competitive research universities in the coming several decades.

Both countries show signs of making better use of their academic diasporas, as large numbers of often highly qualified Chinese and Indian researchers and scholars are working abroad. This key group can be mobilised to assist academic development and link with the international academic community.

While it is certain that China and India are two of the world's largest academic systems, it is less clear that these systems will be globally competitive. As noted, China has made considerable progress with its top institutions and India has illustrated with the Indian Institutes of Technology and a few other institutions that high standards are possible. Yet, the overall excellence and effectiveness of the systems themselves need improvement. The problem of quality, and the related issues of whether graduates are qualified for the labour market, remain in question. Generally, the overall standards tend to decline in an academic system that is expanding dramatically. It is rather unlikely that these countries can avoid that phenomenon. It seems that China and India will, at the least, not see significant reform in the overall academic quality of higher education. An effective quality-assurance system can help to ensure standards, but neither country has such a system in place currently capable of overall supervision. The systems will probably become more stratified, with a small number of research universities at the top and very large numbers of fairly unselective colleges and universities at the bottom.

A complex and diversified higher education system that includes some world-class universities is needed for the future economic development of China and India as both countries build more sophisticated economies and require larger numbers of highly educated personnel and research. Future expansion of numbers and institutions can be anticipated. Qualitative improvement is likely as well, but less assured. It is clear that higher education in China and India will undertake a significant impact both within these key countries and on the global higher education system.

Note

1. *www.mckinsey.com/ideas/mgi/.*

Bibliography

Agarwal, P. (2006), "Higher Education Services and Trade Liberalization," in R. Chanda (ed.), *Trade in Services and India: Prospects and Strategies.* Wiley-India, New Delhi, pp. 299-358.

Agarwal, P. (2008), "India in the Context of International Student Circulation: Status and Prospects," in H. de Wit *et al.* (eds.), *The Dynamics of International Student Circulation in a Global Context,* Sense, Rotterdam, pp. 83-112.

Agarwal, P. (2009), *Indian Higher Education: Envisioning the Future,* Sage, New Delhi.

Altbach, P. G. (2005), "The Private Higher Education Revolution: An Introduction," in P. G. Altbach and D. C. Levy, *Private Higher Education: A Global Revolution,* pp. 1-13. Sense Publishers, Rotterdam, the Netherlands.

Altbach, P. G. (2006), "The Foreign Student Dilemma," in P. G. Altbach, *Comparative Higher Education,* pp. 225-48. Center for International Higher Education, Boston College, Chestnut Hill, MA.

Altbach, P. G. (2006), "Tiny at the Top." *Wilson Quarterly,* Autumn, pp. 49-51.

Altbach, P. G. (2007), "Fostering Asia's Brightest," *Far eastern Economic Review,* January-February, pp. 53-57.

Altbach, P. G. and J. Balán (eds.) (2007), *World Class Worldwide: Transforming Research Universities in Asia and Latin America,* Johns Hopkins University Press, Baltimore.

Basu, A. (1974), *The Growth of Education and Political Development in India, 1898-1920,* Oxford University Press, Delhi.

Ben-David, J. and A. Zloczower (1962), "Universities and Academic System in Modern Societies," *European Journal of Sociology,* Vol. 3, No. 1, pp. 41-82.

Chen, X. (2003), "The Academic Profession in China," in P. G. Altbach (ed.), *The Decline of the Guru: The Academic Profession in Developing and Middle-Income Countries,* Palgrave-Macmillan, New York, pp. 107-35.

China Scholarship Council (2007), *Annual Report 2007,* China Scholarship Council, *http://en.csc.edu.cn/uploads/20080813132840281.pdf.*

China, Ministry of Education (2007), *National Statistical Gazette of Educational Development,* Ministry of Education, Beijing.

Fazackerley, A. (2007), *British Universities in China.* Agora: The Forum for Culture and Education, London.

Gupta, A. (2008), "Judicial Interventions and Private Higher Education in India," in Gupta, A., D. C. Levy, and K. B. Powar (eds.), *Private Higher Education: Global Trends and Indian Perspectives.* pp. 239-53. Shipra, Delhi.

Gupta, A., D. C. Levy, and K. B. Powar (eds.) (2008), *Private Higher Education: Global Trends and Indian Perspectives.* Shipra, Delhi.

Hayhoe, R. (1999), *China's Universities, 1895-1995: A Century of Cultural Conflict.* Comparative Education Research Centre, University of Hong Kong, Hong Kong.

He, Q. (2002), "Academic Freedom in China." *Academe* (May-June).

Helms, R. M. (2008), *Transnational Education in China: Key Challenges Critical Issues and Strategies for Success,* Observatory on Borderless Higher Education, London.

Hindu (2008), "Manmohan: We are Destined to Become Knowledge Superpower," 20 December 2008.

Indiresan, P. V. (2007), in P. G. Altbach and J. Balán (eds.), *World Class Worldwide: Transforming Research Universities in Asia and Latin America,* Johns Hopkins University Press, Baltimore, pp. 95-121.

Jayaram, N. (2003), "The Fall of the Guru: The Decline of the Academic Profession in India," in P. G. Altbach (ed.), *The Decline of the Guru: The Academic Profession in Developing and Middle-Income Countries,* Palgrave-Macmillan, New York, pp. 199-230.

Jayaram, N. (2004), "Higher Education in India: Massification and Change," in P. G. Altbach and T. Umkoahi (eds.), *Asian Universities: Historical Perspectives and Contemporary Challenges.* Baltimore, MD: Johns Hopkins University Press, pp. 85-114.

Jayaram, N. (2007), "Beyond Retailing Knowledge: Prospects for Research-Oriented Universities in India," in P. G. Altbach and J. Balán (eds.), *World Class Worldwide: Transforming Research Universities in Asia and Latin America,* Johns Hopkins University Press, Baltimore, pp. 70-94.

Jha, A. (2009), "Abysmal Global Ranking of India's Best University" *Education World* (February), pp. 64–72.

Kapur, D. and M. Crowley (2008), *Beyond the ABCs: Higher Education and Developing Countries.* Working Paper Number 139, Center for Global Development, Washington, DC.

Kaul, J. N. (1974), *Higher Education in India, 1951-1971: Two Decades of Planned Drift.* Indian Institute of Advanced Study, Simla.

Knight, J. (2008), *Higher Education in Turmoil: The Changing World of Internationalization.* Sense Publishers, Rotterdam, Netherlands.

Li, Y., J. Whalley, S. Zhang, and X. Zhao (2008), *The Higher Educational Transformation of China and Its Global Implications,* Working Paper 13849. National Bureau of Economic Research, Cambridge, MA.

Liu, N. C. (2007), "Research Universities in China: Differentiation, Classification, and Future World-Class Status," in P. G. Altbach and J. Balán (eds.), *World Class Worldwide: Transforming Research Universities in Asia and Latin America,* Johns Hopkins University Press, Baltimore, pp. 54-69.

Ma, W. (2007), "The Flagship University and China's Economic Reform," in P. G. Altbach and J. Balán (eds.), *World Class Worldwide: Transforming Research Universities in Asia and Latin America,* Johns Hopkins University Press, Baltimore, pp. 31-53.

Mahajan, N. (2007), "The Cream of India's Colleges Turns Sour," *Far eastern Economic Review,* January-February, pp. 62-65.

Marcucci, P.N. and D.B. Johnstone (2005), "Tuition policies in a Comparative Perspective: Theoretical and Political Rationales", State University of New York at Buffalo.

Marginson S. and M. Van Der Wende (2009), "Europeanisation, International Rankings and Faculty Mobility: Three cases in Higher Education Globalisation", in *Higher Education 2030, Volume 2: Globalisation,* OECD Publishing, Paris.

McBurnie, G. and C. Ziguras (2009), *Transnational Education: Issues and Trends in Offshore Higher Education,* Taylor and Francis, London.

Min, W. (2004), "Chinese Higher Education: The Legacy of the Past and the Context of the Future," in P. G. Altbach and T. Umkoahi (eds.), *Asian Universities: Historical Perspectives and Contemporary Challenges,* Baltimore, MD: Johns Hopkins University Press, pp. 53-84.

Ministry of Human Resource Development, India (2009), *India: UNESCO Country Report,* Ministry of Human Resource Development, New Delhi.

Organisation for Economic Co-operation and Development (OECD) (2007a), *Cross-border Tertiary Education: A Way Towards Capacity Development,* OECD Publishing, Paris.

OECD (2007b), *Thematic Review of Tertiary Education: China,* OECD Publishing, Paris.

Rumbley, L. E., I. F. Pacheco, and P. G. Altbach (2008), *International Comparison of Academic Salaries: An Exploratory Study,* Boston College Center for International Higher Education, Chestnut Hill, MA.

Shanghai Jiao Tong University Institute of Higher Education (SJTUIHE) (2008), *Academic Ranking of World Universities, http://ed.sjtu.edu.cn/ranking.htm*

Surowiecki, J. (2007), "India's Skills Famine." *New Yorker,* April 16, p. 54.

Tilak, J. B. G. (2007), "Knowledge Commission and Higher Education," *Economic and Political Weekly,* 24 February 2007, pp. 630-32.

Times Higher Education (2008), World University Rankings, *The Times Higher Education Supplement, www.thes.co.uk.*

Trow, M. (2006), "Reflections on the Transition from Elite to Mass to Universal Access: Forms and Phases of Higher Education in Modern Societies since World War II," in J. J. F. Forest and P. G. Altbach (eds.), *International Handbook of Higher Education, Vol. 1.* Springer, Dordrecht, pp. 329–46.

UNESCO Institute of Statistics (UIS) (2009), Education Statistics, accessed in February 2009. *http://stats.uis.unesco.org/unesco/ReportFolders/ReportFolders.aspx.*

World Bank (2008a), World Bank Data and Statistics, accessed in July 2008. *http://go.worldbank.org/4C55Z0H7Z0.*

World Bank (2008b), *World Development Indicators Database*, revised 10 September 2008, *http://go.worldbank.org/1SF48T40L0.*

Higher Education to 2030
Volume 2: Globalisation
© OECD 2009

Chapter 7

European Higher Education Reforms in the Context of the Bologna Process: How did We Get Here, Where are We and Where are We Going?

by

Johanna Witte*, Jeroen Huisman** and Lewis Purser***

This chapter takes a detailed look into the Bologna Process in Europe and reflects it against the wider global context. It first provides an overview of the complex dynamics of the process, after which it takes stock of the main reforms related to it. The chapter concludes by discussing the persisting challenges, different opportunities and alternative scenarios for the future of European higher education, reflecting also on the potential of the Bologna example to diffuse to the other parts of the world.

*   The Bavarian State Institute for Higher Education Research and Planning (IHF).
** The International Centre for Higher Education Management (ICHEM), University of Bath.
*** Irish Universities Association.

7.1. Introduction

The Bologna Process is a strange and complex undertaking. On the one hand, almost ten years after its inception, it is so well known and thoroughly discussed as the most encompassing and profound set of reforms of European higher education ever, that writing something new and interesting about it seems a real challenge. On the other hand, there are still some deep-rooted misunderstandings about its content, such as that it would prescribe the implementation of a three-year Bachelor and a two-year Masters degree (see Gürüz, 2008, p. 147) – which is definitely not true. There is also confusion about its nature as a fuzzy, continuously evolving, multi-level and multi-actor process. This particular nature makes it difficult to judge its importance, its relevance and its success.

This chapter hopes to do the impossible: write an encompassing overview on the state of the art of reforms on the verge of the magic date "2010" – set as the formal target by which the declaration aims are to be achieved – explain and reflect how this state was achieved and what makes up for the specific, confusing nature of the process, and develop some scenarios for possible futures of the process after 2010. In doing so, it hopes to be interesting reading for audiences both within and outside of higher education, and both within and outside of Europe – as the Bologna Process is increasingly of interest to other regions in the world, who wonder how to judge it and what it means for them (see *e.g.* Adelman, 2008).

The chapter draws on a wide spectrum of available sources, ranging from the self-reports of national governments compiled in the *Bologna Process Stocktaking Report* (2007), and – somewhat more independent – the European University Association's (EUA) periodic Trends reports, through a major study commissioned by the European Commission in 2006 (Huisman *et al.*, 2006) to some purely academic studies such as Witte (2006).[1] All sources have their limits, either because of the thin empirical base upon which their assessments are based, because of the political constraints set by the commissioning institutions, the small range of countries covered, or their limited perspective. The comparably thin empirical basis of this major process is in itself a reflection of its nature: permanently in motion, complex and hard to trace, chronically underfunded, and so political and involving that it is hard to achieve independent assessments by members of the higher education policy and research communities.

But let us turn to how it all developed.

7.2. How did we get here: the Bologna Process in motion

How it all started

While the Bologna Process owes its name to the place of a conference of 29 European ministers in charge of higher education in 1999, its beginning can be traced back to earlier times. One year previously in May 1998, the education ministers of Germany, Italy and England accepted the invitation of their French colleague Claude Allègre to celebrate the 800th anniversary of the Sorbonne, and together they signed the Sorbonne declaration.

The Sorbonne declaration already contained nearly all the important elements of the Bologna Process: the idea of a European higher education area, the convergence aim (referred to as "harmonisation"), the idea of "two main cycles, undergraduate and graduate", that "should be recognised for international comparison and equivalence", the vision of "mutual recognition of higher education degrees for professional purposes" and increased flexibility through the use of a common credit transfer system. It also contained the call for curriculum reform with "multidisciplinary studies, the development of a proficiency in languages and the ability to use new information technology", the concept of lifelong learning ("acquire degrees in due time throughout life") and a call for widening access ("from diverse backgrounds") (Sorbonne joint declaration, 1998).[2]

At the time of the Sorbonne meeting, the four ministers probably did not expect that the initiative would develop into such a far-reaching European reform. For the Italian, German, British and French ministers, signing the declaration was an attempt to join hands to render European higher education more competitive *vis-à-vis* other parts of the world, notably the United States, but also to solve different problems in their own higher education systems by using the declaration for leveraging national reforms (Ravinet, 2006; Witte, 2006, p. 124-28). In the Sorbonne declaration, the four ministers called upon other European colleagues to join the initiative. However some other ministers did not want to sign a document they had not helped to formulate, and therefore a new declaration was drawn up (see Ravinet, 2006 and Hackl, 2001).

But the content of the Bologna declaration came very close to that of the Sorbonne text. Its aims were to realise a European Higher Education Area (EHEA), to promote European citizens' mobility and employability, to achieve "greater comparability and compatibility of higher education systems", and to increase the "international competitiveness" of European higher education. The signatories committed themselves to "co-ordinating... [their] policies" to achieve six objectives by 2010:

- the "adoption of a system of easily readable and comparable degrees, also through the implementation of the Diploma Supplement";
- the "adoption of a system essentially based on two main cycles, undergraduate and graduate";
- the "establishment of a system of credits";
- the "promotion of mobility" of students and academic and administrative staff;
- the "promotion of European co-operation in quality assurance"; and
- the "promotion of the necessary European dimensions in higher education" (Bologna declaration, 1999).

These objectives were later referred to as "action lines". The ministers made a pledge to meet again in two years time "in order to assess the progress achieved and the new steps to be taken" (Bologna declaration, 1999). They would actually meet every two years from then on. The Bologna declaration's action lines provided the benchmark against which progress was measured, and the operational backbone that has triggered reform in the signatory countries.

The particular nature of the policy process

The ensuing policy process stands out for a range of peculiar features that make "Bologna" special, but also hard to grasp and easy to misunderstand. Starting as an intergovernmental initiative of four ministers, the process has become a multi-level, multi-actor, multi-ownership, path-dependent, long-term, and comprehensive policy game, in which the objectives as well as rules of the game are surrounded by some ambiguity and subject to change during the game. It is important to understand a number of these complicating factors, for they not only are key elements of the process itself, they have also largely determined the current state of the art.

The agenda of the Bologna Process has evolved considerably over the past decade, through its biannual conferences. At each Bologna conference, new action lines were added, new aspects highlighted, or the phrasing of existing fields of action adjusted. In Prague (2001), the promotion of lifelong learning, the active participation of higher education institutions and students in the Bologna Process, and the promotion of the attractiveness of the European Higher Education Area were formally included as new action lines, and the need for co-operation in quality assurance endorsed and made more concrete. In Berlin (2003), the "third cycle", i.e. doctoral level education, was added to the agenda and the importance of taking care of the "social dimension" was stressed. In Bergen (2005), the integration of higher education and research, the social dimension, student mobility, and the attractiveness of the European Higher Education Area and co-operation with other parts of the world were highlighted as priorities. Also, the "Standards and Guidelines for Quality Assurance in the European Higher Education Area" were adopted and a European register of quality assurance agencies called for. In London (2007), the establishment of this register was agreed and a strategy for "the European Higher Education Area in a Global Setting" was adopted. In Leuven (2009), the themes of lifelong learning, higher education access, and mobility were emphasised. As a concrete target, it was indicated that at least 20% of those graduating in the European Higher Education Area by 2020 should have had a study or training period abroad. By 2009, the fields of activity had been reorganised into the following eleven "action lines": qualifications frameworks/ the three-cycle system, joint degrees, mobility, recognition, quality assurance, the social dimension, employability, lifelong learning, the European Higher Education Area in a Global Context, stocktaking activities, and plans for "Bologna beyond 2010".[3] The evolving nature of the process' content and the shifting formulations in the communiqué texts make it hard to grasp the process' reach and borders.

The geographical reach of the Bologna Process, too, has significantly expanded within a decade, while new groups of stakeholders have been gradually included. The number of signatory countries increased from 29 to 46 between 1999 and 2007.[4] It reaches far beyond the 27 members of the European Union and now encompasses all signatories of the Council of Europe's European Cultural Convention except for Monaco and San Marino.[5] At the same time, further groups of stakeholders were included in the Bologna Follow-up Group (BFUG), made up of the representatives of all member states of the Bologna Process, the European Commission, and an increasing range of consultative members such as the representative organisations of higher education institutions, students and labour organisations.[6] The follow-up group is chaired by the EU Presidency with the host country of the next Ministerial Conference as vice-chair. In the future this will change to co-chairing by the country holding the EU presidency and a non-EU country (Leuven Communiqué, 2009). A Board, chaired by the EU Presidency and with the next host country as vice-chair, oversees the work between the meetings of the Follow-up Group.

It is clear that a process with such a large and widely varied geographic range of participants, as far as systems and cultures are concerned, has to make compromises regarding the rigour of agreements reached. Furthermore, the involvement of various stakeholders and the change in the composition of the multi-partner consortium contribute to blurring who actually is in charge of the process, who has been in the driving seat and who has been affected. For example, by publishing a series of "Trends reports" with financial support from the European Commission, the European University Association has significantly shaped perceptions and expectations regarding the course of events (Crosier *et al.*, 2007; Haug and Tauch, 2001; Reichert and Tauch, 2003, 2005).

In addition to this, the Bologna Process has a complicated relationship with the EU and the Lisbon Process. Until today, many observers think of Bologna as an "EU process", which it is not. But indeed its relationship with the EU is not trivial. By inviting ministers from both within and outside the EU to join, the initiators of the Bologna conference initially stressed the process' intergovernmental nature. However, the European Commission soon increased its influence in the process through the coinciding Lisbon Process, in addition to taking of a seat in the Bologna Follow-up Group as well as to the sponsoring of conferences, seminars and studies. The Lisbon Process goes back to a meeting of the EU heads of state or government in March 2000 where they launched the ambitious aim to render the EU "the most competitive and dynamic knowledge-based economy in the world" by 2010. The Lisbon agenda primarily focuses on research and development and includes the concrete goal to raise expenditure in this area to 3% of gross domestic products in all countries. While there are clear differences between the Lisbon and Bologna Processes, the similarity of aims and policy modes has led to convergence between them (Van der Wende and Huisman, 2004, pp. 33-34). The European Commission increasingly appropriates the Bologna Process as part of its Lisbon agenda (European Commission, 2005, 2006), under which it sees higher education reforms in Europe through three main lenses: "curriculum", "governance" and "funding".

The Bologna Process is characterised by several inherent ambiguities that simultaneously contain potential for encompassing change. Given the process' intergovernmental nature and the huge number of participating countries, the declarations and communiqués include vague and contradictory paragraphs, leaving some guesswork, interpretation and political scope for those in charge of adaptations at the national level. This has contributed to the unavoidable ambiguities in the process, right from the beginning. At the same time, the ambiguities around the Bologna agreements' significance – legally non-binding but in fact highly committing – together with the multi-level nature of the process gave actors ample room for playing the level game in different ways: either to use the international commitments to push for national reform, or to use the non-binding nature of these commitments to avoid implementing them. The Bologna policy agenda arguably is one of the most encompassing attempts to bring about change in higher education.[7] In most countries, the changes of degree structure have considerable repercussions for other elements of the system, such as funding, curricular cultures, and labour market linkages (see Witte, 2006, p. 77-92), partly due to necessary issue linkages, partly because "the Bologna Process has been [intentionally] used by various actors to address existing imbalances and problems in their inherited higher education systems far beyond the core of the Bologna agreements" (Witte, Van der Wende and Huisman, 2008, p. 228-29). So many governments have used the Bologna Process as a lever to bring about change also in areas only marginally related to the elements of the Bologna Process, or not at all "prescribed" by its agenda. This has led to confusion in national debates about what the Bologna Process really is, and yielded many national interpretations (see also Gornitzka, 2006, and Musselin, 2006).

The difficulty of the Bologna agenda to overcome national institutional structures can be seen as a form of path dependence, but the Bologna Process is also path-dependent in another sense. Its outcomes are to a large extent the result of adaptive and self-fulfilling expectations, learning effects and co-ordination effects (Arthur, 1989; Pierson, 2000). This led to the "lock-in" of sometimes unexpected and not always fully intended solutions. Because of the linkages between national and supra-national policies, the speed of take-up by national governments had feedback impacts on the supra-national agenda (see Witte, 2006, Chapter 5).

To conclude, the Bologna Process will not enter the history books as a reform characterised by clear-cut objectives, instruments, steering and ownership. It is a far cry from a straightforward policy to be implemented by the relevant stakeholders at national and institutional levels. Given its broad agenda and the complex linkages from policy formulation to actual change, it is hard to judge which changes actually go back to the Bologna Process and which ones would have taken place anyway (see also Neave, 2001, pp. 186-87 on Bologna as an act of appropriation). This should be taken into account when judging the process' outcomes.

7.3. Where are we: the state of change

There are too many aspects of the Bologna Process to sketch them all here; a choice has to be made. Degree structures – the move to a common three-cycle system – is certainly what is associated most with the Bologna Process at an aggregate level. We also discuss the state of implementation of some core elements from the "Bologna tool-kit" such as Diploma Supplements, ECTS, and qualification frameworks, and summarise the reforms in the area of quality assurance.[8] The section concludes with some reflections on the implications of the reforms for achieving the Bologna Process's broader objectives.

Achievements in operational aims

Degree structures

While the reform of degree structures certainly is at the heart of the Bologna Process, the length of degrees is not set out in the formal Bologna documents. The Bologna declaration said that a first-cycle degree should last "a minimum of three years" (Bologna declaration, 1999), the only specification we find on the issue. It is only in the accompanying documents such as notes from Bologna seminars or European University Association (EUA) Trends reports, that we find views and expectations formulated on the issue. For example, the first EUA Trends report state that there was "a high degree of convergence towards a duration of five years for master-level studies" (Haug et al., 1999, p. 10). Neither do the official texts state that the first degree should be called "Bachelor", and only the second degree is specifically referred to as "Master and/or doctorate degree" (Haug et al., 1999).[9]

So if we do not find the "3 + 2" model in the Bologna texts, what does the empirical picture look like? It actually looks quite diverse. True, the 3 + 2 model can be conceived of as the "basic model" (Marginson and Van der Wende, 2009), but the considerable number of exceptions to this rule actually undermines this idea, and it seems more adequate to speak of a reference point in the minds of actors. Besides the 3 + 2 structure, 4 + 1 and 3 + 1 models are widespread across the Bologna countries, and there are also models in which "half years" appear. For example, in England and the Netherlands most Masters programmes are one year full-time. The extent of regulation of degree structures also varies: in France, the 3 + 2 model is *legislated* for universities, while in England the picture is the result of institutional choice. Some countries such as Spain and Romania have both opted for the 4 + 1/1½/2 model, where in both cases the Bachelor is fixed by law at four years and the Master is defined less prescriptively between one and two years.

It should however be noted that these models are not implemented across the board, and that for many disciplines, national exceptions are accepted. This is most frequent in health-related fields like medicine, but also *e.g.* in law, engineering and sometimes teacher training (see *e.g.* Huisman *et al.*, 2006). For example in Germany, medical studies are so far fully exempted from the reform of degree structures, in law the debate about possible models has just started, and in teacher training a wide range of pioneering models exists but no agreement has yet been reached. We also see variations between models by institutional type, *e.g.* in the Netherlands, the Bachelor degree lasts four years at *hogescholen* and three years at universities. In Germany, at *Fachhochschulen* many Bachelor programmes last 3½ years to make room for an internship semester, in order to maintain the applied nature of these programmes. In some countries, certain institutional types are more or less exempt from the reform, *e.g.* the *grandes écoles* in France.

Also, implementation paths and speed vary: in some countries, full transition to the new degree structure was legislated early on – in 1999 in Italy, in 2001 in the Netherlands – while in others, a legislative framework was created for the new degrees, but it has been left up to institutions to opt for the transition. This was the case in France and Germany. Even in systems that opted for the Bachelor-Master structure early on, implementation mostly started only for the new first-year undergraduate intake. In most European countries, significant numbers of Bachelor and Master graduates therefore have not yet reached the labour market, and little hard data on their acceptance and success is available. Depending on speed, path and scope of implementation, we still find patchworks of different degree structures co-existing in a range of countries.

Finally, the meaning and implications of the new degree structures also vary: in many European countries, the long "pre-Bologna" university programmes led directly to the Master level, so that the labour market acceptance of the new shorter Bachelor degrees is a challenge. In several European countries the gap between the Bachelor and Master programme at universities is still rather *pro forma*: almost all university students continue to the Master level, sometimes even supported by governmental regulation. For example in law, access to professional training is still at the Master level in nearly all European countries, even where the Bachelor-Master structure has been implemented (Huisman *et al.*, 2006). So overall, it is too early to speak of success or failure, given the recent and limited experiences of Bachelor graduates (Alesi, 2007).

According to the latest EUA Trends report (Crosier *et al.*, 2007, pp. 16-21), based on a survey conducted in winter 2005/2006 to which over 900 European higher education institutions of all descriptions across all Bologna countries responded, 83% of institutions had the three-cycle structure in place, and only 2% did not plan to implement it. While 85% thought that the new degree structure functioned extremely or reasonably well, respondents in institutions also highlighted a range of issues related to the transition. These included difficulties in relationship with national authorities regarding the degree of autonomy and support, feelings that structural reforms are divorced from their objectives, lack of attention to student centred learning, and incoherent and incomplete implementation of the new system. These issues certainly constitute challenges for the future.

Diploma Supplements

The Diploma Supplement is an instrument that dates back to before the Bologna Process, and which was developed by the European Commission, the Council of Europe and UNESCO/CEPES.[10] It is an example of how the Bologna Process has integrated such elements in order to contribute to the realisation of its aims. Basically, the Diploma Supplement is a supplement to the degree certificate, explaining the meaning and status of the qualification achieved to those not familiar with the structure of that higher education system, its grading system, etc., helping them to judge how hard it was to enter and pass the programme. By doing so, the Diploma Supplement is hoped to facilitate the mutual recognition of qualifications for further study and on the labour market, and consequently to encourage greater mobility of students and graduates. At their 2003 meeting in Berlin, the ministers in charge of higher education set the goal that all students would be issued a Diploma Supplement automatically and free of charge by 2005. Table 7.1 gives an overview of the state of the art, drawn from three official reports published by stakeholders of the Bologna Process.

As Table 7.1 shows the implementation phase of Diploma Supplement has been more complicated than originally expected. This reflects the need for effective institutional information systems linking to student records and other data, often requiring considerable investment at local and national levels. The clear differences between levels of implementation across different higher education systems suggest that national initiatives in this area have been important in ensuring effective roll-out and delivery. There appears to be significant work still to be done in the area of communication at local, national and European levels.

Table 7.1. **Implementation of diploma supplement in 2007**

	Report		
	Bologna Process Stocktaking Report	*European University Association Trends Report V*	*Survey by National Unions of Students in Europe (ESIB)*[1]
Focus of the survey	Bologna countries	Higher education institutions in Bologna countries	Students in Bologna countries
State of implementation	Fully implemented in 25 countries	60% of institutions have implemented	
	Implementation underway in 20 countries	40% of institutions plan to implement	n.a.
	Implementation not yet started in one country		
Main challenges identified	n.a.	Lack of effective institutional information systems	Low levels of general awareness regarding Diploma Supplement among students, employers and the general public

n.a.: not applicable.

1. Later European Student Union (ESU).

Sources: Bologna Follow-up Group (2007); D. Crosier, Lewis Purser, and H. Smidt (2007); ESIB Bologna Process Committee 2005-07 (2007).

European Credit Transfer System (ECTS)

The European Credit Transfer System (ECTS) is another Bologna instrument that was developed beforehand and integrated into the process – in this case building on the previous work undertaken by the European Commission in the context of its student mobility scheme ERASMUS. It is now used both as a credit transfer and accumulation scheme, and assigns 60 credits per year based on a notional student workload varying in a range from 1 500 to 1 800 hours. It is not based on contact time with teachers, but is a student-centred instrument, requiring teachers to think about the notional time needed by their students to prepare, understand and study the subject matter both in and outside the classroom. ECTS credits as such do not include measures of level or grades achieved, but there is an ECTS grading scheme recommended for use in the context of international exchange that is based on relative, not absolute achievement. A requirement for proper implementation of ECTS is that institutions modularise their programmes – only then they are able to define learning outcomes for each module and assign credits (see Gehmlich, 2007). Table 7.2 presents the state of the art regarding ECTS implementation.

Table 7.2. **Implementation of European Credit Transfer System (ECTS) in 2007**

	Report		
	Bologna Process Stocktaking Report	European University Association Trends Report V	Survey by National Unions of Students in Europe (ESIB)[1]
Focus of the survey	Bologna countries	Higher education institutions in Bologna countries	Students in Bologna countries
State of implementation	Fully implemented ECTS in 27 countries	75% of institutions use ECTS as a transfer system	n.a.
	Close to fully implemented ECTS in 15 countries	Over 66% of institutions use ECTS as an accumulation system	
	Implementation of ECTS less than 50% in 6 countries		
Main challenges identified	Linking credits with learning outcomes	Linking credits with student workload	Linking credits with learning outcomes
		Linking credits with learning outcomes	Measuring student workload
			Using ECTS for both transfer and accumulation

n.a.: not applicable.
1. Later European Student Union (ESU).
Sources: Bologna Follow-up Group (2007); D. Crosier, Lewis Purser, and H. Smidt (2007); ESIB Bologna Process Committee 2005-07 (2007).

Table 7.2 shows that, by 2007, there was no higher education system remaining in Europe without a credit system in place. This in itself is a major achievement, given that in 1999, at the beginning of the process, very few countries used ECTS for more than to facilitate the exchange of individual students on European mobility schemes such as Erasmus, and overall knowledge in Europe of credit systems as a way of measuring and recording student learning was extremely limited. Despite clear progress since the 2005 reports in terms of the use of ECTS across entire higher education systems, the 2007 reports highlight the challenges of linking credits with learning outcomes, and of measuring student workload.

Qualifications frameworks

Qualifications frameworks are also part of the "Bologna architecture" of compatible and understandable degree structures across Europe, designed to help make qualifications more transparent and learning paths more flexible. They build on other tools such as ECTS and the Diploma Supplement, and like these, are based on the concept of learning outcomes rather than educational input factors. In 2005, an overarching Framework of Qualifications for the European Higher Education Area was formally adopted at the Bologna Process ministerial conference in Bergen. After some initial tensions, the more recent European Qualifications Framework for Lifelong Learning (EQF-LLL) – developed by the European Union within the Lisbon Strategy, covering all levels and areas of education and training systems – is now fully compatible with the Bologna qualifications framework for higher education. At the Bergen conference in 2005, each Bologna country agreed to start developing its own qualifications framework within the overarching European Higher Education Area framework, with the goal that, little by little, all qualifications across each higher education system in Europe could be mapped for the benefit of learners and wider society.

As shown in Table 7.3, the national implementation work for qualification frameworks – in line with the overarching qualifications framework for European Higher Education Area – was still at early stages in most countries in 2007. The awareness of this Bologna tool was low among institutions and there was a lack of effective stakeholder involvement in national discussions. Given that learners should be the major beneficiary of such a framework, there is an understandable unease regarding the early stages of this work so far in a number of countries. Indeed, the Stocktaking report went so far as to express concerns that the goal of having national frameworks in place by 2010 might unduly rush the national process, given that although the principles of a framework can be introduced in legislation relatively quickly, it is likely to take some years before these are fully implemented. Thus one of the important Stocktaking recommendations to participating countries focused on linking the development of these qualifications frameworks to other Bologna action lines, including quality assurance, credit transfer

Table 7.3. **Implementation of national qualification frameworks in line with the overarching Qualifications Framework for European Higher Education Area (EHEA) in 2007**

	Report		
	Bologna Process Stocktaking Report	*European University Association Trends Report V*	*Survey by National Unions of Students in Europe (ESIB)*[1]
Focus of the survey	Bologna countries	Higher education institutions in Bologna countries	Students in Bologna countries
State of implementation	National qualifications frameworks in place in 7 countries	Many institutions unaware of the existence of qualifications framework as well as of a clear concept of what the framework should be	Slow pace of implementation
	A proposal for a national qualifications framework discussed with all relevant stakeholders and a timetable for implementation agreed in 6 countries		
	Development process started in 23 countries		
	Development process not started in 1 country		
Main challenges identified	Risk of conducting the national process too hastily against the target date 2010	Lack of awareness	Lack of effective stakeholder involvement in national discussions

1. Later European Student Union (ESU).

Sources: Bologna Follow-up Group (2007); D. Crosier, Lewis Purser, and H. Smidt (2007); ESIB Bologna Process Committee 2005-2007 (2007).

and accumulation systems, lifelong learning, flexible learning paths and the social dimension.

Quality assurance

The area of quality assurance is one of those within the Bologna Process where huge advances have been made in terms of both policy and implementation since 1999. A major milestone in this development was the statement in the 2003 Berlin Ministerial communiqué that "the primary responsibility for quality assurance lies within each institution itself, and this provides the basis for real accountability of the academic system" (Berlin Communiqué, 2003). The implicit situation in many countries of Europe until then had been that quality assurance had been the job of government or a governmental agency rather than an intrinsic element of institutional responsibility. The explicit ministerial statement can be seen "to have sparked a significant change in attitude and perception" (Crosier *et al.*, 2007), particularly in those countries where university autonomy was previously somewhat limited.

The gradual evolution of existing and newly established national quality assurance systems was given an additional impetus by the adoption by Ministers, at their 2005 meeting in Bergen, of "Standards and guidelines for quality assurance in the European Higher Education Area" (ENQA, 2005). These standards and guidelines were developed during the period 2003 to 2005 as a collaborative project involving the main stakeholder groups (European Association for Quality Assurance in Higher Education – ENQA, European university Association – EUA, European Association of Institutions in Higher Education – EURASHE, European Student Union – ESU), and provide European-wide references for internal quality assurance processes within institutions, for external quality assurance processes carried out by agencies, and for the quality assurance of these agencies themselves.

The standards and guidelines have since then been widely disseminated, discussed and by 2008, referenced more or less explicitly to quality assurance processes and procedures at institutional and national levels across most countries of Europe. They have also become the *de facto* criteria for membership of ENQA, and the explicit standards by which an agency can be deemed of sufficient trustworthiness for inclusion on the recently created European Quality Assurance Register – EQAR (Tück, 2008). The mission of EQAR is to publish a list of legitimate and credible quality assurance agencies that operate in Europe.

The architecture for a transparent and coherent approach to quality assurance, based on common principles, is thus now mostly in place at both European and national levels. These will translate, where not already the case, into revised procedures at institutional level also. At the same time, the quest for the "optimal" balance between state control and institutional autonomy, between quality "assurance" and quality "enhancement", between systems targeted predominantly at the programme versus the institutional level, and between accreditation and evaluation/audit approaches, has not yet come to an end in European higher education. For example, in Germany currently programme accreditation is being complemented – and might one day be replaced by – accreditation of institutional quality assurance systems, while in Sweden institutional evaluation is being replaced by programme evaluation. So while the general trend is one towards more institutional responsibility, the pendulum continues to swing in one or the other direction in different systems (see also Bienefeld *et al.*, 2008; Schwarz and Westerheijden, 2004; Costes *et al.*, 2008; Schwarz and Westerheijden, 2004).

Implications for broader Bologna objectives

Based on the reforms happening in so many areas, it is safe to say that European higher education systems currently find themselves in a particularly dynamic reform period. A great deal of these reforms is taking place in the context of the Bologna – and Lisbon – Processes. When judging their success, it should however be kept in mind this is only partly because these processes have triggered the reforms, but also because the necessary adjustments in reaction to global economic challenges that would take place anyway are framed by these two increasingly interlocking processes.

It is also important to keep in mind that the reforms in the specific areas described above are "only" steps in place to reach broader objectives, such as increasing mobility, employability, and the compatibility and comparability of systems – or, to put it in the context of the Lisbon agenda – the objective of becoming the most competitive and dynamic knowledge-based economy in the world. And this is precisely the area where – at the moment – answers cannot be provided. The intentions of coming to terms with the Bologna Process have primarily focused on the tangible aspects of the reform process and hardly on the outcomes. For most elements of the process, it is too early to measure impact (see Huisman *et al.*, 2006). For example, whether Bachelor graduates will find a suitable place in the labour market, both to their own liking and that of the employers, is still an open question (Alesi, 2007). Cohorts of students need to graduate from converted programmes and labour markets need to be given time to adjust before jumping to conclusions. In some European countries, such as Germany, the government is concerned with study time and is pushing to make the Bachelor degree the regular entry point into the labour market. On the other hand, Adelman (2008) in his study from the US perspective forecasts that studying up to the Master degree will become pervasive on both sides of the Atlantic. Of course the future regarding the Bachelor's degree will not only depend on student preferences, but to a large degree on public and institutional policies on funding and access at Master level.

In light of all this, what can we expect from the future?

7.4. Where are we going: future scenarios

In the Bologna declaration, the year 2010 has been set as the formal target date by which the declaration aims are to be achieved. While it has become clear in the meantime that a reform process as broad as this does not suddenly come to an end at a specific date, there is still something magic about the deadline. Certainly the date has the function of making higher education systems and institutions hurry to get certain reform elements implemented by then, but also to trigger reflections on how far the process has got and where it will move beyond 2010. The Bologna Follow-up Group (BFUG) has already set up a working group whose task it is to deal with both aspects: evaluate the state of reforms and develop avenues for the future.[11]

This chapter cannot anticipate what the BFUG will decide on the formal future of the Bologna Process. However, the Bologna work programme (Bologna Follow Up Group, 2008) makes clear that the current action lines will be important in the near future as well. The BFUG takes almost all elements of the London communiqué as a point of departure for its work programme 2007-09. The host of the Leuven 2009 meeting, the Flemish vice-premier Vandenbroucke, emphasised the issues of transparency, global attractiveness, and social responsibility and responsiveness (ScienceGuide, 2008), topics in line with the BFUG work programme. This begs the question how different the post-2010 process will be. We have argued above that path dependencies play a crucial role in the Bologna Process. For the future this means that once the ship has been set in motion and concrete actions have been taken, the interests of large groups of stakeholders become vested and it will be difficult to change the course of the ship radically.

Three areas in which most interesting tensions and issues will highly likely continue to exist beyond 2010 are: 1) diversity and convergence, 2) profile-building and mobility, and 3) inward and outward orientation. We offer some reflection on the current situation in these areas, where the process might move, and how the tensions might play out in the future.

Diversity and convergence

The current situation

From the beginning, a fundamental contradiction was inherent in the Bologna Process (Huisman, 2009; Witte, 2008). On the one hand, a certain degree of harmonisation and convergence of higher education systems and structures was aimed at to realise the objectives of transparency, mobility, flexibility, comparability and compatibility. On the other hand, these objectives should be reached "within the framework of national competences and taking full respect of the diversity of cultures, languages, national education systems and of university autonomy" (Bologna Declaration, 1999). How to balance the two aims in concrete terms was never defined and has remained subject to continuous negotiation during the ongoing process. Also, it was never made explicit which aspects of higher education systems should be covered by the convergence aims: only "curricular" features such as length of degree programmes, degree titles and levels, or also more general characteristics of higher education systems such as the types of institutions they entail, the way quality of higher education is assured, and the governance of the system? Not being clear about these issues has led to unnecessary misunderstandings and frustrations, as those who measure the success of the process solely by the achievement of system or structural convergence tend to be disappointed, if not upset, by what they regard as little degree of goal achievement so far. Until today, many actors in national higher education systems are confused about what is really required by the "Bologna guidelines" and what is up to the individual signatories.

Empirically, several convergence developments related to the Bologna Process can be found – even if only to a certain extent (Witte, 2006). Certainly the fact that most countries are moving to the three-cycle degree structure, albeit in different forms, is a convergent development, as is the introduction of ECTS and the Diploma Supplement as well as the far-spread efforts to improve quality assurance regimes and coordinate them at European level. Other convergent developments are to be found in the discourses on internationalisation, competitive pressure and marketisation, which permeate all European higher education systems, and in the according trends towards profile-building of individual institutions and competition between them. The latter goes hand in hand with the blurring of boundaries between state-defined institutional types (Witte, Van der Wende and Huisman, 2008).

But when looking in more detail at the actual manifestations the elements of the Bologna Process, we see an enormous level of variety within and across systems – and even within institutions. There are different lengths of cycles across countries and disciplines, the use of degree titles varies and remains non-transparent to the foreign observer and the function and status of the Bachelor degree in national systems varies greatly. Diploma Supplements are sometimes supplied automatically, sometimes only upon request, some are only in the national language. Some quality assurance mechanisms rely largely on institutional audits, others on programme accreditation; some quality assurance mechanisms stress quality enhancement, whereas others stress quality control, etc.

While the situation can be judged as "a glass half full or half empty",[12] we should not solely focus on the convergence issue, because there is a risk of forgetting about other merits of the Bologna Process (Witte, 2008), notably the necessary reforms it has set in motion in many European higher education systems. In all countries, the Bologna Process has been used to address the diverse problems of each national system, and this alone is an important driver to improve the competitiveness of European higher education. At the same time it may ensure a positive impact on the experience of future students through a more student-centred organisation of studies.

The future

From a birds-eye perspective, two scenarios can be imagined for the process beyond 2010. One is that the actors involved in the Bologna Process agree to engage in another round of reforms aimed at further convergence, and maybe in a more precisely targeted way than before. The other is that no such commitment can be reached at European level, and that the pervasive pressures towards diversification and profile-building within systems outweigh any convergence efforts of the past.

In the first scenario, we might one day see a European higher education area which truly resembles a European higher education *system*, as daringly formulated in the original Bologna declaration, with similar categories for institutional types, degrees of similar length and type and with similar titles, a vivid discourse at European level on curricular contents and programme design, similar quality assurance regimes and quality labels for degree programmes, the same way of calculating and transferring European credits and a common template for the Diploma Supplement across the board, and fully coherent qualifications frameworks for higher education. In a such a world, student and graduate mobility would be easy across Europe (note however that students may also be less mobile, because of the "similarity" of other national systems [Teichler, 2009]), and students coming to Europe from other parts of the world would find very transparent conditions, irrespective of which country they choose as their destination. Such a European higher education system would be an attractive orientation mark for other systems in the world.

In the second scenario, the state of convergence that has been achieved so far gets lost again as pressures towards diversification prevail: after the first disillusionment about the degree of convergence achieved up to 2010, the "Bologna argument" does not function any more as a lever for national reforms, and each national system falls back into its own logic and dynamics to an even larger extent than pre-2010. Governments and other Bologna actors do not manage to agree on another round of binding targets, and the coordination mechanisms developed in the course of the Bologna Process are lost. As a result, in ten years' time European higher education systems are as diverse as ever. For example, there will continue to be national-specific and nationally-regulated institutional types such as

Fachhochschulen in Germany, Austria and Switzerland, *hogescholen* in the Netherlands, *ammattikorkeakoulu* in Finland and *grandes écoles* and IUTs in France, and the orientation, value and length of degrees will continue to vary greatly. At the same time, the systems will be speckled with a range of elements that stem from the Bologna Process such as Bachelor degrees, ECTS or accreditation. But behind these "labels", very different contents and ways of functioning can be found in each system. These are driven by the pressures of national problems and national cultures rather than by common goals. Within national systems, diversification is advanced and counteracts further convergence: competition between higher education institutions seeking different market niches and promoting their increasingly specialised profiles increasingly works against any state-defined classifications of institutional types. Such competition is even pushed for by the state under the quest for more efficiency and simple cost-cutting measures. Positively speaking, the strength of the European higher education area, its immense diversity and wealth of national cultures, is as vivid as ever.

So which of the two scenarios is more likely? Commitment to the first scenario is delicate to achieve, first because it requires a clear will to subscribe to a vision that entails a higher degree of convergence than achieved in the past, and second because it implies an implicit confession that actors – governments, administrators and academics – "have not done their homework properly" in the past. While there is considerable endorsement for the process (Huisman *et al.*, 2006), how much buy-in would there be for future change? The position paper of the European University Association (2008), for example, expresses a clear commitment to an engaging continuation of the process beyond 2010, and for "the maintenance of the present BFUG structure" – with an emphasis on broader challenges rather than mere implementation of concrete reform measures, and avoiding to address the convergence versus diversity issue.[13] If a higher degree of convergence was to be achieved in the future, it is obvious that this would require more clarity in which areas (further) convergence should take place, what the timeline is or should be, and which instruments are most suitable to make progress. And when it comes to instruments, it seems clear that those bringing about the change should have a clear perspective on costs (investment of time and energy of academics, managers and administrators to bring about the change) and benefits.

In any case, a European meta-state in the field of higher education – as wrongly assumed already today by some observers – is not in sight. The degree of convergence we will find in the future will continue to be the result either of voluntary agreements of national governments or other actors united in European associations, or of global (market) pressures that affect all European higher education systems in very similar ways. The level of organisational diversity can be even expected to increase rather than decrease in the future (Huisman, 2009). At the same time, when looking at the clear commitment to the overall process of one of its major actors, the European University Association, one may say that the European Higher Education Area and the associated structures are unlikely to fall apart. It rather looks as if the ambivalence of the past regarding convergence versus diversity is carried forward into the future.

Profile building and mobility

The current situation

Another closely related tension inherent in the Bologna Process is the one between the aim to increase the mobility of students, graduates and academic staff on the one hand,

and the strengthened efforts of European higher education institutions, departments, institutes and degree programme to enhance their individual profiles on the other, often at the expense of compatibility and thus mobility. While the increased profile-building of individual institutions need not necessarily impede student mobility, it will do so if individual institutions and programmes find it more important to stress how unique they are than to ensure compatibility with other programmes. This can show in restrictive entry requirements, both with respect to the contents and level of prior knowledge and competences achieved.

While mobility is an official aim of the Bologna declaration texts, profile-building efforts are an indirect consequence of the process. They are triggered by the enlargement of the relevant organisational field and market space through the creation of a European Higher Education Area as well as by the increasing dominance of a competition-oriented paradigm in higher education policy. The trends towards increasing diversity discussed in the previous section point in the same direction.

So far little hard data is available on the effect of the Bologna reforms on student mobility: while higher education institutions themselves report ongoing relative increases in both incoming and outgoing student mobility, longitudinal data gathered by European University Association and the 2006 ACA Eurodata study provide no such evidence and point to the lack of reliable data (Reichert and Tauch 2003; Crosier *et al.*, 2007; Kelo *et al.*, 2006). It has nevertheless become clear that the move to a three-tier degree structure as such and the introduction of ECTS do not automatically ease and increase student mobility. For example, according to the European University Association Trends V report, 47% of the 900 European higher education institutions that responded to the survey acknowledged that "some students have problems with the recognition of their credits gained abroad" (and this is the answer of institutions, not students) (Crosier *et al.*, 2007, p. 38). At the same time, the effects on mobility are actually quite complex. One needs to distinguish between horizontal mobility, that is mobility *within* degree programmes, and vertical mobility, that is *between* degree programmes, meaning between the Bachelor and the Master degrees. For both, national and international mobility can be distinguished.

As for international horizontal student mobility, in a nutshell it looks as if the Bologna reforms so far have had at best a neutral effect. An international comparative study undertaken in 2005 on behalf of the German Academic Exchange Service (DAAD) showed that student mobility was not suffering from the Bologna Process as "felt" in some countries such as Germany (Bürger *et al.*, 2006). Nevertheless there are issues: with the introduction of shorter first degrees in systems that previously had long integrated programmes leading directly to the Masters level, the time pressure felt by students has increased. The introduction of ECTS and continuous assessment has also contributed to this tendency. There are signs that students become more conscious of the adverse effects of study-abroad periods on time-to-degree, if these periods are not organised in the framework of co-operation agreements with guaranteed recognition of study achievement. This means that horizontal student mobility – during degree programmes – only increases if institutions develop new partnerships with compatible programmes that ensure the recognition of credits earned abroad (see also DAAD, 2005). There is also evidence that ECTS can help ease recognition difficulties, but is not a substitute for trust of academics in the compatibility of content and level of courses passed abroad (Witte and Huisman, 2008). Subject-specific qualifications frameworks, developing ECTS further to differentiate credits earned at different levels, and university networks for organised student mobility, will surely all help in the future to increase international horizontal student mobility. It will also help to communicate to students that a study abroad experience is worthwhile even if it implies a longer time to degree.

The most difficult effects are currently experienced in the field of national horizontal student mobility. By pushing their institutions into profile-building and competition, at the same time as implementing the Bologna reforms, governments in countries such as France (Mignot-Gérard and Musselin, 2005) and Germany have created contradictions. In these countries as well as in Spain, standardised national subject-specific curriculum frameworks have been given up, in order to stimulate curricular innovation at institutional level. This has come at the expense of comparability. The challenge for the future is to find a new balance between diversity and comparability, and to develop larger "zones of trust" (Teichler, 2008) to enable recognition in the face of a higher degree of diversity.

As for vertical student mobility, the Bologna Process has created new opportunities by making the transition from the Bachelor to the Master degree a natural occasion for national and international mobility – and, it is important to stress, for trans-disciplinary mobility as well. For students, including those from outside Europe, this creates new opportunities. For weaker institutions this can be perceived as a threat, as they have lost the guarantee that they can retain their students up to the Master level. A "logistical" problem for students is that if they want to start their Master programme directly upon completion of the Bachelor degree, they need to apply a year before on the basis of achievements in their – uncompleted – first degree. In this respect, the situation has ultimately not changed so much compared to "before Bologna", where institutions in such cases also made the assessment on the basis of transcripts rather than completed degrees. At the same time, a more profound challenge for the future is that institutions need to develop entry requirements to Master programmes that allow students with a range of prior qualifications to enter. Here, a healthy balance between homogeneity of intake and tolerance of diversity of prior achievements needs to be found. There are indications that academics coming from the previous system tend to define entry requirements to Master programmes too narrowly, thus impeding vertical student mobility. It is probably easier to live this "tolerance" in social science and humanities programmes than in the "hard" sciences and engineering.

The future

For the future, it seems that the most likely scenario would combine elements from two extremes. One of these extremes has a strong emphasis on institutional profiles and diversity, so that student mobility only exists in terms of "organised mobility" in *ex ante* defined networks. In the other extreme, "Bologna tools" such as ECTS, qualifications frameworks, competence-based learning, etc. are developed to such an extent that student mobility within and between degrees becomes the norm, even outside of organised networks.

The Bologna tools will no doubt be developed further in the future. Particularly the development of European-wide subject-specific qualifications frameworks that are tuned with national qualifications frameworks and ultimately with the European one may be helpful regarding mobility. The TUNING projects provide prototypes for these developments, and European subject associations and networks have a challenging task here for the future. Also, ECTS will likely be further developed to depict credits earned at different levels and thus provide greater depth of information about a student's learning.

In England, credit frameworks other than ECTS have already developed the necessary specifications.

However, even with such developments it is unlikely that the "automatic recognition" of student achievements earned in other institutions, be it national or international, will ever become the norm in Europe. While much investment is needed for further work on necessary tools such as qualification frameworks, level-specific ECTS, compatible modularisation at the national and disciplinary levels, such tools are not sufficient conditions for easy recognition. They will ease the process outside of organised mobility in institutional networks, but the smoothest transition for students between institutions – both horizontal and vertical – will always take place in organised networks. This is even more so since the level of organisational diversity can be expected to increase rather than decrease in the future (Huisman, 2009).[14] At the same time, this does not mean that student mobility is threatened. On the contrary, ensuring student mobility in "networks of equals" will be an important element of institutional strategies for profile-building themselves, as it will make individual institutions and their degree programmes more attractive. Ultimately the tension between mobility and profile-building is not unsolvable.

Inward and outward orientation

The current situation

Another example of the multiple goals of the Bologna Process is the tension between "internal" and "external" aspirations, between making European higher education systems more compatible among each other, and making them more attractive to students from other parts of the world. Making European higher education more attractive and competitive in a global scale, notably *vis-à-vis* the United States, was an important initial motive behind the Bologna Process – an aim often referred to vaguely as "the external dimension" of the Bologna Process (Zgaga, 2006). Introducing degrees that were compatible with the dominant global role model – provided by the "Anglo-American" Bachelor-Master structure – was a means to this end. At the same time, the introduction of a two- (and later three-) tier degree structure was meant to improve the "compatibility and comparability of the [European] systems of higher education" (Bologna declaration, 1999) among themselves.

Through the path dependent, contingent process discussed earlier, the "3 + 2 model" of three-year undergraduate and two-year Master degrees has emerged as a dominant reference point within the European Higher Education Area. This model can now be perceived as in tension with the four-year Bachelor's degrees in the United States. Some argue that this will ironically make the mobility of European graduates to the United States more difficult than before (see Witte and Huisman, 2008). Others say that shorter undergraduate education might actually improve the competitive position of European higher education *vis-à-vis* the United States. For example, at the time of the Sorbonne declaration, the German higher education minister Rüttgers argued that "European students can do it in less time", and thus favoured the three-year degrees as a sign of competitive strength (see Witte 2006, p. 127). However if the level of achievement after a three-year undergraduate degree is questioned – as it was done by a range of graduate schools in the United States in recent years – then the strength can turn into a disadvantage (see Denecke, 2006). The complexity of considerations was however not present in the European debates that preceded the lock-in of the "3 + 2 model".

The future

Future developments depend significantly on which arguments will win predominance in the perceptions of European degrees in the rest of the world. Two options can be envisaged in this regard – one where the current situation prevails, and another other, where European degrees increase their external attractiveness in relation to, and even within, the United States. Under the first option, most international students would continue to opt for the United States as a destination for their first degree "to play it safe" with regard to entry to US Master programmes. Under the second scenario, however, students from South East Asia and other dynamic regions of the world would come to see the shorter European degrees as a way to gain a high-level undergraduate degree in less time than in the United States, and therefore prefer Europe as a location over the United States. At the same time, US universities would move to competency-based assessment of prerequisites, rather than counting years (Redd, 2008). They might even come to accept the argument that "it is the freshman year, not the senior year that is missing in the three-year European degree" (Jaschik, 2006) and therefore routinely accept graduates from Europe into their Masters programmes. And, as a consequence, they might start considering that in the United States, too, undergraduate degrees might be reached within three years, as now already practiced in exceptional cases for talented individuals This might even be linked to reforms of the school system: a common, albeit not undisputed argument is that the general education that is currently taught in the first year of US Bachelor degrees takes place in European high schools already (Bollag, 2004), and therefore similar levels of competence can be reached in three years (see Witte, 2007 on which this section is largely based). This might easily link up with the debate in the United States on how well the school system prepares for college, and on college achievement and drop-out (Adelman, 2007).

These and other effects are not unrealistic. A major recent report of the Washington-based Institute of Higher Education Policy (IHEP) portrays the European reform efforts as potential model for US higher education in many areas, reaching from qualification frameworks through ECTS and the diploma supplement to degree structures (Adelman, 2008). The general tenor is "if they could do this in light of the immense diversity of languages, cultures and traditions, why don't we try to achieve something similar?" What is regarded as exemplary for US higher education is the effort to develop shared and practical denominators for assessing and recognising student achievement across a wide range of learning paths and institutions. Already now, the European University Association (EUA) – Association of International Educators (NAFSA) dialogue points in the direction of greater acceptance of "Bologna degrees" in the US (see *e.g.* NAFSA, 2008).

In other regions of the world, too, the Bologna experience is discussed as a potential role model. In the ASEAN (Association of South-East Asian Nations) region and in Latin America, and the introduction of tools such as ECTS and the Diploma Supplement is being considered (see also Group of Eight, 2006). North African countries whose higher education systems are oriented towards France are also following the Bologna reforms. So the Bologna Process has already developed into a world reference point – and might develop into a world role model both in process and in substance terms: process with regard to the way a common language or currency for comparing and exchanging education achievement is being developed, and substance with regard to the concrete tools in use. One vision is that other integrated world regions – such as North America, South America, and South East Asia – will develop similar international higher education areas as Europe is currently doing. Another – even more far-reaching vision – is that these higher education areas will be one day be linked more intensely than they are today by the use of instruments modelled upon the Bologna Process.

7.5. Summary and conclusions

We have seen that the Bologna Process is a complex and fuzzy undertaking. It is characterised by highly ambitious, vague and partly contradictory goals, a developing agenda, formally non-binding but *de facto* highly committing implementation structures at European level, a wide range of actors involved at several policy levels, and a wide spectrum of national interpretations, as well as implementation modes and patterns.

While the empirical evidence on the achievements so far in the 46 signatory countries is thin,[15] what we know from the evidence available is that the Bologna reforms have developed unprecedented reform dynamics in European higher education and a considerable amount of profound reform in national higher education systems. Degree structures are being changed, ECTS introduced, Diploma Supplements issued, qualifications frameworks designed, quality assurance systems reformed. In many countries, even more profound changes have been initiated, changing curricular designs by introducing generic skills trainings and orientation phases, changing curricular cultures by introducing continuous assessment and competence-based learning, changing teaching modes by moving to project work and information technology and the like.

We also know that in spite of immense reform efforts, in some higher education systems the structural transition will not be complete by 2010. This includes for example the implementation of three-cycle degree structures in all subject areas and across all institutions, ECTS systems at all institutions that fulfil the European guidelines, and guaranteed Diploma Supplements for all students. For some subject areas, such as medicine and law, it is still an open question whether Bologna-type three-cycle structures will be applied at all in all countries (Huisman *et al.*, 2006).

At the same time, while the cultural transition is still ongoing in even more systems, the impulses for this cultural transition provided by the Bologna Process are maybe its most important achievement. By cultural transition we refer for example to reforming curricula to reflect the new paradigm of student-centred learning, with learning outcomes defined for all modules, suitable student guidance and orientation phases as well as to inclusion of general skills and labour-market orientation in the curriculum, while maintaining the academic nature or even improving research training. Through European tools such as ECTS and qualification frameworks, these impulses are institutionalised to such a degree that they cannot be ignored even by sceptical academics.

What can we then expect from the future? As discussed in this text, the Bologna Process on the verge of 2010 remains torn between convergence and diversity, mobility and profile-building, and inward and outward orientation. So many possibilities exist for the future. Two simplified extremes shall be depicted to conclude. A pessimistic scenario would see little or no advances made in achieving the ultimate objectives of the Bologna Process. The European Higher Education Area would be chronically inward-looking, busy only with internal problems and debates, but not solving them. The European higher education landscape would continue to lack transparency for the foreign student and observer, while the institutional landscape would be fragmented with hurdles for mobility of students, graduates and academic staff. Curricular cultures in most higher education systems would be teacher-centred. There would be little acceptance of the Bachelor degree on labour markets. Obsession with uniqueness of individual institutions and programmes would hamper student mobility. In other words, we would see the ongoing search for local solutions to European-wide problems, which would make the realisation of supra-national objectives difficult if not impossible. Such a European Higher Education Area would have little appeal to the rest of the world and little positive effect on European societies and economies. We would see a piecemeal realisation of the Bologna action lines, but the *outcomes* – for which the whole process was begun – would be lost to sight. The danger of this is evident as so far, the Bologna Process has often been characterised by an uncritical acceptance of the causal links between action lines and objectives. It is true that in 2009, we do not know the answers yet to questions concerning employability, increased mobility, transparency, attractiveness, etc.... neither do we know whether they have been affected by the reform elements.

Nevertheless, there is also a chance for an optimistic scenario. In this scenario, the European Higher Education Area will consolidate internally with true convergence. Such convergence would not be solely around shared goals such as increased access and better graduation rates, improved relevance of studies and employability of graduates, but would include true structural convergence improving both the quality and compatibility of European higher education. For example, module sizes used in ECTS would match, ECTS would be developed to include level indicators, qualifications frameworks would be specified at subject level and developed in European associations, and the academic year would start and end at about the same dates throughout Europe. In all that, the right balance between convergence and diversity would be found. Entry requirements to Masters degrees would be competence-oriented and there would be programmes allowing for student intake with different backgrounds. Qualifications frameworks would be broad enough to allow for local variation and innovation. Both highly specialised and more generalist Bachelor degrees would exist, as well as programmes designed for immediate labour-market entry and others primarily meant to prepare for further academic studies, with permeability between both. Degree titles would be transparent and understandable for international observers, and Diploma Supplements readable and meaningful. Such a European Higher Education Area would be attractive to students and institutions in other parts of the world, and would be a role model for regions such as North America, South America and the Caribbean, South East Asia, and Africa. These regions would also develop Bologna-like frameworks fostering regional mobility and co-operation, so that we would ultimately see fruitful competition for innovation and an enhanced exchange between several international higher education areas in the world.

As discussed earlier in the chapter, many seeds and signs for this optimistic scenario can already be found. However, achieving this vision requires continuing and deepening the co-operation of European higher education systems in the current Bologna follow-up structure – with intensified attention to tuning national reforms to each other, to involving academics, students and other stakeholders in the reforms on the ground, as well as to improving recognition and increasing student mobility. It is to be hoped that after the first eleven years of Bologna reforms, energy, including sufficient funds, can be mobilised for such a "second round". A clearly phased process, with clear priorities and the necessary financial support, seems prerequisite for a potentially successful next stage of the reform process.

Notes

1. Besides these, a wealth of evaluation studies, policy reports, institutional cases, handbooks, etc. is available at national levels and often in national languages, and therefore not always accessible at an international scale.

2. Of course the Sorbonne declaration had important forerunners too, elements of which have been integrated into the Bologna Process. These include the Council of Europe/UNESCO Lisbon recognition convention of 1997 and the CRE's Magna Charta of European Universities in 1988 on the core values of European higher education. One can also go back further and think of 1971, when ministers committed themselves for the first time to co-operation in (vocational) education (De Wit and Verhoeven, 2001), or even to the early thoughts in the 1950s about founding a European university (see Corbett, 2005 for an account of this often forgotten period in the European history of higher education). And the European Community programmes of the mid-1980s, focusing on student and staff mobility in higher education (ERASMUS and COMETT), definitely contributed to preparing the ground for "Bologna", too (Neave, 2003). Elements out of this context, such as the European Credit Transfer System (ECTS), entered the Bologna action lines in very concrete terms.

3. See www.ond.vlaanderen.be/hogeronderwijs/bologna/#, retrieved on 21 November 2008.

4. The number of signatories was four at the Sorbonne (1998), 29 in Bologna (1999), 33 in Prague (2001), 40 in Berlin (2003), 45 in Bergen (2005), and 46 in London (2007).

5. As being a signatory to the Council of Europe's Cultural Convention is a condition for joining the process, this dynamic has come to a preliminary end unless the rules were to be changed.

6. The consultative members include the Council of Europe, the European University Association (EUA), the organisation representing non-university higher education institutions (EURASHE), the body representing European students' organisations (ESIB, now ESU), UNESCO/CEPES, and – since the Bergen meeting – also the European Association for Quality Assurance in Higher Education (ENQA) and the European representative organisations of employers and higher education staff. These are the Union of Industrial and Employers' Confederations in Europe (UNICE, now Business Europe) and Education International (EI) (see Witte, 2006, pp. 133-35, p. 146).

7. As shown in Gornitzka, Kogan and Amaral (2007), national higher education policies mostly focus on specific aspects of the system and change is incremental.

8. We are aware that there are other reform areas as well as e.g. lifelong learning, the social dimension, access, and employability, but it is impossible to discuss all these issues in this chapter.

9. For the sake of easy reading, we will refer to the first and second degree as "Bachelor" and "Master", implying also first degrees with other titles such as e.g. the French "licence".

10. See www.hrk.de/de/download/dateien/Muster_DiplSupplAcr5.pdf for the sample format.

11. At a seminar in Ghent in spring 2008, the views of independent higher education researchers on the topic were presented (Kehm, Huisman, and Stensaker, 2009). Furthermore, the BFUG – with funding from the European Commission – has commissioned an independent evaluation of the Bologna Process that will be available in early 2010.

12. The current mix of convergence and diversification can be judged positively, since full convergence – in the meaning of reaching identical systems – has never been an aim of the Bologna Process or because without the Bologna Process, diversity (read: lack of transparency, flexibility, etc.) would have remained far greater. On the other hand, one could argue that one of the process' major objectives has not been realised.

13. There is recognition in the text that "careful attention must be given to following up on 'unfinished business'" to "avoid the risk of achieving only superficial structural change" and achieve the "major shift to student-centred learning". However the main impetus is not on improving the implementation details of concrete reform measures such as three-cycle degree structures, ECTS and Diploma Supplements, but on broader overarching challenges. These include: improving the research base of education, opening access to higher education to at least 50% of an age cohort, rebalancing public responsibility and institutional autonomy and facing global competition. All these aims can be pursued while avoiding the issue of convergence versus diversity. Regarding student mobility, the paper proposes further research, not concrete measures.

14. A European classification similar to the Carnegie classification in the United States, as currently developed by a research team funded by the European Commission (CHEPS, 2008; Van Vught, 2009) might ultimately replace the national distinctions between institutions, so that we will one day find one highly differentiated institutional landscape in Europe with institutions competing and cooperating in one organisational field. It seems likely that classifications like this and

international rankings contribute to a further blurring of boundaries between institutional types, as already happening in the context of the Bologna Process (Witte, Van der Wende and Huisman, 2008). This could possibly also impact on the way state delineations are defined, but would not lead to their abolishment.

15. This is due to the immense resources a systematic broad-scale assessment would cost and that no institution has been willing to provide so far. Given the continuously evolving reforms, such an assessment would soon be outdated anyway.

Bibliography

Adelman, C. (2007), "Do We Really Have a College Access Problem?" *Change*, July/August 2007.

Adelman, C. (2008), *The Bologna Club: What U.S. Higher Education can Learn from a Decade of European Reconstruction*, May 2008, Institute for Higher Education Policy (IHEP), Washington.

Alesi, B. (2007), "Bachelor Graduates on the Labour Market. A Cross-national Comparison of the Employers' Viewpoint", *Tertiary Education and Management*, 13(2), 85-98.

Arthur, W. B. (1989), "Competing Technologies, Increasing Returns, and Lock-in by Historical Events", *Economic Journal*, 99, 116-91.

Berlin Communiqué (2003), *Realising the European Higher Education Area: Communiqué of the Conference of Ministers Responsible for Higher Education*, September 19, Berlin.

Bienefeld, S., N. Harris, E. Helle, A. Hopbach, B. Maguire, B. Michalk *et al.* (2008), *Quality Assurance and Qualification Frameworks*, ENQA, Helsinki.

Bollag, B. (2004), "Degrees of Separation: Many American Graduate Schools are Cool to Europe's New Three-Year Diplomas", *The Chronicle of Higher Education: Today's News*, A36.

Bologna declaration (1999), "The European Higher Education Area: Joint Declaration of the European Ministers of Education", convened in Bologna on the 19th of June 1999.

Bologna Follow-up Group (2007), *Bologna Process Stocktaking London 2007*, Report from a working group appointed by the Bologna Follow-up Group to the Ministerial Conference in London, May 2007, *www.ond.vlaanderen.be/hogeronderwijs/bologna/documents/WGR2007/Stocktaking_report2007.pdf*

Bologna Follow Up Group (2008), *Bologna Work Programme 2007-2009*, BFUG.

Bürger, S., M. Günther, B. Kehm, F. Maiworm, and A. Schelewsky (2006), "International Study on Transnational Mobility in Bachelor and Master Programmes", in DAAD (Ed.), *Transnational Mobility in Bachelor and Master Programmes* (pp. 1-65), DAAD, Bonn.

CHEPS (2008), *Mapping Diversity: Developing a European Classification of Higher Education Institutions*, Enschede.

Costes N., F. Crozier, P. Cullen, J. Grifoll, N. Harris *et al.* (2008), Quality Procedures in the European Higher Education Area and Beyond – Second ENQA Survey, European Association for Quality Assurance in Higher Education, Helsinki, *www.enqa.eu/files/ENQA%20Occasional%20papers%2014.pdf*

Crosier, D., L. Purser, and H. Smidt (2007), *Trends V: Universities Shaping the European Higher Education Area*, EUA, Brussels.

DAAD (2005), *www.daad.de/en/index.html*, retrieved 20 February 2005.

De Wit, K., and J. C. Verhoeven (2001), "The Higher Education Policy of the European Union: With or Against the member states", in J. Huisman, P. Maassen, and G. Neave (Reds.), *Higher Education and the Nation State. The International Dimension of Higher Education*, Pergamon, Oxford.

Denecke, D. (2006), "The Bologna Process, Three Year Degrees and US Graduate Admissions", in E. Froment, J. Kohler, L. Purser and L. Wilson (Eds.), *EUA Bologna Handbook*, Raabe Verlag, Berlin.

ENQA (2005), *Standards and Guidelines for Quality Assurance in the European Higher Education Area*, Helsinki.

European Commission (2005), *Mobilising the Brainpower of Europe: Enabling Universities to Make their Full Contribution to the Lisbon Strategy*, EC, Brussels.

European Commission (2006), *Delivering on the Modernisation Agenda for Universities: Education, Research and Innovation*, European Commission, Brussels.

European University Association (2008), "EUA Policy Position: The Future of the Bologna Process Post 2010", EUA position paper, *www.eua.be/fileadmin/user_upload/files/Newsletter_new/ 2008_C_4_EUA_Bologna_post_2010.pdf*

Gehmlich, V. (2007), "The Added Value of Using ECTS – Article C 3.3-1", in E. Froment, J. Kohler, L. Purser and L. Wilson (Eds.), *EUA Bologna Handbook – Making Bologna Work*, Raabe Verlag, Berlin.

Gornitzka, A. (2006), "What is the Use of Bologna in National Reform? The Case of Norwegian Quality Reform in Higher Education", in V. Tomusk (Ed.), *Creating the European Area of Higher Education. Voices from the periphery* (pp. 19-41), Kluwer, Dordrecht.

Gornitzka, A., M. Kogan, and A. Amaral (eds.) (2007), *Reform and Change in Higher Education*, Kluwer, Dordrecht.

Group of Eight (2006), The Bologna Process and Australia: Submission to the Department of Education, Science and Training. May 2006, available at: *http://aei.gov.au/AEI/GovernmentActivities/ BolognaProcess/Go8_pdf.pdf*, retrieved on 11 November 2008.

Gürüz, K. (2008), *Higher Education and International Student Mobility in the Global Knowledge Economy*, State University of New York Press, Albany.

Hackl, E. (2001), *Towards a European Area of Higher Education: Change and Convergence in Higher Education*, Robert Schuman Centre for European Studies Working Paper No. 2001/09, San Domenico.

Haug, G., J. Kirstein, and I. Knudsen (1999), *Trends in Learning Structures in Higher Education I*, Danish Rectors' Conference, Copenhagen.

Haug, G., and C. Tauch (2001), *Trends in Learning Structures in Higher Education II*. Follow-up report prepared for the Salamanca and Prague Conferences of March/May 2001, EUA, Geneva/Brussels.

Huisman, J. (2009), "Institutional Diversification or Convergence?" in B. Kehm, J. Huisman and B. Stensaker (Eds.), *The European Higher Education Area: Perspectives on a Moving Target,* Sense Publishers, Rotterdam.

Huisman, J., J. Witte, and J. File (2006), *The Extent and Impact of Higher Education Curricular Reform across Europe*, CHEPS, Enschede.

Jaschik, S. (2006), "Making Sense of 'Bologna Degrees'", *Journal,* (November 6),

Kehm, B., J. Huisman, and B. Stensaker (Eds.) (2009), *The European Higher Education Area: Perspectives on a Moving Target*, Sense Publishers, Rotterdam.

Kelo, M., U. Teichler, and B. Wächter (2006), "Towards Improved Data on Student Mobility in Europe: Findings and Concepts of the Eurodata Study", *Journal of Studies in International Education,* 10(3), 194-223.

Leuven Communiqué (2009), *The Bologna Process 2020 – The European Higher Education Area in the New Decade*, Communiqué of the Conference of European Ministers responsible for Higher Education, Leuven and Louvain-la-Neuve, 28-29 April 2009.

Marginson S. and M. Van Der Wende (2009), "Europeanisation, International Rankings and Faculty Mobility: Three Cases in Higher Education Globalisation", in *Higher Education 2030, Volume 2: Globalisation*, OECD Publishing, Paris.

Mignot-Gérard, S., and C. Musselin (2005), *Chacun cherche son LMD : L'adoption par les universités françaises du schéma européen des études supérieures en deux cycles*, École Supérieure de l'Éducation Nationale (ESEN).

Musselin, C. (2006), The National Institutional Side-effects of the Bologna Process and their Implications for Systems Convergence, *CHER 19th Annual Conference: Systems Convergence and Institutional Diversity*, September 7-9, University of Kassel, Germany.

NAFSA (2008), NAFSA and the Bologna Process, *2007 Online*, available at *www.nafsa.org/ knowledge_community_network.sec/recruitment_admissions/bologna_process_network/ events_training_19/nafsa_and_the_bologna*, retrieved on 11 November 2008: Association of International Educators [NAFSA].

Neave, G. (2001), "Anything Goes: Or, how the Accommodation of Europe's Universities to European Integration Integrates an Inspiring Number of Contradictions", *Tertiary Education and Management,* 8(3), 181-197.

Neave, G. (2003), "The Bologna Declaration: Some of the Historic Dilemmas Posed by the Reconstruction of the Community in Europe's Systems of Higher Education", in *Educational Policy*, Vol. 17, No 1.

Pierson, P. (2000), "Increasing Returns, Path Dependence, and the Study of Politics", *American Political Science Review*, Vol. 94, No. 2, pp. 251-67.

Ravinet, P. (2006), *When Constraining Links Emerge from Loose Co-operation: Mechanisms of Involvement and Building of a Follow-up Structure in the Bologna Process*, paper presented at the Third International Euredocs Conference.

Redd, K. (2008), "Data Sources: Changes in Policies Regarding Bologna Three-Year Bachelor's Degrees, 2005 to 2006", *Journal*, December 2006.

Reichert, S., and C. Tauch (2003), *Trends 2003: Progress towards the European Higher Education Area*, EUA, Geneva/Brussels.

Reichert, S., and C. Tauch (2005), *Trends IV: European Universities Implementing Bologna*, EUA, Brussels.

Schwarz, S., and D. Westerheijden (eds.) (2004), *Accreditation and Evaluation in the European Higher Education Area* (Vol. 5), Springer, Dordrecht.

ScienceGuide. (2008), *Vandenbroucke zet agenda* "Leuven 2009".

Teichler, U. (2008), *Student Mobility: Where Do We Come From, Where Are We, Where Are We Going to Inside the EHEA?* Paper presented at the Bologna Conference "Fostering Student Mobility: Next Steps? Involving Stakeholders for an Improved Mobility Inside the EHEA", 29-30 May 2008, Brussels.

Teichler, U. (2009), "Student Mobility and Staff Mobility in the EHEA beyond 2010", in B. Kehm, J. Huisman and B. Stensaker (Eds.), *The European Higher Education Area: Perspectives on a Moving Target*, Sense Publishers, Rotterdam.

Tück, C. (2008), "European Quality Assurance Register: Enhancing Trust through Greater Transparency – Article C 4.3-3", in E. Froment, J. Kohler, L. Purser and L. Wilson (Eds.), *EUA Bologna Handbook – Making Bologna Work*, Raabe Verlag, Berlin.

Van der Wende, M., and J. Huisman (2004), Europe. In J. Huisman and M. Van der Wende (Eds.), *On co-operation and Competition. National and European Policies for the Internationalisation of Higher Education* (pp. 17-49), Lemmens, Bonn.

Van Vught, F. (Ed.) (2009), *Mapping the Higher Education Landscape: Towards a European Classification of Higher Education*, Springer, Dordrecht.

Witte, J. (2006), *Change of Degrees and Degrees of Change. Comparing Adaptations of European Higher Education Systems in the Context of the Bologna Process*, CHEPS, Enschede.

Witte, J. (2007), *European and US-American Higher Education: The Bologna Process between Internal and External Aspirations*, paper presented at the ASHE Conference 2007, International Forum, Symposium "Lenses on Bologna: Critical Analyses, Implications, and Higher Education Reform".

Witte, J. (2008), "Aspired Convergence, Cherished Diversity: Dealing with the Contradictions of Bologna", *Tertiary Education and Management*, Vol. 14, No. 2, pp. 81-93.

Witte, J., and J. Huisman (2008), "Curriculum Reconstruction by German Engineers", in E. Froment, J. Kohler, L. Purser and L. Wilson (Eds.), *EUA Bologna Handbook. Making Bologna Work* (7th ed., Vol. C 5.1-2, pp. 1-20), EUA. Stuttgart.

Witte, J., M. Van der Wende and J. Huisman (2008), "Blurring Boundaries: How the Bologna Process Changes the Relationship between University and Non-university Higher Education in Germany, the Netherlands, and France", *Studies in Higher Education*, Vol. 33, No. 3, pp. 217-31.

Zgaga, P. (2006), *Looking out: The Bologna Process in a Global Setting. On the "External Dimension" of the Bologna Process*, Norwegian Ministry of Education and Research, Bergen.

Higher Education to 2030
Volume 2: Globalisation
© OECD 2009

Chapter 8

Mass Higher Education and Private Institutions

by

Pedro Teixeira*

This chapter takes a long historical perspective on the global emergence of private higher education. It first provides an overview of the history of private higher education worldwide by examining it within the context of the evolution of the modern State. The chapter then focuses on the driving forces behind the recent expansion of private provision in several regions of the world and explores the related challenges. It concludes by discussing the different roles private higher education could play in the future.

* University of Porto and the Centre for Research in Higher Education Policies (CIPES).

8.1. Introduction[1]

Higher education has been facing significant and persistent pressures towards expansion in recent decades, which has led to the emergence of mass higher education – even in countries that until recently enrolled very small portions of their younger populations. This trend towards expansion has raised significant economic and academic challenges for both higher education institutions and governments. The challenges are even more significant since higher education has traditionally been dominated by public provision in many countries. Higher education is being asked to cater to a growing and increasingly diverse population and to do so in a more economic and efficient way. Higher education institutions have also been asked to strengthen their responsiveness to the demands of the economic and social environment.

One response to these challenges has been to promote the adoption of market elements in higher education systems, in particular through increased privatisation. Even though the concept of privatisation is often used to mean the transfer of ownership and/or financial responsibilities from the public sphere to the private, this is only one of its possible meanings when referring to higher education (see Williams, 1991). Others include the development of private providers concurrently with public provision, the diversification of funding mechanisms, and the use of private management in public organisations. In this chapter, we concentrate on exploring the development of private sector provision as part of higher education systems (Geiger, 1986 and Altbach 1999), which is one of the main dimensions of the privatisation trend.

Section 8.2 starts by briefly reflecting on the historically small role of private higher education and its recent emergence as a significant player in many systems (Levy, 2006). In order to better understand the motivations and expectations underlying this growth, it will then be placed against the larger background of increasing *marketisation* in higher education. Section 8.3 will then present some of the main trends associated with the expansion of private higher education. Finally, the conclusion (Section 8.4) will point out the main emerging issues about the role of private higher education in mass higher education systems.

8.2. The long history and recent expansion of private higher education

Private higher education is at times an old and a new reality. Many of the earliest universities were a product of non-governmental initiatives taking place in Europe during the second half of the Middle Ages. From a material and organisational point of view, even when founded by royal or papal decree they were normally set up as autonomous institutions. However, these same universities were not private in the way we understand them nowadays. They had been set up with a public orientation that made them accountable to religious and secular authorities in a way that would not fit into what is presently the norm in private higher education. The separation between the public and private sphere was far less clear in medieval times, especially between the European monarchies and the Catholic Church. Thus the dichotomy between public and private higher education was in some respects also less clear than today. On the other hand, private institutions today are more accountable to public authorities since they tend to face the same regulation and regulatory bodies as public ones. In fact, the more we advance in the history of higher education, the more pronounced the role of public authorities becomes (see Hammerstein, 1996, and Gerbod, 2004). This reached a height in the nineteenth and early twentieth century when the modern state explicitly expanded its functions to include higher education in what Neave (2000) calls the "nationalisation" of higher education. By the mid-twentieth century private institutions were absent from most countries worldwide, and even when they existed, their relative size was small in comparison to the public sector.

European legacy and public hegemony

One of the major forces that contributed to the (small) role that private forces came to play in higher education has to do with its European origins. The way educational needs were provided in Europe would be determinant not only for higher education on this continent but also worldwide since most universities were modelled upon their European forerunners. The first universities were established in medieval Europe at the end of the eleventh century and then grew significantly during the following centuries under the patronage of secular and religious authorities. This support was important for various reasons, not least of which for material ones, since it tended to be vital for universities' subsistence and survival.

This involvement of national and local authorities grew and strengthened universities' role in training local and national secular elites. At the same time, the more the modern State (emerging from the late 1600s) regarded the university as a supplier of qualified labour, the more its appetite grew to increase its control over university life (see Neave, 2001). Higher education institutions were increasingly regarded as an instrument for training elites whose usefulness was growing. In order to train the new members of administration, European states, especially in Continental Europe, started to either establish institutions to regulate more visibly the already existing institutions. This was vividly illustrated by the tensions with the Jesuit order throughout the eighteenth century, whose prominence in educational institutions at that time put them on a collision course with public authorities and contributed to their expulsion from many European countries.

Thus, the turn to the nineteenth century saw the emergence of a growing state bureaucracy aiming at regulating in significant detail universities' organisation, syllabus, teaching staff and student recruitment. Nowhere was this process taken further than in France, with the emergence of the so-called Napoleonic university model, referring to State involvement in steering its specialised higher education institution, which was considered to have an important role to play in the modernisation of society as well as in nation-building (Neave and van Vught, 1994). The Napoleonic model was to have a lasting influence in many countries such as Spain and Italy. At the same time, the so-called Prussian or Humboldtian university model, although established in the early 1800s against the Napoleonic model with the view to protect academic freedom, presented as well the new pattern of strong administrative influence by the State over university life. In some cases, this steady process of persistent State control over universities started to be reversed in the last decades of the twentieth century.

The new type of relationship between universities and the State emerging in the nineteenth century and largely persisting throughout most of the twentieth century, forged a new and strong state of dependence of universities towards secular authorities (see Wittrock, 1993). This dependence, particularly noticeable in Europe, was visible at the financial, administrative, educational and political levels. The growing role of the government in funding universities was encompassed by a much greater administrative oversight of the former. One of the most visible signs was the slow but steady establishment of Ministries of Education or similar public administrative structures that would develop a detailed control of university life. In continental Europe, this had already taken place throughout the nineteenth century whereas in Britain it was more gradual and was not accomplished until after the Second World War. Universities became increasingly accountable to state authorities and had to ask for governmental authorisation for a wide set of organisational procedures, which in the mid-twentieth century became the so-called model of rational planning and control (Van Vught, 1989). This reached its height in the post-Second World War decades with the so-called legal homogeneity (Neave and Van Vught, 1991), meaning that governments defined a standard curriculum and syllabus for each institution aiming at providing higher training in a specific field. These developments were particularly pronounced in continental Europe.

In addition to national equality, this strong governmental regulation of higher education training envisaged ensuring that universities would provide the training that governmental officials deemed most appropriate, especially bearing in mind the future role of university graduates within public administration (Neave, 2001). The growing influence of governments in higher education was significantly shaped by the development of modern administrative and political structures (Middleton, 1997). The expansion of a government's economic and social roles, especially after the Second World War, created significant needs for qualified personnel that could be provided by higher education. This demand for some types of qualified individuals was already present in the nineteenth century, especially as regards those with some type of legal training and also some engineers. However, the post-war expansion of the State, especially with the construction of the so-called Welfare State, required that governments hire an enormous amount of highly qualified people, such as teachers, social workers, doctors, nurses and accountants. The post-war times of macroeconomic demand management also enhanced the governmental demand for individuals with economic training. As governments became the major employer for many of these careers, they became increasingly interested in adjusting the training provided by higher education to the needs of the increasingly expanding governmental structures and sought to accomplish this either in the syllabus or even in the type of programmes available.

This expansion of the governments' role in higher education was itself part and parcel of the post-war expansion of the State, particularly visible in western countries. The post-war expansion in governments' expenditures in public education clearly went beyond merely encompassing the rising number of students. It corresponded to a growing willingness to support education, turning it eventually into a political and budgetary priority (Gosden, 1983). The Second World War was a kind of turning point, showing the importance of a pool of skilled labour and the potential achievements of scientific research for military, economic and social life. Higher education therefore became a major concern for many governments (Wittrock and Wagner, 1996). These multiple and complex expectations fuelled a steady and rapid expansion of public higher education in the second half of the twentieth century, leading to the emergence of mass higher education in North America, Japan and then in western Europe.

By the early twentieth century, there were very few universities outside Europe and the Americas. Although higher learning has a long history in the Arab and Islamic World, there were very few higher education institutions in the Middle East by the mid-twentieth century aside from Islamic seminaries. The situation in Africa was similar. In North Africa there were very old and important theological institutions of advanced learning, but secular higher education only appeared in the nineteenth century with the emergence of some colleges and separate faculties. The first North African universities were established only in the twentieth century, while in most of Sub-Saharan Africa the first higher education institutions were founded very recently, mostly after independence in the post-Second World War decades. In Asia, the first western style universities date from the mid-nineteenth century. In the nineteenth and twentieth centuries, the learning and diffusion of western science was linked with the idea of western culture (Altbach and Umakoshi, 2004).

The dissemination of university-like institutions outside Europe was linked with the European influence around the world. Even in the twentieth century, universities were often modelled on and deeply influenced by those existing in Europe (Neave, 2000) as the authorities, frequently a product of the European universities themselves, tended to replicate those institutional structures (Neave and van Vught, 1994). The influence of European university models was in some cases indirect, as when certain organisational types of higher learning institutions, originally modelled from European patterns, absorbed other influences and characteristics under the influence of local needs and local elites. This was already the case, especially in North and South America, in the nineteenth century. While Latin America was more inclined to follow trends similar to those in Europe regarding the role of the State in higher education, the increasing involvement of local elites in higher education in North America made institutions much more diverse and more oriented towards their external environment. In the case of North America, the development of a federal state and its limited role in higher education also contributed to the increasing divergence with Europe and Latin America. These developments eventually lead to an emergence of a different, "North American" higher education institution, which would be imitated in other parts of the world.

The worldwide expansion of the private higher education sector

Both in Europe and outside Europe, the earliest universities came increasingly under the influence of governments although many of them were first established as autonomous institutions. This was also the case with the many religiously affiliated institutions that were prominent, particularly in southern Europe and Latin America. These institutions were increasingly supervised by secular authorities, either due to the growing share of public funding or their actual transfer to the public domain. Hence, by the early twentieth century, not only was the number of universities still small, especially outside Europe and North America, but the number of private institutions was even less significant.

By the end of the twentieth century many higher education systems included some type of private higher education institutions. Thus, though in the early twentieth century the existence of private higher education institutions was rather uncommon, they became increasingly part of the higher education landscape throughout the last century, especially during its last quarter. For a significant number of countries the first private institutions to emerge were still nurtured by the traditional role that religion had played in higher education. Although secularisation and the growth of the modern state since the eighteenth century had created an environment much less favourable to religiously affiliated institutions, in many countries the first private institutions were established by the churches, especially the Catholic Church, in the late nineteenth and early twentieth century.

The role of religion was particularly important in the Americas. In Latin America, the so-called first modern wave of private universities prior to the nineteenth century was clearly dominated by the Catholic Church (Levy, 1986). However, with the ascent of the modern State, most of these universities were eventually taken by the State and, during the nineteenth century, higher education became almost a state monopoly. Yet, the 1920s and 1930s saw a slow but visible resurgence of Catholic universities in several Latin American countries, namely Colombia, Chile, Bolivia and Peru. This new set of private Catholic universities established throughout Latin America was often regarded as a way of fighting against the growing secularisation of societies and an attempt by the Catholic Church to retain some of its prior social and political influence.

In North America, the role of religion was also very important for the establishment of the first private higher education institutions. Many of the institutions established in the colonial period and thereafter had strong links with the various protestant denominations (Thelin, 2004). The first institution was a college established in 1636 by the Massachusetts General Court, renamed three years later as Harvard College in honour of a generous donor, John Harvard, and chartered in 1650 by the General Court. The religious dimension was not only clearly present in the motivations for its establishment but also in the frequent controversies regarding the degree of its faculty's – and especially its administration's – compliance to religious orthodoxy. The establishment of Harvard was followed by a series of colleges created along the East Coast.[2] In the Canadian provinces no higher education institutions were established until the end of the eighteenth century except for a seminary in Quebec and a few grammar schools (Roberts *et al.*, 1996). However, religion had lost significant ground in higher education by the nineteenth century. Although many colleges were still sponsored on a private denominational basis, they had developed a system of lay government (Hofstadter, 1996) where trustees held fiduciary control of the institution. Moreover, many of the private institutions established in North America had a much less confessional tone in the twentieth century, even if they often were a product of fervent religious individuals.

In other parts of the world, private higher education is clearly a twentieth century phenomenon, following a later development of higher education as a whole. The first private higher education institutions in the Middle East were only established in the mid-nineteenth century. Throughout the twentieth century, especially after independence, almost all new universities were established as public universities in many Arab countries, according to a widespread belief that higher education was a state responsibility. As in many other parts of the world, higher education was regarded as an instrument for training elites, especially with regard to the senior ranks of civil service and public administration. Private higher education institutions either were not allowed to continue to function or were prevented from being established. The trend of public sector dominance continued until the 1980s and 1990s, when the emergence of massive growth in higher education demand strained the States' ability to meet the rising demand (UNESCO/OECD, 2006). For example, between 1995 and 2003 the participation rate almost tripled in Egypt and almost doubled in Jordan. This led to the re-emergence and rapid increase of private universities and institutions.

The development of private higher education in Africa also followed the lagging development of its overall higher education structures. The number of universities in Sub-Saharan Africa was minimal until the mid-twentieth century. The British imperial achievements in Africa were very limited concerning higher education; the only exception was South Africa with the establishment of the University of Cape of Good Hope in 1873, followed by a couple more in the turn to the twentieth century. In the French colonies in Africa, the efforts were even more limited. Hence, most private higher education institutions in Africa are a recent development, mainly dating from the 1990s. The emergence of the private higher education sector seems to have benefited from the slow development of the public sector and the financial constraints of many African governments, which prevents them from keeping pace with the growing demands for higher education. This has been illustrated by explosive expansions of enrolments in countries such as Kenya, Uganda or Zimbabwe, especially since the 1980s (Neave and Van Vught, 1994; UNESCO/OECD, 2006). However, widespread poverty – in 2005, 50% of the population in Sub-Saharan Africa was living with less than USD 1.25 a day (in Purchasing Power Parity terms, World Bank, 2009) – has prevented a fast development of the private sector in many Africa countries.

In Asia, where western-style higher education developed in the nineteenth century, private higher education became a significant feature of systems from an early stage on and attained a prominent role in several countries (Shils and Roberts, 2004). The Philippines, the first Asian country to have a university inspired by western models, was also pioneer in Asia as regards private higher education with the establishment of a for-profit institution – the Far Eastern University, first established as the Institute of Accountancy in 1928 (attaining university status in 1934). In both China and Japan, private higher education developed quite early, in the turn to the twentieth century, following quite rapidly the establishment of their public counterparts in the last decades of the nineteenth century. Thus, by 1949 around 40% of the 205 universities and colleges existing in China were private with a significant proportion of them based on prior missionary colleges founded under European and American influence (Min, 2004). Japan also developed a tradition of private universities, several of which were created in the second half of the nineteenth century. The private higher education sector also started to expand rapidly in other Asian countries, such as Viet Nam and Malaysia, where until recently their role was small or non-existent. Private higher education is therefore not a new development in a number of Asian countries; this sector often represents more than half of the total higher education enrolment, as in the cases of Japan, Korea and the Philippines. Some of these private higher education institutions are very prestigious.[3]

As regards most OECD countries, we observe that for a long time Europe remained a bastion of public dominance in higher education with a large majority of higher education students still being enrolled in public higher education institutions in most European countries today (see Table 8.1 below). Even those confessional institutions that survived until modern times in Europe came to be assimilated into the public sector during the twentieth century, often through financial mechanisms. This was the case, for example, of several institutions in the Netherlands and Belgium. Although these institutions were nominally private, they were funded and supervised as any other public universities in the same system, being considered mainly as government-dependent private institutions. This means that a private entity has control over the institution, but the institution receives 50% or more of its core funding from governmental sources or a government

Table 8.1. **Tertiary education students enrolled by type of institution in 2006 (full and part-time students)**

	Total number of students	Public institutions (%)	Government dependent private institutions (%)	Independent private institutions (%)
Australia	1 040 153	97.8	0.3	1.9
Austria	253 139	86.7	13.3	0.0
Belgium	394 427	44.6	55.4	0.0
Canada	1 014 837	100.0	0,00	0.0
Czech Republic	337 405	92.3	3.0	7.7
Denmark	228 893	98.1	1.9	0.0
Finland	308 966	89.5	10.5	0.0
France	2 201 201	83.4	2.5	14.0
Germany	2 289 465	91.1	9.0	0.0
Greece	653 003	100.0	0.0	0.0
Hungary	438 702	85.0	15.0	0.0
Iceland	15 721	80.3	19.7	0.0
Ireland	186 044	92.1	0.0	7.9
Italy	2 029 023	92.8	0.0	7.2
Japan	4 084 861	20.1	0,00	79.9
Korea	3 204 036	19.9	0.0	80.1
Luxembourg	2 692	100.0	0.0	0.0
Mexico	2 446 726	67.3	0.0	32.7
New Zealand	23 778 262	90.9	9.1	0.0
Norway	214 711	86.4	13.6	0.0
Poland	2 145 687	69.2	0.0	30.8
Portugal	367 312	75.0	0.0	25.0
Slovak Republic	197 943	95.6	0.2	4.2
Spain	1 789 254	86.6	2.1	11.3
Sweden	422 614	92.2	7.8	0.0
Switzerland	204 999	81.4	11.5	7.1
Turkey	2 342 898	95.2	0.0	4.8
United Kingdom	2 336 111	0.0	100.0	0.0
United States	17 487 475	74.5	0.0	25.5

Source: *OECD Education Database.*

agency pays its teaching personnel. Thus, the existence of private institutions remained minimal in most of the western European higher education systems, despite the increasing willingness of governments to adopt market-like mechanisms (Teixeira *et al.*, 2004)

Table 8.1 shows that a surge of student enrolments in private higher education institutions has occurred in the part of Europe where its establishment was prevented for several decades. Since the collapse of the communist regimes in the end of the twentieth century, private higher education has became a significant feature of many higher education systems in central and eastern Europe (Wells *et al.*, 2007). In 2006, independent private institutions enrolled 30.8% of all higher education students in Poland and 7.7% in Czech Republic. Besides these countries, the only European country in which a large private sector has developed since the mid-1980s is Portugal, where one fourth of higher education students were enrolled in private institutions in 2006. However, demographic patterns seem to be contributing to the slowing down of demand in countries such as Poland and Portugal, with severe negative effects on those private sectors (Teixeira and Amaral, 2007).

The data presented in Table 8.1 also reflect some of the aforementioned historic patterns. They show the current relevance of private higher education in those countries, in which private institutions were at the centre of the historic development of the higher education sector. This is for example the case of the United States. Moreover, the data also suggest that in those countries, in which the private sector was an important part of the development of mass higher education, the former has retained a very relevant role regarding enrolments. This is notably the case of Asian countries like Korea and Japan, where private sectors represent the backbone of the system, with independent private institutions enrolling roughly 80% of the higher education student population. This significance of the private sector in terms of student enrolments remains also very visible in many Latin American countries, such as Mexico, Brazil and Chile, where independent private institutions enrolled 32.7%, 71.8% and 60.3% of higher education students in 2006, respectively (*OECD Education Database*).

Rationales behind the recent expansion of private higher education

As we have seen, higher education has traditionally been strongly dominated by public provision and government regulation, especially in Europe. This has been influenced by the parallel evolution of the modern State and its growing interplay with the university's missions. In this context, historically, the role of the private sector in higher education remained modest until the last three decades, when all around the globe private higher education has been experiencing a notable growth. This phenomenon has been especially visible in central and eastern Europe, Latin America and eastern Asia. While religion was an important driver behind the emergence of the first private higher education institutions, especially in the Americas, its recent massive growth can be explained by a set of other contextual factors that have shaped higher education worldwide in recent decades.

One of the major forces promoting the role of private higher education has been the continuous and strong expansion of this sector globally, even in countries and regions where until recently access to higher education was restricted to a very small minority. Student numbers surged from 68 million in 1991 to 132 million in 2004 worldwide (UNESCO, 2006). This expansion of higher education has been fuelled by societal and individual forces. At the policy level, governments have increasingly regarded the advanced qualification of human resources as a key factor in promoting national economic competitiveness. The recent economic discourse based on models of endogenous growth has but strengthen this view that the accumulation of human capital can improve the economic prospects of a certain community (see Romer, 1986). In times of growing globalisation, the improvement of the qualification of human resources has become one of the few factors through which governments can actually contribute to enhance national economic performance (Blöndal and Girouard, 2002).

The expansion of higher education is visible in Table 8.2. On average, there are more tertiary graduates in the younger age groups than in the older age groups in OECD countries, which reflects the growing qualifications of their work force. This pattern has expanded beyond developed countries and has stimulated major expansions of higher education enrolments in many developing countries. Whereas in OECD countries tertiary enrolment rose sharply in the last decades, growing by 43% between 1995 and 2003, in many developing countries the expansion was even larger. A study by UNESCO and OECD found that for a selection of 17 developing countries from Latin America, Asia and Africa, the increase during the same period was 77% (UNESCO/OECD, 2006).

This expansion of higher education has also been pushed significantly by the behaviour of individuals. A higher education degree has remained an attractive personal

Table 8.2. **Population having attained tertiary education in OECD countries in 2006**
(%)

	Age groups				
	25-64	25-34	35-44	45-54	55-64
OECD average	27	33	28	24	19
EU19 average	24	30	25	21	17

Source: OECD (2008a).

investment, as shown by persistently high private rates of return observable in many countries. For several decades, this has nurtured the view among the public that higher education graduates should expect enviable prospects regarding long-term income and employability, especially when compared to individuals with much lower formal qualifications (see Mincer, 1993).

As Table 8.3 indicates, higher education graduates hold a significant income premium over individuals with lower educational qualifications. This is particularly the case in Germany, Switzerland, Ireland, the United Kingdom, the United States, Czech Republic, Poland, Portugal and Israel. Despite variations, this pattern holds across different geographical and economic contexts worldwide. The high rates of return of higher education have been very important in fuelling demand in developing countries, where the

Table 8.3. **Relative earnings of the population with tertiary education (upper secondary and post-secondary non tertiary education = 100)**

	Year	Age group 25-64	Age group 30-44
Australia	2005	131	134
Austria	2005	152	148
Belgium	2004	134	134
Canada	2004	138	134
Czech Republic	2005	181	191
Denmark	2004	126	122
Finland	2004	149	138
France	2005	144	148
Germany	2005	156	150
Hungary	2005	215	225
Ireland	2004	164	159
Israel	2005	151	156
Italy	2004	160	143
Korea	2003	141	148
Luxembourg	2002	145	152
Netherlands	2002	148	147
New Zealand	2005	132	131
Norway	2004	136	134
Poland	2004	163	169
Portugal	2004	179	179
Spain	2004	132	130
Sweden	2004	127	122
Switzerland	2005	156	157
Turkey	2004	141	135
United Kingdom	2005	155	161
United States	2005	175	175

Source: OECD (2007).

scarcity of qualified labour has tended to further enhance the premium for more educated workers (Psacharopoulos and Patrinos, 2002). However, as we can see in Table 8.3, the income advantage of more educated individuals has persisted even in countries where there has been a significant and persistent expansion in the number of individuals with a higher education degree. Altogether, this has contributed to keep the social demand for higher education very strong.

This persistent high demand has led to the so-called *massification* of higher education, meaning not only growing rates of enrolment, but also more heterogeneous and complex higher education systems. In order to respond adequately to an increasingly diverse demand, higher education systems have developed new and diverse programs and institutions (Teichler, 1988); thus, diversity has become an increasingly important dimension in higher education policy. On the other hand, massification also meant that it was no longer possible, or at least not advisable, for most governments to maintain a pattern of detailed regulation of higher education institutions (Neave and van Vught, 1991). Hence, governments needed to explore new forms of steering that would be effective within the new context of mass higher education.

Another factor critical to understanding the relative decrease in the dominance of public higher education is the fact that the recent expansion of higher education has coincided with a period of increasing constraints on public expenditure that has affected higher education as well. The difficulties in funding the continuous expansion of higher education have posed a problem for both richer and poorer countries alike. In the case of the former, the so-called crisis of the welfare state has challenged the sustainability of the traditional financial reliance of higher education on public funding (see Barr, 2004). In the case of countries with lower levels of income, the financial limitations associated with a lower fiscal basis have been regarded as a significant obstacle to the ambition of expanding the higher education system on the basis of public funding.

The changes in the funding of higher education were also influenced by the changing political mood that has affected western countries since the early 1980s and then progressively extended to other parts of the world. In the aftermath of the economic turmoil of the 1970s there was an increasing debate about the type and degree of government intervention, with the ideological pendulum swaying towards increasing liberalisation and market regulation and restrained government regulation (Middleton, 1997). This was initially more visible in macroeconomic policy, but then started to pervade social policy in general and educational policy in particular (Barr, 2004). The discourse about public services became populated by managerial jargon and customer orientation.

The so-called neo-liberal revival has long and important roots in educational policy. Already in the mid-1950s, Milton Friedman started to question what he called the nationalisation of the education sector. In his *Capitalism and Freedom* (1962), he launched the contemporary debate on the role of markets and governments in (higher) education. According to Friedman, the role of government would be largely unjustified in types of education such as higher education that clearly enhanced the individual's productivity since in these cases the individual would reap a major benefit through enhanced lifetime income and, therefore, should be called on to bear most of the costs. In this case, Friedman believed that the argument for nationalisation was weak, particularly as it would introduce some major distortions into the functioning of the higher education system. This led him to develop the controversial proposal of a voucher scheme for funding. Friedman believed that the shift from institutional to individual funding would enhance the competition between higher education institutions and encourage better use of resources. Moreover, it would promote a greater diversity of types of higher education, which he largely associates with private provision.

These arguments would face an increasingly congenial audience with the so-called crisis of the welfare state since the 1980s. In OECD countries and elsewhere, there were mounting pressures towards greater efficiency in the allocation of public resources and in the management of public institutions (Cave *et al.*, 1990). Although higher education institutions were recognised as a peculiar type of organisation (Winston, 1999), many policy makers have been keen to promote a more managerial behaviour by higher education institutions (Amaral *et al.*, 2003). Moreover, in several countries the promotion of private institutions has been regarded as an instrument to foster the assimilation of more efficient practices among public higher education institutions through better management of resources. This type of rationale can frequently be found in discussions about the emergence of a strong private sector in regions as diverse as eastern and central Europe, Latin America and South-East Asia (see Geiger, 1986).

The arguments used in favour of the development of private higher education were not only related to issues of internal efficiency but also to the debates about the degree of external efficiency of the higher education system (Levy, 2002). The private sector was supposed to demonstrate an increased capacity for exploring new market opportunities and occupying market niches by using its higher administrative flexibility and financial motivation. Private and private-like institutions – meaning those institutions treated as if they were privately owned – were to promote a better balanced supply of higher education from a geographical and disciplinary perspective. A similar rationale was present as regards labour market demands, as the expected greater responsiveness of private-type higher education institutions was regarded as a powerful force driving institutions to supply qualifications more suitable to labour market needs. The changes aiming at strengthening market forces and a more prominent role for private initiative in higher education were expected to favour the emergence of innovative behaviour (Geiger, 1986).

These arguments have been persistently repeated in recent decades to justify the growing role of market competition and privatisation in higher education. This political and economic context has led many governments to test different approaches to managing the higher education system, most often through the introduction of some market mechanisms.[4] An important dimension of these market mechanisms has been the growing *privateness* of the higher education system. In several countries, especially in Asia and South America, but also in southern and eastern Europe, this has taken place notably with the emergence of a significant private sub-sector in higher education.

A good illustration of this kind of development is provided by the Portuguese higher education system, the only case in western Europe of higher education massification through a strong private sector. Table 8.4 shows that the system multiplied its overall enrolment number more than seven-fold between 1971 and 2006 and almost two-fold since 1991. The fastest growing higher education sub-sector in a long term (1971-2006) were the public polytechnics (more than 35-fold increase), followed closely by private institutions (almost 28-fold increase). Between 1981 and 2006, the fastest student enrolment increase took place in the private higher education sector. By 2006, private

Table 8.4. **Evolution of enrolments in Portuguese higher education from 1971 to 2006**

	1971		1981		1991		1996		2006	
	Number	%	Number	%	Number	%	Number	%	Number	%
Public universities	43 191	87.3	64 659	76.8	103 999	55.7	147 340	44.1	169 449	46.2
Public polytechnics	2 981	6.0	12 195	14.5	31 351	16.8	65 377	19.6	105 872	28.9
Private institutions	3 289	6.7	7 319	8.7	51 430	27.5	121 399	36.3	91 408	24.9
Total	49 461	100.0	84 173	100.0	186 780	100.0	334 868	100.0	366 729	100.0
Gross enrolment rate % (20–24 year olds)		7.9		11.0		24.4		44.3		46,4

Source: Teixeira and Amaral (2008).

higher education institutions enrolled roughly one fourth of all Portuguese higher education students. This represents a notable increase in share from 1971 as well as from 1981.

Either due to a change in the ideological and political context or to pressing financial constraints, privatisation of higher education has become a fast-growing reality in many countries worldwide since the 1980s. In most higher education systems in western Europe, the trend towards privatisation has occurred mostly by increasing the private-like aspects of the dominant public system through stimulating competition in terms of students and funds rather than by promoting or even allowing the emergence of a significant sub-sector of private higher education (see for example Vincent-Lancrin, 2009; OECD, 2008b). In other regions, impressive increases of enrolments have become common, partly as a result of the expansion of the private higher education sector (Altbach, 1999). For some systems, such as those in eastern Europe, this has meant the emergence of a completely new reality.

Also in Africa and South-East Asia, this new wave of privatisation engulfed the previous experiences (which consisted mainly of religiously affiliated institutions) and changed the almost insignificant presence of private higher education into a sizeable part of the system. During the last two decades (see also Table 8.5), private higher education has become a significant force in higher education worldwide. This change was expected to shape the development of higher education in many instances.

Yet, the role of religion, which had been so important in earlier, played a less prominent role in this recent wave of privatisation. This does not mean that there was no growth of religiously affiliated higher education institutions but that this group lost the dominant role it had in most of the countries where the private sector had deeper roots (Levy, 1986 and 2006). There was certainly a revival of church-affiliated institutions in parts of the world where the political situation had clearly restricted or prevented it, as in several eastern European countries (Wells et al., 2007). However, even in those countries that type of private institution often became a minority in the private sector. The process of secularisation in many societies meant that, despite some religious revival, most members no longer regarded higher education as the sole province of the churches. Moreover, the most commercially aggressive approach of many of the new private players clearly outpaced the growth of the church-affiliated institutions, which often preferred to model themselves on their more established and respected public counterparts.

Table 8.5. **Main features in development of private and public higher education provision in a global scale**

Development of private provision			Time line				Development of public provision		
Features	Regional focus	Driving factors					Driving factors	Regional focus	**Features**
First modern wave of private universities	Latin-America North-America	Influence of the Catholic Church Influence of protestant denominations	18th century				Growth of the modern state – Need for trained elites	Continental Europe	**Establishment and/or visible regulation of institutions by public authorities**
Development of private higher education	Asia	Influence of missionary colleges and increasing westernisation	19th century				Quest for national homogenisation – Increasing need for qualified personnel	Europe – Latin America – Arab countries	**Increased State control over higher education institutions**
Resurgence of Catholic Universities	Latin-America	Addressing growing secularisation		*First half*	20th century	20th century			
Emergence or rapid growth of private higher education	Eastern, central and southern Europe – Latin America – South-East Asia – Africa	Budgetary constraints – Demand for access and high private rates of return – Quest for increased efficiency		*Post-Second World War decades* *Recent decades*			Acknowledgement of the strategic importance of higher education – Increasing need for qualified personnel	Western Europe – North America Worldwide trend	**Higher education expansion** **Mass Higher Education**

8.3. Some stylised facts on private higher education

The recent surge of private higher education requires a new look on privatisation and its impact on higher education worldwide. In particular, one needs to go beyond some of the "myths" surrounding private higher education in order to understand the complexity of this important part of higher education. This section tries to identify some of the most significant patterns emerging with this recent wave of private higher education institutions.

Diverse private sector

One of the most significant aspects regarding private higher education is its striking diversity. This is not an exclusive characteristic of the private sector, but its degree of institutional diversity is significant. Whereas the public sector is often under significant homogenisation rules, through instruments of regulation such as legal framework, funding, staff policies, and student recruitment, private institutions often present a reasonable degree of institutional diversity.

Size

One of these main differences refers to size since we can find very small and large institutions in most if not all private sectors worldwide. The private higher education sector is characterised by the frequent existence of some very small institutions, often in large numbers (Levy, 2002). The size regarding enrolments is normally far smaller in an average private sector institution than in its public counterpart. An analysis of the Database compiled by PROPHE – Program of Research on Private Higher Education – confirms that this is a very common pattern. The average size of private institutions is often one half or one third of the average size of public institutions. This is even the case in those countries that have a well-established private sector such as the United States, where the number of private institutions represents around 60% of the total institutions though they enrol less than 25% of the students.

For-profit nature

Another important source of diversity among private higher education institutions has to do with their for-profit nature. Although historically private institutions were established as not-for-profit institutions – as is the case with the old private universities in the United States – recent growth of private provision has introduced increasing shades of profit-seeking behaviour. The for-profit private sector has in some cases attained reasonable success regarding enrolments Examples of this expansion of the for-profit private sector can be found in Brazil, the Philippines, Malaysia and South Africa where the majority of the private sector is for-profit (Kinser and Levy, 2005).

Furthermore, although in many countries for-profit institutions are not allowed, many private institutions, established with a not-for-profit status, have behaved as if they were for-profit. This is the case, for example, with Portugal, Poland and Russia, where institutions have focused their activities on areas where demand in very high end risk and investment is very low (see more on this below). This has introduced important dynamics, not only to the private higher education sector, but also to the whole higher education system as the for-profit provision has often become a challenge to regulatory powers that have shown difficulty in dealing with this emerging type of private institution. The degree of commercialisation brought by this type of institution make the role of government crucial in providing reliable information and ensuring the quality of provision.

The available information on for-profit private higher education is still very limited as well as data on its actual size on a global scale. One of the few studies on the subject has shown that private for-profit higher education covers roughly 5% of all higher education enrolments in the United States and employs roughly 3% of the faculty, even though at the same time almost 50% of all American higher education institutions are private for-profit establishments (Kinser and Levy, 2005; see Table 8.6). The shares in relation to all private higher education providers are clearly higher, 24%, 9.5% and 62% respectively. The study also indicates that a large part of enrolment in this type of small institution tends to be in the non-university sector, even if the most visible growth has taken place through a only few universities (Kinser, 2006), such as, for example, the University of Phoenix, which is the largest US university.

Table 8.6. **Scale of for-profit higher education in the United States**

Indicator	Year	For-profit higher education		
		Number	% of total higher education	% of total private higher education
Enrolment	2001	765 701	4.7	23.9
Part-time		*126 720*	*1.9*	*14.9*
Full-time		*638 981*	*6.6*	*27.2*
Faculty	1999	30 000	2.9	9.5
Institutions	2000	4 338	46.9	61.7
Degrees awarded	2001/2002	77 712	13.1	62.9

Source: Kinser and Levy (2005).

Some of the developments in for-profit private higher education outside the United States do often take the form of international collaboration stimulated by the fast expanding demand for higher education in many parts of the world, especially in Asia and Latin America. In some cases this is done by the establishment of new campuses; in others, by the acquisition of local institutions that keep their brand name although they are managed by the international owners (Kinser and Levy, 2005). Sometimes, the international dimension can actually be interpreted as a mechanism for circumventing national regulations and restrictions.

Institutional profile

Another significant source of diversity within private sectors is its institutional profile. Although in many public sectors there are also institutional differences, this is even more the case within the private sector. Many private higher education institutions are not universities, but rather specialised institutions that provide higher training in one or a few fields of studies. Moreover, the role model of the university as an institution with a research mission is largely mitigated in the private sector. Whereas some private institutions try to obtain legitimacy, both regarding the public authorities and society, through some research, this is not the most common situation. The US experience with prestigious private not-for-profit research universities, often cited in policy circles as the example to follow in the development of the private sector, remains quite unique as regards the significance and relevance of private institutions for the development of graduate education and research (Levy, 2006). There is nothing similar to that in most other countries with a sizeable private sector, even though countries such as Japan and Korea also have some prestigious private research universities.

However, one can observe a few examples of private institutions trying to strengthen their reputation through more intensive research activity. Some examples in this respect have been emerging in Latin America, which is not surprising given the size and maturity of the sector in that part of the world. In his extensive study about the research activity of the private sector in Latin America, Levy (1996) noted an increasing research intensity in recent years, especially in social sciences and public policies. In his study he identifies and analyses the important role played by private research units in those fields. These units are often associated with higher education institutions, for example, in Mexico, Brazil, Argentina and Chile. However, even where some research activity is discernible, it is highly contingent on the concentrated disciplinary pattern, mostly in the social sciences, that on the one hand tend to have less public visibility and on the other hand tend to attract fewer funds.[5]

In addition to the concern for reputation, another motivation for research efforts by private institutions has been the possibility of earning additional income, especially as regards applied research. In the early phase of the private sector's development there is usually resistance to channelling public funding to private institutions, not the least from public universities that fear their share of funding will diminish. For example, in many western European countries, where private supply is still recent and tends to be very limited, there are often significant obstacles keeping private institutions from qualifying for national research funding (though not for EU funding). However, the availability of funding for private institutions has become more frequent in those systems where the presence of the private sector has become a common feature of the landscape of higher education. This is the case in most Latin American countries (Balán and Fanelli, 2002). The change can be explained by various factors, not least the growing influence of a more established private sector or even the realisation by the public sector that the shape of the private sector (and especially its disciplinary composition) does not mean that it will become a major competitor for research funding.

Great expectations, policy omissions and mixed results

One of the main characteristics of the recent expansion of private higher education is that, in many countries with very different levels of income, governments alike have allowed the private sector to develop rapidly in order to fulfil objectives of higher levels of enrolment. This has been done either because those governments were financially unable to support a massive expansion of higher education or because they attempted to mitigate the effects of massification on the public sector.

This pattern of expansion, also called demand-absorption (see Levy, 2002 and 2006), is normally the result of strong social demand and lax regulation by political decision makers. The lax regulatory forces often stimulate opportunistic behaviour from many of these newly established institutions by lowering entry requirements or simply by not enforcing regulatory rules that are in place (Teixeira and Amaral, 2007). Accordingly, private institutions are allowed to mushroom and rapidly expand the number of programmes and size of enrolments, at times outpacing the expansion of the public sector, as in the case of Portugal (see Table 8.4). The private sector may move from an almost non-existent role to a prominent role in the mass sector, as has happened in several eastern European countries. This kind of evolution may also correspond to a strategy that gives pre-eminence to quantity rather than quality in the development of private higher education institutions.

However, the relationship between policy makers and the private sector can often be ambiguous. On the one hand, many governments create the conditions for the rapid development of the private sector through lax regulation of the sector. On the other hand, they may maintain close bureaucratic control over private institutions that often have less autonomy in some respects than their public counterparts. There are many examples of this pattern to be found in very different political contexts such as Poland or Brazil. Although there is a perception that governments do not seem very effective in regulating higher education institutions, there is also a pervasive opinion that they should not be trusted in the same way as public institutions (see Castro and Navarro, 1999).

Moreover, the positioning of the private sector as a demand-absorbing sector presents other risks. Governments may use the development of the private sector in order to insulate the public sector from an uncontrolled expansion. However, in some cases, such as that of Portugal, once the demand stabilises, mainly due to demographic reasons, private institutions may be the most vulnerable to that changing context (Teixeira and Amaral, 2007). In Portugal, the number of enrolments to private higher education institutions decreased by 25% between 1996 and 2006, having first expanded since the early 1970s (see Table 8.4). In relative terms, the size of the private provision declined from 36% to 25% of all higher education enrolments during that ten-year period. This happened in the context of a modest growth of overall higher education student population.

Another important dimension in recent processes of the rapid expansion of the private sector has been the diversification of access to higher education. In many South American countries for example, where public higher education institutions attempted to retain some of their elitist nature, the expansion of the public sector often relied on the recruitment of more students from social groups with high economic and cultural capital (see Altbach, 1999 and Wells *et al.*, 2007). These groups have traditionally been over-represented in the elitist part of higher education system (Cohn and Geske, 2004).

This has led many students from families with lower academic qualifications to enrol in private institutions due to the difficulty in getting access to highly contested places in the most prestigious public universities. The presence of significant portions of students from families with lower income and/or lower cultural capital in private higher education institutions can be found in different parts of the world. For example, in the case of Portugal, Teixeira *et al.* (2006) have found that, at the height of its market share (in the mid-1990s), the private sector's enrolment was relatively less elitist than that of public universities as regards the level of schooling of the student's parents and not significantly different as regards the household's level of income (though clearly less inclusive on both accounts than the public vocational sector). In the case of Latin America, where the private sector often caters to a majority of students, there are several examples of this positive contribution to access. For instance, in the case of Brazil it was found that the share of private universities' enrolments coming from the most affluent groups was slightly lower than their public counterparts (Sampaio, 1999). As in the Portuguese case, the difference between public and private universities was even more noticeable when comparing the parents' levels of schooling, with the latter enrolling a larger proportion of students whose parents were illiterate or had less than secondary education.

These examples suggest that families regard a higher education degree as a good long-term investment due to the high private rates of return (Psacharopoulos and Patrinos, 2002). These positive private rates of return tend to increase significantly in those countries where the average level of schooling is low and when a small portion of the population has attained higher education. Individuals and families are willing to take a short-term financial burden because they expect the long-term return will largely compensate that.

However, these expectations have to be managed carefully since they are not always fulfilled. The data on rates of return are often an average result that hides significant differences according to degree. This is a problem that in the medium term may create significant frustration, especially if the pattern of disciplinary and geographical concentration of private institutions creates an excessive supply of graduates in certain areas. Moreover, since the cost of attending a private institution tends to be much higher than that of a public institution, the expansion of the private sector does not guarantee that disadvantaged groups will see their educational opportunities greatly enhanced.

External efficiency of the higher education system

One of the most significant and discussed results of the recent privatisation has also to do with its contribution to the external efficiency of the higher education system (see for example Meek *et al.*, 1996). The expectation was that the development of the private sector would contribute to making higher education more responsive to labour market demands. It was argued that privatisation could make higher education supply better balanced from a disciplinary perspective, reaching a wider geographical area than traditional institutions and turning out graduates better suited to foreseeable labour-market needs (Meek *et al.*, 1996). However, the strategy towards quantitative expansion and demand absorption seems to have undermined those expectations.

Initially there were strong expectations regarding the extent to which private institutions brought a more diversified supply at the regional level. However, more recent research in higher education has questioned this embedded belief. In the specific case of countries, where a late process of privatisation played a role in the massification process, there are indications that the private sector has had an overall negative effect in the diversity of the higher education system (Teixeira and Amaral, 2002). This is the case not only in those European countries with a large private sector, but also in Latin America and in many South-East Asian countries. For instance, in the case of Poland, Duczmal and Jongbloed (2007) found that the regional distribution of the post-transition wave of private institutions was largely concentrated in the capital and major metropolitan areas (see Table 8.7).

Table 8.7. **Emergence of private higher education institutions in Poland**

	Type of institution	Location				Total
		Warsaw	Large cities	Medium size cities	Small cities	
Period of establishment						
Pre-1991	Public	5	22	17	0	44
1991-97	Public	0	2	0	0	2
	Private	34	34	32	28	128
1997-2004	Public	0	0	7	17	24
	Private	24	41	25	42	133
Number of Institutions in 2004	Public	5	24	24	17	70
	Private	58	75	57	70	261

Source: Duczmal and Jongbloed (2007).

The analysis of recent waves of private institutions indicates that the data for Poland are not unusual and that the private sector tends to be strongly concentrated in the region of the capital city and in major urban areas. The analysis of recent waves of privatisation shows that private supply tends to be highly concentrated in the wealthiest and most highly populated regions (see Geiger, 1986 and Altbach, 1999). For instance, in the case of Portugal half of vacancies in private institutions are located in the capital city (Teixeira and Amaral, 2007). In the case of Brazil, the distribution has traditionally been concentrated in the southeast and southern parts of the country, which are also the wealthiest regions (Sampaio, 1999). In the case of Mexico, the dominant number of states in which the enrolment's share of the private sector is above the national average also have a per capita income higher than the average (Kent and Ramírez, 1999). In contrast, the public sector presents in general a more diversified distribution from a regional point of view due to the influence of local and regional authorities on governments.

Another result that tends to contradict most policy expectations concerns the disciplinary diversity of institutions emerging with privatisation. For example, Meek *et al.* (1996) considered that institutional responses to growing private provision and increased market competition could lead institutions not only to diversify in an attempt to capture a specific market niche, but also to imitate the activities of their successful competitors. The private higher education supply is frequently concentrated in low-cost programs with strong student demand such as social sciences (*e.g.* law, economics and management) (Wells *et al.*, 2007; see Table 8.8). Private institutions do not tend to invest in programmes with less promising employment prospects or in more technical and costlier areas, where their presence is relatively lower than that of the public sector (Levy, 2002).

Table 8.8. **Most common/popular study fields in private higher education institutions in selected countries**

High enrolment | Low enrolment | Insignificant enrolment

	Field of study[1]						
	Law	Economics	Social sciences	Humanities	Arts	Technical sciences	Health sciences
Albania							
Austria							
Bulgaria							
Estonia							
Germany							
Italy							
Poland							
Portugal							
Romania							
Russia							
Spain							
Turkey							
Ukraine							

1. Economics includes business, commerce, finance, and banking. Social sciences include political science, administration and management, international relations, pedagogy, psychology, and sociology. Technical sciences include information technology, engineering, architecture, biotechnology, transportation, and mathematics.

Source: UNESCO-CEPES project on Private Higher Education in Europe (2005), in Wells *et al.* (2007).

Almost every country portrayed in Table 8.8 presents high enrolment for the private sector in the areas of social sciences, law and economics and business. In countries with a significant private sector, it is not unusual to find that more than half of enrolled students are concentrated in the social sciences. In contrast, the presence in more technical and costlier areas tends to be lower than in the public sector (see individual country studies in Wells *et al.*, 2007). The costs of running programmes in those areas would imply very high tuition fees and in many cases this is hardly viable in terms of attracting enrolments. At the same time, these areas tend to be much more regulated, both by governments and professional associations, and it takes time for private institutions to obtain public and professional recognition of their degrees. Thus, the pattern of regional concentration of the private sector is coupled with a strong concentration also on the disciplinary distribution of enrolments.

Quality issues in recent privatisation

The quality of private higher education is one issue that has received greater attention with the recent development of the sector (see Wells *et al.*, 2007). Concerns with quality have been receiving increasing support among the private institutions themselves (Castro and Navarro, 1999) since many private institutions find it hard to compete with public institutions, notably because students pay more substantial tuition fees in private institutions.

One of the most contentious aspects of the development of the private sector is the scarce research activity in many private higher education institutions worldwide. This is particularly striking in light of the US experience where private higher education has been critical for the importance that research activities and graduate education have attained. The growth of research universities, many of which were established at the turn of the twentieth century was until the Second World War largely funded by private sources.[6] Although these universities enrol a small portion of students, their visibility within the United States and abroad has remained quite significant with many of them often leading international lists ranking universities' reputations. This situation has contributed to forging many of the ideas (and myths) about the United States and about private higher education.

The low priority given to research by many emerging private institutions in most countries is due to various factors of a financial and administrative nature. Research activities, especially basic research ones, have a very limited short-term economic return, despite their often high social value. Since in most countries private institutions have limited or no access to public research funding (and cannot find alternative sources through philanthropic institutions), they have to fund those activities themselves. Thus, when some private institutions develop research activities, it is based on cross-subsidisation from teaching funds and done mainly to enhance their prestige and attain some degree of academic legitimacy. It is not unlikely that, as they mature, some of those institutions will tend to give more attention to research activities, especially as an instrument of social and political recognition or under the presence of quality assurance labels.

A large part of the reason for the low research profile in recent development of the private sector has to do with staff issues. Many private institutions depend heavily on part-time staff (Levy, 2006). This issue tends to be particularly visible in the early phases of development of the private sector, since recently established institutions often find it difficult to recruit new staff and therefore tend to rely on staff already committed to other institutions, often public ones. This practice of "moonlighting" has created tensions between private and public higher education institutions (Altbach, 1999) and has raised concerns about the quality of the educational provision in places as diverse as eastern Europe, Latin America and South Asia. On the other hand, some parts of the private sector may be inclined to recruit part of the academic staff among professionals in the area of the academic programme. Thus, the private sector tends to present higher percentages of part-time staff (especially academic staff) clearly above those observed in their public counterparts (Levy, 2006); this is true even in countries with more mature processes of privatisation although it is more visible in Mediterranean and Latin American countries. The main rationale for this is the cost advantage. Not only does part-time staffing cost less, but it also provides a more flexible cost-structure that may help the institution to adapt to changes in student demand (see for example Wells *et al.*, 2007 and Altbach, 1999).

As many private institutions have a very limited capacity to develop research activities due to organisational factors, a large part of recent private sector institutions has remained focused on undergraduate programs designed to serve the short-term needs of the labour market. The most recently established private institutions do not have sufficiently qualified staff to develop post-graduate or advanced research programs, which are far more demanding in terms of academic and legal requirements than undergraduate programs. Traditionally, the private higher education sector has a less qualified staff and the better-qualified academic staff includes a number of retired professors from the public sector. For example, in the case of Brazil the percentage of academic staff with a Masters or PhD degree is above 50% in public universities and in private ones was around one third

(Sampaio, 1999). This is one of the reasons why postgraduate studies is still a minor activity in the sector.

In addition, not only is there the problem of good quality faculty, there are also shortages in sheer numbers which increases the ratio of faculty to students and dilutes quality. For example, in the case of Hungary, whereas the percentage of part-time staff was found to be above two-thirds in the recent private sector, it was 10% in the state universities (Nagy-Darvas and Darvas, 1999). In Japan, the private sector has for many years dominated the supply of undergraduate teaching, but private institutions have struggled to diversify into the postgraduate market (Goodman and Yonezawa, 2007). Other problems include a perceived lack of investment in infrastructure (buildings, libraries, laboratories and equipment) and dependence on traditional models of teaching, learning and assessment.

8.4. What future role for private higher education in times of mass higher education?

Although private higher education has a long historical significance, until recently its role was rather small in many higher education systems. However, during the last decades this situation has changed significantly, mainly due to the massive and continuous expansion of higher education worldwide. Pressed by increasing financial constraints and by an increasing cost-burden due to the massive expansion of the higher education sector, governments searched for ways of coping with this paradoxical situation, redefining not only their financial role but also their administrative and political roles. In many parts of the world, the promotion of private higher education has emerged as a viable policy alternative to the often over-stretched public sector.

Although in some cases it has been seen as a transitory phenomenon, the evidence seems to suggest that private higher education is becoming a permanent feature of the higher education landscape. As discussed earlier, the resilience of private higher education is strengthened not only in developing countries where the limitations in resources prevent governments from major expansions of their public higher education systems but also in many developed countries, where fiscal constraints conflict with the rising cost of (largely subsidised) public higher education. Thus it is important to identify some of the expected major issues of debate in the coming years concerning the role of the private sector in higher education.

A growing necessity

Arguably the most important feature of the future perspectives facing private higher education is that it is likely to become a more necessary part of the higher education landscape in the coming years. Higher education is expected to persist as an important priority in policy terms and, therefore, the expansion of higher education is also likely to continue to be pushed significantly by both social and individual behaviour. These expectations pose financial challenges on how to further expand higher education supply. One of the most likely responses to those financial challenges will be through strengthening market mechanisms in higher education, namely by increasing the *privateness* of the system.

This is likely to be a complex and controversial issue, especially in those countries where the existence of private institutions remained minimal, such as in most of western

Europe. The relevance of private higher education may be strengthened not only due to the financial constraints, but also in response to some of the shortcomings of past massification. In those countries where patterns of enrolment are still growing rapidly, the expansion of the private sector will tend to focus on the absorption of unfulfilled demand. However, in the more common post-massification cases, private institutions may position themselves as a high-quality/high-cost alternative to the mass/low-cost public higher education.

The acceptance of private higher education may also be enhanced by changes in the role of the state. The likely strengthening of a market orientation in higher education, especially in funding, will tend to position governments increasingly as contractors of higher educational services from autonomous institutions, which in many cases happen to be publicly owned, rather than as a provider of public higher education.

A changing profile

Although much of the recent expansion of private higher education has been characterised as a demand-absorption pattern, in the systems where the private sector has emerged after the consolidation of the massification process, this type of expansion does not seem to be a very plausible strategy of development. This is particularly the case in western Europe. In these post-massification cases, private institutions tend to prefer catering to market niches and presenting alternatives to mass higher education instead of reinforcing it. This more specialised approach may be expressed in such aspects as the type of programmes offered or the methods of teaching. Private institutions tend to position themselves as an elite alternative to a mass public system, rather than as a second-choice for those who could not get a place in the latter. While this does not mean that the former situation will disappear, there are signs that in some countries different types of private institutions are emerging, often in order to obtain a renewed academic and political legitimacy. This has been the case, for example, in western European countries such as Germany and Italy (Levy, 2006)

The consolidation of the private sector and its battle for growing acceptance is linked with another potential force of differentiation among private higher education institutions, namely a stronger commitment to research activities. In most examples of recent expansion of private higher education, the teaching mission has been dominant in these institutions have, which has been pointed out as a sign of weakness. However, a growing number of private institutions are increasingly aware that this undermines their legitimacy. These institutions have been trying to improve their academic pedigree such efforts as better qualification of their academic staff, an increase in the number of research centres affiliated with them, and the development of postgraduate programs. For example, in Spain, efforts have been focused on the qualification of the academic staff because the quality assurance system has increased the requirements. In Colombia, private institutions have anticipated this happening. In several Latin American countries where the presence of the private sector is both older and quantitatively strong, many have observed examples of this changing profile trend. Levy (1996) has documented a visible trend towards a more active role of the private sector in the social sciences and in the analysis of public policies. Although these developments are often still small (and mostly present in those systems where the expansion of the private sector is older and has stabilised its size), they are an important element to be followed and may become an important pattern of reconfiguration of the private sector in the future.

The quest for legitimacy

As private higher education grows and become more prominent, its quest for greater legitimacy will strengthen, an issue which is relevant on several levels for emerging private institutions. First, it is certainly relevant on the level of the teaching mission. Although many private institutions emerged in contexts of rapid expansion of higher education demand, many private institutions are already facing a more adverse situation where demand has tightened due to changes in demographic trends. Thus they have to demonstrate a significant capacity to attract students and, as a result, the quality of their programmes will become of greater concern. Second, it is relevant as private higher education institutions become entitled to benefit from public support to develop research activities. Finally, there is the issue of student support mechanisms. Many private institutions have been lobbying for their students to benefit from mechanisms of social support, which is often restricted to students enrolled in public institutions. Overall, it is an ambition of many private institutions to attain treatment similar to that awarded to most public institutions.

The implications of political and social legitimacy are fundamental for the capacity of higher education institutions to develop their mission. In many countries the level of institutional autonomy is not high and, in fact, is often below that of their public counterparts due to a difficult relationship with public authorities. The frequent mistrust of public authorities regarding private institutions has often been anchored in concerns about several controversial features of private higher education development (geographical and disciplinary distribution, balance between teaching and research, quality of the degrees provided), which have often been quite different from political expectations and created tensions within the higher education system.

Due to these concerns, governments have been increasingly willing to implement evaluation and accreditation mechanisms, often as an instrument to curtail the proliferation of private institutions. For example, in Spain the government has seized on the Bologna Process to increase the requirements regarding the qualification of the academic staff. Although this applies to all higher education institutions, it has been a challenge to many private institutions that frequently relied less on permanent staff and ranked research lower within their institutional priorities. Recent years have seen accreditation becoming a major policy focus in Latin American higher education. In Mexico, the national government and the public and private sectors' representative bodies have developed a new national accreditation system, namely because a very small portion of private institutions are not yet accredited (Kent, 2007). This increasing relevance of accreditation mechanisms as a way of regulating the private sector is likely to be strengthened with the consolidation of the private sector expansion.

The question of accreditation is likely to gain additional relevance due to two major developments that are emerging in private higher education sector. The first is the increasing visibility of for-profit private higher education or, in some cases, not-for-profit private institutions behaving like for-profit ones. This has become a major issue of debate in higher education policy in some countries, such as Brazil, the Philippines, South Africa and Malaysia, where a large share of the private providers are nowadays reportedly for-profit (Kinser and Levy, 2005). Secondly, there is the development of transnational private higher education. On this front the task of governments will also be difficult, balancing, on the one hand, the need to protect customers in a traditional opaque market such as higher education and, on the other hand, the potential of those purveyors to suppress the limitations of national providers.

There is some evidence that private institutions have been rather active in applying for accreditation, since accredited private institutions are often granted greater autonomy (Kim *et al.*, 2007). An analysis of the institutional responses in the case of Mexico suggests that, although some older private institutions fear that the trend towards accreditation may introduce further governmental intervention and regulation, several recently established institutions see national accreditation procedures as a necessary and useful step to enhance their academic reputation and gain political recognition (Kent, 2007). Some examples, like Chile, also point out that this process of academic and political legitimisation through accreditation tends to be more complex in the case of non-university private institutions (González, 1999).

A necessary partnership

After initial disconcertion, there is a growing recognition (Kim *et al.*, 2007) that private higher education will become a more integral part of the reality of mass higher education. The main force contributing to an acceptance of this realisation may be the blurring division of public and private higher education sectors. The growing pervasiveness of market elements in many higher education systems, namely the growing *privateness* of the public sector, has been slowly making it more difficult to distinguish between public and private institutions. Although this will make life more difficult for private institutions, who face more proactive behaviour from public institutions, it will also contribute to eroding resistance to including them as part of the higher education system.

Overall, one cannot help but expect that the role of private higher education in mass higher education systems will be strengthened in the coming years. Although the recent privatisation has often been characterised by controversy and some mismatches between expectations and results, private higher education may play an important role in mass higher education. This includes major aspects such as the expansion of higher education to respond to growing demand, the broadening of access and the development of some innovative programmes.

This strengthening of privatisation and *marketisation* forces does not mean that governments will retreat from any kind of regulation. On the contrary, as in any other market, some kind of regulation is needed, and higher education is no exception to that (Teixeira *et al.*, 2004). The more governments strengthen the role of markets and private initiative in higher education, the more they will need to give attention to issues such as the quantity and quality of the information available in the system, the consequences of enhanced institutional competition and the level of equity (either at the individual or at the institutional level).

The challenges for policy makers will be to learn how to use this rapidly expanding sector in the best possible manner, to steer it in a way that will contribute to social welfare and to fulfil the social expectations regarding the higher education sector. This will only be possible if governments are able to develop an integrated view of the higher education system in which different types of institutions could coexist. Easier said than done, this will be one of the major future challenges in higher education policy in many parts of the world.

Notes

1. Some of the arguments developed in this chapter were initially nurtured by my participation in the Fulbright New Century Scholar Group of 2005/2006 and its excellent team of scholars. The summary of the results produced by the various working groups are published in Altbach and Paterson (2007).

2. In 1693 was chartered by the Crown the College of William and Mary (Virginia), in 1745 the Connecticut College (later renamed Yale College also in honour of a private benefactor). In 1746 was chartered the College of New Jersey (that would eventually become Princeton University), in 1756 the King's College of New York (nowadays Columbia University). In 1755 was established the College of Philadelphia, which became the University of Pennsylvania in 1791. The last ones to be established in the colonial period were the College of Rhode Island in 1764 (nowadays Brown University), the Queen's College in New Jersey in 1766 (now Rutgers University), and finally Dartmouth College in 1769.

3. This is the case of some old universities in Japan, Korea, Philippines, and Indonesia. Even some of the new private universities in Asia have been able to reach a prestigious level such as the Aga Khan University in Pakistan. In addition, there are also a few high-quality specialized technical institutes in the Philippines, and Thailand. In Singapore there are elite business schools established in collaboration with prestigious counterparts in Europe and the United States. Unlike other countries, Indian private higher education institutions are heavily subsidized by the state (Altbach and Toru, 2004; Altbach, 1999).

4. A market mechanism is usually presented by economics as mechanism of allocation of resources based on a multiplicity of individual decisions that, through the interaction of supply and demand forces. A market system is normally associated with significant degree of competition between individuals, a high degree of freedom for each agent, and a strong economic motivation of individuals to obtain gains from those activities.

5. For an illustration of this see the analysis of the Japanese case in Goodman and Yonezawa (2007). Levy (1996) also points out that the private sector traditional concentration in certain fields is clearly reflected in its research activity.

6. This changed after the Second World War with the emergence of the so-called Federal Research Economy, through which federal government came to play an increasing and dominant role in funding of research activities inside and outside these universities.

Bibliography

Altbach, Philip and Patti McGill Peterson (eds.) (2007), *Higher Education in the New Century – Global Challenges and Innovative Ideas*, Center for International Higher Education – Boston College and UNESCO.

Altbach, Philip and T. Umakoshi (eds.) (2004), *Asian Universities – Historical Perspectives and Contemporary Challenges*, John Hopkins Press.

Altbach, Philip G. (ed). (1999), *Private Prometheus: Private Higher Education and Development in the 21st Century*, Greenwood Publishing, Westport, CT.

Amaral, Alberto, V. Lynn Meek and Ingvil M. Larsen (eds.) (2003), *The Higher Education Managerial Revolution?*, Kluwer, Dordrecht.

Balán, Jorge and Ana Fanelli (2002), "El Sector Privado de la Educación Superior", in Rollin Kent (ed.) *Los Temas Críticos de la Educación Superior en América Latina en los Años Noventa*, FCE, Mexico.

Barr, Nicholas (2004), *The Economics of the Welfare State*, Oxford, OUP.

Blöndal S., S. Field and N. Girouard (2002), "Investment In Human Capital Through Post-Compulsory Education and Training: Selected Efficiency and Equity Aspects", *OECD Economics Department Working Paper* No. 333.

Castro, Claudio de Moura and Juan Carlos Navarro (1999), "Will the Invisible Hand Fix Private Higher Education?", in Altbach (ed.), pp. 45-63.

Cave, M., M. Kogan and R. Smith (1990), *Output and Performance Measurement in Government. The State of the Art*, Jessica Kinsgley, London.

Cohn, Elchanan and Terry Geske (2004), *The Economics of Education*, Thomson South-Western.

Duczmal, Wojciech and Ben Jongbloed (2007), "Private Higher Education in Poland: A Case of Public-Private Dynamics", in Enders and Jongbloed (eds.), pp. 415-42.

Friedman, Milton (1962), *Capitalism and Freedom*, University of Chicago Press, Chicago.

Geiger, Roger (1986), *Private Sectors in Higher Education*, Ann Arbor, The University of Michigan Press.

Gerbod, Paul (2004), "Relations with Authority", in W. Rüegg (ed.) *An History of the University in Europe, Vol. III*, Cambridge University Press, Cambridge.

González, Luis Eduardo (1999), "Accreditation of Higher Education in Chile and Latin America", in Altbach (ed.), pp. 65-83.

Goodman, Roger and Akiyoshi Yonezawa (2007), "Market competition, Demographic Change, and Educational Reform: The Problems Confronting Japan's Private Universities in a Period of Contraction", in Enders and Jongbloed (eds.), pp. 443-70.

Gosden, Peter (1983), *The Education System since 1944*, Oxford, Martin Robertson.

Hammerstein, Notker (1996), "Relations with Authority," in H. de Ridder-Symoens (ed.), *An History of the University in Europe, Vol. II*, Cambridge University Press, Cambridge.

Hofstadter, Richard (1996), *Academic Freedom in the Age of College*, Transaction Publishers, New Brunswick.

Kent, Rollin and Rosalba Ramírez (1999), "Private Higher Education in Mexico: Growth and Differentiation", in Altbach (ed), pp. 85-99.

Kim, Sunwoong; G., Zulfikar, P. Landoni, N. Musisi and Pedro Teixeira (2007), "Rethinking Public-Private Mix in Higher Education: Global Trends and National Policy Challenges", in Altbach and Peterson (eds.), pp. 79-108.

Kinser, Kevin (2006), *From Main Street to Wall Street – The Transformation of For-Profit Higher Education*; ASHE Higher Education, Reports, Vol. 31, No. 5.

Kinser, Kevin and Daniel C. Levy (2005), "The For-Profit Sector: U.S. Patterns and International Echoes in Higher Education"; PROPHE Working Paper #5.

Levy, Daniel C. (2006), "An Introductory Global Overview: The Private Fit to Salient Higher Education Tendencies", PROPHE Working Paper #7.

Levy, Daniel C. (2002), "Unanticipated Development: Perspectives on Private Higher Education's Emerging Roles", PROPHE (Program for Research on Private Higher Education) Working Paper #1.

Levy, Daniel C. (1996), *Building the Third Sector – Latin America's Private Research Centers and Nonprofit Development*, University of Pittsburgh Press, Pittsburgh.

Levy, Daniel C. (1986), *Higher Education and the State in Latin America: Private Challenges to Public Dominance*, University of Chicago Press, Chicago.

Meek, V. L., L. Goedegebuure, O. Kivinen, and R. Rinne (eds.),(1996), *The Mockers and the Mocked: Comparative Perspectives on Differentiation, Convergence, and Diversity in Higher Education*, Pergamon Press, Oxford.

Min, Weifang (2004), "Chinese Higher Education: The Legacy of the Past and the Context of the Future", in Altbach and Umakoshi (eds.), pp. 53-84.

Mincer, Jacob (1993), *Studies in Human Capital*, Edward Elgar, Aldershot.

Middleton, Roger (1997), *Government Versus the Market: The Growth of the Public Sector, Economic Management and British Economic Performance*, Edward Elgar, Aldershot.

Nagy-Darvas, Judit and Peter Darvas (1999), "Private Higher Education in Hungary: The Market influences the University", in Altbach (ed.), pp. 161-80.

Neave, Guy (2001), "The European Dimension in Higher Education: An Excursion into the Modern Use of Historical Analogues", in Jeroen Huisman, Peter Maassen and Guy Neave (eds.) *Higher Education and the Nation State*, Oxford: Pergamon, pp. 13-73.

Neave, Guy (2000), "Universities' Responsibilities to Society: An Historical Exploration of an Enduring Issue", in Neave (ed.) *The Universities' Responsibilities to Society – International Perspectives*, Pergamon/Elsevier, London, pp. 1-28.

Neave, Guy and Van Vught, Frans (eds.) (1994), *The Winds of Change – Government and Higher Education Relationships Across Three Continents*, Pergamon Press, London.

Neave, Guy and Van Vught, Frans (eds.) (1991), *Prometheus Bound: The Changing Relationship Between Government and Higher Education in Western Europe*, Pergamon Press, London.

OECD (2007), *Education at a Glance*, OECD Publishing, Paris.

OECD (2008a), *Education at a Glance*, OECD Publishing, Paris.

OECD (2008b), *Tertiary Education for the Knowledge Society. Volume 1 Special Features: Governance, Funding, Quality*, OECD Publishing, Paris.

Psacharopoulos, G and H. A. Patrinos (2002), *Returns to Investment in Education: A Further Update*, World Bank Policy Research Working Paper 2881, September 2002, pp. 29.

Roberts, John, Á. M. Cruz and J. Herbst (1996), "Exporting Models", in Hilde de Ridder-Symoens (ed.), *A History of the University in Europe*, Vol. II, (1500-1850), Cambridge, CUP, pp. 256-82.

Romer, Paul (1986), "Increasing Returns and Long-Run Growth", *Journal of Political Economy*, Vol. 94, No. 5, pp. 1002-37.

Sampaio, Helena (1999), *Ensino Superior no Brasil*, FAPESP/Editora HUCITEC, São Paulo.

Shils, Edward and Roberts, John (2004), "The Diffusion of European Models Outside Europe," in W. Rüegg (ed.), *An History of the University in Europe*, Vol. III, Cambridge University Press, Cambridge.

Teichler, U. (1988), *Changing Patterns of the Higher Education System: The Experience of Three Decades*, London, Jessica Kingsley Publishers.

Teixeira, Pedro, B. Johnstone, M. J. Rosa and H. Vossensteyn (eds.) (2006), *Cost-Sharing and Accessibility in Higher Education – A Fairer Deal?*, Springer, Dordrecht.

Teixeira, Pedro, D. Dill, B. Jongbloed and A. Amaral (eds.) (2004), *The Rising Strength of Markets in Higher Education*, Kluwer, Dordrecht.

Teixeira, Pedro and A. Amaral,(2008), "Can Private Institutions Learn from Mistakes? – Some Reflections based on the Portuguese Experience", *DieHochschule*; forthcoming.

Teixeira, Pedro and A. Amaral (2007), Waiting for the Tide to Change? Strategies for Survival of Portuguese Private HEIs, *Higher Education Quarterly*, Vol. 61, No. 2, pp. 208-22.

Teixeira, Pedro, and A. Amaral (2002), "Private Higher Education and Diversity: An Exploratory Survey", *Higher Education Quarterly*, Vol. 55, No. 4, pp. 359-95.

Thelin, John R. (2004), *A History of American Higher Education*, Baltimore, John Hopkins University Press.

UNESCO Institute for Statistics (UIS) (2006), *Global Education Digest 2006*, UIS, Montreal.

UNESCO/OECD (2006), *Education Trends in Perspective – Analysis of the World Education Indicators,* UNESCO Institute For Statistics, OECD, World Education Indicators Programme.

Van Vught, Frans (ed.) (1989), *Governmental Strategies and Innovations in Higher Education*, Jessica Kingsley, London.

Vincent-Lancrin, S. (2009), "What is Changing in Academic Research? Trends and Prospects", in *Higher Education 2030, Volume 2: Globalisation*, OECD Publishing, Paris.

Wells, P. J., J. Sadlak and L. Vlăsceanu (eds.) (2007), *The Rising Role and Relevance of Private Higher Education in Europe*, UNESCO – CEPES, Bucharest.

Williams, Gareth (1991), "The Many Faces of Privatisation", *Higher Education Management*, Vol. 8, pp. 39-56.

Winston, Gordon C (1999), "Subsidies, Hierarchy and Peers: The Awkward Economics of Higher Education", *Journal of Economic Perspectives*, Vol. 13, No. 1, pp. 13-36.

Wittrock, Bjorn (1993), "The Modern University: The Three Transformations", in Rothblatt and Wittrock (eds.) *The European and American University since 1800 – Historical and Sociological Essays*, Cambridge University Press, Cambridge, pp. 303-62.

Wittrock, B. and W. Peter (1996), "Social Science and the Building of the Early Welfare State: Toward a Comparison of Statist and Non-Statist Western Societies", in Dietrich Rueschemeyer and Theda Skocpol (eds.) *States, Social Knowledge and the Origins of Modern Social Policies*, Princeton University Press, Princeton, New Jersey.

World Bank (2009), *World Bank Statistics*, accessed 15 July 2009, *http://go.worldbank.org/RQBDCTUXW0*.

Higher Education to 2030
Volume 2: Globalisation
© OECD 2009

Chapter 9

Finance and Provision in Higher Education: A Shift from Public to Private?

by

Stéphan Vincent-Lancrin*

This chapter examines to what extent there has been a shift away from public provision and funding in higher education in OECD countries in the past decade. It first focuses on relative enrolments in the public and private sectors to show that enrolments in the public sector have not significantly declined, and only marginally benefited the private for-profit sector. It then analyses changes in the funding of tertiary education from the perspectives of tertiary education institutions, students and governments. It shows that only students have experienced a shift away from public funding. Finally, the paper points to other possible reasons for the perceived decline of the public model of higher education.

* OECD, Directorate for Education, Centre for Educational Research and Innovation (CERI). The author gratefully acknowledges Kiira Kärkkäinen for her helpful comments and a background paper on private and public funding carried out for the OECD project on the future of higher education (Kärkkäinen, 2006).

9.1. Introduction

There is growing concern that public higher education institutions, and particularly public research universities, are losing ground compared to private research universities: this is the so-called "crisis of the publics". There is also a feeling of a "crisis" of public higher education, relating to the perception of an underfunding of public tertiary education, especially when compared to US tertiary education, and some concerns about the rise of competition, trade, private providers and market mechanisms. Many observers see the traditional public model governing tertiary education changing, for better or for worse. Something is changing in tertiary education and tertiary education currently ranks higher in policy debates than it used to: anecdotal evidence is that OECD Education Ministers decided to devote their 2006 meeting to higher education. Several projects discussing the possible future of higher education, such as the Spelling Commission on the Future of Higher Education in the United States (US Department of Education, 2006) also point to this widespread perceived urge to engage a dialogue about recent trends and possible and desirable changes in higher education in the coming decades.[1]

Is the public model of tertiary education really declining, and, if yes, in what sense? This chapter gives an answer to this question by analysing international aggregated data and examining how the public provision and funding of tertiary education has evolved in the OECD area in the past decade – with an emphasis on research universities when the data enable it. The first section focuses on relative enrolments in the public and the private sector and shows that enrolments in the public sector have not significantly declined and only marginally benefited the private for-profit sector. The second section analyses changes in the funding of tertiary education from the perspectives of tertiary education institutions, students and governments. It shows that students have to some extent experienced a recent decline in the public funding of their studies. Otherwise, there has been a remarkable stability. The third section concludes by pointing to other possible reasons for the perceived decline of the traditional model of public higher education.

9.2. Trends in enrolments in public and private higher education

Along with the discussion on the inclusion of education services in the General Agreement on Trade in Services (GATS) under the World Trade Organization (WTO) and on the "commodification" of higher education (OECD, 2004), there has been a lot of public concern about the emergence of new types of providers, in particular for-profit providers (Cunningham *et al.*, 2000; Knight, 2004). There is a perception of an expansion and increasing competition from the private for-profit sector in a sector which has traditionally been public or not-for-profit. This perception is pervasive in all segments of the tertiary education sector, from research universities to community colleges (Bailey, 2007).

To what extent is public tertiary education losing ground? Is the private sector becoming more attractive to students? One way to answer these questions is to look at the relative importance of enrolments in private and public tertiary education institutions in OECD countries and how this has changed over time. Given the way international statistics are collected (and that the concept of a "research university" does not exist in all OECD countries), enrolments in advanced research programs (ISCED 6) will be the closest indicator of what happens in research universities.

Public and private, for-profit and not-for-profit, institutions refer to different animals across OECD countries, with different conditions of operation and relationships to public authorities and their stakeholders. In international statistics (OECD, 2008a), the definitions of public and private are the following:

- A *public* institution is "controlled and managed directly by a public education authority or agency, or is controlled and managed either by a government agency directly or by a governing body (Council, Committee etc.), most of whose members are appointed by a public authority or elected by public franchise."

- A *private* institution is "controlled and managed by a nongovernmental organisation (*e.g.* a Church, Trade Union or business enterprise), or its Governing Board consists mostly of members not selected by a public government agency but by private institutions."

The source of funding is an additional dimension of what defines private institutions. Otherwise, the difference between public and private could be purely formal or legal. There is thus an additional distinction between private institutions: depending on their funding, some are *government-dependent* while others are *independent* private institutions. Government-dependent private institutions receive (by definition) more than 50% of their core funding from government agencies. Independent private institutions receive less than 50%. Hence, independent private institutions are the institutions generally referred to as private (or the closest to the common understanding).

Public and government-dependent private institutions are not necessarily very different, at least in public perception. For example, in the United Kingdom, higher education institutions are generally considered public, although they are technically government-dependent private. Australia has a very close system to the British system, but almost all institutions are actually public, although their funding comes to a larger extent from private sources than in the United Kingdom. In 2004, a new law incurring some changes in the composition of the governing boards of Dutch universities including more members from non-governmental organisations has changed the formerly "public" higher education institutions into government-dependent private institutions, although most observers would not describe this particular aspect of the reform as a radical change in the Dutch university system. In statistical terms, it implies that the public sector has become a "not applicable" category. The recent (2004) "incorporation" of Japanese public universities will lead to the same outcome in future international statistics about Japan. A recent law (July 2007) that gives full autonomy to public universities in France might lead to the same result.

First of all, higher education is (still) structurally a public enterprise in almost all OECD countries (Figure 9.1). Independent private institutions are a small segment of the system in most OECD countries, even when growing. The (independent) private sector represents slightly more than 10% of total tertiary education enrolments in Spain and France, about 30% in Poland, the United States and Mexico, and over three quarters of enrolments in Japan and Korea. While it is more important in other economically advanced non-OECD countries, especially in Asia and South America, it is only in Japan and Korea that it

Figure 9.1. **Distribution of all tertiary education enrolments (full-time equivalent) by control of institution, 2006**

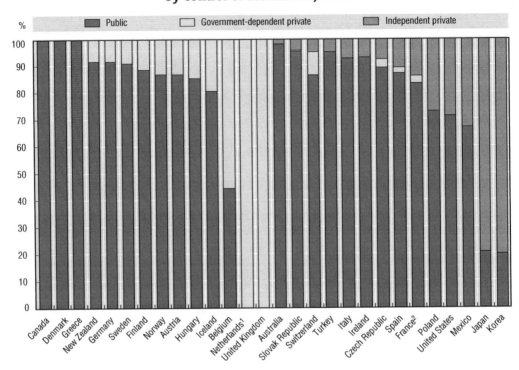

1. 2005 instead of 2006.
2. 2004 instead of 2006.

overtakes the public sector within the OECD area. The share of enrolments in the private sector is consistently and significantly lower for advanced research programs, except in the United States, where the share of enrolments in independent private institutions increases to 42% (Figure 9.2), against 28% for total tertiary education. In many countries, independent private institutions are on average smaller and less prestigious (and thus often less research intensive) than public institutions (see *e.g.* Teixeira, 2009; Levy, 2002). Japan and Korea are good counter-examples though, as they have a good public/private balance at the top of their national institutional hierarchy – and some other countries have their counter-examples too, but more scattered. The Table 9.A1.1 in annex presents the underlying enrolment data.

Although most students are enrolled in public or government-dependent private tertiary education institutions, a rapid change in the distribution of enrolments in favour of independent private higher education institutions would certainly be a sign of an OECD-wide decline of the public tertiary education sector. Table 9.1 shows recent changes in the distribution of enrolments: the share of total enrolments in public institutions has dropped by 3% points on average between 1998 and 2006 (or 1.8% without the Netherlands). The independent private sector benefited from 1.5% points of this average shift. Most of the enrolment shift went to government-dependent private institutions. Poland, the Czech Republic, Slovak Republic, Mexico, Turkey and France are the countries where private institutions have expanded their share the most against both public and government-dependent private institutions. In Belgium and Italy, the public sector has regained ground. At the same time, the structure of enrolments in advanced

Figure 9.2. **Distribution of enrolments in advanced research programs (full-time equivalent) by control of institution, 2006**

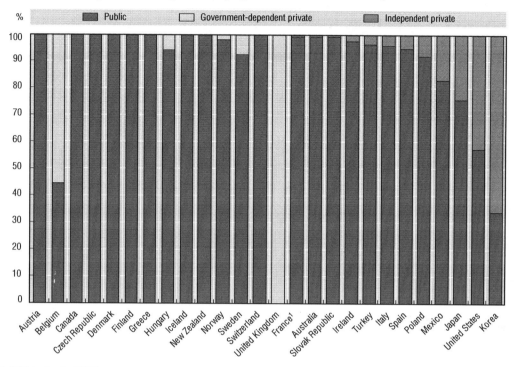

1. 2005 instead of 2006.

research programs (ISCED 6), that is those which are typically the most relevant for research universities, has changed very little (when data are available). In Mexico, however, there has been a significant increase (18.3% points) in the share of public advance research programme enrolments.

While data have the advantage of being comparable over this eight-year period, as they were all collected according to the latest ISCED classification, it is possible that the time series is too short to show the erosion of the public sector in terms of enrolments. At this aggregated level, one can also look further back without too many comparability problems, but for a smaller number of countries. One should be cautious with the data though. It is only in 1992 that the distinction between government-dependent and independent private was introduced. However, data were already collected between public and private institutions in 1985 and are available for 1985 and 2004 in 18 OECD countries. Over this 21-year period, the drop in the share of tertiary education enrolments in public institutions is more marked, at about 4% points, but it is still modest (see Table 9.2). What the data indicate too is a slowdown of the decreasing share of public institutions in most countries: Norway and Japan are the sole countries were the relative decrease has accelerated in the most recent period.

It is noteworthy that a loss in the relative share of public institutions in total tertiary education enrolments does not imply an absolute decrease in enrolments. In almost all countries, enrolments in public institutions have increased in the same period, sometimes significantly (OECD, 2008b). Again, it does not imply either that students haemorrhaged to the independent private sector.

Table 9.1. **Change in the distribution of students (full-time equivalent) enrolled in tertiary education and in advanced research programs by control of institutions between 1998 and 2006 (% points)**

	All tertiary education programs			Advanced research programs		
	Type of institution			Type of institution		
	Public	Government dependent private	Independent private	Public	Government dependent private	Independent private
Australia	m	0.0	1.7	−0.4	m	m
Austria	−7.5	7.5	m	0.0	m	m
Belgium	24.8	29.8	m	25.7	11.9	m
Canada	1.0	m	m	0.0	m	m
Czech Republic	−6.2	−1.4	m	0.0	m	m
Denmark	0.1	m	m	0.0	m	m
Finland	−0.3	0.3	m	0.0	m	m
France	−3.5	−0.2	3.7	−0.4	m	m
Germany	−3.1	m	m	m	m	m
Greece	0.0	m	m	0.0	m	m
Hungary	−3.5	3.5	m	−4.2	4.2	m
Iceland	−14.9	14.9	m	0.0	m	m
Ireland	−1.4	m	1.7	−2.2	m	2.2
Italy	5.6	m	−5.6	−0.2	m	0.2
Japan	−0.4	m	0.4	−0.1	m	0.1
Korea	−0.2	m	0.2	−2.4	m	2.4
Mexico	−6.1	m	6.1	18.3	m	−18.3
Netherlands	−32.2	32.2	0	m	m	m
New Zealand	−5.3	7.2	m	0.0	m	m
Poland	−10.6	m	10.6	−0.1	m	0.1
Slovak Republic	−4.3	0.1	m	m	m	m
Spain	−1.4	1.9	−0.5	−1.3	m	1.3
Sweden	−3.0	3.0	m	−0.8	0.8	m
Switzerland	0.7	−0.4	−0.4	0.0	m	m
Turkey	−3.3	m	m	m	m	m
United Kingdom	m	0.0	m	m	0.0	m
United States	0.0	m	0.0	−3.8	m	3.8
OECD country mean	**−3.0**	**6.6**	**1.5**	**1.3**	**4.2**	**−1.0**

m = missing data.

Notes: Belgium and Slovak Republic, 1999 instead of 1998; France, 2005 instead of 2006; Netherlands, 2004 instead of 2006.

These enrolment patterns may be interpreted as a relative decline of the public higher education sector, but arguably not a critical one, and one that has only modestly benefited the independent private sector. Moreover, the change is almost negligible for advanced research programs so that there is less evidence of a decline of public research institutions (by this indicator).

Although Korea relies more heavily than any other OECD country on independent private institutions for its research training, the United States ranks second and is the only country where the private sector seems to have a strong presence and competitive advantage in advanced research programs compared to other types of institutions. One reason why the decline of public "research universities" is (generally) not perceived in relation to private education outside the United States may come from this difference: there are few countries where public research universities have strong private competitors, just because the (independent) private sector is generally much less important. This does not mean that public research universities do not feel ill equipped to compete with US

Table 9.2. **Change in the share of tertiary education students (full-time and part-time) enrolled in public institutions (% points)**

	1985-2006	1998-2006
Austria	−10.5	−7.5
Belgium	7.6	24.0
Canada	10.2	0.9
Czech Republic	−7.7	−3.5
Denmark	−1.9	−1.8
Finland	−7.8	0.6
France	−5.3	−3.6
Hungary	−13.9	−3.3
Ireland	−5.6	−2.4
Italy	−0.8	5.6
Japan	0.9	−1.1
Luxembourg	0.0	0.0
Netherlands	−12.7	−3.3
New Zealand	−9.1	−6.6
Norway	4.1	−3.0
Portugal	−11.6	9.5
Spain	−4.3	−2.6
Sweden	−6.3	−2.1
Switzerland	−2.1	−1.3
Turkey	−4.8	−3.3
United States	−3.0	0.7
OECD country mean	**−4.0**	**−0.2**

Notes: Japan and Luxembourg, 1986 instead of 1985; Sweden, 1989 instead of 1985; Czech Republic and Hungary, 1991 instead of 1985; Belgium, 1999 instead of 1998; the Netherlands, 2002 instead of 2006.

private research universities, as US public universities sometimes do, but this is rather perceived as a loss of *global* competitiveness and a challenge to their domestic public higher education in a changing global environment (Salmi, 2009a).

Three conclusions follow from this section:

1. The (independent) private sector has grown, sometimes significantly in some countries, but it is relatively small in most OECD countries and even less so for advanced research programs.

2. The growth of the government-dependent private sector is likely a sign of a change in public governance and management of higher education rather than an evidence of a rapid growth of the private sector. Public institutions are increasingly changing status to become more autonomous and less reliant on public authorities, without becoming "independent private". This shift is not pervasive though, and the traditional public sector remained the norm in most OECD countries as of 2009.

3. Except in the United States, public research universities have little domestic competition for their enrolments in advanced research programmes. This might explain why the "competitiveness of research universities" is not debated in terms of a public-private competition in most OECD countries, but rather in terms of funding and of a transformation of its public governance (*e.g.* Aghion *et al.*, 2008; Ferlie *et al.*, 2007).

9.3. Is public funding declining in higher education?

More than a decrease in enrolments and attractiveness to students, higher education may have experienced a shift away from public funding. Private US research universities topping international rankings are more affluent than their public counterparts. Yale University, one of the top private US universities, had an operating budget of USD 1.96 billion in 2006-07, for 11 358 undergraduate and graduate students and 3 384 faculty, and an endowment of USD 22.5 billion. By comparison, the University of California, Berkeley, one of the top public US research universities, had revenues of USD 1.7 billion in 2006-07, for 34 953 students (Fall 2007) and 2 028 hired and international faculty. The University of Vienna, one of the top Austrian research universities, had an operating budget of USD 354 million (EUR 309 million, transformed in PPPs) for about 72 000 students and 6 200 academic staff in 2006-07.[2] In other words, Yale had 3.5 times as much resources per student as Berkeley, and 35 times as much as the University of Vienna. Per faculty, however, Berkeley had 1.4 times as much resources as Yale and almost 15 times as much as Vienna. In addition, US public universities tend to be more affluent than other public universities in the OECD: Berkeley had also almost 10 times as much resources per student as Vienna. In Austria, a system relying almost exclusively on public funds, the operating budget for all tertiary education institutions equated USD 3.6 billion (in PPPs) in 2005, for 244 410 students and about 29 000 faculty (in 2003) – that is, twice as much as Yale University to serve more than twenty times more students and almost 9 times more faculty. Austria is the 7th best resourced system per student within the OECD area (see Figure 9.6). The figures speak for themselves.

There is a wide consensus in some OECD countries that the expansion of higher education systems has led to its underfunding, especially where it relies on a traditional public governance model. However, it should be reminded that there is no objective benchmark in this respect. While more money certainly means better resources, it does not necessarily imply better quality or cost-effectiveness; some less well funded systems might compare favourably to better resourced ones. Nobody knows what the optimal level of tertiary education funding ought to be.

The funding issue has many facets and varies according to the standpoints. Typically, governments, students (and their families), higher education institutions and their staff will have different perspectives/interests on this. In other words, a decline in public funding does not necessarily imply a decrease in funding generally and several conflicting perceptions may be accurate (depending on one's perspective). This section explores how the funding of tertiary education has changed at the macro-level. Here, international statistics do not allow one to see what happened in "research universities": the only thing that can be looked at is what happened in the funding of academic research (Vincent-Lancrin, 2009).

The institutional perspective

A "crisis" of public funding could take different forms from the perspective of tertiary education institutions: an absolute and/or relative decline in public funding, and, in countries where there is a significant private sector, a relative impoverishment of public higher education institutions compared to their independent private counterparts. This can have broad-reaching effects on education funding, research funding, as well as education and research facilities.

The funding of tertiary education institutions has increased in all OECD countries between 1995 and 2005, in real terms. On average, countries have spent 58% more for tertiary education institutions in 2005 than in 1995 (see Figure 9.3). Research expenditures in the academic sector have not suffered either: overall, research universities and academic centres have increased their share of research and development compared to other sectors between 1981 and 2006, and their funding accounted for 0.39% of GDP in 2006, against 0.28% in 1981. In real terms (constant prices), research expenditures have tripled during that time (Vincent-Lancrin, 2009).

Figure 9.3. **Change in expenditures on tertiary education institutions between 1995 and 2005 (Index of change 1995 = 100, GDP deflator and GDP, constant prices)**

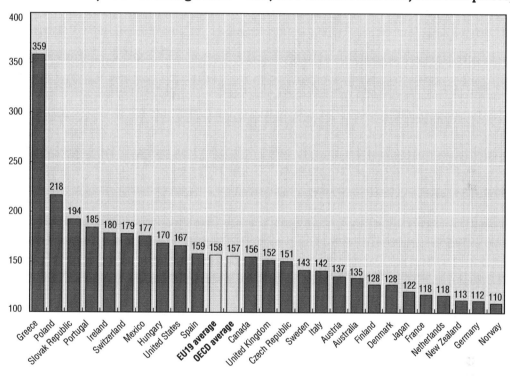

Source: OECD (2008a).

However, the budget growth has been more modest when the expansion of enrolments is taken into account, and has even decreased in six countries between 1995 and 2005. The budget per student of tertiary education institutions has increased by 13% on average over the same period of time, and by 11% since 2000 (Figure 9.4).

While the resources of tertiary education institutions have actually increased in recent years, the share of their public resources have on average diminished by 2.2 % points between 1995 and 2005 (Figures 9.5 and 9.6). However, in most OECD countries, their resources remain overwhelmingly public. Only in four countries do public resources represent less than 50% on average of an institution's budget, whereas they represent more than 70% in 16 countries. Table 9.3 shows that there were marked differences in changes across countries: the decrease in the share of public funding has been significant (over 25% points) in some countries (Poland and Portugal), but more modest or very small in most countries.

A relative decrease in public funding does not necessarily imply an absolute decrease in public funding: it can also result from the development of other funding

Figure 9.4. **Change in expenditures on tertiary education institutions for all services per student between 1995 and 2005 (Index of change 1995 = 100, GDP deflator and GDP, constant prices)**

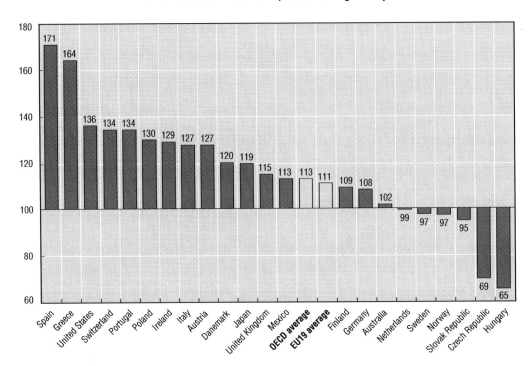

Source: OECD (2008a).

sources. Between 1995 and 2005, there was virtually no absolute decrease in direct public funding to tertiary education institutions (among those for which information was available on both years). Over the same period, the public funding *per student* has, however, decreased in absolute terms in six countries (with only one overlap with the decrease in direct public funding): Australia, Czech Republic, Finland, Hungary, the Netherlands and Sweden. If one looks at a shorter period of time, between 2000 and 2005, the picture changes slightly: in Japan there has been a decrease in public funding, while institutions have experienced a decrease in public funding per student in nine OECD countries.

Research performed by the higher education sector is largely government-funded in the OECD area. In 2006, the government sector funded directly or indirectly 72% on average of academic research: that year, government funding amounted to more than 80% of academic research in 15 out of the 30 OECD countries for which information is available. Between 1981 and 2006, the share of government funding has dropped by 6% points, most of the decrease having occurred before 1992 where this share was at 73%. In the United States, 70% of the funding for academic research came from public sources in 2006, against 67% in 1992 and 74% in 1981 (Vincent-Lancrin, 2009).

Changes in the allocation of expenditures within institutions could also explain the perception of a decreased funding. Some expenditures are more visible than others. International data on institutional cost structure are available, but they are difficult to interpret in this light without being supplemented by institutional case studies. Between 1998 and 2005, the share of capital expenditures in institutional budgets has decreased

Table 9.3. **Change in the distribution of funding to higher education institutions by stakeholder between 1995 and 2005 and change in public funding and public funding per student to higher education institutions (1995-2005)**

	2005			Shift 1995-2005 (% points)			Change in public funding 1995-2005 (1995 = 100, constant prices)	Change in public funding per student 1995-2005 (1995 = 100, constant prices, FTE)
	Government	Households	Other private entities (firms, etc.)	Government	Households	Other private entities (firms, etc.)		
Australia	47.8	36.3	15.9	−17.3	16.3	0.9	99	81
Austria	92.9	5.5	1.6	−5.0	3.4	1.6	132	126
Belgium	90.6	5.0	4.4	m	m	m	m	m
Canada	55.1	22.3	22.6	−6.0	8.7	−2.5	151	m
Czech Republic	81.2	9.4	9.4	10.9	4.9	−15.9	170	86
Denmark	96.7	3.3	n	−2.5	2.5	m	125	102
Finland	96.1	m	m	−3.9	m	m	126	61
France	83.6	10.3	6.1	−0.8	−1.5	2.3	114	m
Germany	85.3	m	m	−6.8	m	m	106	103
Greece	96.7	0.4	2.9	−3.3	0.4	2.9	365	167
Hungary	78.5	6.9	14.6	m	m	m	166	70
Iceland	91.2	8.8	m	−1.8	1.8	m	m	m
Ireland	84.0	14.1	1.9	16.9	−13.1	1.9	219	144
Italy	69.6	18.0	12.5	−13.9	5.8	8.3	118	105
Japan	33.7	53.4	12.9	−9.1	−3.8	12.9	117	114
Korea	24.3	52.1	23.6	8.7	−10.8	2.1	m	m
Luxembourg	m	m	m	m	m	m	m	m
Mexico	69.0	30.6	0.5	−8.4	7.9	0.5	158	m
Netherlands	77.6	12.0	10.4	−10.7	0.4	10.3	113	99
New Zealand	59.7	40.3	m	m	m	m	113	m
Norway	m	m	m	m	m	m	110	103
Poland	74.0	26.0	m	−26.0	26.0	m	218	m
Portugal	68.1	23.4	8.5	−28.4	23.4	8.5	132	m
Slovak Republic	77.3	9.1	13.6	77.3	9.1	13.6	149	m
Spain	77.9	18.7	3.4	1.5	1.3	−2.8	166	151
Sweden	88.2	n	11.8	−4.1	m	5.4	132	95
Switzerland	m	m	m	m	m	m	179	133
Turkey	m	m	m	m	m	m	m	m

m = missing data

Notes: Canada year of reference 2004 instead of 2005.

Source: OECD Education at a Glance 2008; OECD Education Database.

on average by 3% points (and represented 9% on average of an OECD country's institutional budget in 2005). On one hand, a decrease in the share of capital expenditure can correspond to an underinvestment in capital (and thus be interpreted as an evidence of budget pressures), but it can also mean there is more available income for current teaching and research activities (budget relief). Conversely, a significant increase in the share of capital expenditures could correspond to an upgrade of facilities having a positive impact on work conditions for teaching and research. Between 1998 and 2005, the share of current expenditures other than staff compensation has increased by 2% points in institutions' budget (to 29.6% of their budget on average). In Czech Republic, France, Mexico and Sweden, where the expenditures have actually fallen more than 8% points, the drop could indicate that available income for teaching and research has diminished. Such a decrease could be due to the ageing of staff (whose compensation grows more quickly than the total budget). But more compensation for staff could also be

Figure 9.5. **Distribution of direct funding for higher education institutions by source 2005 (%)**

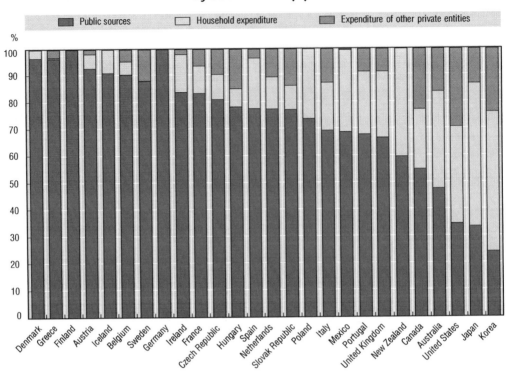

Note: Canada, 2004 instead of 2005.
Source: OECD (2008).

due to the expansion of staff and represent less rather than more pressure on institutional budgets and conditions of work. No conclusions about budget pressure can thus be drawn from these data alone.

The main conclusion is a trend towards a smaller share of public resources in institutional budgets, generally because of a quicker growth of other sources of income: this has happened in 19 countries (with different magnitudes). Tertiary education institutions have experienced an increase in their budget (or expenditures) in all OECD countries over the past decade, but their funding per student has decreased in six countries. Overall, their public funding has increased (or remained the same) as well as their public funding per student (except in six countries). Seven countries stand out and may indeed experience a public funding decline: in Australia, there was a decrease in public funding per student, in the share of public funding, as the overall level of public funding has virtually remained the same over the ten-year period; in Italy, Finland and Sweden, there was a decrease in the share of public funding, but also in public funding per student (and, in the case of Sweden, in funding per student); finally, the Hungarian and Czech institutions experienced a drop in funding per student as well as in public funding per student. In 9 other OECD countries, tertiary education institutions only experienced a decrease in their share of public funding between 1995 and 2005: while this may be the consequence of insufficient public funding, it is not a strong evidence of a major public funding crisis.

Figure 9.6. **Annual expenditure per student on core services, ancillary services and R&D by source of funding (2005) (in equivalent US dollars converted using PPPs for GDP, based on full-time equivalents [FTE])**

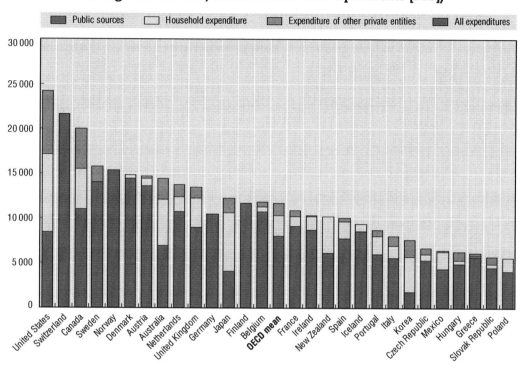

Note: Canada: year of reference 2004 instead of 2005; Canada, Hungary, Italy, Poland, Portugal, Slovak Republic: including subsidies attributable to payments to educational institutions received from public sources; Switzerland and Norway: all expenditures, no breakdown available.

Source: OECD (2008a).

A caveat to this discussion is that averages can hide big variations within countries and the average story can vary greatly from the individual ones. The distribution of public funding within countries may have become more concentrated and left a majority of institutions less well off than they used to be (even if the average story is different). Conversely, the distribution of public funding may have become less concentrated and some top research universities may feel they have been inadequately funded compared to other national institutions or their foreign counterparts.

The student (household) perspective

From a student perspective, there has been a small decrease in (public) funding in recent years in the sense that, overall, students (and their families) have made a greater contribution to the cost of their higher education than in the past, both in absolute and relative terms. In most OECD countries though, their tertiary education is still subsidised to a great extent.

In international statistics, the best estimate of the cost of tertiary education to students is the households' contribution to the expenditures (or budget) of tertiary education institutions. This contribution typically consists of tuition fees but it can include other components like boarding fees and all other payments made to institutions (*e.g.* for meals, textbooks and other instructional material, etc.). Given the differences of habits regarding boarding and provision of other services than teaching by the institutions themselves, the data are only imperfectly comparable: an institution offering catering or boarding to students will for example get more student contribution than one where catering and housing are left to external providers, although the cost of tertiary education to the student would in all cases include living costs. However, in most countries non-fee revenues are small enough to make it a fairly good proxy.

While institutions' resources have increased, the share coming from households has increased by 4% points on average between 1995 and 2005. Figure 9.7 shows that there have been marked differences across countries: in most countries, this share has been fairly stable. Changes towards more household contribution have occurred in Australia, Portugal and Poland – while changes in Korea and Ireland have taken the opposite direction.

Figure 9.7. **Change in the share of resources coming from households in tertiary education institutions' expenditures, 1995-2005 (% points)**

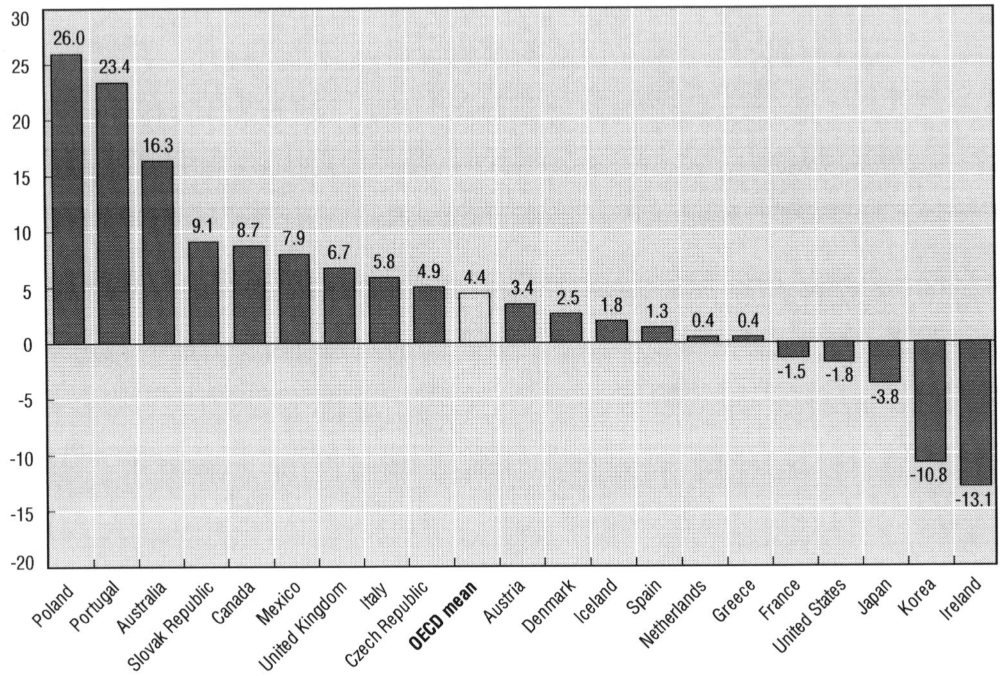

Source: OECD Education Database and OECD (2008a).

The relative stability of students' share to the expenditures of tertiary education institutions in most countries does not mean that there was no change in the cost to students and their families. Indeed, as shown in the previous section, the expenditures of tertiary education institutions have risen. In absolute terms, the level of the household contribution in constant prices has increased in almost all countries for which information was available for both 1995 and 2005 – with the exception of Ireland (–70%). It is noteworthy that tuition fees were first introduced in several countries since the early 1990s: before 1998, tertiary education students did for example not pay fees in the United Kingdom, while student payments represented 25% of British institutions' budget in 2005. Given that the distribution of enrolments in the private and public sector has remained more or less stable over that period, the increase has occurred across the board rather than as a mechanical impact of the growth of the private sector.

In power purchasing parities, the average contribution of students to tertiary education institutions' expenditures amounted to USD 2 348 in 2005, while the median was at USD 1 776. Figure 9.8 shows that household contribution varies significantly across countries. These average costs can also hide a large variance within countries. The cost of tertiary education to students is significantly higher in the United States and in Japan than in other countries. US households contribute the most to tertiary education institutions, with an average contribution per student of USD 8 795. While boarding costs probably weigh more than in many other countries, this is mainly due to higher tuition fees. In 2008 tuition fees represented 46% of US undergraduate students' contribution to public four-year institutions, 74% for private four-year institutions (while there is typically no boarding at two-year institutions that enrol about 40% of US students) (College Board, 2008). In the United States, the cost of tertiary education to families (including tuition fees) varies significantly for public two-year colleges, public four-year institutions, and private four-year institutions. In 2008, costs to *undergraduate* students averaged USD 2 402 at public two-year institutions (tuition only), USD 14 333 (including USD 6 585 of tuition and fees) at public four-year institutions, USD 13 046 (tuition fees only) at private for-profit institutions, and USD 34 132 (including USD 25 143 of tuition fees) at private four-year institutions.[3]

The cost of tertiary education to students (and their families) can be alleviated by student aid, but student aid does not have a big impact on the cost per student on average (although it has a big positive impact on those receiving it according to many studies (*e.g.* Dynarski, 2003, 2004). Only 1.44% of the private funding of tertiary education institutions was actually an indirect public subsidy in 2005 on average in OECD countries (OECD, 2008). In many countries, student aid is supposed to support living costs rather than tuition fees (especially

Figure 9.8. **Contribution of households to the expenditures of tertiary education institutions, 2005 (USD and PPPs, based on FTE)**

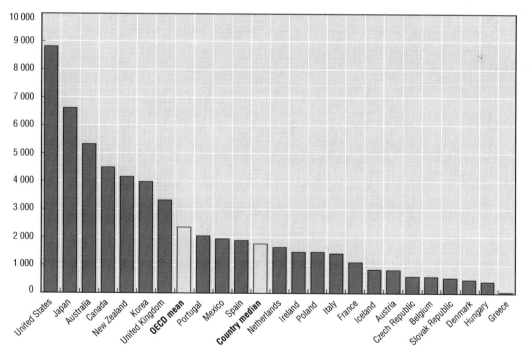

Note: Same as Figure 9.6.

Source: OECD (2008a).

as they are often low and publicly subsidised in the OECD area). Moreover, part of it can take the form of loans which will be repaid (and are thus a temporary aid). While the contribution of students to tertiary education institutions increased, the public student aid also increased per student by 66% on average between 1995 and 2005 (when excluding Poland, where the increase was exponential. There are strong variations though: the median increase is 49%. It amounted to an average USD 2 339 in 2005 (with a median at USD 2 130).

However, in spite of their increasing contribution to the expenditures of tertiary education institutions, students and their families still benefit from generally high levels of public subsidisation. Student payments represent on average 16% of tertiary education institutions' expenditures in OECD countries. There are only 6 countries where students (and their households) contribute more than 30% on average to the tertiary institutions' budgets, with only two (Japan and Korea) where they are the main income source in institutions' budgets (Figure 9.9). This means that students are still publicly subsidised in most (but not all) OECD countries. However, it is noteworthy that students would legitimately have to contribute less than 100% of institutions' expenditures even in a system in which they were unsubsidised: tertiary education institutions produce non-teaching services like research and services to the community (participation in boards, peer reviewing, work with private companies, etc.) which would not necessarily be paid for by (all) students and their families.

In conclusion, students and their households have experienced a small decrease in public funding in OECD countries, actually only significant in few countries. However, in most OECD countries students are still very far from paying unsubsidised prices for their tertiary education. It is likely that tuition fees will be raised in the coming years, particularly in public education systems where fees are very low or nonexistent. For

Figure 9.9. Share of direct expenditures to tertiary education institutions coming from households, 2005 (%)

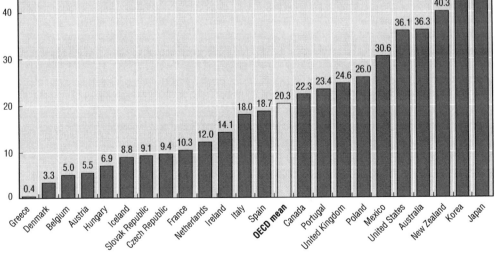

Source: OECD (2008a).

example, Germany has introduced tuition fees in 2005. However, this may take a long time in some countries, for political reasons. The financing models of Australia, New Zealand and now England have become the most appealing to many tertiary education experts and economists, with higher tuition fees paid after graduation through a public (income-contingent) loan scheme (see for example Santiago *et al.*, 2008; Johnstone, 2006).

The debate takes an opposite direction in the United States and Japan: the affordability of tertiary education to students has become a big concern and the question is more about cost containment or, in the case of Japan, a possible increase of public funding (see for example Yonezawa and Kim, 2008). While tertiary education can be expensive to students in the United States, notably if they study in private selective universities, it remains largely subsidised for the bulk of tertiary education students: in 2008, about 56% of US full-time undergraduate students at four-year institutions (public and private) attended institutions charging less than USD 9 000 for tuition fees (College Board, 2008). Given the coming demographic pressure on US tertiary education, whose enrolments are projected to increase significantly, costs to students and their families are likely to remain a big issue in the coming decades (Anderson and Cook).

The government perspective

From a government perspective, a decline in public spending will be less likely regarded as a problem than a rapid increase (although a decrease could also be a sign of underfunding). Overall, government spending on higher education and on academic research has increased in the past decades, but not in a critical way. The share of public expenditures on tertiary education (including all transfers to students, other private entities, and tertiary education institutions) has increased by about 0.2% points on average since 1993, to reach 3.0% in 2005. Canada, the Czech Republic, Hungary and the United States are the only four countries (for which information is available on both years), where the public spending on higher education has declined as a share of total public spending. These public expenditures represented on average 1.3% of an OECD country's GDP in 2005, as they did in 1998. And as real GDP has grown in all countries over that period (net of inflation), this is also the case of real public expenditures on tertiary education (Table 9.4).

Between 1995 and 2005, there has been little change in the pattern of public funding allocation for higher education. On average, 82.4% of a country's public budget for tertiary education still funds directly tertiary education institutions in the OECD area. This share has slightly decreased (–1.2% points on average) between 1995 and 2005 (Table 9.5). Governments and other public authorities have spent a higher proportion of their budget for financial aid for students (part of which is only a temporary disbursement when it takes the form of a student loan that will typically be repaid and later represent a source of public income). In some countries (Australia, Austria, Germany, Italy, Japan and Norway), this shift towards student financial aid (and less direct funding to institutions as a share of their budget) has been above 8% points. The opposite trend (a shift of more than 9% points) could be observed in a smaller number of countries (Ireland and the United Kingdom). The structure of spending did not change much in other countries.

Between 2000 and 2005, the share of public expenditures for financial aid to students also remained stable at 17% of public expenditures for tertiary education – corresponding to 0.25% of countries' GDP in 2005. A noticeable change is that the relative importance of funding for grants and scholarships has decreased by 2% points and benefited student loans, with 10.4% of public funding being devoted to grants and 7.8% to student loans in

Table 9.4. **Total public expenditure on tertiary education as a percentage of public expenditure and as a percentage of GDP**

	Public expenditure on tertiary education as a percentage of total public expenditure		Public expenditure on tertiary education as a percentage of GDP	
	1993	2005	1994	2005
OECD countries				
Australia	3.8	m	1.4	1.1
Austria	2.1	3.0	0.9	1.5
Belgium	1.7	2.6	1.0	1.3
Canada	4.7	4.2	2.3	1.7
Czech Republic	2.1	2.0	0.8	0.9
Denmark	3.4	4.5	1.4	2.4
Finland	3.6	4.0	1.5	2.0
France	1.8	2.2	0.9	1.2
Germany	2.1	2.4	0.9	1.1
Greece	2.3	m	0.7	1.4
Hungary	3.0	2.1	0.9	1.0
Iceland	2.9	3.4	0.7	1.5
Ireland	2.9	3.3	1.1	1.1
Italy	1.5	1.6	0.7	0.8
Japan	1.1	1.6	0.5	0.6
Korea	1.3	2.1	0.3	0.6
Luxembourg	m	m	m	m
Mexico	m	4.1	0.9	1.0
Netherlands	2.9	3.0	1.3	1.4
New Zealand	4.4	4.8	1.1	1.5
Norway	3.9	m	1.4	2.3
Poland	m	2.8	m	1.2
Portugal	m	2.1	0.8	1.0
Slovak Republic	m	4.1	m	0.8
Spain	2.1	2.5	0.8	0.9
Sweden	2.9	3.5	1.5	1.9
Switzerland	3.3	3.3	1.1	1.5
Turkey	m	m	1.3	m
United Kingdom	2.6	2.7	1.0	1.2
United States	3.6	3.5	1.1	1.3
OECD average	**2.8**	**3.0**	**1.0**	**1.3**
EU19 average	**2.5**	**2.8**	**1.0**	**1.3**

m: missing data

Note: Canada, 2004 instead of 2005.

Source: OECD Education Database; OECD Education at a Glance 2008.

2005. That being said, in 2005, publicly subsidised (and/or administrated) student loans were still unavailable or of negligible amount in 9 of the 26 OECD countries (for which information was available), including some of the countries where the share of household contribution to tertiary education rose the most between 1995 and 2005.

In most countries for which information is available, only a small part of financial aid to students seems to ultimately go to educational institutions (OECD, 2008): it can thus generally not be seen as a new way of indirectly financing tertiary education institutions through more competitive market mechanisms or vouchers. In the case of research, there is more evidence of a shift towards a different allocation of public funding: between 1981 and 2006, the percentage of public research funding allocated through general university funds has dropped from 78% to 64% in the 13 OECD countries for which information is available for both years. While general university funds still funded over 70% of academic

Table 9.5. **Public expenditures for tertiary education by category, 2005 (and change)**

	Direct expenditure for institutions	Subsidies for education to private entities						Change (% points) in the share of direct expenditures for institutions (1995-2005)
		Financial aid to students				Transfers and payments to other private entities	Total	
		Scholarships/ other grants to households	Student loans	Total	Scholarships/ other grants to households attributable for educational institutions			
OECD countries								
Australia	67.7	14.7	17.7	32.3	1.0	n	32.3	–9.9
Austria	81.2	16.8	m	16.8	m	2.0	18.8	3.2
Belgium	84.8	15.2	n	15.2	4.3	n	15.2	
Canada	84.5	11.5	2.8	14.4	m	1.2	15.5	19.4
Czech Republic	94.1	5.9	a	5.9	m	n	5.9	4.6
Denmark	69.2	25.8	5.0	30.8	n	n	30.8	1.9
Finland	82.9	16.6	n	16.6	n	0.5	17.1	2.4
France	92.1	7.9	a	7.9	m	a	7.9	1.1
Germany	80.9	14.1	5.1	19.1	m	n	19.1	–9.6
Greece	98.6	0.8	0.7	1.4	m	a	1.4	0.3
Hungary	84.3	15.7	m	15.7	n	n	15.7	–1.6
Iceland	76.9	m	23.1	23.1	m	n	23.1	6.6
Ireland	85.2	14.8	n	14.8	4.8	n	14.8	9.3
Italy	83.2	16.8	n	16.8	5.5	n	16.8	–8.5
Japan	78.5	0.7	20.9	21.5	m	n	21.5	–21.5
Korea	97.1	1.4	1.2	2.7	0.8	0.3	2.9	–2.9
Luxembourg	m	m	m	m	m	m	m	
Mexico	93.6	3.7	2.7	6.4	1.2	n	6.4	–2.6
Netherlands	72.3	12.3	15.5	27.7	1.2	n	27.7	–1.2
New Zealand	58.5	11.6	30.0	41.5	m	n	41.5	–5.8
Norway	57.4	10.9	31.7	42.6	m	n	42.6	–9.2
Poland	98.4	1.1	a	1.1	m	0.4	1.6	–1.1
Portugal	91.1	8.9	a	8.9	m	m	8.9	–5.3
Slovak Republic	85.9	12.1	1.6	13.7	a	0.4	14.1	
Spain	91.8	8.2	n	8.2	2.2	n	8.2	–1.4
Sweden	72.9	10.3	16.8	27.1	a	a	27.1	0.3
Switzerland	95.0	2.2	0.2	2.4	m	2.6	5.0	–0.7
Turkey	m	m	m	m	m	m	m	
United Kingdom	74.2	6.7	19.1	25.8	m	n	25.8	12.7
United States	76.5	14.9	8.6	23.5	m	m	23.5	–11.6
OECD average	**82.4**	**10.4**	**7.8**	**17.3**	**1.6**	**0.3**	**17.6**	**–1.2**

Notes: Turkey, 2003 instead of 2005; m: missing, n: negligible, a: not applicable.

Source: OECD Education at a Glance 2008; OECD Education Database.

research in 2006 in 10 OECD countries, they have decreased by more than 13% in New Zealand, Ireland, the United Kingdom, Canada, Finland and Turkey since the early 1990s as well as in Australia, Denmark, Norway, Sweden, Greece and Spain since the early 1980s (Vincent-Lancrin, 2009). Moreover, the allocation of these general university funds have been increasingly (partially) performance-related in many countries, generally based on university research evaluation that were introduced in several countries in the late 1980s and 1990s (Geuna and Martin, 2003; Santiago et al., 2008).

In conclusion, in the past decade the structure of public expenditures for higher education has remained fairly stable on average in most OECD countries. In some countries, there was a notable decrease of the share of direct public expenditures for tertiary education institutions at the beginning of the 1990s. In recent years, while the share of public expenditures devoted to student financial aid has remained stable, there has been a tendency towards less expenditures for grants and more for student loan programs in relative terms. However, the structure of public expenditures for tertiary education varies considerably across countries (Table 9.5).

Table 9.6 summarises the evolution of expenditures and funding in the past decade in synthetic form, while Table 9.A1.2 in the annex presents some additional data from a stakeholder perspective.

Table 9.6. **Changes in funding according to several indictors**

	Change in total funding to institutions	Change in total funding to institutions per student	Change in public funding to institutions	Change in public funding to institutions per student	Change in share of public funding to institutions vs. total institution funding	Change in public funding of tertiary education as share of GDP	Change in direct public funding to institutions	Change in share of public funding to tertiary education vs. total government expenditure	Change in expenditure of private households to higher education institutions
	1995-2005	1995-2005	1995-2005	1995-2005	1995-2005	1994-2005	1995-2005	1995-2005	1995-2005
Australia	++	+	–	– –	– –	– –	–	m	++
Austria	++	++	++	++	–	+++	+	++	+
Belgium	m	m	m	m	m	++	m	+++	m
Canada	+++	m	+++	m	–	– –	++	– –	+
Czech Republic	+++	– –	+++	– –	+	++	+	–	+
Denmark	++	++	++	+	–	+++	+	++	+
Finland	++	+	++	– –	–	++	+	++	m
France	++	m	++	m	–	++	+	++	–
Germany	++	+	+	+	–	++	–	++	m
Greece	+++	+++	+++	+++	–	+++	+	m	+
Hungary	+++	– –	+++	– –	m	++	–	– –	m
Iceland	m	m	m	m	–	+++	+	++	+
Ireland	+++	++	+++	++	++	=	+	++	– –
Italy	++	++	++	+	– –	++	–	+	+
Japan	++	++	++	++	–	++	m	++	–
Korea	m	m	m	m	+	+++	–	+++	++
Luxembourg	m	m	m	m	m	m	m	m	m
Mexico	+++	++	+++	m	–	++	–	m	+
Netherlands	++	–	++	–	++	+	–	+	+
New Zealand	++	m	++	m	m	++	–	+	m
Norway	+	–	+	+	m	+++	–	m	m
Poland	+++	++	+++	m	– –	m	–	m	++
Portugal	+++	++	++	m	– –	++	–	m	++
Slovak Republic	+++	–	++	m	+++	m	m	m	+
Spain	+++	+++	+++	+++	+	++	–	++	+
Sweden	++	–	++	–	–	++	+	++	m
Switzerland	+++	++	+++	++	m	++	–	=	m
Turkey	m	m	m	m	m	m	m	m	m
United Kingdom	+++	++	++	+	–	++	++	+	+
United States	+++	++	+++	++	– –	++	– –	–	–
OECD average	+++	++	++	+	–	++	–	+	+

Note: "+++" indicates a change greater than +50%; "++": between +10% and +50%; "+": between 0 and +10%; "=": no change; "–": between 0 and –10%; "– –": between –10% and –50%; m: missing data.

9.4. Concluding remarks

The present analysis shows that there is no general decline in enrolments, funding or public funding in public tertiary education in OECD countries. At the macro level, on the contrary, there was remarkable stability overall in the distribution of enrolments and in the funding patterns of tertiary education in the past decade. Except for Japan and Korea, tertiary education is still predominantly a public enterprise in the OECD area; the private for-profit sector is still marginal in a large majority of countries, and even more so for advanced research programmes. However, the small shift towards enrolments in private government-dependent institutions corresponds to recent shifts in policy thinking and policy reforms making tertiary education institutions more autonomous from public authorities and more remote from traditional administrative models of public governance.

Tertiary education institutions have not faced a major decline in public funding either: their budgets have increased over the past years, in most cases per student, and their public funding per student has also increased in most countries. The share of public funding in their budget has decreased on average, but this is mainly due to the quicker growth of (additional) private funding. Students (and their households) have arguably faced the most serious changes as they contribute more to the expenditures of tertiary education institutions than they used to. However, in most countries their tertiary education is still significantly publicly subsidised. In brief, the decline in the public provision and funding of higher education is limited – and actually limited to a few countries.

Does this mean that there is no transformation of public tertiary education? Not necessarily. Country averages can hide large variations within countries and case studies or less aggregated data could help better understand this widespread perception of the decline of the public model. In the case of academic research, there is for example a well established trend towards allocating public research funding through competitive bids, as this has long been the case in the United States, whereas a large share of public research funding used to go directly to tertiary education institutions (Vincent-Lancrin, 2009; Geuna and Martin, 2003). As a result, public funding may become more concentrated in a few institutions, leaving a large number of public universities with less resources and research facilities (even if the public funding increases): most institutions could thus legitimately feel they are in crisis, a few being better off.

Another important reason could be that the decline of the public model rests with other factors than enrolments or funding levels (Ferlie *et al.*, 2007). A mental revolution is underway in tertiary education with the qualitative transformation of the public governance and economics of tertiary education, the frontrunners countries being Australia, New Zealand and the United Kingdom. The United States follows a different trend because of a different tradition and history of its higher education. So do also other countries such as Japan and Korea. This can be seen through several changes in the way institutions, governments and experts think about tertiary education, regardless of the implementation of these changes. These changes can take the following forms:

- changes in the legal and funding relationships of (public) tertiary education institutions and public authorities, which are encouraged to raise more private funds and act in a more entrepreneurial way: this results in a cost sharing that is less favourable to students compared, to more endeavours to raise (or use) private funds for academic research, and in new ways of publicly funding tertiary education;

- changes in the employment system and job content of academics: while they are still civil servants or tenured professionals in a number of OECD countries, tertiary education institutions use more temporary or adjunct professors than in the past, and the academic profession is changing to become closer to a business-like employer-employee relationship (Enders and Musselin, 2008; Schuster and Finkelstein, 2006); and

- changes in the perception of the sector, which is increasingly seen as a regular economic sector: while the sector can hardly be described as a regular marketplace, some ways of thinking about it would have been difficult decades ago: the inclusion of tertiary education it the General Agreement on Trade in Services (GATS), the competition for foreign (and sometimes domestic) fee paying students and for funding are indeed transforming the perception (and to a large extent self-perception) of tertiary education from a public service into a service industry, even in countries which are not directly affected by these changes.

In most countries, these changes are driven (or at least viewed as driven) by globalisation, either directly or indirectly, as a response or preparation to it – demography being another important factor (OECD, 2008b). Public governance practices have got closer, though not converged, as information and "best practices" circulate more quickly internationally. Globalisation has also brought innovation and human capital development to the fore of public policies. As a result, tertiary education is now perceived as playing a major role for maintaining the economic standards of economically advanced nations – and governments now try to make their public education competitive globally. International rankings have recently been prominent in policy reform discussions and explain why some countries try to establish "world class" universities (although a few world class departments located in different universities may actually be enough if excellence was to be the only objective). While international competition and competitiveness become more important in public tertiary education, perhaps is it not so surprising to see public tertiary education transforming itself. Given that relatively affluent US universities top international rankings, giving the rest of the world a benchmark of what world class universities are, most OECD countries try to help their institutions to raise as much resources and to be able to compete with them by attracting (or retaining) their best faculty: this will probably remain a major driver of change in public tertiary education in the coming decade.

Because of the prominence of US research universities worldwide, the pressure of globalisation and competitiveness is not perceived in the same way in the United States and in most other OECD countries. While US public research universities find it more difficult to compete financially with US private research universities, some US public research universities belong to these "world class" universities and are much more affluent than the most affluent public universities in other countries. Many of the changes underway in other OECD countries have long been features of US tertiary education. Whereas research funding becomes more concentrated in many countries, this has long been the case in the United States; whereas countries are starting to openly differentiate their public tertiary education hierarchically, this hierarchy has long been in place in the United States; whereas private funding becomes more important in the economy of tertiary education institutions, this has long be part of public tertiary education in the United States; whereas many countries are considering having students covering a more significant share of the cost of their tertiary education in order to increase their institutions' resources, this has long been the case in the United States.

In the United States, the major challenge related to globalisation lies in the qualification or tertiary educational attainment of its workforce: in spite of a high access to tertiary education, tertiary educational attainment has stagnated while it has continued to increase in most other OECD countries. The cost (or "affordability") of tertiary education to students is part of the equation: while many OECD are in the process of increasing the contribution of household to their public tertiary education, the policy agenda in the United States is about maintaining or reducing it. While the research excellence of US research universities makes the United States a benchmark for other countries, one question about the US model is whether quality in teaching and excellence in research can be achieved at a lower cost to students and taxpayers. The search for the answer will probably lead to a further transformation of public tertiary education in all OECD countries, though not necessarily to less diversity in country models.

Notes

1. Other examples are the "Futures project" in the US (Newman *et al.*, 2004), foresight studies on European higher education (Enders *et al.*, 2005), on Japanese higher education (Arima, 2002), or on global higher education (Weber and Dudderstadt, 2008), but also two OECD project on tertiary education: the OECD thematic review of tertiary education (Santiago *et al.*, 2008) and the project on the Future of higher education (*www.oecd.org/edu/universityfutures*).

2. The figures come from the respective institutional websites (and from the common dataset for faculty figures for Yale and Berkeley). For University of Vienna: *Tätigkeitbericht* 2005.

3. The price has continued to rise since 2003. Total charges to families amounted to USD 1 735 at public two-year institutions, USD 9 663 at public four-year institutions (including USD 4 081 of tuition and fees), and USD 25 052 at private four-year institutions (including USD 18 273 of tuition and fees) in 2003 (College Board, 2003).

Bibliography

Aghion, P., M. Dewatripont, C. Hoxby, A. Mas-Colell and A. Sapir (2008), *Higher Aspirations: An Agenda for Reforming European Universities*, Bruegel, Brussels.

Anderson E. and B. Cook (2008), "Access to Post-secondary Education in the United States: Past, Present, and Future Perspectives", in *Higher Education to 2030, Volume 1: Demography*, OECD Publishing, Paris.

Arima, A. (2002), "The Future of Higher Education in Japan", United Nations University, Tokyo. *www.unu.edu/hq/public-lectures/arima.pdf*.

Bailey, T. (2006), "Increasing Competition and Growth of the For-Profits", in Thomas Bailey and Vanessa Smith Morest (ed.), *Defending the Community College Equity Agenda*, Johns Hopkins, Baltimore.

College Board (2003), *Trends in College Pricing*, Washington DC.

College Board (2008), *Trends in College Pricing*, Washington DC.

Cunningham, S., Y. Ryan, L. Stedman, S. Tapsall, S. Bagdon, T. Flew and P. Coaldrake (2000), *The Business of Borderless Education*, Australian Department of Education, Training and Youth Affairs, Canberra.

Dynarski, S. (2003), "Does Aid Matter? Measuring the Effect of Student Aid on College Attendance and Completion", *American Economic Review*, Vol. 93, No. 1, pp. 279-88.

Dynarski, S. (2004), "The New Merit Aid", in Caroline Hoxby (ed.), *College Choices. The Economics of Where to Go, When to Go, and How to Pay for it*, The University of Chicago Press, Chicago and London.

Enders, J., J. File, J. Huisman, and D. Westerheijden (2005), *The European Higher Education and Research Landscape 2020. Scenarios and Strategic Debates*, CHEPS, Twente, *www.utwente.nl/cheps/publications/Publications%202005/Enders05european.pdf*.

Enders, J. and C. Musselin (2008), "Back to the Future? The Academic Professions in the 21st Century", in *Higher Education to 2030, Volume 1: Demography*, OECD Publishing, Paris.

Ferlie, E., C. Musselin, and G. Andresani (2007), "The 'Steering' of Higher Education Systems: A Public Management Perspective", in European Science Foundation, *Higher Education Looking Forward: Relations between Higher Education and Society*, Strasbourg.

Geuna A. and B. R. Martin (2003), "University Research Evaluation and Funding: An International Comparison", *Minerva*, Vol. 41, pp. 277-304.

Johnstone, D. B. (2006), *Financing Higher Education: Cost-sharing in International Perspective*, Sense Publishers, Boston and Rotterdam.

Kärkkäinen, K. (2006), "Emergence of Private Higher Education Funding in the OECD Area", mimeo, *www.oecd.org/dataoecd/19/20/38621229.pdf*.

Knight, J. (2004), "Internationalization Remodeled: Definition, Approaches, and Rationales", *Journal of Studies in International Education*, Vol. 8, No. 1, pp. 5-31.

Levy, D.C. (2002) "Unanticipated Development: Perspectives on Private Higher Education's Emerging Roles", Working Paper PROPHE, No. 1.

Marginson S. and M. Van Der Wende (2009), "Europeanisation, International Rankings and Faculty Mobility: Three Cases in Higher Education Globalisation", in *Higher Education 2030, Volume 2: Globalisation*, OECD Publishing, Paris.

Newman, F., L. Couturier and J. Scurrie (2004), *The Future of Higher Education. Rhetoric, Reality, and the Risks of the Market*, Wiley and Sons, San Francisco.

Salmi, J. and A. Saroyan (2006), "League Tables as Policy Instruments: uses and misuses", mimeo.

OECD (2004), *Internationalisation and Trade in Higher Education*, OECD Publishing, Paris.

OECD (2008a), *Education at a Glance*, OECD Publishing, Paris.

OECD (2008b), *Higher Education to 2030, Volume 1: Demography*, OECD Publishing, Paris.

Santiago P., K. Tremblay, E. Basri E. and E. Arnal (2008), *Tertiary Education for the Knowledge Society, 2 Volumes*, OECD Publishing, Paris.

Schuster, J. and M. Finkelstein (2006), *The American Faculty. The Restructuring of Academic Work and Careers*, Johns Hopkins, Baltimore.

Salmi, J. (2009a), *The Challenges of Establishing world-class universities*, World Bank, Washington DC.

Teixeira P. (2009), "Mass higher education and Private Institutions", in *Higher Education to 2030, Volume 2: Globalisation*, OECD Publishing, Paris.

US Department of Education (2006), *A Test of Leadership. Charting the Future of US Higher Education*, Washington DC, *www.ed.gov/about/bdscomm/list/hiedfuture/reports/final-report.pdf*.

Vincent-Lancrin (2008), "What is the Impact of Demography on the Size, Budget and Policies of Higher Education Systems? A Forward-looking Approach for OECD Countries", in OECD, *Higher Education to 2030, Volume 1: Demography*, OECD Publishing, Paris.

Vincent-Lancrin, S. (2009), "What is Changing in Academic Research? Trends and Prospects", in *Higher Education 2030, Volume 2: Globalisation*, OECD Publishing, Paris.

Yonezawa A. and Kim T. (2008), "The Future of Higher Education in the Context of a Shrinking Student Population: Policy Challenges for Japan and Korea", in *Higher Education to 2030, Volume 1: Demography*, OECD Publishing, Paris.

Weber, L. and J. Dudderstadt (2008), *The Globalization of Higher Education (Glion Colloquium)*, Economica, Paris.

ANNEX 9.A1

Supplementary Tables

Table 9.A1.1. Change in number of students (full-time equivalent) enrolled in tertiary education and in advanced research programs by control of institutions between 1998 and 2006

	Total tertiary education						Advanced Research Programmes					
	Enrolments to all types of institutions			Change in enrolments by type of institution (from 1998 to 2006)			Enrolments to all types of institutions			Change in enrolments by type of institution (from 1998 to 2006)		
	1998	2006	Change 1998 = 100	Public	Government dependent private	Independent private	1998	2006	Change 1998 = 100	Public	Government dependent private	Independent private
Australia	626 518	737 047	118	96 235	328	12 550	20 147	28 492	141	8 221	m	m
Austria	247 498	253 139	102	−13 718	19 359	m	22 167	16 819	76	−5 348	m	m
Belgium*	327 143	341 048	104	87 356	105 046	m	5 933	7 482	126	2 223	1 558	m
Canada	949 604	831 912	88	−108 113	m	m	24 250	33 109	137	8 859	m	m
Czech Republic	204 841	336 441	164	105 038	1 147	m	11 969	22 646	189	10 677	m	m
Denmark	183 274	209 545	114	26 473	m	m	4 290	4 751	111	461	m	m
Finland	250 047	227 524	91	−20 769	−1 755	m	17 930	10 319	58	−7 611	m	m
France**	2 027 422	2 187 383	108	63 692	−413	96 682	97 311	82 696	85	−14 915	m	m
Germany	2 072 880	2 224 072	107	75 159	m	m	m	m	m	m	m	m
Greece	374 125	653 003	175	278 878	m	m	2 175	22 483	1034	20 308	m	m
Hungary	205 794	340 317	165	107 673	26 851	m	4 005	6 540	163	2 223	312	m
Iceland	8 100	13 887	171	3 459	2 328	m	14	149	1064	135	m	m
Ireland	127 478	168 836	132	36 696	m	5 193	2 190	5 146	235	2 843	m	113
Italy	1 869 095	2 029 023	109	252 880	m	−92 952	12 363	38 262	309	24 796	m	1 103
Japan	3 826 887	3 892 598	102	−385	m	66 096	52 141	74 968	144	17 264	m	5 563
Korea	2 636 388	3 204 036	122	108 167	m	459 481	26 291	43 443	165	5 227	m	11 925
Mexico	1 727 484	2 446 726	142	378 187	m	341 055	107 149	13 458	13	−58 403	m	−35 288
Netherlands	423 617	531 411	125	m	m	m	m	3 738	m	m	m	m
New Zealand	127 183	172 258	135	34 604	12 767	m	2 648	5 362	203	2 715	m	m
Poland	939 497	1 759 080	187	499 317	m	320 266	16 419	32 725	199	15 010	m	1 296
Slovak Republic*	99 752	197 943	198	89 553	306	m	2 884	10 739	372	7 768	m	m
Spain	1 654 055	1 649 196	100	−28 089	31 936	m	60 136	74 002	123	12 390	m	1 476
Sweden	243 550	302 581	124	46 528	12 503	m	11 892	13 233	111	1 147	194	m
Switzerland	121 639	183 184	151	54 152	4 921	2 472	12 275	17 234	140	4 959	m	m
Turkey	1 409 627	2 342 898	166	842 800	m	m	20 038	32 575	163	m	m	m
United Kingdom	1 526 151	1 663 454	109	m	137 303	m	48 158	60 702	126	m	12 544	m
United States	9 955 146	13 323 301	134	2 411 166	m	956 989	214 952	310 353	144	46 940	m	48 461
OECD	**34 166 616**	**42 407 393**	**124**	~	~	~	**799 728**	**976 443**	**122**	~	~	~

m: missing data.
* 1999 instead of 1998.
** 2005 instead of 2006.

Table 9.A1.2. **Tertiary education expenditures by stakeholder source of funding (selected indicators)**

	Funding for institutions			Funding from government				Funding from households	
	Total expenditure	Change in overall funding	Expenditure per student for all services	Total funding	Change in overall funding	Funding per student to institutions	Share of funding	Funding per student to institutions	Share of funding
	2005	1995-2005	2005	2005	1995-2005	2005	2005	2005	2005
	% of GDP	1995 = 100 (constant prices)	USD (PPPs, FTE)	% of GDP	1995 = 100 (constant prices)	USD (PPPs, FTE)	% of direct expenditures	USD (PPPs, FTE)	% of direct expenditures
Australia	1.6	135	14 579	1.1	99	6 969	48	5 288	36
Austria	1.3	137	14 775	1.5	132	13 727	93	808	5
Belgium	1.2	m	11 960	1.3	m	10 836	88	597	5
Canada	2.6	156	m	1.7	151	11 097	55	4 502	22
Czech Republic	1.0	151	6 649	0.9	170	5 399	81	628	9
Denmark	1.7	128	14 959	2.4	125	14 466	97	493	3
Finland	1.7	128	12 285	2	126	11 810	96	m	0
France	1.3	118	10 995	1.2	114	9 190	83	1 129	10
Germany	1.1	112	12 446	1.1	106	10 616	84	m	0
Greece	1.5	359	6 130	1.4	365	5 928	97	24	0
Hungary	1.1	170	6 244	1	166	4 900	78	431	7
Iceland	1.2	m	9 474	1.5	m	8 640	91	834	9
Ireland	1.2	180	10 468	1.1	219	8 791	82	1 477	14
Italy	0.9	142	8 026	0.8	118	5 586	69	1 442	18
Japan	1.4	122	12 326	0.6	117	4 155	34	6 582	53
Korea	2.4	m	7 606	0.6	m	1 848	24	3 965	52
Luxembourg	m	m	m	m	m	m	m	m	m
Mexico	1.3	177	6 402	1	158	4 416	69	1 957	31
Netherlands	1.3	118	13 883	1.4	113	10 776	78	1 666	12
New Zealand	1.5	113	10 262	1.5	113	6 125	60	4 136	40
Norway	1.3	110	15 552	2.3	110	m	100	m	0
Poland	1.6	218	5 593	1.2	218	4 138	74	1 455	26
Portugal	1.4	194	8 787	1	132	5 985	66	2 058	23
Slovak Republic	0.9	185	5 783	0.8	149	4 473	76	525	9
Spain	1.1	159	10 089	0.9	166	7 859	78	1 886	19
Sweden	1.6	143	15 946	1.9	132	14 072	85	m	0
Switzerland	1.4	179	21 734	1.5	179	m	100	m	0
Turkey	m	m	m	m	m	m	90	m	10
United Kingdom	1.3	152	13 506	1.2	128	9 037	67	3 329	25
United States	2.9	167	24 370	1.3	155	8 464	35	8 795	36
OECD average	~	**157**	**11 512**	**1.3**	**150**	**8 050**	**75**	**2 348**	**16**

m = missing data

Source: OECD Education at a Glance 2008; OECD Education Database.

Chapter 10

Scenarios for Financial Sustainability of Tertiary Education

by

Jamil Salmi*

This chapter explores how tertiary education worldwide could develop in a financially sustainable manner. The chapter starts by discussing the potential impact of demographic changes as well as of new provision and delivery models on higher education financing in different parts of the world. It then provides an overview of the main alternatives for higher education financing today, with an emphasis on different allocation models. The chapter concludes by developing three future scenarios for higher education financing.

* The World Bank.

10.1. Introduction

*My interest is in the future
because I am going to spend the rest of my life there.*
Charles Kettering

Three critical dates will always stand out in human history: 7 July 1947, when the first UFOs were sighted in Roswell, New Mexico; 21 July 1969, the day man landed on the moon for the first time; and 7 July 2021, when the first encounter with an extraterrestrial being took place on the island of Maui. One of the odd questions the alien creatures asked was how humans organise and finance their education systems. They were quite impressed when told that, from birth onwards, each new human being is entitled to a Learning and Competitiveness Account that is alimented over the course of his/her life by contributions from the State, employers and the person's own savings.

Will such innovative financing mechanisms, which exist today on a limited scale in few OECD countries, remain in the realm of science fiction? Or will they gradually become the norm to finance education in a lifelong learning setting?

The trends suggested by recent headlines on the state of tertiary education financing make it doubtful that many nations will be able to implement such innovative mechanisms. Developing countries typically lament the deteriorating quality in their universities, due to rapidly expanding enrolment in a situation of limited funding. Even in the richest economies, the massification of tertiary education has not been systematically matched by growing fiscal resources, as symbolised by the front page title of the daily paper *Le Monde* on 24 January 2004, which denounced "the great misery of French universities".

Yet, expanding and improving tertiary education is increasingly seen as an important priority in both industrial and developing countries. In Europe, for example, the Lisbon agenda calls for renewed focus on the role of human capital in support of innovation and competitiveness (Schleicher, 2006).

Nothing will matter more to Europe's future than the ability of countries, governments, workers and companies to innovate – a process which will depend in no small degree on the efficiency of our decision-making and the quality of our human capital (Ederer, 2006).

Similarly, in the developing world, there is increased recognition that achieving the Millennium Development Goals is not feasible unless all countries, especially the poorest ones, build up the capacity of their tertiary education system to train the technicians, specialists and professionals needed to improve health and education systems, protect the environment and reduce poverty.

Against this background, this chapter sets out to explore how tertiary education can develop in a financially sustainable way in order to ensure its positive contribution to economic growth and social development. The chapter starts by exploring recent trends likely to have a significant impact on the future of tertiary education financing. It then outlines the main factors that shape the way in which tertiary education is financed today, focusing in particular on sources of funding and allocation mechanisms. Finally the chapter proposes three alternative financing scenarios and outlines the conditions under which each one could become reality.

10.2. Trends and factors shaping tertiary education financing

Student demographics

The tertiary education sector has experienced a rapid demographic transition characterised by three main movements: accelerated enrolment growth especially in developing nations, extension of the college-age period in a lifelong learning perspective, and shrinking of the cohort of secondary school graduates in a number of industrial countries.

Between 1991 and 2004, the world tertiary student population almost doubled from 68 million to 132 million (UNESCO, 2006). As seen in Figure 10.1 below, a large part of the increase is due to the massification of tertiary education in industrial countries. But the gross enrolment ratio for developing and emerging nations has also been increasing at a fast pace.

The rapid growth in the developing world is likely to continue because of continuous demographic pressure and progress in reaching the Education for All (EFA) goals,[1] especially since the launch of the Fast-Track Initiative[2] in 2004. The potential for further expansion is therefore enormous, particularly in Sub-Saharan Africa and South Asia. Data from Pakistan, for example, illustrate the enormous challenge faced by countries trying to keep up with the rising demand for tertiary education. Table 10.1 projects the number of students under two scenarios. In the first case, even if the enrolment rate stays stable at 2.9%, the number of students would almost double by 2018. In the second case, if Pakistan succeeds in reaching an enrolment rate of 8% by 2018, it would mean multiplying the present number of students three-fold.

At the other extreme are countries whose aging population is gradually translating into smaller school-age groups. OECD and US Census Bureau population statistics and demographic projections for 2050 show starkly aging populations in countries such as Spain and Portugal, and several nations in East Europe and the former Soviet Union. According to the US Census Bureau (2008), East European nations like Poland, Bulgaria, and the Czech Republic were bottom-heavy in their population pyramids in 2000. Projections for 2050 indicate a reversal of this trend with more of the population concentrated in older age groups of 65 and above. For example, 32% of Poland's population in 2050 will belong to the age group of 65 and above.

Alongside birthrate, the other operative factor in the economic equation is lifespan. People everywhere are living longer than ever, and lifespan is continuing to increase beyond what was once considered a natural limit. Policy makers fear that, taken together, these trends forecast a perfect demographic storm. According to the Rand Europe research group: "Demographers and economists foresee that 30 million Europeans of working age will 'disappear' by 2050. At the same time, retirement will be lasting decades as the number of people in their 80s and 90s increases dramatically." The crisis, they argue, will come from a "triple whammy of increasing demand on the welfare state and health-care systems, with a decline in tax contributions from an ever-smaller work force." That is to say, there won't be enough workers to pay for the

Figure 10.1. **Evolution of tertiary education gross enrolment ratio from 1985 to 2007 (%)**

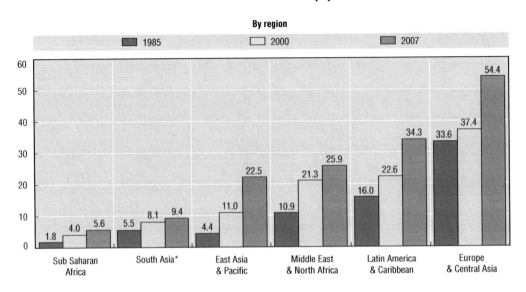

By region

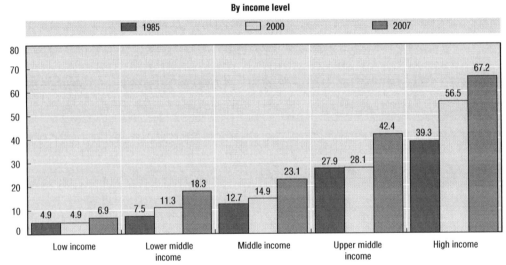

By income level

* 2005 instead of 2007.

Source: World Bank Education Statistics.

Table 10.1. **The demographic challenge in Pakistan, two scenarios**

Year	17-23 years age-group	Number of students with fixed enrolment rate at 2.9%	Number of students if enrolment rate increases to 8%
2002	19.3 million	560 000	560 000
2006	22.1 million	640 000	880 000
2010	25.4 million	740 000	1 270 000
2014	29.1 million	840 000	1 750 000
2018	33.4 million	970 000	2 340 000

Source: Higher Education Commission (2008).

pensions of all those long-living retirees. What's more, there will be a smaller working-age population compared with other parts of the world; the U.S. *Census Bureau*'s International Database projects that in 2025, 42% of the people living in India will be 24 or younger, while only 22% of Spain's population will be in that age group. This, in the wording of a Demographic Fitness Survey by the Adecco Institute, a London-based research group, will result in a "war for talent" (Shorto, 2008).

The former Soviet Union shows a similar picture. In countries like Georgia, Russia, and Ukraine, the pyramids for 2000 were bottom heavy and included high proportions of the very young age groups of 10-15. Fast forwarding to 2050, the trend shows a dramatic bias towards the older populations. Russia is facing grim prospects even earlier, as illustrated by Box 10.1.

Box 10.1. Demographic Impact on the Student Age Population in Russia

Russian universities and colleges are expecting a 30% slump in applications for next year and in some regions students may be accepted virtually without entrance examinations. A decline in the birth rate in the difficult decade of the 1990s is starting to be felt now.

Official statistics show that 1.05 million young people will leave school this summer compared with 1.32 million in 2005. In 2009, the number of school leavers will fall to 930 000 and the year after to a mere 808 000.

Reporting on the issue, the newspaper *Trud* said the problem of filling places was compounded by the fact that the number of institutions of higher education had grown considerably since Soviet times. For a while, the extra colleges had achieved capacity with adults who missed out on their education in the Communist era or who had not had time to study in the turbulent 1990s. But this stream of people was also now drying up.

"Today's school leavers and their parents can draw two conclusions," the paper reported. "One is that in the near future, it will be easier to get into university or college. And the other is that the institutions of higher education will be competing more fiercely for potential entrants, both fee-paying students and those supported by the state." The established, elite universities, such as Moscow State University, will obviously have a big advantage. The regions will have a harder time competing for applicants.

Source: Womack (2008).

Of particular concern in this regard are Asian OECD countries such as Korea and Japan. Population pyramids for the two nations are becoming almost completely inverted. It is projected, for instance, that more than 30% of the Japanese female population will be seventy years old or more, and almost 25% of the male population will be in the same age group (OECD, 2007b). The population pyramids for Korea and Denmark are presented below by way of illustration of the contrast between the two types of demographic structures (Figure 10.2). While Korea is geared towards the relative growth of its population aged 50 and above, Denmark shows a steady state with a majority of its population still in the younger age groups that are in an education/employment phase.

While countries with aging populations will feel more pressure in terms of health and pension expenditures, funding requirements at the tertiary education level will diminish. In fact, Korea is already considering the possibility of reducing the number of institutions of higher learning through mergers or closures. Efforts to attract larger numbers of foreign students are also part of its coping strategy.

Figure 10.2. **Current and projected population pyramids for Korea and Denmark**

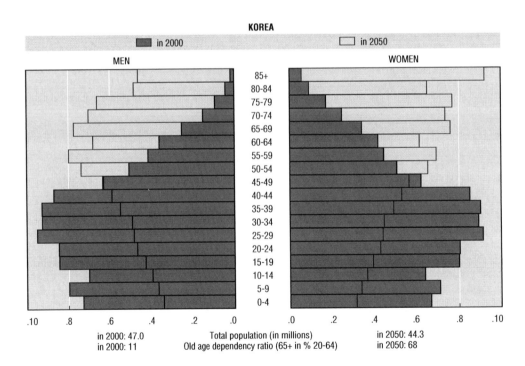

Source: OECD (2007b).

The unknown factor in this changing demographic picture is the extent to which the lifelong learning agenda will result in significantly higher levels of demand for training and retraining opportunities in high- and middle-income countries. In 1996, OECD adopted a comprehensive view of education including the goal of "lifelong learning for all". This paradigm shift signalled the importance of learning opportunities from "cradle to grave" for

Figure 10.3. **Enrolment rates by age for full-time and part-time students in public and private institutions in 2005**

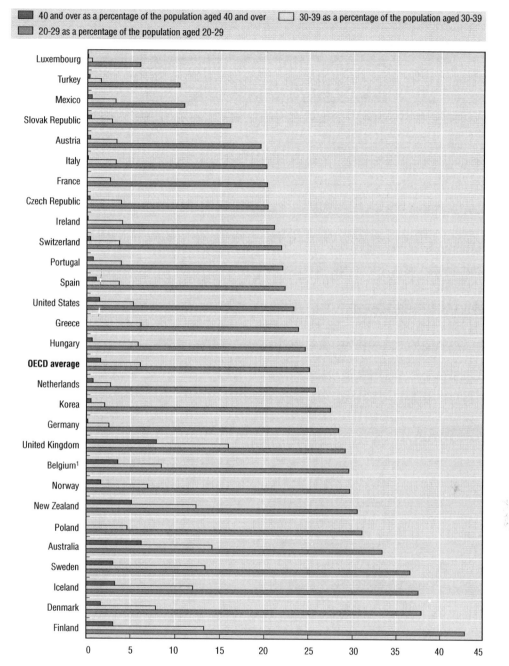

1. Excludes German speaking community of Belgium
Source: OECD (2007a).

those who wished to participate in gaining knowledge and competencies across all stages of their life and career. Larsen and Istance (2001) in the *OECD Observer* stated that "in our rapidly changing world, educational equity can no longer be addressed only in terms of what happens in schools and colleges but throughout our lives. The scope is now much more ambitious as countries aim to make lifelong learning available to all". The European Union also recognises the importance of lifelong learning for the future of their knowledge economy (Osborn, 2008).

Lifelong learning is not a phenomenon limited to the industrial nations alone. Emerging and developing countries like China have also recognised the significance of lifelong learning, including retraining of the labour force to adapt to economic restructuring, in order to successfully compete in the global economy. Dahlman, Zeng, and Wang conclude in their report on lifelong learning in China (World Bank, 2007) that while China has made enormous progress in education and training, the nation "now needs a more integrated system of lifelong learning" with a concentrated effort from all stakeholders including the government and education authorities. Some of the key requirements to make the lifelong learning agenda in China a success are for the government to take on the role of architect and facilitator; focusing on making reliable information available and mobilizing private resources.

One of the specific challenges faced by China is the fact that the average educational attainment of the working age population is still very low, as depicted in Figure 10.4 below. The report indicates that of the total population of 1.3 billion, only 260 million have formal training of any kind (basic, secondary and higher education included). Lifelong learning from childhood through retirement will require concentrated training efforts for all population groups – especially for the 770 million who have no formal training of any kind, and training for the adults and unemployed. It is estimated that approximately two-thirds of the Chinese population will be involved in both formal education activities and non-formal training after entering the labour force.

Figure 10.4. **Average educational attainment of the Chinese and OECD working-age population (2001)**

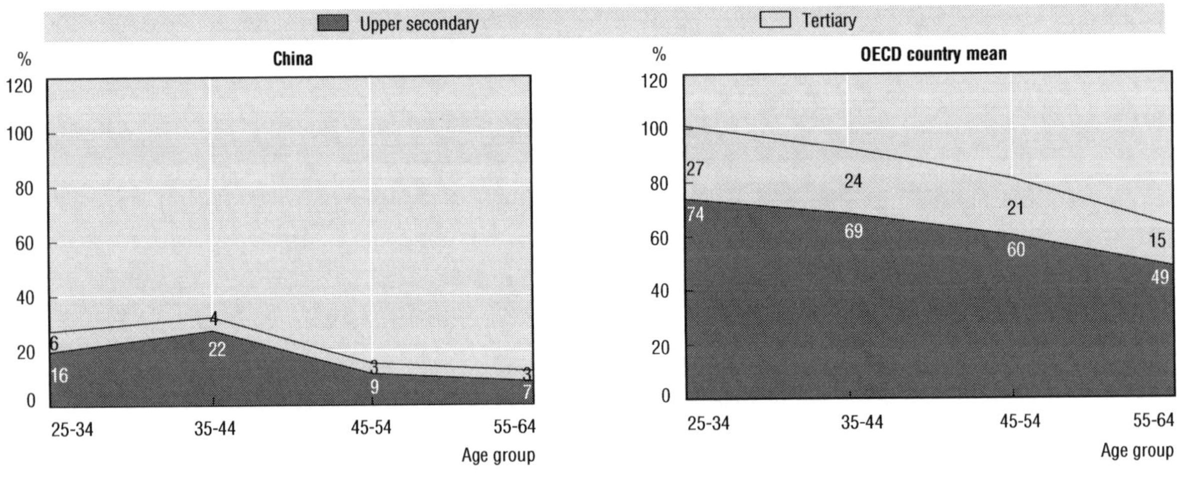

Source: OECD (2003).

The growing importance of lifelong learning means that traditional students coming out of secondary education would gradually cease to be the primary clientele of tertiary education institutions. As a result, universities and other institutions would need to organise themselves to accommodate the learning and training needs of a very diverse clientele: working students, mature students, stay-at-home students, travelling students, part-time students, day students, night students, weekend students, etc. One can therefore expect a significant change in the demographic shape of tertiary education institutions, whereby the traditional structure of a pyramid with a majority of first degree students, a smaller group of post-graduate students, and finally an even smaller share of participants in continuing education programs would be replaced by an inverted pyramid with a minority of first time students, more students pursuing a second or third degree, and the majority of students enrolled in short-term continuing education activities, as illustrated by Figure 10.5 below. Already in the United States, almost half of the student population consists of mature and part-time students, a dramatic shift from the previous generation.

Figure 10.5. **Demographic shape of tertiary education in the future**

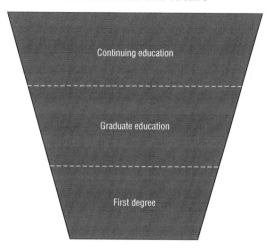

Achieving economies of scale through new providers and delivery modes

Studying in a foreign country or through virtual education is among the most promising options to absorb the increasing demand for tertiary education. Between 1999 and 2004, international student enrolment went up by 46% for the host nations of United States, the United Kingdom, Germany, France, Australia, and Japan (Kapur and Crowley, 2008). Overall, OECD nations hosted 93% of the students studying abroad (OECD, 2005). But other countries are also trying to capture a share of this market, as illustrated by the success of private tertiary education institutions in Malaysia which in 2007, only 11 years after being allowed to operate, boasted a 25% proportion of foreign students (World Bank, 2007). Another model is Singapore's attempt to create a tertiary education hub through partnerships with well reputed universities from industrial nations. This prompted international tertiary enrolment in Singapore to increase in 2005 to 72 000 students. In 2003, Dubai launched a "Knowledge Village" housed in the Dubai International Academic City (DIAC), hoping to become "the focal point of the knowledge economy in the Middle East" (Kapur and Crowley, 2008). This initiative has encouraged participation from over twenty universities from across the world.

Franchise universities are at the forefront of new developments in international education (Kapur and Crowley, 2008). In many parts of the world, but predominantly in South-East Asia and the formerly socialist countries of eastern Europe, overseas "validated courses" offered by franchise institutions operating on behalf of British, American, Canadian and Australian universities have proliferated. In 2007, one quarter (71 000) of the 273 000 international students enrolled in Australian universities were studying at offshore campuses, mainly in Malaysia and Singapore. Even though these foreign campuses charge relatively high fees compared to domestic institutions, the cost of attending these franchise institutions is usually one-fourth to one-third what it would cost to enrol in the mother institution overseas.

With the advent of the Internet, physical distance has been all but abolished. This means that the best universities in any country can open a branch anywhere in the world or reach out across borders using the Internet or satellite communication links, effectively competing with any national university on its own territory. With 90 000 and 500 000 students respectively, the (public) University of Maryland University College and (private) University of Phoenix have been the fastest growing distance education institutions in the United States in the past five years. It is estimated that, in the United States alone, there are already more than 3 000 specialised institutions dedicated to online training. Thirty-three states in the United States have a state-wide virtual university (Olsen, 2000).

Distance education is sometimes delivered by a specialised institution set up by an alliance of universities, as is the case with western Governor University in the United States and the Open Learning Agency in British Columbia. In Thailand and Turkey, the national open universities enrol respectively 41 and 38% of the total student population in each country (World Bank, 2002).

Corporate universities represent another form of education and training provision which can complement traditional tertiary education institutions, especially in the area of continuing education. It is estimated that there are more than 2 000 institutions in the world functioning today as corporate universities, up from 1 600 in 2002 and 400 fifteen years ago. Some 80% of *Fortune* 500 companies either already have a corporate university or are in the process of establishing one (World Bank, 2002).

Box 10.2. **Foreign competition in Indian higher education**

India has been struggling to meet the increased demand for tertiary education. In the field of engineering, for example, only a quarter of the 300 000 engineering graduates are considered employable. Added to this is the problem that faculty are seeking employment in the private sector leaving 5 000 job vacancies in the university sector. Diplomas from foreign institutions of higher education are highly sought after in India. According to the National Institute for Education Planning and Administration (NIEPA), 131 institutions, a majority being Business schools, are currently partnering with American and British universities to attract foreign competition. India's Minister for Commerce and Industry, Kamal Nath, is championing a pending vote since 2006. The intent of the vote is "opening of higher education to foreign institutions" in order to meet recruiting needs which can be met through an "estimated 1 500 additional universities by 2015". This idea has been severely debated, and decision is still pending.

Source: Montgomery (2008).

The introduction of new pedagogical approaches supported by alternative delivery mechanisms has just begun to revolutionise teaching and learning in tertiary education. The concurrent use of multimedia, a variety of computing devices (PCs, low-cost laptops, and soon mobile phones), and communication networks (*e.g.* the Internet, and increasingly mobile phone networks) can make possible more active and interactive learning experiences through, for example, peer tutoring and self-directed learning, experiential and real-world learning, resource-based and problem-based learning, reflective practice and critical self-awareness, or any combination of these approaches. Traditional in-person teaching can be replaced by or associated with asynchronous teaching in the form of online classes that can be either scheduled or self-paced. The new pedagogical model involves active engagement of the students rather than passive reception of information; it offers opportunities to apply new knowledge to real-life situations, to represent concepts and knowledge in multiple ways rather than with text only, to learn as a collaborative activity rather than as an individual act, and emphasises learning processes rather than memorisation of information (World Bank, 2002).

The transformational impact of technology on tertiary education is not a new phenomenon. What is new is the type of technologies that are being adopted by universities and colleges to increase access and improve student involvement in the ever expanding learning networks of "formal" higher education. New student cohorts are technically savvy and their methods of learning are relatively new-age. Older student cohorts are also more sophisticated and are looking for wider and deeper networks and communities of learners. In April 2008, the University of New South Wales, Australia, pioneered an educational channel on You Tube (UWN, April 2008). The UNSW channel is being used to share research and teaching materials and "has become one of the most watched local online sites, scoring more hits than television competitors such as Channel Ten, Beat TV and SkyNewsShowbiz". The university has also added an eLearning channel and a community channel to provide a venue for teaching / learning with a platform to communicate and share ideas. The information has also been "uploaded to China's number one education site, Tigtag, which has 1.5 million visitors every day, and was featured on Pakistan's premier education website Ilmkidunya".

Along similar lines, INSEAD, the top European business school with campuses in France and Singapore, has established a virtual campus in the online 3-D universe of Second Life to facilitate the interaction among professors and students in the two physical campuses. The Second Life campus, designed for a cost of about USD 15 000, includes a virtual amphitheatre, a research lab and lounge areas for social interaction. MBA students of HEC (École des Hautes Etudes Commerciales), one of France's leading business schools, routinely uses iPods to review lessons, publish presentations and get feedback from their professors (Business Week, 23 March 2006).

The adoption of pedagogical approaches and modes of delivery that rely significantly on information technology have far-reaching implications, both positive and negative, with respect to the design and the cost of the physical infrastructure of tertiary education institutions. The new technologies require considerable investment in equipment and in terrestrial or wireless networks, followed by high costs for infrastructure maintenance, training, and technical support. In addition, there are typically significant costs over time related to reengineering existing practices and organisational structures to take advantage of the investments in technology. While few rigorous studies of the total cost of ownership or operation of the use of informational technologies in educational institutions exit, it is estimated that the initial capital outlays represent only 10-20% of the total costs associated with the purchase, use, and maintenance of information and communication hardware and software; the recurrent costs can thus represent as much as 80%-90% of the life-cycle costs of technology investments (Du Vivier, 2008; Twinomugisha, 2005).

It should be noted that various costs related to technology use can in many circumstances be much greater in developing countries than they are in OECD countries. The 2006 African Tertiary Institutions Connectivity Survey (ATICS) found that "The average African university has bandwidth capacity equivalent to a broadband residential connection available in Europe, pays 50 times more for their bandwidth than their educational counterparts in the rest of the world" (Gakio, 2006). Such important capital investments and recurrent costs present major fiscal challenges for tertiary institutions in developing countries. Realigning the programs and curricula of universities on the basis of interdisciplinary and multidisciplinary learning and research similarly entails significant modifications in the organisation of the laboratory and workshop infrastructure supporting basic science and engineering programs.

At the same time, the judicious use of new technologies can be a source of major savings. In the United Kingdom the cost of producing an Open University graduate is about one-third that at a regular university. Traditional libraries are evolving into multifunctional information centres as digitisation of information transforms their core work. Many academic libraries are now using networked information resources such as commercially available electronic databases as a means of expanding access to relevant information for all members of the academic community. Together with other departments and institutions, libraries are also engaged in the preservation of educational materials in digital form. Some of these projects can help academic libraries in developing countries cope with the pressure of the ever-increasing costs of reference documents, especially scientific journals. The Korean Education and Research Information Service (KERIS), a government-funded organisation established in 1999, supports the purchase and sharing of quality international academic databases and online academic journals to help tertiary institutions and research institutes conserve financial resources.

In this context, the global movement to produce and disseminate "open educational resources" – educational materials and resources offered freely and openly for anyone to use and under some licenses re-mix, improve and redistribute – is of increasing relevance to tertiary institutions, especially in developing countries. The MIT OpenCourseWare project (ocw.mit.edu), which makes available MIT course materials for free, and the MERLOT Network (Multimedia Educational Resource for Learning and Online Teaching, www.merlot.org) are prominent examples of initiatives in this area.

Utilizing networked databases and portable media (DVD, USD flash drives) can partially replace expensive journal and book collections and alleviate the shortage of storage space that many libraries face. In Canada 64 universities recently pooled their resources to establish nationwide site licenses for online scholarly journals. This project should give access to a larger pool of digital information to smaller universities that may not have the financial capacity to maintain a large stock of journals (Paskey, 2001). Some options are of great attractiveness to tertiary institutions where Internet connectivity is too expensive and/or unreliable. The eGranary Digital Library (www.widernet.org/digitallibrary) is one example of how organisations are taking advantage of the steep decline, in storage prices to cache vast amounts of digital content locally, obviating the need for Internet access altogether. Under any circumstances, however, whether to subscribe to particular networked information resources or to purchase their off-line equivalents has to be determined on the basis of the potential benefits and the cost implications of using digitised resources or printed resources.

Some observers see the future of tertiary education in achieving both economies of scale and scope by engaging with new technologies like Second Life, iTunes, wiki's, blogs, and open source knowledge sharing. Colleges and universities worldwide are grappling with the issue of how to harness the power of new information and communication technologies while maintaining the "feel of a community" for students and institutions alike. In that sense, tertiary education in its modern complex form has also come full circle, and is aiming to bring back for the student the Socratic model of exploration and engaged learning.

The rising cost of tertiary education

The financial impact of the demographic and technological factors analyzed in the previous sections will depend on country circumstances. In many developing countries, rapid demographic growth, fuelled by high social and economic returns, will continue to boost the demand for tertiary education. The ability to meet this demand is largely dependent on financial resources available. In most industrial and transition countries, the changing age structure could translate into a decline in tertiary enrolment but also in diminishing fiscal resources. Whether countries manage to take advantage of cost-effective education technologies tends to be a function of the behaviour of individual tertiary education institutions. But in all cases, the net effect will be influenced by the trend of rising costs in tertiary education.

As observed by Johnstone and Marcucci (2007), the costs of providing tertiary education have, in many cases outpaced inflation. Tertiary education finance "is burdened with a natural unit cost trajectory that in normal years will exceed the average rate of increase of consumer prices generally: that is, *will naturally exceed the rate of inflation* year-in and year-out". Johnstone explains that this annual increment is to be expected given the costs composition that characterises the provision of tertiary education, including faculty salary, technology and connectivity, the increasing importance bestowed on research even in non-research universities, and rapidly escalating expenses towards student programs, services, and facilities.

This situation of increasing costs can be observed across most OECD nations, as illustrated by Figure 10.6 which displays the rise in total per student costs in constant prices between 1995 and 2004. Developing countries have also experienced a similar trend of rising costs, especially as the non-salary inputs (laboratory equipment, textbooks, journals, etc.) must usually be bought at international prices.

Figure 10.6. **Change in number of students and total per student expenditures from 1995 to 2004 (2004 constant prices, Index of change 1995 = 100)**

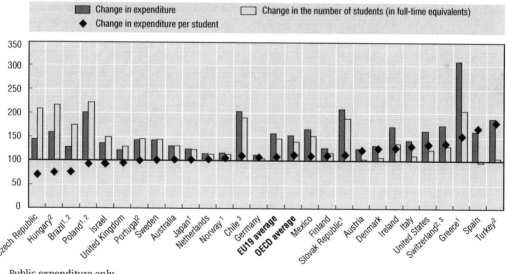

1. Public expenditure only.
2. Public institutions only.
3. Year of reference 2005.
Source: OECD (2007a).

10.3. The changing face of public financing: funding approaches and instruments

Most nations have invested a lot of effort and resources in providing increased educational access to students from all walks of life, not just to those who can afford it. While this approach has positively impacted individual and economic prosperity, it has also left states hard pressed for resources to meet the ever increasing and evolving demand for tertiary education. This in turn has called for new and innovative ways to finance tertiary education. The following two fundamental paradigm shifts have taken place over the past decade:

● Reduced dependence on state funding and increased resource diversification.

● Search for performance-based allocation mechanisms.

Sources of funding

Johnstone (2001) discusses how worldwide "fiscal austerity" in tertiary education is caused by the "increasing scarcity of public revenue". The chief cause for this scarcity is competition from other public needs like health, infrastructure, public order, and poverty alleviation programs. Additionally, as some segments of transition economies become private, or as some economies become stagnant, funding from tax sources decline and become more difficult to collect. Figure 10.7 illustrates the declining expenditures for tertiary education as a percentage of GDP in several OECD nations, including Australia, Finland, the Netherlands, and Norway for example.

Figure 10.7. **Evolution of total expenditures on tertiary education institutions as a percentage of GDP from 1995 to 2004**

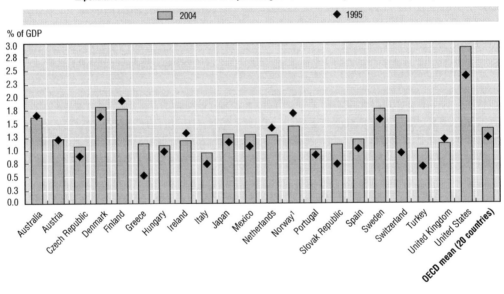

Expenditure on educational institutions as a percentage of GDP for tertiary education (1995, 2004)

1. Year of reference 2005 and 1995.

Source: OECD (2007a).

Overall, the average proportion of public funding of total tertiary education funding in OECD countries fell by 6% points between 1995 and 2005, decreasing in 22 out of 28 OECD member countries, for which information was available (OECD, 2008).

The combination of increasing costs and declining public funding has pushed colleges and universities to look for alternative sources of funding and encouraged the growth of private tertiary education worldwide. As state funding decreases, educational institutions diversify their revenue through various channels, starting with tuition. The *Chronicle of Higher Education* (Supiano, 2008) stated that "most college financial officers", at 100 private colleges in the United States, "expect tuition increases to continue outpacing inflation". Many cite competition to provide the best facilities, health-care costs, and salaries as important contributing factors. Infrastructure, investments, sustainability, and planning, are some of the other concerns discussed in the report "Finance Officers on Tuition, Student Debt, and Cost Cutting". While one half of the respondents are of the opinion that tuition increases will lead to improved access, the other half is concerned about the resultant debt burden.

The US Department of Education published a report entitled "A Test of Leadership: Charting the Future of Higher Education". According to the report, tuition fees have continued to outpace inflation, family income levels, and even cost of health care. The report further elaborates that in the decade leading to 2005, average tuition in four-year public institutions rose by 51% after inflation adjustment; the same figure for private educational institutions was 36%. Along the same lines, a recent report by the College Board (2007) demonstrates that tuition and fees have more than doubled when compared to inflation rates for United States. In comments on this report, the *New York Times* (*Glater* 2007) writes that "in recent years, consumer prices have risen less than 3% a year, while net tuition at public colleges has risen by 8.8% and at private ones, 6.7%".

Figure 10.8 hereafter shows the increase in tuition fees and the cost of room and board in the United States for the past three decades. Such enormous tuition and fee hikes have prompted parents and students into much higher levels of borrowing.

Figure 10.8. Average tuition fees and room and board at four-year institutions in the United States from 1975-76 to 2008-09 (Constant dollars, enrolment-weighted)

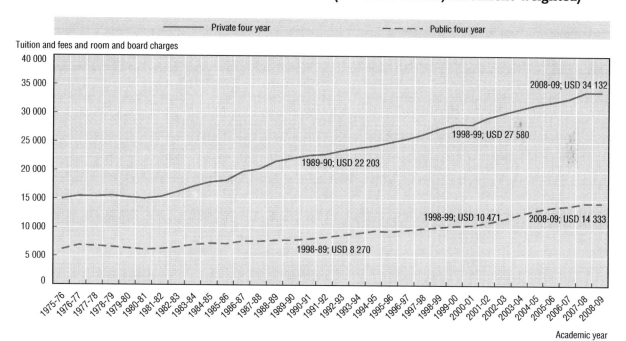

Source: College Board (2008); data online, *www.collegeboard.com/trends.*

According to the Institute for Higher Education Policy, "the world is seeing a historic swing from public to private financing of higher education" (Bollag, 2007). Despite the controversies attached with the idea of cost-sharing in nations across Africa, Latin America, and Europe, more students are paying tuition even in developing countries. South

Africa, for example, witnessed a fee increase "from an average of 24% to 29% of total university income" in the early years of this decade (McGregor 2008). In Ghana, "the increases in student loan amounts over the years… were necessary to cover the high inflation rate as well as the gradual increase in fees" (ICHEFAP 2006).

Institutions are also diversifying revenue from other private sources like businesses. All private sources "accounted for 43% of all spending on higher education" in eight middle-income countries, for which data was analyzed.[3] This figure was lower at 23% for the richer nations but it was growing. Between 1995 and 2003, "private finance as a part of total expenditure increased on average by five percentage points" for industrialised nations, especially, Australia, Italy, and England. Even in France, where there is no official policy of cost-sharing, the students union recently complained that 40% of the universities charged fees in one way or the other (Lemoine, 2008). Only Norway and Ireland have actually reduced private investment in tertiary education due to their high economic growth. Table 10.2 below shows the level of fees paid by students in selected OECD and non-OECD countries.

Table 10.2. **Average fees in public universities in selected countries in academic year 2004-05 (USD converted using PPPs)**

> USD 5 000	United States
USD 3 000 to USD 4 000	Australia, Canada, Chile, Hong Kong, Japan, Korea
USD 2 000 to USD 3 000	Israel, United Kingdom
USD 1 000 to USD 2 000	Italy, New Zealand, Netherlands, South Africa
USD 500 to USD 1 000	Austria, Belgium, China, Colombia, Costa Rica, Spain
< USD 500	Bolivia, El Salvador, France, Kenya, Mexico, Peru, Philippines, Turkey
No significant fees	Argentina, Brazil, Czech Republic, Cuba, Denmark, Finland, India, Indonesia, Ireland, Iceland, Norway, Poland, Russia, Sweden, Venezuela

Sources: OECD (2007a); for non OECD countries (outside Latin America), data from the International Comparative Higher Education Finance and Accessibility Project (2006), *http://www.gse.buffalo.edu/org/IntHigherEdFinance/*; Chilean Ministry of Education Statistics (2007), *http://www.mineduc.cl/index0.php?id_portal=1#*; for other Latin American countries, field visits by Jamil Salmi (2002-08).

Beyond tuition fees, tertiary education institutions have displayed a lot of ingenuity in diversifying their income sources through continuing education, productive activities and fund-raising. Table 10.3 below presents the range of income diversification resources that can be observed across the world. Figure 10.9 complements the picture by showing the proportion of self-generated resources (including tuition fees) for a number of Latin American and other countries.

With respect to the growth in the share of funding from private sources, OECD (2008) data indicate that roughly 26% of funding distributed to tertiary education institutions came from private sources for OECD nations on average in 2005, up from roughly 20% in 1995. The same figure for EU19 nations increased from roughly 14% in 1995 to 19% in 2005. The presence of the private sector is even stronger in other parts of the world, especially in Latin America and East Asia. Figure 10.10 shows the impressive growth of private enrolment in Latin America between 1970 and 2006.

As a result of this evolution, in most countries tertiary education typically receives funding from various sources comprising the government, students, commercial banks, companies, and philanthropists (Johnstone, 2004). While the mix of sources does vary across nations, Figure 10.11 provides a schematic representation of how the various

Table 10.3. **Resource diversification matrix for public tertiary institutions by category and source of income**

Category of income	Source of income				
	Government	Students and families	Industry & services	Alumni/ philanthropists	International co-operation
Budgetary contribution					
General budget	X				
Dedicated taxes (lottery, tax on liquor sales, tax on contracts, tax on export duties)	X				
Payroll tax			X		
Fees for instructional activities					
Tuition fees					
Degree/non-degree programs		X	X		
On-campus/distance education programs		X	X		
Advance payments		X			
Chargeback	X				
Other fees (registration, labs, remote labs)		X			
Affiliation fees (colleges)			X		
Productive activities					
Sale of services					
Consulting	X		X		X
Research	X		X	X	X
Laboratory tests	X		X		
Patent royalties, share of spin-off profits, monetised patent royalties deal			X	X	
Operation of service enterprises (television, hotel, retirement homes, malls, parking, driving school, Internet provider, gym)			X		
Financial products (endowment funds, shares)			X		
Production of goods (agricultural and industrial)		X	X	X	
Themed merchandises	X	X	X	X	X
Rental of facilities (land, classrooms, dormitories, laboratories, ballrooms, drive-through, concert halls, mortuary space, movie shooting)			X	X	
Sale of assets (land, residential housing, art treasures)					
Fund raising					
Direct donations					
Monetary grants (immediate, deferred)			X	X	X
Equipment			X	X	
Land and buildings	X			X	
Scholarships and student loans	X		X	X	X
Endowed chairs, libraries, mascot			X	X	
Challenging/matching grants		X	X	X	
Indirect donations (credit card, percentage of gas sales, percentage of stock exchange trade, lectures by alumni)					
Tied donations (access to patents, share of spin-off profits)			X		
Concessions, franchising, licensing, sponsorships, partnerships (products sold on campus, names, concerts, museum showings, athletic events)			X		
Lotteries and auctions (scholarships)		X	X		
Loans					
Regular bank loans	X		X		X
Bond issues		X	X	X	

sources contribute to the overall financing picture. Government funding consists of both direct transfers (entitlements, formula funding, performance contracts, competitive funds, etc.) and indirect transfers (scholarships, loans, vouchers, tax and saving benefits, etc.). Amongst the remaining sources, students contribute to tertiary education through tuition fees, and commercial banks, firms and philanthropists through loans, research and consultancy contracts and donations respectively (Salmi and Hauptman, 2006).

Figure 10.9. **Self-generated income in public tertiary education institutions as a proportion of total resources in 2005**

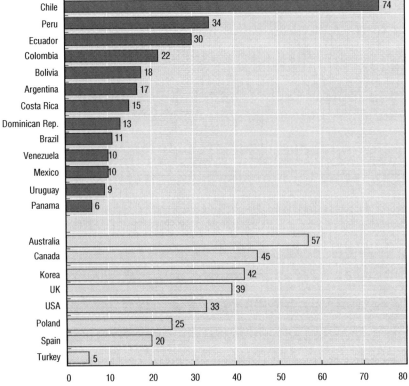

Source: OECD/World Bank (2008).

Figure 10.10. **Evolution of the share of private tertiary education enrolment from 1970 to 2006**

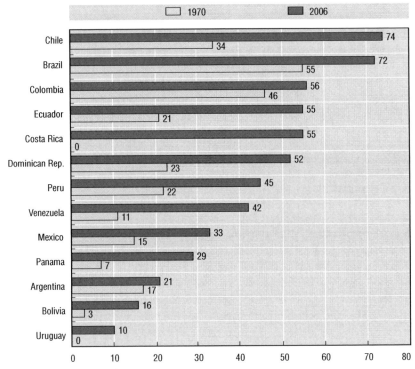

Source: OECD/World Bank (2008).

Figure 10.11. **Schematic representation of tertiary education financing**

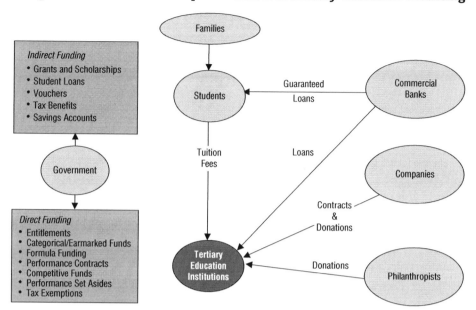

Allocation mechanisms

To promote greater efficiency and innovativeness in the use of public resources, many governments have moved to performance-based funding mechanisms. These approaches attempt to allocate funds to the best performing institutions or most promising investment proposals. They rely on performance indicators that reflect public policy objectives rather than institutional needs, and provide incentives for institutional improvement, not just maintaining *status quo*. In tertiary education systems that are sufficiently large and a have relatively high degree of institutional diversification, some of the new allocation mechanisms also have a built-in element of competitiveness.

These various allocation mechanisms can be broadly categorised along the two key dimensions of performance and competitiveness. A quadrant-based representation is proposed in Figure 10.12. Performance refers to whether or not the allocation mechanism is directly linked to some measure of results. Thus, the X-axis runs between two extremes of tertiary education institutions having no performance criteria through those whose resource allocation is based on performance criteria. The second dimension reflects the degree to which resources are allocated on a competitive basis. The Y axis denotes degrees of competitiveness, with two ends of the spectrum being negotiated allocations and competitive mechanisms. Items within the quadrants have been labelled as Institutional (I), Student-based (S), and Family-based (F) to denote which of these parties receives the allocated resource. The four quadrants, which have been numbered from Quadrant 1 through Quadrant 4 for ease of discussion, are briefly presented hereafter.

Following that logic, Quadrant 1 represents the most traditional allocation approach, such as historical entitlements or negotiated budgets, where no objective performance criteria are taken into consideration. These are the most common funding allocation mechanisms, especially in developing countries. Other types of mechanisms in Quadrant 1 are input-based funding formulas (number of students and/or faculty) and funds that are

Figure 10.12. **Funding matrix: dimensions of performance and competitiveness**

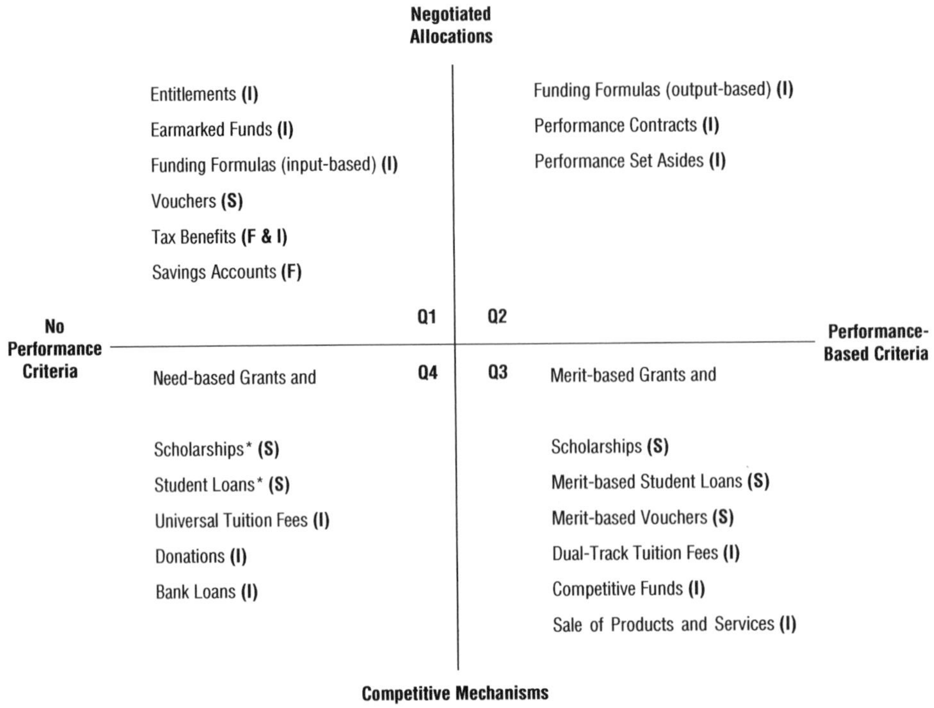

Notes: I = Institutions, S = Students, F = Families

* In countries where there is no rationing, need-based scholarships and student loans would move up to quadrant Q1, as everyone would be eligible.

Source: Adapted from Brunner (2007).

earmarked by the government and allocated to universities by virtue of them belonging to certain defined categories. A fairly innovative system, the universal voucher scheme that was implemented in Colorado in the United States a few years ago, would also belong in this quadrant. Under the scheme, by virtue of being a resident in the State, any student is entitled to a certain amount that he / she can apply towards paying fees at their university of choice. In other words, no performance or competition consideration comes into play from the viewpoint of the students' eligibility for the voucher.

Quadrant 2 lists mechanisms, where the amounts are still controlled by the State and the resources are transferred directly to the institutions, but the allocation is based on specific performance criteria. Output-based formulas are good examples of this kind of mechanism. Examples of countries that have built performance into their funding formulas include:

- England, where the recurrent expenses formula is paid on the basis of the number of students who complete each year of study;

- Denmark, which has a "taximeter model" in which 30 to 50 % of recurrent funds are paid for each student who passes exams;

- Netherlands, where half of recurrent funding is based on number of degrees awarded;

- South Africa, where the funding formula takes both the number of students enrolled and the number of graduates into consideration; and

- Norway, where some funding has been based on the number of credits obtained and beginning in 2007 a portion of funding will be based on the number of graduates.

Performance contracts, used for example in Austria, Chile, Denmark, France, Spain and Switzerland, also come under this category. Despite their name, performance contracts typically are not legally enforceable documents. Instead, they are more often non-binding regulatory agreements negotiated between governments or buffer bodies and tertiary education institutions. Performance contracts allow the institutions to receive additional funding against their commitment to fulfil a number of national objectives measured with specific targets agreed between the ministry of education and the institutions. The agreements may be with entire systems of institutions or individual institutions. All or a portion of funding may be based on whether institutions meet the requirements in the contracts. The agreements can be prospectively funded or reviewed and acted upon retrospectively.

Box 10.3. **Performance contracts in Spain: the "contract program" in Madrid**

The first "contract program" in Spain was signed in 2005 between the autonomous government of Madrid and the six public universities operating in the Spanish capital city. This agreement combines the elements of a funding formula and a performance contract with a multi-year horizon (five years). Not only does the formula allocate resources for both teaching and research, amounting to 85% of the total budget contribution, but it also provides funding against a number of policy objectives (restructuring of studies in accordance with the Bologna Process, better deployment of teachers, improvement in pedagogical practices and use of education technologies, continuing education, etc.). The "contract" includes as well a clause for compensatory payments to the universities less favored by the new allocation model in order to reduce past resource disparities.

Source: Interview with Rector of Universidad Autónoma de Madrid, 28 November 2005.

Quadrant 3 regroups the direct and indirect allocation mechanisms that embody a combination of performance and competitiveness. Among the principal examples are the various competitive funds, to which tertiary education institutions can apply, such as the innovation funds developed in Indonesia and Chile or the competitive research funds in most OECD countries, and the range of merit-based grants, scholarships and loans that the better academically qualified students can receive. Well-designed competitive funds can greatly stimulate the performance of tertiary education institutions and serve as powerful vehicles for their transformation and innovation. Argentina's Quality Improvement Fund (FOMEC), established in the mid-1990s with World Bank financing, has encouraged universities to engage in strategic planning for the strengthening of existing programs and the creation of new interdisciplinary graduate programs. Within universities, faculties that had never worked together started cooperating in the design and implementation of joint projects. In Chile, a second wave of tertiary education reforms is being supported by a competitive fund for diversification (development of the non-university sector, including private technical institutes) and quality improvement of all tertiary institutions (Salmi and Hauptman, 2006).

The voucher-like education grants that Kazakhstan rely on to allocate public funds also fall under this category. About 20% of the students receive education grants that they carry with them to the public or private institution of their choice, so long as they choose to study a grant-carrying subject. For the students, eligibility is determined by their score in the highly competitive Unified National Test and their subject choice. For the tertiary education institutions, eligibility is a function of their standing with the quality assurance unit of the Ministry of Education and Science, and the subjects they offer. Even after only a few years of operation, the voucher system appears to be functioning as an effective allocation instrument to reward those institutions that are perceived as better performing and offer national priority subjects (OECD /World Bank, 2007).

Finally, Q4 includes mechanisms which are competitive but have no specific performance criteria connected to them. Examples are needs-based grants and scholarships that are linked essentially to particular social characteristics of the students. Donations from businesses and philanthropists, and bank loans to tertiary education institutions also fall into this category (Salmi and Hauptman, 2006).

Table 10.4 presents the main categories of innovative allocation mechanisms implemented in recent years in various parts of the world.

Table 10.4. **Innovative allocation models in tertiary education, selected countries**

	Negotiated allocations	Competitive mechanisms
Direct funding (supply-side)	*Performance contracts* Austria, Denmark, France, Finland, Spain, Chile, United States (Colorado, Virginia) *Performance set-asides* South Africa, United States (States including Missouri, New Jersey, Tennessee, South Carolina, and Ohio)	*Competitive funds** Indonesia, Sri Lanka, Ghana, Mozambique, Argentina, Chile, Bolivia, Bulgaria, Hungary, Egypt, Tunisia
Indirect funding (demand-side)	*Income-contingent student loans* Thailand, South Africa, United States, Sweden, *New Zealand*, Australia *Human capital contracts* Chile, Colombia, Germany, United States *Universal vouchers* United States (Colorado), Bulgaria *Lifelong learning accounts* Canada, Sweden, United Kingdom	*Merit-based vouchers* Kazakhstan, Chile, Georgia, Hungary

* Research funding allocation mechanisms are not included in this table.

Sources: Oosterbeek and Patrinos (2008); Schuetze (2007); Salmi and Hauptman (2006).

In summary, many countries have witnessed important higher education financing reforms in recent years. The majority of these reforms had to do with changes in allocation mechanisms, with a general move towards a more direct relationship between public resources and institutional performance and a more competitive approach to resource distribution overall.

10.4. Three scenarios for the future

Based on the study of recent trends in the world of tertiary education, this chapter proposes three alternative scenarios to consider the likely evolution of higher education financing in future years. The first one, called the supply-side scenario, explores consequences and varied conditions for continued reliance on traditional kind public funding. The second scenario, entitled the transformation scenario, extrapolates likely developments in countries having already moved away from – or sometimes towards – the traditional approach of government financing as the main source of funding. The third scenario, called the demand-side scenario, envisages bold reforms to allow tertiary education institutions to compete for most of their resources. This section considers the pros and cons of each scenario, as well as some of their governance implications.

Supply-side financing scenario

More than any other time in history, mankind faces a crossroads. One path leads to despair and utter hopelessness. The other to total extinction. Let us pray we have the wisdom to choose correctly.

Woody Allen

Supply-side financing scenario reflects the traditional financing model that has had as an objective to support the public good functions of higher education, especially with regard to fundamental research, and to provide equal opportunities for access to tertiary education. Under this model, higher education institutions are mainly funded directly from public sources, often coupled with largely input-based allocation without performance criteria. Still today, higher education is largely financed from the public purse in many OECD countries, especially in Europe (see Table 10.5 below). Yet, the future sustainability and quality of higher education under the supply-side scenario can be put in question, as experiences with regard to this type of financing model have been very varied in a global scale.

Table 10.5. **OECD countries with the highest proportion of public funding for tertiary education in 2005**

	% of public funding of total funding for higher education institutions	Level of public funding, as % of GDP
Switzerland	100.0	1.4
Finland	99.4	1.7
Denmark	94.1	1.6
Sweden	93.8	1.5
Greece	93.3	1.4
Austria	92.3	1.2
Belgium	92.3	1.2
Iceland	91.7	1.1
Ireland	91.7	1.1
France	84.6	1.1
Germany	81.8	0.9
OECD average	73.3	1.1

Source: OECD (2008).

The Nordic countries and Switzerland represent the few countries, which have managed to maintain good quality tertiary education institutions and programs financed almost entirely from public resources. If international rankings are used as proxy of quality, the results achieved by these countries are much better than the rest of the world when seen in relative terms, i.e. compared to their size. A population-based analysis of the 2008 world ranking of universities published by Jiao Tong University in Shanghai demonstrates that Sweden has the highest number of top universities (number of universities among the 500 best universities in the world relative to the population size). Table 10.6 illustrates the relatively better performance compared to the United States, even though the latter country has the largest number of top universities.

But this is the case not only because these countries finance tertiary education from public sources, but also because they devote high levels of resources to tertiary education. As Table 10.5 illustrates, Switzerland and the Nordic countries spend at least 1.5% of their GDP on tertiary education from the public coffers.

However, as shown in Table 10.5, the absolute level of public investment is significantly lower in Ireland, France and Germany. The case of Ireland is very telling in

Table 10.6. **World rankings and population size**

Population per top 500-listed University in 2008	
Sweden	822 000
Finland	874 000
Switzerland	948 000
Norway	1 161 000
Denmark	1 371 000
Australia	1 373 000
United States	1 900 000

Source: Gerritsen (2008).

that respect. After being a pioneer for many years in terms of cost-sharing in Europe, the Irish government made the decision to abolish tuition fees in 1995. This has compromised the financial sustainability of the tertiary education sector, as noted in the 2006 OECD evaluation of higher education in Ireland (OECD, 2006).

Until recent years, university leaders in France and Germany, for example, were observing with concern the worsening financial and infrastructure situation in their institutions, translating sometimes in the same kind of overcrowding circumstances that are usually found in poor developing countries. In September 2007, for example, several French medical schools had to introduce a double shift teaching system using videotaped lectures in order to accommodate the growing number of students without sufficient teaching and infrastructure resources. The autonomy reforms that have just been launched in several German states and in France, as well as the fresh injection of resources through the German Excellence Initiative[4] and the French "Opération Campus"[5] are testimony to deliberate efforts to escape drawbacks in supply-side financing scenario through increased public, but more competitive , investment to higher education.

Another example comes from the United States, where the state of Texas has experienced very rapid demographic growth in recent years. After California, Texas is the second largest state in size and the second fastest growing state. But public investment to create new tertiary education institutions or consolidate existing ones has been lagging. In the eyes of the leadership of the University of Texas system, "… the kind of growth that Texas is experiencing […] is likely to make it overall a poorer and less educated state" (Malandra, 2008). Industrial nations are not free from the danger of falling into the spiral of deteriorating conditions that risk taking place with the supply-side scenario, if the high enough level of public higher education funding cannot be guaranteed.

However, the prospects are darker especially for many developing countries, in Sub-Saharan Africa, North Africa, the Middle East, Central and South America, and South Asia.

Almost fifteen years ago, the World Bank (1994) observed that tertiary education was "in crisis throughout the world" and highlighted the fiscal distress faced by the sector in many countries in the developing world. The supply-side financing scenario can be a tragic scenario for those countries, which have been in crisis for a long time and are incapable of changing the intractable equation which defines the parameters of their situation. In the future, countries with a predominantly public tertiary education sector typified by rapidly increasing secondary school enrolment and limited budgetary resources (or insufficient political commitment to tertiary education) could escape the downward path only, if they manage to regulate access to tertiary education and introduce significant levels of cost-sharing. Otherwise, they are likely to continue to experience unsustainable growth, deteriorating quality and, in many cases, high levels of graduate unemployment due to the slow rate of job creation.

Box 10.4. Enrolment growth and quality crisis in Egyptian tertiary education

"The monthly salary Tareq Al Desouki earns from his job as a medical professor at a university in Egypt's Nile Delta barely covers his family's needs for one week. He depends on his earnings from a private clinic to make both ends meet. But what about the thousands of university professors who do not have a private clinic to earn enough to cope with the soaring costs of living?"

The case of Egypt, where the Constitution stipulates that education should be free at all levels, exemplifies the situation faced by public universities in many nations, which is one of deteriorating quality as a result of unsustainable enrollment growth against a background of limited funding.

One of the most pressing concerns in Egypt's current higher education system is the appallingly weak salary structure, which caused the first ever half-day strike, by lecturers, in March of 2008. Egyptian academics have been struggling to conduct research on salaries which have remained unchanged since 1972 – as reflected in starting salaries of USD 93 for assistant professors. While some faculty have been able to augment their income with outside consultancies, others have not been that lucky. This has prompted many faculty members to seek employment in the private sector or even overseas, impacting student-teacher ratio and the quality of education.

Source: Khaled (2008).

In the developing world, even though some countries following this dangerous path of supply-side higher education financing may continue to have small islands of quality among their tertiary education institutions, they are at risk of further marginalisation and are unlikely to be able to establish or maintain any institution recognised at the international level. The growing lack of resources is a deterrent to hiring high quality staff in sufficient numbers and offering facilities and equipment of good standards, including broadband for universal connectivity.

Reliance on public funding has traditionally been justified in terms of the State's responsibility to support the public good functions of the university. However, if the State is not able to devote sufficient public resources for the sector, it is likely to fall short of meeting the needs of society and the economy. In many countries, especially in developing countries, the traditional model of financing tertiary education would be a bleak scenario for the future, assuming that they are unable to meet the economic and political conditions that would ensure enough political resources to achieve quality and equity.

Transformation scenario

> *A bend in the road is not the end of the road... unless you fail to make the turn.*
>
> Anonymous

The transformation scenario applies to countries and tertiary education institutions that have gone through first generation reforms towards cost-sharing but need to make adjustments to improve the impact of these earlier reforms or address some negative, often unanticipated consequences. This applies in particular to the Latin American region, countries in transition in eastern Europe and Central Asia, some East Asian nations.

At the country level, examples would include situations where, a few years after the introduction of cost-sharing and the establishment of a student loan scheme to help low-income students, a country would face rising default on loan reimbursement because of high graduate unemployment. One of the causes could be, as happened in the United States in the 1980s, that many student loan beneficiaries are enrolled in low-quality proprietary institutions. This would call for strengthening accreditation procedures to eliminate sub-standard institutions. Another such situation would arise when a government that has adopted a funding formula to allocate public resources among tertiary education institutions feels the need to modify the formula to reflect new conditions. In Poland, for example, the funding formula introduced in the early 1990s was very effective in boosting the recruitment of full-time teaching staff with PhDs. But fifteen years later it had become a barrier for university departments wanting to rely on part-time industry professionals without a doctorate.

Many countries throughout the world have encouraged the growth of private universities and colleges to complement, sometimes even substitute for public investment in tertiary education. But they have not always removed existing barriers that prevent private sector providers from operating effectively. In Azerbaijan, for example, the Ministry of Education controls the number of students in each private university and the type of programs that they are allowed to offer. Along the same lines, there is a need for increased financial autonomy in African and South Asian countries, where the government calls on public tertiary education institutions to diversify their resources but still requires that they transfer to the Treasury any surplus money they raise by themselves.

The case of Chile is also illustrative of the need for second generation reforms. A recent joint OECD/World Bank review of tertiary education (OECD/World Bank 2008) found that, while successive governments over the past twenty years have introduced several innovative ways of allocating resources (competitive fund, performance contracts, vouchers, student loans), these funding instruments lack consistency in terms of policy objectives, operational modalities and intended beneficiaries. For example, low-income students have access to two distinct loan schemes with different interest rates depending on whether they attend an older or newer university. Similarly, only the oldest private universities are eligible for grants through the competitive fund.

At the institutional level, a good example would be the case of universities that have introduced tuition fees on a selective basis, thereby creating a dual track system that can have negative effects from an efficiency and equity viewpoint. This is the case in most former socialist countries (for instance Viet Nam, Russia, Poland, Armenia and Azerbaijan) and in several eastern African countries (Uganda, Tanzania). What happens in these cases is that success at the competitive entrance examination to public universities determines who has to pay fees and who is exempted. The equity effect of this apparently purely meritocratic selection system is that students from wealthier families have better chances to be among the highest scoring students, either because they studied in good private secondary schools, were able to spend money on private tutoring, and/or come from families with a higher cultural capital. The efficiency argument is linked to the risk of a "dumbing" down effect as fee-paying students with lower exam scores study side by side with fee-exempt students with higher scores. The reform in this case would be to shift to universal tuition fees accompanied by a comprehensive student aid program of fee exemption, scholarships and loans for needy students.

Sometimes governments may also find it more suitable to re-introduce some elements of the supply-side model of higher education funding than to move on with additional reforms towards cost-sharing. This may be due to particular cultural or social characteristics of a country – or, at times, simply a result of political convenience. The Irish case has already been mentioned, but it is not the only recent example of removal of fees and return to public higher education funding. In the late 1990s, Hungary cancelled the tuition fees that had been introduced for repeating students and Togo halved its fees in 2005. Senegal reinstituted universal scholarships in 2005 only two years after having rationalised the eligibility criteria to eliminate leakage. *New Zealand* went back to a zero interest rate in its income-contingent student loan scheme. In each case, reversal of the reform has meant additional pressure on the public budget and less resources to expand higher education coverage and improve the quality and relevance of education and training.

The advantage of second generation financing and governance reforms is that they can provide countries and institutions with the opportunity to adjust to the changing environment by correcting distortions and preparing better to confront new challenges. On the down side, some of the reform proposed changes may challenge existing practices and acquired privileges. The success of implementing reforms that entail redistribution of funds is directly proportional to the ability of ensuring a smooth transition from old to new policies. To deal with these disruptions, it may be advisable to introduce "grandfather" provisions or minimal funding levels that guarantee all institutions a proportion of the funds they would have received under previous arrangements at least for some period of time.

As the recent reform experience in Pakistan has shown, it is much easier to impose redistribution measures, when there is additional funding than when it is carried out under a fixed budget. But even in richer countries, where additional private resources could be easily found, the political obstacles for cost-sharing can be daunting. For example in France, in spite of stretched public finances, the resistance to the increase in tuition fees is so fierce that it is firmly ruled out.

The Bologna Process has also been a powerful force to induce European countries and institutions to consider reforms – especially in the area of quality assurance – that would have been difficult to envisage in the purely national context. This trend can be observed beyond the European higher education space, not only in the Caucasus and Central Asia, but also in the Maghreb countries and in Sub-Saharan Africa. Similarly, the development of the Mercosur *(Mercado Común del Sur)* agreement in the southern Cone has prompted countries such as Uruguay and Bolivia to move faster towards building a national quality assurance system because of the degree recognition requirements for the mobility of professionals across Mercosur countries (Argentina, Brazil, Paraguay and Uruguay).

In conclusion, the transformation scenario is likely to be adopted by a growing number of countries facing the need to align their resource mobilisation and allocation strategies for higher education with changes in the economic and social environment.

Demand-side financing scenario

> *Innovation is to see what everybody sees, to think what someone thinks, and to do what*
> *no one does.*
>
> Patricio Montesinos

The third scenario envisages a funding system predominantly based on market mechanisms, whereby public resources follow the students rather than being transferred directly to tertiary education institutions, as is presently the case in almost all countries in the world. Also, in a lifelong learning perspective, public funding would not apply exclusively to first-time students moving from high school to tertiary education, but would be made available as well to mature students participating in retraining or skill updating programs throughout their working life.

A variety of instruments can be relied upon to implement this approach, including grants and scholarships, student loans, human capital contracts, vouchers, and savings accounts. Although no country has moved fully to this type of demand-side funding, there are relevant precedents in several parts of the world.

- *Scholarship and grants*. Most countries and tertiary education institutions offer non-reimbursable financial aid in the form of means-tested grants or merit scholarships.

- *Student loans*. Student loans exist in one form or the other in more than 60 countries. A large number of tertiary education institutions organise and finance their own student loans.

- *Human capital contracts*. Offered by private firms, human capital contracts are a different modality of student loans. Student participants agree to repay a portion of their incomes to investors who have an equity stake in the student's post graduation income. Human capital contracts exist on a pilot basis in Chile, Colombia, Germany and the United States (Oosterbeek and Patrinos, 2008).

- *Vouchers*. At least six countries[6] (or regions within a country) have implemented a form of voucher for tertiary education. Students receive an entitlement which can be used to study at the tertiary education institution of their choice. Annex 10.A1 lists the principal voucher experiences that have taken place so far, and outlines their main characteristics.

- *Education savings accounts*. Education savings accounts, sometimes called Individual Learning Accounts, are aimed at promoting savings from families or individuals for tertiary education. The State encourages families to contribute into the savings accounts for their children by offering either tax advantages or matching donations. The learning accounts are used for vocational training purposes too; employees and employers are encouraged to open up accounts and use the money to further their training. Savings accounts have been established, with uneven success, in nine countries.[7] Annex 10.A2 lists the principal experiences with regard to education savings accounts.

The demand-side approach presents several potential advantages. First, it puts students and firms, the "consumers" of tertiary education services, in the driving seat. The assumption is that, as tertiary education institutions compete for students, they become more sensitive to the need for improving the quality and relevance of their course offerings. Demand-side mechanisms could also provide incentives to encourage institutions to be more cost-effective. Students, in turn, would be more aware of the value of their education and better motivated to study hard, which in turn could lead to better academic results and increased internal efficiency (Salmi and Hauptman, 2006).

Second, demand-side mechanisms may be used regardless of the source of funding. They can be applied equally to allocate public resources and to capture private funding from employers or from students and their families. It is doubtful that governments can significantly expand lifelong learning opportunities through public funding alone. Reliance on demand-side financing mechanisms could facilitate resource mobilisation efforts to raise private funding from individuals and firms, since they are able to see the direct connection between their financial contribution and the training benefits that they can derive.

The main drawback of demand-side mechanisms is that they cannot be used to finance tertiary education programs serving a public good purpose. Institutions that compete for students are naturally going to offer courses directly linked to the professional interests of the majority of students. They have no incentive to spend resources on programs with low market value or to fund basic research unless competitive grants are available for that purpose. These issues have come up clearly in several former Soviet Union republics, such as Armenia, Azerbaijan or Kazakhstan, where most of the public resources transferred to State universities come in the form of merit scholarships (usually called "state orders"). The downside is that the public universities are starved for research funding and have difficulty maintaining disciplines in the humanities for which there is limited demand and which are not considered as high priority professions by the government itself.

Another limitation of this approach is that it would be difficult to implement in countries that are part of a regional higher education agreement unless all the countries concerned adopt the same financing model. The Erasmus Mundus controversy in Denmark in 2007 highlights the potential conflicts when partner countries do not share the same financing rules. One of the conditions of Erasmus Mundus, an EU scheme that allows students to enrol in joint and double degree programs offered by universities from at least three countries, is that the students be subject to the same access and financing rules. But since in Denmark public universities are entirely financed through tax money, the Parliament is strongly opposed to the country's participation in a program that requires students to contribute to the cost of their education (Jongsma, 2008).

It seems likely that this financing scenario can evolve only in countries with a diversified tertiary education system that includes both public and private institutions and where it is (or becomes) socially and politically acceptable to transfer public resources to private institutions through the students. Chile is perhaps the one country in the world whose financing model comes closer to the demand-side financing scenario (see Box 10.5).

Figure 10.13 shows the variety of levels private resource mobilisation to fund tertiary education and the absence of correlation with enrolment rates. Opportunities for moving towards increased demand-side funding seem greater in countries with a high proportion of students enrolled in private institutions, in particular in Latin America and East Asia. Conversely, the availability of demand-side financing through scholarships and student

---

Box 10.5. **Demand-side funding in Chile**

Chile has one of the highest proportions of students enrolled in the private sector in the world (73%) and the second highest level of self-generated income in public universities (74%) after Armenia (82%). Tuition fees charged in public institutions represent 28% of per capita GDP, compared to 16% in Korea and about 11% in the United States, Australia and Japan.

Chile is also the country in the world with the highest proportion of public resources transferred through demand-side mechanisms: 48.7% in 2007, up from 33.7% in 2000. Three instruments are used for that purpose. The first one, a voucher-like scheme called *Aporte Fiscal Indirecto* (AFI), goes to the top 15% students selected on the basis of their results in the national university admissions test. The AFI mechanism has encouraged universities to compete on the basis of quality and has also pushed more institutions to adopt the national admission test results as their principal selection criterion.

Need-based scholarships represent the second demand-side instrument used in Chile. About 12% of the overall student population receives a scholarship. Finally, the Chilean government operates two student loan programs which, together, reach close to 11% of the student population.

Source: OECD/World Bank (2008).

Figure 10.13. **Private enrolment and expenditures in tertiary education: a comparison between OECD and selected other countries (2004)**

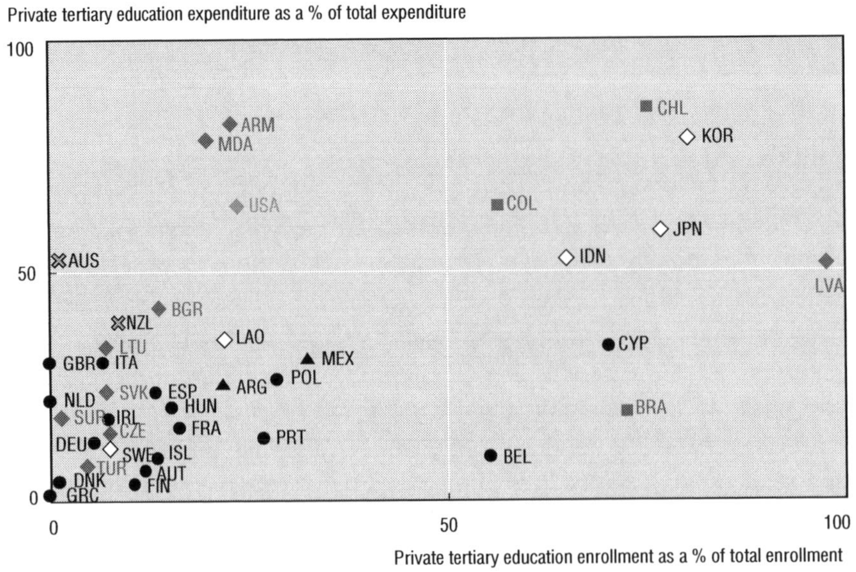

Private tertiary education expenditure as a % of total expenditure

Private tertiary education enrollment as a % of total enrollment

Sources: OECD (2007a); *OECD Education Database*; UNESCO Institute for Statistics; World Bank Education Statistics.

loans is a strong factor to facilitate the growth of private tertiary education. It is significant to observe that the two African nations where private enrolment in tertiary education has soared, Botswana and the Ivory Coast, are among the few countries where the government does not restrict scholarships to students at public institutions only.

By the same token, the prospects for the demand-side scenario are less solid in countries with a predominant public tertiary education sector mostly financed by the State. Only in countries with substantial levels of cost-sharing is there room for increased demand-side funding through grants, scholarships and student loans. Interestingly, student mobility in the European Higher Education Area could be a factor that would stimulate growing reliance on demand-side financing, as governments try to find better ways to account for the costs and financial contributions for students from other European countries.

The other key requirement for moving towards demand-side funding is the existence of adequate quality assurance and accountability mechanisms to inform and guide the decision of students. This means effective evaluation/accreditation instruments and independent observatories to monitor and disseminate information about student experiences and labour market outcomes. Countries lacking reliable and comprehensive quality assurance and information systems face the risk that rankings might become a driving force of accountability and influence over university offerings, despite their methodological limitations (Salmi and Saroyan, 2007). In some countries, private companies are already preparing and disseminating their own list of approved tertiary education institutions eligible for providing reimbursable training to their employees, as illustrated by a recent initiative by Intel in the United States, while Boeing announced its intention to compile its ranking of top universities and colleges.

Global trends and the financing scenarios

Resource mobilisation and utilisation are priority concerns for tertiary education leaders in all parts of the world, reflecting several converging trends that have a direct impact in terms of additional financing needs: changing demographic structures, the rising demand for tertiary education especially in developing countries, the move towards a lifelong learning approach to education, and the growing cost of tertiary education delivery.

In that context, the evolution of tertiary education financing strategies seems to follow several generic patterns. The first one is increased cost-sharing in various forms. The second one is the growing reliance on performance-based funding mechanisms. The third one is a greater mix of financing instruments within a given country context, including the emergence of demand-side funding mechanisms.

However, the responses of countries and institutions vary a lot depending on local economic, social and cultural circumstances, political conditions, and the existence of a strategic vision on the role of tertiary education. In order to capture the range of possible reactions and approaches, three main scenarios were constructed. Table 10.7 below summarises the principal features of each scenario.

When attempting to gauge the probability that a given scenario will happen in a particular country setting, it is important to look not only at these characteristics within national boundaries, but also at several international phenomena that are increasingly influencing the national debate on tertiary education. Competition for international students, the presence of cross-border tertiary education institutions, the emergence of multi-national higher education areas, and international rankings all play a non-negligible role in shaping strategic decisions on the future of tertiary education.

Table 10.7. **Main characteristics of the financing scenarios**

Characteristics / Scenarios	Supply-side scenario	Transformation scenario	Demand-side scenario
Rationale	Provide equal opportunities for access to tertiary education Support the public good functions of higher education, especially with regard to fundamental research	Improve or correct the impact of earlier reforms in order to adjust to changing circumstances	Allow sufficient and efficiently used resources for improved quality and relevance of higher education
Features	Main part of higher education funding going directly from public sources to institutions Non-performance based resource allocation	Forward-looking vision to implement second-generation reforms to address quality and equity concerns Unintended consequences of earlier reforms	Growing share of public resources allocated indirectly through demand-side mechanisms
Advantages	Strong and diversified tertiary education participation in high-income countries with sufficient fiscal resources	Flexibility and adaptability	More choice for users Increased responsiveness of institutions Higher efficiency in resource use Greater motivation among students
Drawbacks	Negative outcome in terms of coverage, quality and equity, especially in less-developed countries Little incentive to improve system and institutional performance	Risk of inequity of access	Lack of attention to public goods programs (research and training)
Risk Factors	Growing gap between funding needs and funding capacity Inertia and resistance to change	Political opposition to change among groups whose interests are threatened Little incentive to improve cost-efficiency	Insufficient institutional differentiation to allow for competition
Corrective action	Increase in public investment to higher education Resource mobilisation through cost-sharing and other forms of income diversification	Likely to work better if additional public resources are available	Careful government oversight and sufficient public funding for public goods programs

10.5. Conclusion

The trouble with our times is that the future is not what it used to be.

Paul Valéry

"Hi there. My name is Ron Steen. I am selling 2% of my future earnings for a chance to go to college." This provocative invitation, posted on eBay in August 2006 by an incoming freshman at California State University, Fullerton, stirred up a controversial debate on the financing challenges faced by US tertiary education (Hess and Carey, 2008). Even though eBay did not allow Mr. Steen to keep his ad, his creative initiative illustrates the need to explore new funding solutions. And if this is true in one of the richest countries in the world, the urgency is even greater in many if not most middle- and low-income nations where the rapidly growing demand for tertiary education opportunities against a background of constrained fiscal situation threatens to blow into a severe financial crisis.

The structure of the world economy is rapidly changing. For most industries, success is increasingly depending on the creativity of firms and their capacity to harness new technologies. In the own words of the 2007 US Commission on the Skills of the American Workforce (NCEE, 2007):

> "producing the most important new products and services depends on maintaining the worldwide technological lead, year in and year out... This is a world in which a very high level of preparation in reading, writing, speaking, mathematics, science, literature, history, and the arts will be an indispensable foundation for everything that comes after for most members of the workforce. It is a world in which comfort with ideas and abstractions is the passport to a good job, in which creativity and innovation are the key to the good life, in which high levels of education – a very different kind of education than most of us have had – are going to be the only security there is."

In this context, tertiary education cannot play its renewal role without adequate financing on a sustainable basis. This chapter looked therefore at key factors affecting the cost of tertiary education and the financial needs faced by countries and institutions, and proposed, on that basis, three scenarios: the supply-side scenario, the transformation scenario, and the demand-side scenario.

As with any scenario exercise, the three possible paths to financial sustainability considered in this chapter reflect choices on the part of decision-makers at the national and institutional levels. Even the lack of willingness to address present or expected crises is a choice in itself, if only by default. Therefore, the usefulness of these scenarios is to help governments and institutional leaders think through what they can and should do today to undertake the kinds of reforms and adjustments that are more likely to bring about sustainable financing in the near and medium future.

Regardless of the path chosen in any given country, governments need to keep in mind five general principles of good funding which could guide their financing policies:

- mobilise sufficient resources, public and private, to meet the needs for quantitative expansion and quality improvement on an equitable basis;

- guarantee that cost-sharing is always accompanied by adequate student aid;

- rely on funding mechanisms that are performance-based and, when appropriate, allocated in a competitive manner;

- ensure full compatibility among the various funding instruments used; and

- offer transparency in the design and operation of all funding mechanisms (policy objectives sought, rules of procedures for resource allocation).

Finally, it is important to underline that financing reform is not an end in itself. It serves the purpose of ensuring sustainability in funding in order to expand tertiary education opportunities and improve the quality and relevance of programs offered. It needs therefore to be part of a national vision about the future of tertiary education and its contribution in support of economic and social development. Sustainable financing is a key pillar of balanced tertiary education development.

Notes

1. 1) Expand early childhood care and education, 2) provide free and compulsory primary education for all, 3) promote learning and life skills for young people and adults, 4) increase adult literacy by 50%, 5) achieve gender parity in primary and secondary education by 2005, gender equality in education by 2015, and 6) improve the quality of education.

2. The Fast Track Initiative is aimed to help low-income countries meet the Education For All goal of all children completing a full cycle of primary education by 2015 and the Education Millennium Development Goals, namely the goal for achieving universal primary education and the goal to promote gender equality and empower women.

3. The eight countries are Argentina, Chile, India, Indonesia, Jamaica, Paraguay, Peru and Thailand.

4. The Initiative, launched in 2005, seeks to strengthen top-level research as well as improve the quality of universities and research institutions in Germany. Within this framework, additional grants (in total worth of 1.9 billion euro, of which 75% from the Federal government) will be allocated in particular to nine German universities, namely Technical University of Aachen, Free University of Berlin, University of Freiburg, University of Göttingen, University of Karlsruhe, University of Konstanz, University of Heidelberg, University of Munich, and the Technical University of Munich.

5. The initiative aims at renewing and increasing the dynamics of existing campuses through massive, targeted investments. This would translate into lively and modern learning spaces and increase their international visibility.

6. Bulgaria, Chile, Georgia, Hungary, Kazakhstan and the United States (especially the State of Colorado).

7. Belgium (Flanders), Canada, Malaysia, The Netherlands, Singapore, Spain, Sweden, the United Kingdom and the United States.

Bibliography

Bollag, B. (2007), "Financing for Higher Education Shifts to Private Sector Worldwide", *The Chronicle of Higher Education,* Vol. 53, Issue 50, p. A36, *http://chronicle.com/weekly/v53/i50/50a03601.htm.*

Brunner, J. J. (2007) "Mercados Universitarios: Los Nuevos Escenarios de la Educación Superior", Informe Final de Proyecto FONDECYT No. 1050138, Santiago de Chile.

Du Vivier, Ed. (2008), *Costs and Financing in Open Schools,* Vancouver, Commonwealth of Learning.

College Board (2007). *Trends in College Pricing,* College Board, *www.collegeboard.com/prod_downloads/ about/news_info/trends/trends_pricing_07.pdf.*

College Board (2008), *Trends in College Pricing,* College Board, *http://professionals.collegeboard.com/ profdownload/trends-in-college-pricing-2008.pdf.*

Ederer, P. (2006), *Innovation at Work: The European Human Capital Index,* Lisbon Council Policy Brief, p. 4.

Gakio, K. (2006), *African Tertiary Institutions Connectivity Survey (ATICS),* Ottawa, IDRC.

Gerritsen, J. (2008), "The Real Shanghai Jiao Tong Winners", *University World News,* 31 August 2008.

Glater, Jonathan (2007), "College Costs Outpace Inflation Rate", *New York Times,* 23 October 2007, *www.nytimes.com/2007/10/23/education/23tuition.html?_r=1&oref=slogin.*

Hess, F.M. and K. Carey (2008), "Popping the Tuition Bubble", Australian Education International *(AEI) Online,* 18 June 2008, *www.aei.org/publications/pubID.28160/pub_detail.asp.*

Higher Education Commission (2008), Unpublished presentation by Soheil Naqvi, Executive Director of the Pakistani Higher Education Commission, at the International Workshop on Diversity and Funding, Islamabad, April 2008.

International Comparative Higher Education Finance and Accessibility Project (ICHEFAP) (2006), ICHEFAP website, *www.gse.buffalo.edu/org/IntHigherEdFinance.*

Johnstone, B. (2001), *Worldwide Reforms in the Financing and Management of Higher Education,* ICHEFAP publication.

Johnstone. B. (2004), "The Economics and Politics of Cost Sharing in Higher Education: Comparative Perspectives", *Economics of Education Review,* Vol. 20, No. 4, pp. 403-10.

Johnstone, B. and P. Marcucci (2007), *Worldwide Trends in Higher Education Finance: Cost-Sharing, Student Loans, and the Support of Academic Research,* UNESCO Forum on Higher Education, Research and Knowledge, *http://portal.unesco.org/education/en/files/53752/11842449745Johnstone.pdf/Johnstone.pdf.*

Jongsma, A. (2008), "*Erasmus Mundus on a Collision Course*", *University World News,* 8 June 2008, *www.universityworldnews.com/article.php?story=20080605160500554.*

Kapur, D. and M. Crowley (2008), *Beyond the ABCs: Higher Education and Developing Countries,* Washington, DC, Center for Global Development, Working paper No. 139.

Khaled, Ashraf (2008), "Egypt: Academics Struggle with No Pay Rise for 25 Years", *University World News,* 27 April 2008, *www.universityworldnews.com/article.php?story=20080424151856999.*

Larsen, Kurt and David Istance (2001), "Lifelong Learning for All", OECD *Observer,* No. 225, *www.oecdobserver.org/news/fullstory.php/aid/432.*

Lemoine, Camille (2008), "35 universités escroqueraient les étudiants", *L'Express,* 23 July 2008, *www.lexpress.fr/actualite/societe/education/35-universites-escroqueraient-les-etudiants_535902.html.*

MacGregor, Karen (2008), "South Africa: Universities Warn against Fee-Capping", *University World News,* 2 March 2008, *www.universityworldnews.com/article.php?story=20080229100527689.*

Malandra, G. (2008), "*Creating a Higher Education Accountability System: The Texas Experience.*" Unpublished paper presented at the OECD/IMHE Conference on Higher Education Outcomes, September 2008, Paris.

Montgomery, Jessica (2008) "Indian Higher Education Debates Opening Its Doors to Foreign Competition", *The American Association of Collegiate Registrars and Admissions Officers (AACRAO),* 24 April 2008, *www.aacrao.org/transcript/index.cfm?fuseaction=show_view&doc_id=3841.*

National Center on Education and the Economy (NCEE) (2007), *Tough Choices Tough Times: The Report of the New Commission on the Skills of the American Workforce,* NCEE, Washington, DC.

OECD (2003), *Education at a Glance,* OECD Publishing, Paris.

OECD (2005), *Education Trends in Perspective: Analysis of the World Education Indicators,* OECD Publishing, Paris.

OECD (2006), *Reviews of National Policies for Education - Higher Education in Ireland,* OECD Publishing, Paris.

OECD (2007a), *Education at a Glance,* OECD Publishing, Paris.

OECD (2007b), *OECD Population Pyramids in 2000 and 2050,* OECD Directorate for Employment, *www.oecd.org/LongAbstract/0,3425,en_2649_33933_38123086_1_1_1_37457,00.html.*

OECD/World Bank (2007), *Higher Education in Kazakhstan,* OECD Publishing, Paris and Washington, DC.

OECD (2008), *Education at a Glance,* OECD Publishing, Paris.

OECD/World Bank (2008), *Tertiary Education in Chile,* OECD Publishing, Paris and Washington, DC.

Olsen, J. (2000), "Is Virtual Education for Real?", *TechKnowLogia,* January-February 2000, pp. 16-18, *www.techknowlogia.org/tkl_active_pages2/CurrentArticles/main.asp?IssueNumber=3&FileType=PDF&ArticleID=59.*

Oosterbeek, H. and H. A. Patrinos (2008), *Financing Lifelong Learning,* Policy Research Working Paper 4569, the World Bank, Washington, DC.

Osborn, Alan (2008), "Europe: Lifelong Learning to Benefit from New Rule", *University World News,* *www.universityworldnews.com/article.php?story=20080314090826122.*

Paskey, H. 2001. "Canadian Universities Band Together in a Giant Journal-Licensing Deal", *Chronicle of Higher Education* (September 14), *http://chronicle.com/free/2001/09/2001091401t.htm.*

Salmi, J., and A. M. Hauptman (2006), "Innovations in Tertiary Education Financing: A Comparative Evaluation of Allocation Mechanisms", Education Working Paper Series No. 4, September 2006, the World Bank, Washington, DC.

Salmi, J., and A. Saroyan (2007), "League Tables as Policy Instruments: Uses and Misuses", *Higher Education Management and Policy,* Volume 19, No. 2, OECD Publishing, Paris.

Schleicher, A. (2006), *The Economics of Knowledge: Why Education is Key to Europe's Success,* Lisbon Council Policy Brief, March 2006, the Lisbon Council, Brussels.

Schuetze, H. (2007), "Individual Learning Accounts and Other Models of Financing Lifelong Learning", *International Journal of Lifelong Education,* Vol. 26, No. 1, pp 5–23.

Shorto, R. (2008), "Childless Europe: No Babies?", *New York Times,* 29 June 2008, *www.nytimes.com/2008/06/29/magazine/29Birth-t.html.*

Supiano, B. (2008), "College Finance Chiefs Say Tuition Increases Will Keep Rising Faster Than Inflation", *The Chronicle,* 30 April 2008, *http://chronicle.com/daily/2008/04/2671n.htm.*

Twinomugisha, A. (2005), *Deploying ICTs in Schools: A Framework for Identifying and Assessing Technology Options, their Benefits, Feasibility and Total Cost of Ownership,* GeSCI.

UNESCO Institute for Statistics (UIS) (2006), *Global Education Digest 2006,* UIS, Montreal.

University World News (2007), "US: Room for Improvement", *University World News,* 16 December 2007, *www.universityworldnews.com/article.php?story=20071213154422566.*

University World News (2008), "First University You Tube Channel", *University World News,* 8 April 2008, *www.universityworldnews.com/article.php?story=20080424152925285.*

US Census Bureau (2008), *Statistical Abstract of the United States,* US Census Bureau, *www.census.gov/compendia/statab/index.html.*

US Department of Education (2006), *A Test Of Leadership: Charting the Future of U.S. Higher Education,* A Report of the Commission Appointed by Secretary of Education Margaret Spellings, Pre-Publication Copy, September 2006, *www.ed.gov/about/bdscomm/list/hiedfuture/reports/pre-pub-report.pdf.*

Womack, H. (2008), "Russia: Demographic Time Bomb Empties Colleges", *University World News,* 18 May 2008, *www.universityworldnews.com/article.php?story=20080515161214914.*

World Bank (1994), *Higher Education: Lessons of Experience,* Washington, DC, World Bank, p. 1.

World Bank (2002), *Constructing Knowledge Societies: New Challenges for Tertiary Education,* World Bank, Washington, DC.

World Bank (2007), *Enhancing China's Competitiveness Through Lifelong Learning,* WBI Development Studies, World Bank, Washington, DC.

World Bank (2007), *Establishing a World-Class Higher Education System in Malaysia,* EASHD Report, World Bank, Washington, DC.

ANNEX 10.A1

Matrix of Voucher Systems

Country or State	Year established	Institutional eligibility	Eligibility criteria	Beneficiaries (number or % of student population)	Amount	Comments
Bulgaria	2001	Public only	Master's level only	90%	USD 1 300	Same per student amount for all institutions penalises more expensive research universities, in the absence of separate research budget
Chile (*Aporte Fiscal Indirecto*)	1981	Public and traditional private only	Top scores at national university entrance examination	27 500 students (15% of new entrants)	USD 900 on average (5 sub-categories with variable amounts linked to academic score)	Selection through university entrance examination that is closely correlated with family income
Colorado – United States (College Opportunity Fund Stipend)	2004	Public and private	Resident of the state	100% of Pell Grant eligible students	USD 2 670 (public) USD 1 335 (private)	Overarching goals were access and generation of revenue
Georgia	2005	Public and private	Students with highest score at National Entrance Examination	8 270 students (about 58% of total student population)	USD 800 on average	Only 4 years since operation – too early to determine outcome of this initiative
Hungary	2007	Public and private	Students with highest score at National Entrance Examination			
Kazakhstan	1999	Public and private	Bachelor level students with highest score at National Entrance Examination	14.6%	USD 1 200 (public) – USD 4 000 (top private)	Working well to facilitate the growth of good quality private institutions and provide actual choice to students
Unites States (GI Bill)	1944	Public and private	2-3 years of active duty	2.2 million veterans (former active duty soldiers, within 10 years of leaving the military)	Up to USD 30 000 towards tuition expenses (45 months of education)	
Unites States (new GI Bill)	2008 (benefits will apply from 2009)	Public and private	3 years of active duty after 9/11 or discharge due to service disability	All former active duty soldiers within 15 years of leaving the military	Tuition covered up to the most expensive public university in the veteran's home state, housing and living expenses (monthly) and money for books	

ANNEX 10.A2

Matrix of Education Savings Accounts

Country or State	Program name	Year established	Main financier	Incentives	Comments
Flanders (Belgium)	Bijblijfrekening (Individual Learning and Development Account)	2002 (two-year project)	State, employer, employee	One-time contribution of 1 000 (euro) from the State The account grows with contributions from the employee and the employer	The project is targeted towards low-qualified, disabled, immigrant and the training must be vocational The account can only be opened if the employee requests it
Canada	Registered Education Savings Plan (RESP)	1974	Family	Returns on savings are tax-free	Since 1998, the govt. matches contributions to the RESP through the Canada Education Savings Grant (CESG)
	Learn$ave	2000	Individual, government	The government matches an individual's savings USD 2 to USD 3 for every USD 1 saved	The project is only offered in select cities because it is a research project Eligible participants have a low to modest income and are between 21 to 65 yrs
Alberta (only)	Alberta Centennial Education Savings Plan (ACES)	2005	Alberta Government	USD 500 or USD 100 (for children born before 2005; must be matched by parents)	To get USD 500, children have to be born 2005 or after; children turning 8, 11 and 14 in 2005 or after get USD 100
Malaysia	National Education Savings Scheme (SSPN)	2004	Family	Returns on savings are tax free; Govt. matches up to USD 3,073 if family income < USD 615 (1:1)	In 2004, there was a requirement for a min. savings balance of USD 154 to obtain a higher education loan; this requirement was abolished in 2008
The Netherlands	Learning Accounts	2001	Employees, employers, State	Contributions by the individual, USD 130-USD 400/learner (by employers), USD 400/learner (by state)	The money has to be used for specific sectors – education, trade
Singapore	Edusave Pupils Fund	1993	Government	USD 180 – primary pupil, USD 220 – secondary pupil (yearly)	The money in the account can be used to pay approved tertiary fees
Spain (Basque Country)	Individual Learning Accounts	2000	Basque Country, teachers	Secondary school teachers receive vouchers worth USD 130-USD 600. The teachers pay 25% of the training costs	Specifically targeted to improve the computer skills of teachers
Sweden	Individual Learning Accounts	2000	Employees, employers	When money is in the account, it grows tax-free; when withdrawn there is a tax subsidy	The tax subsidy depends on the amount withdrawn and the importance of training
Skandia (firm)	Competency Assurance Accounts	1999	Skandia, employee	Employer matches the employee's contributions	To cover training costs or cover expenses when studying full-time
United Kingdom (UK)	Individual Learning Accounts (ILA)	2000	Government, employee, employer	One-time contribution of GBP 150 for first 1 million account holders (with a contribution of GBP 25; tax advantages for employee and employer if they contribute	The scheme was abandoned in Nov. 2001 due to fraud on part of the providers of learning services

Country or State	Program Name	Year Established	Main Financier	Incentives	Comments
Scotland	ILA Scotland	2004	Government	GBP 200 if you want to study a new course; GBP 500 if you are already a part-time student	Eligible only to Scottish residents over 16 and earning < GBP 18,000 or are on benefits
Wales	ILA Wales	2001	Government	Up to GBP 200/year	Eligible only to Welsh residents over 18, claiming income benefits
United States (USA)	Coverdell ESA (previously Education IRA)	1997	Family	Returns on the savings in the account are tax-free	There are penalties if the account is not used to pay for tertiary education
US States (District of Columbia and 49 states excluding Washington)	College 529 Plans	Varies	Family	The investment grows tax-free; withdrawals for tertiary education are tax-exempt	The plans vary by each state. Wyoming has adopted the 529 plan of Colorado and the state of Washington only offers a pre-paid 5289 plan.
IBM (firm)	Individual Training and Learning Accounts	2007	Employee, employer	Employee can contribute up to USD 1 000 annually with a 50% match from IBM	Only employees with at least 5 years of service are eligible

Source: Sonali Ballal and Jamil Salmi.

Chapter 11

Quality Assurance in Higher Education – Its Global Future

by
Richard Lewis*

This chapter examines the developments in higher education quality assurance worldwide. It starts by providing an overview of different quality assurance models, their characteristics and the differences in their use across countries and regions worldwide. It then reflects on a number of emerging trends with regard to alternative quality assurance approaches and methodologies. The chapter concludes by discussing the future prospects for internationalisation of higher education quality assurance.

* The author is a consultant on quality assurance worldwide and a former President of the International Network of Quality Assurance Agencies in Higher Education's (INQAAHE), from 2003 to 2007.

Quality assurance in Higher Education has undoubtedly got a future but it is by no means clear what that future will be. Will we see an increase of external, often governmental, intervention adopting what might be well described as a "inspectoral" approach, or will it be based on the notion that Higher Education Institutions (HEIs), while needing to be accountable to the wider community, should retain or obtain, a high degree of autonomy?

This chapter will provide a brief history of the development of quality assurance in higher education as well as an exploration of what superficially appears to be the "standard model" which applies in many jurisdictions, but which is in fact operated very differently in different places. A number of significant emerging trends will be identified and their longer term consequences discussed amongst which the more significant include the desire to have more objective evidence of what students have learnt and how their learning has been applied and the ever increasing internationalisation or globalisation of higher education. Finally some speculative thoughts are offered as the longer term future of quality assurance in higher education.

11.1. Terminology

The subject of quality assurance in higher education[1] is bedevilled by the inconsistent use of terminology, and it might be helpful to start the chapter by explicitly defining the key terms or phrases. There are three such phrases.[2]

Quality assurance

Quality assurance is an all-embracing term covering all the policies, processes, and actions through which the quality of higher education is maintained and developed (Campbell and Rozsnyai, 2002, p. 32).

Quality assessment

Quality assessment covers both the means by which a judgement is made about the quality and standards of an institution or a programme and the judgement itself (Vlăscanu, Grünberg and Pârlea, 2004, p. 22).

Accreditation

Accreditation is a form of quality assessment where the outcome is a binary (yes/no) decision that usually involves the granting of special status to an institution or programme (CHEA, 2001).

To an extent any action taken by a university[3] teacher to check on the quality of his or her own work or steps taken to improve it might be said to be an act of "quality assurance" – indeed the same might be said about the actions of students. So an often unstated assumption is that quality assurance is a collective action with more than one person being involved.

And one final comment on terminology, which is on the word "external" when used in phrases such as "external quality assurance" or "external quality assessment". This means that the activity is predominantly being carried by an individual or a team that are from outside the area which is being assessed or assured. In the case of the quality assurance of a programme,[4] the externals may come from other parts of the institution while in the case of the external assessment of an institution the task would be carried out by those from outside the institution.[5]

This paper will be mainly concerned with external quality assurance but the relationship between external and internal is so close that it is impossible to discuss the external element without some reference to internal quality assurance.

One other point needs to be made before the discussion can properly begin. That is that this paper is concerned with quality assurance relating to the learning and teaching process and is not concerned with the quality assurance, or as is usually the case, quality assessment of research.

11.2. The development of quality assurance

Given the virtual universality of external quality assurance systems across the world it is remarkably easy to forget, with very few exceptions, the youthfulness of most of the systems of external quality assurance and of the agencies that operate them.

It may be worth starting by describing the exceptions – that is, the systems that have been around for more than, say, 50 years. It will be noted that the older systems are to be found in the United Kingdom and the United States. This is in part explained by the point that in many other countries the State was more closely involved with the day-to-day operations of HEIs, for example academic staff being employed by the State, than was the case in these two countries and hence there was a far less perceived need for a system of external quality assurance.

The UK external examiner system

It was in 1832 with the creation of the University of Durham and the consequent massive, 50%, increase in the number of universities in England – from two to three – that the external examiner system was introduced (Silver, 1994).[6] The external examiners were mostly drawn from the University of Oxford and, while their main purpose was to increase the local "examining capacity", they also provided some evidence to the outside world of the acceptability of Durham's degrees. Thus, in the 19th century a policy concern was identified which has continued to concern the academic community – namely how to achieve comparability of standards across institutions.

The system after some development has continued to this day and has been adopted either in whole or in part by a few other countries.

Early US accreditation

In her introduction to the accreditation in the United States, Elaine El-Kahwas (2001) explains that the initial purpose of the regional associations, which later developed as regional accreditation agencies, was to establish closer links between the administrators of colleges and schools and to set standards for adequate preparation for college study. The growth in student numbers, and in the number of schools and higher education institutions, towards the end of the 19th century meant that informal and personal links between the institutions and the administrators was no longer sufficient and it was judged necessary to make the system more formal.

Accreditation of institutions was first undertaken by the North Central Association in 1905 but the institutions that were accredited first were schools not colleges, the first list of accredited colleges was not issued until 1913. The main purpose of the exercise was to enable college administrators to evaluate the worthiness of applicants from institutions of which they had no personal knowledge whether they were schools or other colleges. Developments in the 20th century were slow to emerge and it was not until 1952 that the New England Association took on an accrediting function.

Professional bodies

In a number of countries, particularly the United States and the United Kingdom, professional or specialised agencies have developed over the years. The US Council of Higher Education Accreditation (CHEA) recognises about 50 such bodies including the Committee on Accreditation of the American Board of Funeral Service Education and the Accreditation Board for Engineering and Technology. Other countries where professional associations play an important role include Korea where professional accrediting bodies review programmes in the engineering, medical and nursing disciplines (OECD, 2008).

The actual remit and powers of these bodies vary considerably but in general they approve, which normally takes the form of accreditation, programmes of study or specialised institutions that are related to their field of activity. In some cases that approval may be necessary if the programmes' graduates are to obtain a professional qualification or a licence to practice while in others there might be no such relationship.

While some of these bodies have had, and continue to have, a significant influence on parts of the higher education system their effects tended to be localised and did not generally impact on other parts of the institutions.

11.3. The growth in external quality assurance agencies over the last 20 or so years

The ending of the Second World War saw the establishment in Japan and the Philippines of accrediting agencies modelled largely on the US agencies but institutional involvement was largely on a voluntary basis. In the United Kingdom, the Council for National Academic Awards (CNAA) was set up in 1965 to act as the degree awarding and quality assurance body for the Polytechnic and College sector of Higher Education.

The 1980s saw the emergence of external quality assurance agencies, but not necessarily comprehensive systems, in a few countries including France, Jamaica, The Netherlands, Republic of Ireland and Hong Kong but the dam did not really burst until the mid-90s.

The increase in the growth on the number of external quality agencies over the period can be best observed by examining the membership of the International Network of Quality Assurance Agencies in Higher Education (INQAAHE).

INQAAHE, or the Network, was established in 1991. Its core (or full) members are the regional and national quality assurance and accreditation agencies, but it also has a number of associate members which are organisations with a strong interest in quality assurance in higher education.

When it was founded INQAAHE had members from only 11 countries, which represented most of the countries that had at that time systems, in some cases partial systems, of external quality assurance in higher education. In July 2008 it had 154 members from 78 countries.[7] There are in addition some agencies that have not joined the network while there are other countries that are still in the course of developing their systems of quality assurance. It is thus probably not unreasonable to suggest that quality assurance in higher education is close to becoming a universal pastime.

There are a number of reasons why the number of members exceeds the number of countries. One is that although the bulk of the INQAAHE membership consists of agencies that cover the whole discipline range it also has in membership a number of professional or specialist accrediting agencies. But the more significant reasons stem from different national arrangements. In some countries, such as Canada, agencies operate at the state or provincial level rather than the national level while in a few countries, such as Austria, there are different agencies for universities and HEIs without university status while in some countries, in Chile and Kuwait for example, different agencies are responsible for public and private HEIs. Another factor is that in a few countries including Germany and Japan, HEIs can choose the agencies to which they will be subject from a list of approved agencies.

Factors contributing to the growth

The growth of quality assurance has been worldwide involving countries with very different cultures and different stages of economic development. It is worth exploring the possible reasons for this growth and to consider the extent to which the various factors will continue to influence future developments.

There is one important factor that is not unique to higher education. That is the recognition that has occurred in many countries of the need for greater accountability for the use of scarce national resources – in the case of higher education this need has been strengthened by the greater importance that is being placed on higher education in virtually all countries, especially in OECD countries.

Other factors that are more specific to the case of higher education include:

- the substantial growth in higher education that has occurred in many countries;
- the increased diversity in HE provision including the establishment of binary systems,[8] the growth in distance learning and employment based learning from which the student can derive academic credit;
- in some countries a trade-off between the reduction of direct governmental control of higher educational institutions and the introduction of external quality assurance arrangements;
- the increase in some countries in the number of private, including "for profit", providers;
- regional developments, for example in Europe and South America, aimed at creating a higher education space which encourages student mobility and the mutual recognition of qualifications; and
- the ever increasing internationalisation of higher education, including the growth in cross border providers and the need for the mutual recognition of qualifications and higher education credits.

While in some countries, in fact in most OECD countries, the participation rates in higher education are now very high there are other, lower income countries which have still to move away from a "close to elite" system. For such countries continuing growth will be a factor that is likely to influence the development of quality assurance.

The factors that are likely to have a continuing and, in some cases, growing influence in many countries are the increased diversity of provision and the regional and international aspects.

11.4. The "standard model" and the differences within that model

There is, superficially, a standard model of external quality assurance. This is demonstrated by inspecting the INQAAHE database.[9] An analysis of the database was carried out in 2008 (see annex for details) and the results of that review will inform later sections of this paper.

The database provides information about such matters as the constitutional basis, sources of funding and style of operation of the members of INQAAHE and indicates that virtually all agencies adopt the same overall approach which has the following stages:

- a self-study (sometimes called a self-evaluation) prepared by the institution in the light of guidelines and regulations issued by the quality assurance agency;

- the appointment of a peer group whose review of the institution or programme would start with a review of the self evaluation;

- site visits by the peer group, involving meetings with senior academic and administrative staff, staff with special responsibilities relating to quality assurance and representatives of other groups of staff. Meetings with students are usually regarded as very important parts of site visits and meetings are normally held both with elected student representatives and with "ordinary students". The site visit enables the review time to inspect the premises and relevant specialist equipment. In some cases the site visits includes an inspection of the actual teaching and learning process through attendance at lectures and classes or the inspection of students' work; and

- the publication of the decision or recommendation of the agency or, in some countries, of the full report of the review.

There are considerable differences in the ways in which the model is applied. It is probably most helpful to think in terms of a continuum with the two extremes being labelled hard and soft.

Scope of review

Some agencies only undertake reviews at institutional level, others only at the programme level while the majority do both. The numbers that emerge from an analysis of the INQAAHE database are set out in Table 11.1 below.

The "institution only" group can be divided further into those who describe the reviews as "institutional audits" and those who state that they undertake evaluations. The differences between the two approaches can be illustrated by the following quotations from the literature of the UK Quality Assurance Agency (QAA) and the US Higher Learning Commission (HLC).

Table 11.1. **Coverage of quality assurance agencies (2008)**[1]

	Coverage			Total
	Programme	Institution	Both	
Europe (excluding the United Kingdom)	6	1	21	28
Australia, Canada, *New Zealand*, United Kingdom	4	3	8	15
Asia (excluding the Middle East)	3	5	5	13
Others	2	3	13	18
Grand totals	15 (20%)	12 (16%)	47 (64%)	74 (100%)

1. Europe includes Israel. The "Others" category includes countries from African, Caribbean, Pacific, Middle eastern and Latin American region as well as the United States, since information is available only on three of the 14 US agencies. See Annex for details on countries.

Source: INQAAHE (*www.inqaahe.org*).

The audit approach

In its publication "Handbook for Institutional Audit: England and Northern Ireland", the UK Quality Assurance Agency states that one of the four objectives[10] of an institutional audit is to review: "the effectiveness of an institution's internal quality assurance structures and mechanisms, in the light of the UK Academic Infrastructure and the *European standards and guidelines for quality assurance in higher education* (ESG) … and the way in which the quality of its educational provision and academic standards of its awards are regularly reviewed and resulting recommendations implemented. This provides public information on an institution's soundness as a provider of HE qualifications of national and international standing" (QAA, 2006).

The evaluation approach

In contrast, in its *Handbook for Accreditation* the US Higher Learning Commission describes the role of an accreditor as follows: "An institutional accrediting body evaluates an entire organisation and accredits as a whole. It assesses formal educational activities and also evaluates governance and administration, financial stability, admissions and student personnel services, resources, student academic achievement, organisational effectiveness, and relationships with outside constituencies" (HEC, 2003).

The first approach focuses on the effectiveness of the institution's quality assurance processes while the second approach actually assesses the salient features of the institution, which suggests that agencies which follow the first, audit, approach place greater trust in the institution as a whole, or adopt a "softer" approach.

It is only a minority of agencies that restrict their activities to institutional audit or assessment. The majority of agencies directly concern themselves with both programme and institutional review. Typically, in such systems the institutional review will be concerned with those aspects which impact on all programmes, such as student services; in addition it might involve making a judgement about institution's internal quality assurance procedures which would help the external programme reviewers decide on the extent to which they can rely on them. Agencies whose activities are restricted to programme review run the risk of having to duplicate work at each review or of paying insufficient attention to institutional wide issues or, most, probably both.

The nature of the relationship between the external agency and the institution

The hard/soft divide may be reflected in a number of different dimensions.

The format of the self study and the conduct of the site visit

There are very considerable variations in the freedom institutions have in completing their self studies. In some systems institutions are given considerable freedom in the way in which they can tell their story, while in other systems the self study essentially consists of a form with mainly closed questions, many of which are of a quantitative nature. In general, the extensive use of closed questions is more often found in Asian countries, for example in Chinese Taipei. In part the extensive use of such questions may be due to the absence of nationally available data relating to such matters as student numbers, progression rates, etc.

Another difference is the relationship between the academic reviewers and those whose programme or institution is being reviewed. At one extreme the reviewers act very much as inspectors exercising a strong degree of authority while at the other extreme the reviewers and the reviewed act more like equals, without entirely ignoring the fact that it is the reviewers who will report their findings. In general the more inspectorial approach will be used by agencies that require the more structured self study reports.

The standard model features a "big bang" in that if all goes well there is only a single site visit by the academic reviewers. In many systems, there could be follow-up visits to deal with matters of concern that have been identified at some stage of the initial review. This is for example the case in the Nordic countries. But in most cases the next visit, whether it will be focused on the institution or a programme, will not happen for another five or ten years.

In the context of institutional accreditation some US regional accreditors, notably The Higher Learning Commission (also known as the North Central Association of Colleges and Schools) and the Accrediting Commission for Senior Colleges and Universities, of the Western Association of Schools and Colleges, are for example developing new models where the single big bang visit is replaced by a number of less intense interactions between the agency and the institution.

Actual observation

The hard/soft divide can be seen in extent to which the academic reviewers engage in directly reviewing the actual learning and teaching process through such things as the inspection of students' work and physical attendance at lectures and other teaching activities. In some systems, as in Indonesia, actual observation of both is regarded as an essential part of the review process while other agencies place far more emphasis on learning how the institution assures itself of the adequacy of the learning teaching process and of the quality of students' work.

Grading

Some agencies award a grade as a result of their assessment of the institutions or programmes. For example, the National Assessment and Accreditation Council (NAAC) of India which is concerned with the accreditation of institutions grades them on a nine point scale.

The basic argument in favour of grading is that institutions will be encouraged to improve quality if, by so doing, they will receive a higher grade or maintain a high grade if such has been awarded as a result of a previous review (Stella, 2002). It is also suggested that the publication of grades will be of help to students in choosing the institutions to which to apply, as well as providing information of value to other interested bodies such as employers and the government.

The main argument against grading is that institutions will concentrate their efforts on improving their grades rather than improving quality. In a perfect world, of course, all actions that were taken to improve the quality of provision would also improve institutional or programme grading and vice versa, but we do not inhabit a perfect world. One of the imperfections is related to the fact that universities generally employ clever people who are capable of passing assessments. It is the experience of a number of countries that institutions often place more importance on satisfying the assessors than actually seeking to enhance quality.

Institutions that are more interested in putting up a good performance in the eyes of the reviewers rather than improving quality are sometimes referred as adopting a "compliance culture" (Brown, 2004).

In completing the survey forms required for the INQAAHE database agencies are asked whether they graded institutions or programmes. As shown in Table 11.2 below of the admittedly not statistically reliable sample of 74 agencies whose practices were surveyed, 17 agencies had a comprehensive system while five stated that the results of their reviews could be interpreted as constituting grading, e.g. as a result of granting accreditation for a shorter than the usual period, or did apply a grading system where there were doubts as to the institution's capacity to sustain quality.

Table 11.2. **Do agencies grade (2008)?**[1]

	Yes	Yes, but indirect	Yes, but only weaker results	No, but reviewing	No	No answer	Total
Europe (excluding the United Kingdom)	2	2	0	2	21	1	28
Australia, Canada, New Zealand, United Kingdom	2	1	1	0	11	0	15
Asia (excluding the Middle East)	9	0	0	0	9	0	18
Others	4	1	0	4	4	0	13
Grand totals	**17 (23%)**	**4 (5%)**	**1 (1%)**	**6 (8%)**	**45 (61%)**	**1 (1%)**	**74 (100%)**

1. Europe includes Israel. The "Others" category includes countries from African, Caribbean, Pacific, Middle eastern and Latin American region as well as the United States, since information is available only on three of the 14 US agencies. See Annex for details on countries.

Source: INQAAHE (www.inqaahe.org).

A particularly interesting feature of the results is that, of the 51 agencies that did not grade, six were reviewing the matter and were considering introducing a grading policy, while 10 of the 13 of the Asian agencies included in the survey had either adopted a grading policy or were considering introducing one. This indicates that grading is becoming more widely practiced and that there may be quite a sharp distinction between Asia and the rest of the world.

Grading by quality assurance must be distinguished from the various league tables published by universities or, more usually, the press. However, the compilers of the league tables are usually happy to use any of the findings of the agencies that can be converted into a numerical format and included as a factor in determining the institution's score (Salmi and Saroyan, 2007).

Publication of reports

The report of the reviewers will be considered by the agency and, depending on its regulations and procedures, may be modified. If the agency is an accrediting agency it will have to make its own decision. In a number of countries it is the government, normally the Ministry of Education or Higher Education, that formally makes the decision but in so doing normally acts on the basis of the recommendation of the agency. The decision, but not necessarily the report, is normally published, but in some systems some decisions, for example the refusal of accreditation to a new programme, may not be put into the public domain. This is the case for example in Switzerland, Mexico, the Russian Federation and the United States.

There is some difference across the world as to whether reports of evaluations are published. In the survey of the INQAAHE Database, it appears that 27 out of the 74 respondents published their reports of all or some of their reviews. Of the 47 agencies that did not, five were reviewing their policy.

Table 11.3. **Do agencies publish reports of reviews (2008)?**[1]

	Yes	Yes, but only some types of report	No, but reviewing	No	Total
Europe (excluding the United Kingdom)	12	0	1	15	28
Australia, Canada, *New Zealand* and the United Kingdom	4	3	1	7	15
Asia (excluding the Middle East)	3	0	2	8	13
Others	5	0	1	12	18
Grand totals	**24 (32%)**	**3 (4%)**	**5 (7%)**	**42 (57%)**	**74 (100%)**

1. Europe includes Israel. The "Others" category includes countries from African, Caribbean, Pacific, Middle eastern and Latin American region as well as the United States, since information is available only on three of the 14 US agencies. See Annex for details on countries.

Source: INQAAHE (*www.inqaahe.org*).

There seem to be two main reasons for the differences. One is related to the question of to whom the agency is accountable: the wider community or the higher education community. The other is based on the view that public reports are less effective than those whose circulation is restricted.

The European and US attitudes to publication are markedly different and can be encapsulated by the following quotations. The first is from a publication of the European Association for Quality Assurance in Higher Education, which was originally called the European Network for Quality Assurance (ENQA), the European network of quality assurance agencies: "Reports should be published and should be written in a way which is clear and readily accessible to its intended readership" (ENQA, 2005). In contrast, practice in the United States is that: "In most cases, the Commission will not make reports public without the permission of the college or university" (HEC, 2003).

The argument supporting publication is that external quality assurance is very much concerned with accountability and the belief that the wider community is entitled to receive reports on how effectively higher education institutions have used the scarce resources entrusted to them. This is a powerful argument, which is not restricted to publicly funded universities in that the talents and abilities of students and the years of their lives that they invest in higher education are as much national resources as money and that even privately funded institutions need to demonstrate to the community that they have made good use of the resources with which they were entrusted.

The counter arguments are twofold. One is that quality assurance or accreditation is a purely private matter between the institutions and the agency. For the reasons given above this does not seem to be a very sound argument. A second, more respectable, argument is that confidential reports are often more honest than those written for public consumption. There is, it is suggested, a great danger that published reports are written in a sort of code that not all will be able to decipher. A compromise position, which does not appear to be very popular, is to produce two reports, one private and one public.

In general, it seems likely that the worldwide demand for accountability will lead to an increase in the number of agencies that publish their reports. There are special circumstances in Europe. As will be described later, a register of recognised agencies has been created, and in order to be included on that register, agencies will have to subscribe to a code of practice that requires publication of its reports. Table 11.4 summarises the differences between the hard and soft approaches to the model.

Table 11.4. **Differences between hard and soft quality assurance models**

	Hard	Soft
Objective	Accountability	Strengthening of quality enhancing strategies
Observation focus	Teaching and student outcomes	Institutional assessment of learning
Method	Evaluation of institutional factors	Audit or assessment of internal quality assurance mechanisms
Philosophy	Inspectorate	Peers
Type of self study	Closed questions	Open ended questions
Publication of report	Yes	No or partial
Grading	Yes	No
Main risks	Compliance culture	Insufficient responsiveness

11.5. Emerging trends and the future of external quality assurance

In its early days external quality assurance relied heavily on two main elements:

- the intuitive judgement of the academic reviewers based, not on agreed explicit requirements, but on their experience; and

- relatively crude quantitative input measures such as the ratio of academic staff (faculty) to students and the number of books in the library.

But this simple approach is no longer regarded as being adequate and the world of quality assurance is now changing quite rapidly. Some emerging trends are listed below and their implications for the future are discussed in the sections that follow.

- a switch in emphasis from quality assurance for accountability to quality assurance for enhancement (5.1);

- the change in focus from inputs to outputs *via* process (5.2);

- shifts in the balance between institutional and programme review (5.3);

- the move away from the reliance on the intuitive experience of reviewers to an approach based on explicit statements of the requirements imposed on institutions and programmes (5.4);

- the demand to provide more information about graduates' academic performance (5.5); and

- differences in attitudes towards "hard" and "soft" approaches (5.6).

From quality assurance for accountability to quality assurance for enhancement or improvement

Accountability is concerned with the institution or programme being able to demonstrate that it is operating at or above the basic minimum standard to justify its right to receive public funding or other rights (in most instances this would involve an accreditation decision), while quality enhancement is concerned with the continuous process of quality improvement.

While it can be argued that quality assurance systems should, as they mature, place greater emphasis on enhancement, it should be remembered that the most important imperative placed on a quality assurance body is to ensure that the worst programme offered by an institution that comes under its purview is of an acceptable standard.

But is quality assurance more than ensuring that the worst is good enough?

Virtually all the agencies included in the INQAAHE Database stated that they made recommendations for improvement, which implies that they are concerned with improving quality as well as ensuring minimum standards.

The move towards quality enhancement can perhaps best illustrated, if we track progress in an imaginary country after the establishment of a quality assurance agency.

Table 11.5. **Steps towards quality enhancement in quality assurance**

Phase 1	Newly established agency, especially if HE system not previously been subject to any form of oversight	Quality assurance for accountability, the closure, or failure to accredit, institutions and programmes not infrequent
Phase 2	Quality assurance system becomes more established	Quality assurance for accountability but moving to enhancement – closures of existing provision infrequent but new programmes and institutions quite often not approved
Phase 3	Most higher education institutions clearly above the threshold level	Quality assurance for enhancement for most institutions – closures only in rare cases nearly all new programmes approved albeit with conditions
Phase 4	Well-established quality assurance system	Quality assurance for enhancement for most institutions – in some countries move to institutional audit. But still need accountability for new types of institutions and new forms of provision.

And when we arrive at Phase 4 there is the question of whether there is a need to maintain a system of external quality assurance for the well-established institutions, a question that might be more dramatically rephrased by asking: Is there any point in accrediting or otherwise quality assure Harvard or Oxford?

The answer is yes. Elite universities are not always very good in dealing with their undergraduate students and, without the need to be accountable, may well revert to old habits and place undue emphasis on research as compared to learning and teaching.

There is also a question that has as yet not been properly addressed regarding the "value added" by elite institutions. Such institutions are able to recruit very able students who will do well in their final assessments and often go on to successful careers, but would they have been even more successful if their elite institution had been better at facilitating their students' learning?

In countries where participation in the quality assurance or accreditation regime is on a voluntary basis the involvement of elite institutions will encourage other institutions to take part.

From inputs to outputs via process

For many years, before the introduction of external quality assurance, the key, or perhaps only, indicator of quality was an input measure: the ability of the teaching staff.

When external quality assurance was first introduced, input measures retained their primacy. To the quality of staff were added such factors as the number of books in the library and even, in some systems, the extent of the sporting facilities made available to students. It is perhaps not surprising that in those early days there was a focus on input measures. Input measures have a nice comfortable feel about them; they are "objective" and are relatively easy to measure. Moreover, they can help avoid the proliferation of very small institutions, especially in developing countries.

But what was often overlooked was that it was only rarely that the actual input was actually measured; usually some proxy was employed. The prime example is the quality of the teaching staff. In many systems, the qualifications of staff were often used unthinkingly as a measure of staff quality – a practice which is still unfortunately prevalent in many countries. While the more sophisticated quality assurors were always alert to the point that, at the end of the day, it was output that mattered, this was often forgotten. Systems became very formulistic with much of the review being concerned with whether the institution met certain targets, which were not necessarily explicitly stated.

There appear to be a number of factors that encouraged the switch in emphasis from inputs to outputs, including a greater degree of professionalism on the part of quality assurors. But a more significant reason might be the increasing diversity of higher education. Historically, the simple input-based method was based on the traditional higher education model: properly qualified students sitting in classrooms taught by properly qualified staff. But the world of higher education is now much more diverse with students studying at a distance or entering the university without traditional entry qualifications.

Before moving on to discuss outputs, some mention should be made of process and the argument that it is wrong to concentrate only on outcomes because process is also very important.

There is considerable merit in this argument which stems from the fact that some of the "outputs" of a period of higher education, such as intellectual honesty or rigour or the recognition of the need for continuing lifelong learning, cannot be measured directly, but in such cases an assessment of the learning experience might provide an acceptable proxy measure. It may be believed that some learning processes may be more conducive to the development of these attributes than others and hence the programme review should include an assessment of the suitability and effectiveness of the actual learning process.

The point that we should not be obsessed with that which can be measured is well summed up in a quotation attributed to Albert Einstein: "Not everything that counts can be counted and not everything that can be counted counts."

Different types of output measures

There seem to be two fairly distinct groups of outcome measures: one relating to student performance, often referred to as learning outcomes, and the other comprising indirect measures that may be related to institutional performance, which are often measured by performance indicators.

Learning outcomes

The student learning assessment movement has gained considerable strength within the United States accreditation community in recent years while there are pressures from others, especially the Federal Secretary of Education, to go further and faster in that direction.

It might be useful to quote the requirements of US Council for Higher Education Accreditation (CHEA), one of the two bodies (the other being the US Federal Department of Education) responsible for the recognition of accreditation agencies. These requirements are compulsory for accreditors in the United States.

CHEA's requirements are set out in a document entitled *Statement of Mutual Responsibilities for Student Learning Outcomes: Accreditation, Institutions, and Programmes*: "Accrediting agencies should place upon institutions the following expectation that they should:

- Regularly gather and report concrete evidence about what students know and can do as a result of their respective courses of study, framed in terms of established learning outcomes and supplied at an appropriate level of aggregation (*e.g.* at the institutional or program level).

- Supplement this evidence with information about other dimensions of effective institutional or program performance with respect to student outcomes (*e.g.* graduation, retention, transfer, job placement, or admission to graduate school) that do not constitute direct evidence of student learning.

- Prominently feature relevant evidence of student learning outcomes – together with other dimensions of effective institutional performance, as appropriate – in demonstrating institutional or program effectiveness" (CHEA, 2003).

The above statement covers both direct student learning outcomes and the more indirect performance indicators.

The question of the measurement of and reporting on direct student learning outcomes is very closely related to the issues surrounding what should be regarded as the core requirements, both generic and disciplinary, of programmes of study leading to higher education qualifications. The topic of direct student learning outcomes will be addressed later in the paper when dealing with the core requirements of programmes of study.

Indirect measures – performance indicators

The CHEA quotation refers to the requirement imposed on institutions that they consider other dimensions of performance, such as graduation and employment rates, that do not constitute direct evidence of student learning. These measures are recognised as key indicators in a growing number of countries, including Belgium (Flemish community), Korea, the Netherlands, New Zealand, Poland, the Russian Federation and the United Kingdom (OECD, 2008).

But an indicator is only a number if one does not have something to compare it with. An institution can of course compare its current to its past performance through time series analysis, but it is also very useful to be able to make comparisons with the performance of others. A quite common practice is for institutions to select a group of other institutions which they believe are similar to themselves and then compare their performance against that of the "peer group". The comparison may be confined to publicly available data, or the institutions may agree to exchange confidential data for their mutual benefit.

In the United Kingdom, the Higher Education Funding Councils have, for a number of years, published a set of performance indicators covering, as far as teaching is concerned, access (which mainly measures the social mix of the student intake), non-completion rates, efficiency (a measure based on the average time it takes a student to graduate) and employment indicators. An interesting feature of the publication is the use of "adjusted sector benchmarks", which make allowance for various factors which affect the indicators. The main factors used are the subject mix of an institution, the entry qualifications of its students, and the proportions of young (under 21) and mature students entering the institution. The adjusted sector benchmark is an "adjusted" average figure. It is the figure that, based on the overall results of the system, might be expected to be achieved by the particular institution given the institution's subject mix and the entry qualifications and ages of its students. The institution's actual results can then be compared to its adjusted sector benchmark.[11]

The increasing use of quantitative performance measures might suggest to some that quality assurance could be an entirely metrics driven process and, so long as the institution's or the programme's measurable outputs are acceptable then nothing else is required. In this context, however, the above quoted words of Albert Einstein are to be duly kept in mind.

Learning outcomes and the US Department of Education

The debate about learning outcomes took a sharp turn with the publication in 2006 of *A Test of Leadership: Charting the Future of US Higher Education* – the report of the Commission on the Future of Higher Education appointed by Margaret Spellings, US Secretary of Education.

While the report identified the strengths of the US higher education system, it also found it wanting in a number of important respects. One of its key findings was that employers repeatedly report that many new graduates are ill-prepared for work and lack the critical thinking, writing and problem-solving skills that are needed in the workplace. To quote from the report, "unacceptable numbers of college graduates enter the workforce without the skills employers say they need in an economy in which, as the truism holds correctly, knowledge matters more than ever" (Department of Education, 2006).

This view led to the recommendation that higher education institutions should measure student learning by using quality assessment data from instruments such as the Collegiate Learning Assessment, which measures the growth of student learning taking place in colleges, and the Measure of Academic Proficiency and Progress, which is designed to assess general education outcomes for undergraduates.

In other words, externally produced standardised forms of assessment should be used which are primarily intended to allow comparisons to be made between institutions, but which could also be used as the bases for comparing the success of different disciplines in terms of the achievements in general education outcomes or generic competences.

The Commission explicitly asks for a shift of emphasis from the accreditation community: "Accreditation agencies should make performance outcomes, including completion rates and student learning, the core of their assessment as a priority over inputs or processes" (Department of Education 2006, p. 25).

Two of the most important implications of this are the pressure being placed by government on the accreditation community, a pressure that has a particular irony in a country that was proud to refer to the voluntary nature of the accreditation, and the suggestion that universities and colleges use externally produced standardised assessment materials.

Meanwhile, it appears that US Higher Education Institutions are already making increasing use of externally produced instruments of assessment. It was reported in the *Chronicle of Higher Education* (28.09.07) that "hundreds of US colleges are using standardised student achievement tests, allowing comparisons between institutions, while investigating options for creating more such tests". As of 2008, the debate in the United States continues, a debate that is likely to have implications for many other countries in the future.

The 2006 OECD Education Ministerial Meeting echoed the US accreditation debate and the Chairs' summary notes: "We need to develop better evidence of learning outcomes… While various indicators for the quality of research are available, much more would need to be done to establish appropriate measures for the quality of teaching, to avoid bad teaching going unnoticed and good teaching unrewarded.[12]" The OECD Secretariat launched in 2008 a feasibility study to design an international instrument for assessing learning outcomes in tertiary education.

Shift in the balance between programme and institutional review

Another important noteworthy shift in recent years lies in the balance of who has the responsibility for the review of programmes. In many ways the heart of quality assurance is programme review because this is usually the best way to examine student experience. Thus, those agencies that only carry out externally organised Institutional Review or Institutional Audit are very interested in how the institution itself reviews its programmes, indeed a major part of the Institutional visit will be devoted to this subject. As mentioned earlier in the paper (Table 11.1), the majority of agencies themselves review programmes and the majority of agencies who devolve that responsibility to institutions are in the English-speaking world.

There are advantages to both approaches:

Advantages of the Programme Review model

- The review is likely to have greater external credibility if organised by the agency.
- The reviewers will have a more thorough expertise of the programme in question.

Advantages of the Institutional Review model

- It reduces the work load of the agency – a particularly important issue in a large country where the agency has responsibility for many thousands of programmes.
- It is probably a cheaper system to operate but the total costs (borne by the agency and the institution) may not be all that different if there is institutionally organised programme reviews in which reviewers external to the institution are involved.

● The most important potential benefit which depends on the way in which the institution organises its operations is that quality assurance will be designed as an ongoing operation rather than an event that takes place every five or six years.

So is the balance shifting and if so in what direction? This is currently a difficult question to answer.

In the longer term it is likely that as external Quality Assurance systems become more firmly established, the advantages of the Institutional Review approach will encourage some agencies to adopt this approach.

Growth of higher education system and programs is itself likely to have a major impact on external quality assurance systems in particular on the question of whether the external agency itself reviews programmes. As the student numbers increase so will the number of programmes and many countries will find in not only too expensive but also too unwieldy to engage in programme level review (Haug, 2003). Thus, as quality assurance matures, in the sense that institutions and programmes have been subject to number of review cycles, and as the participation rates in higher education increase, it is argued that it is likely that external quality assurance agencies will increasingly focus their attention on institutional audit or institutional assessment. Malaysia provides a recent example in that the Malaysian Qualifications Agency is moving to a system of institutional review.

Not all would agree with that prediction for there are those who wish to encourage the accreditation of programmes across the whole range of disciplines not just those in the professional/vocational areas that have been subject to specialised accreditation. The European Consortium for Accreditation (ECA)[13] is, for example, advocating this approach. The ECA, which includes 13 agencies from ten countries,[14] is interested in the accreditation of programmes and institutions and is particularly interested in the mutual recognition of accreditation decisions.

Explicit statement of requirements

Before considering how to assess student learning outcomes it is first necessary to gain some agreement as to what it is that students should learn. What should a degree programme include?

When 20 or 30 years ago academics considered applications to approve a bachelor's degree in areas such as physics or history they had only their experience, and perhaps a bit of prejudice, to guide them. There were no written expectations of what should be requirements of a bachelor's degree in general, let alone the expectations placed on the holder of a physics degree.

The world has changed considerably in that respect. Many countries have established "National Qualification Frameworks" setting out the attributes required to be demonstrated in order to be granted a degree at the various levels. Since 2002, a multinational initiative, known as the Dublin descriptors, has been developed by quality assurance and accreditation agencies from a number of European countries.[15] The Dublin descriptors set out the generic attributes that should be demonstrated in order to be granted a degree at one of three levels; bachelors, masters or doctoral.

In terms of discipline-specific requirements, in the summer of 2000 a group of universities started a pilot project called "Tuning educational structures in Europe". Subsequently, they have asked the European University Association (EUA) to help widen the group of participants, and they have asked the European Commission for a grant under the Socrates programme. The project aims at identifying points of reference for generic and subject-specific competences of first and second cycle graduates in a series of subject areas: Business Administration, Education Sciences, Geology, History, Mathematics, Physics and Chemistry. Competences are based on learning outcomes: what a learner knows or is able to demonstrate after the completion of a learning process. This covers both discipline-specific competences and generic competences like communication skills and leadership.

By way of example, the specific and generic competences for first cycle (bachelor) degrees in business are:[16]

Table 11.6. **Indicative specific and generic competences for first cycle degrees in business**

Competences	Key generic competences
Students should be able to:	
• Use and evaluate tools for analysing a company in its environment	• Basic knowledge of the profession
• Work in a subject specific field of a company, and be a specialist to some extent	• Basic knowledge of the study field
• Interface with other functions	• Ability to work in interdisciplinary teams
• Have self-awareness	• Capacity to apply knowledge in practice
• Be able to argue for the principles to be used in finding a solution to a problem mainly at an operational or tactical level.	• Ability to adopt to new situations
• Defend the proposed solution	• Elementary computer skills
• Prepare for decision making at mainly operational and tactical levels	• Capacity to learn
	• Capacity to do oral and written presentation in native language

Source: Joint Quality Initiative website, *www.jointquality.nl/.*

Some might feel that the above is stated in such general terms as not to be all that helpful, but it does represent a start to explaining the meaning of the qualification to the outside world.

There is, of course, always the danger that the publication of such statements may encourage rigidity and discourage innovation and development. The United Kingdom Quality Assurance Agency (QAA), which has published what it refers to as subject benchmarks in over 40 fields at the undergraduate level, seeks to avoid this danger by emphasising that it does not require strict adherence to the guidelines but that it does want to be assured that the institution has taken them into account. For example, paragraph 41 of the *Handbook for Institutional Review: Wales* states that:

> ... in respect of Subject benchmark statements, the (review) team enquires into the way in which the statements have been taken into account when establishing and/ or reviewing programmes and awards, as illustrated through programme specifications. The Agency views the statements as authoritative reference points, but not as definitive regulatory criteria for individual programmes or awards (QAA 2003).

In practice this means that institutions can depart from the subject benchmarks, but they will need to supply solid justification for doing so.

The introduction of these guidelines at regional level in, for example, South America as well as Europe is serving to break down national boundaries and helping ensure comparability between the awards of universities in the different countries.

How should the learning outcomes and competences be assessed?

It is all very well to decide the core set of desired student learning outcomes requiring demonstration by a successful graduate of a degree programme, but the issue remains of how to demonstrate that the necessary attributes are, in fact, possessed. Many higher education institutions and, indeed, systems currently face this challenge and much work needs to be done in this area.

A particular problem is the case of generic competences such as communication and team working skills. The general academic tradition is that these competences should be taught, and assessed, alongside discipline-related competences. That means that unless very special care is taken, the generic competences will be swamped by the discipline-related competences. In this context the increasing use of externally produced non-institutionally specific tests of generic competences in the United States (to which reference was made earlier) is of special interest.

Reporting graduates' performance

The idea that the whole of a student's achievements can be summarised by a single measure, whether it be a 3.4 grade point average or an upper second class degree in the United Kingdom, was always a questionable – in fact pretty silly – idea, although this does not mean that many higher education systems do not follow this practice. But things are changing. Europe is introducing the Diploma Supplement which is to be issued to each student and will include the mark or grade obtained for each unit or module studied.

This will obviously give greater information, but unless some of the courses taken as part of a student's programme of study are clearly described as being related to a particular general competence, as is the case with some lower level courses taken by American students as part of the Liberal Education requirement, the Supplements may not be of all that much assistance in gaining an understanding of a graduate's generic competences.

The increasing importance of qualifications frameworks that place strong emphasis on generic competences and the desire, as evidenced by the European Diploma Supplement, to provide more information about the competences achieved by students is likely to have a significant impact on the basic model of higher education. It will surely be more difficult to sustain the traditional academic desire that is found in some parts of the world to incorporate the development and assessment of generic competences with discipline related learning. This might not necessitate a move to the US model but it may involve substantial changes in the ways that student learning is assessed.

Differences in attitudes towards "hard" and "soft" approaches

In the immediate future it seems most likely that the current developments referred earlier such as the increased emphasis on outcomes and the adoption of explicit statements of expectations will continue to develop on a global basis. Important as these features are, the apparent commonality of approach might be masking a more fundamental divide between what was referred to earlier in the paper as the "hard" and "soft" extremes of the continuum or, as the different approaches are sometimes expressed, between the "inspectorial" and "peer review or collegiate" approaches.

There are already significant differences in the hardness of external quality assurance systems on a geographical basis. If one takes, for example, the practice of publishing a grade following institutional or programme reviews, the survey of the INQAAHE Database

(Table 11.3) reveals that this is a far more popular approach in Asia than it is in the rest of the World.

Anecdotal evidence, based on the author's experience of participating in and observing external quality assurance in Asian countries, is that the approach tends to be highly inspectorial. For example, the format of self studies contain many closed questions while during the institutional visits much of the time is spent on the observation of the teaching process and of student work and less on learning about the institution's own internal systems for assuring quality. This may, of course, be due to the fact that the institutions' own internal quality assurance are as yet not fully developed and in a number of countries great emphasis is (still) being placed on the development of internal quality assurance systems. It will be interesting to discover whether the further development of internal quality assurance systems will result in the softening of the external quality assurance approach or whether cultural differences related to "self-criticality", a characteristic on which the softer approach to quality assurance relies, would make it less likely that the differences in national approaches will disappear.

There is an expectation, perhaps more felt than stated, that as quality assurance systems mature they will move towards the softer end of the continuum but there are some interesting examples of hardening of approaches in developed countries. Reference has already been made to the recent desire to enforce changes on the US accreditation system and to make institutions more accountable for the achievements of their graduates. Another example of government influence is Australia, a country with a very well established Higher Education system but with a relatively new system of external quality assurance, as the Australian Universities Quality Agency (AUQA) only commenced operations in 2001. In its first cycle of institutional reviews the AUQA adopted an audit approach but in the second cycle, that commenced in 2008, additional features have been incorporated including "more explicit consideration of the extent to which requirements of external reference points are being met by the institution" (AUQA 2008). One very important set of reference point is the National Protocols for Educational Approval Processes that were issued by a governmental body, the Ministerial Council on Education, Employment, Training and Youth Affairs.

11.6. The breaking down of national boundaries

Quality assurance is increasingly becoming more international. Reference has already been made in this paper to the impact of regional groupings, such as in South America and Europe, that are creating "Higher Education Spaces" within which qualification frameworks are being established with a view to reduce national differences. These regional groupings are having a significant impact on national quality assurance agencies. Europe provides a good example.

Ministers from 29 countries signed the Bologna Declaration in 1999, which established a programme to create a "European Higher Education Area" by 2010; subsequently a further 17 countries have added their names to the declaration. Its effect on quality assurance has been very significant.

The declaration encouraged European co-operation in quality assurance with the aim of establishing common criteria and methodologies. In 2001, the Ministers of Education invited the European Association for Quality Assurance in Higher Education (ENQA) to help establish a common European quality assurance framework by 2010. Considerable progress has been made, and in 2007 the Ministers agreed to set up a European Register for Quality Assurance Agencies.

While the register is voluntary, in the sense that there will be no restrictions placed on the operations of non-members, it is likely that virtually all relevant agencies would wish to be included on the list. In order to be included, agencies will have to agree substantially to comply with the Standards and Guidelines for Quality Assurance in the European Higher Education Area (ESG) published by ENQA[17] and to be subject to an external review every five years.

A great deal of interest is being shown in the Bologna Process in other parts of the world. The Australian Federal Government's Department of Education Science and Training engaged in 2007 in a number of activities that related to the impact of Bologna on both Australia and the Asia Pacific Region. Amongst the outcomes were the allocation of AUD 400 000 for the development of an Australian Diploma Supplement and the establishment of a High Level Steering Group to provide ongoing leadership to the issues and challenges posed by the Bologna Process in Australia.[18]

Further emerging trends in this regard will be examined under the following themes:

- Cross-border reviewers (6.1).
- Transnational or Cross-Border Higher Education (CBHE) (6.2).
- The growth of regional networks of quality assurance bodies (6.3).
- The international market for quality assurance (6.4).

Cross-border reviewers

Another aspect of crossing borders is the use by an agency of academic reviewers from other countries. As shown in Table 11.7 below, the survey of the INQAAHE database revealed that out of the 69 agencies who had answered the question as to whether they used reviewers from other countries, 50 (73%) indicated they did; in fact, 19 agencies (28%) stated that 25% or more came from other countries. This seems to indicate that there is a good deal of exchange of experience across national boundaries. There is, however, some regional imbalance in that, possibly because of the developments discussed above, the practice is found more frequently in Europe than elsewhere. If the European agencies are discounted, 42 agencies remain and, of these, 23 (55%) use reviewers from other countries – while, of these, 8 (18% of the 42 respondents) are in the 25% or over group.

Table 11.7. **Use of cross-border reviewers (2008)**[1]

	Yes, 25% and above	Yes, less than 25%	No	No answer	Total
Europe (excluding the United Kingdom)	11	16	0	1	28
Australia, Canada, New Zealand and the United Kingdom	1	5	8	1	15
Asia (excluding the Middle East)	3	3	7	0	13
Others	4	7	4	3	18
Grand totals	**19 (26%)**	**31 (42%)**	**19 (26%)**	**5 (7%)**	**74 (100%)**

1. Europe includes Israel. The "Others" category includes countries from African, Caribbean, Pacific, Middle eastern and Latin American region as well as the United States, since information is available only on three of the 14 US agencies. See Annex for details on countries.

Source: INQAAHE (*www.inqaahe.org*).

Transnational or cross-border higher education (CBHE)

Another important trend is the growing importance of Cross-border Higher Education (CBHE). One aspect of CBHE is as old as higher education itself, that is, the movement of students across borders, but in the last 20 years or so there has been a substantial increase in other forms of CBHE, for example, distance learning and overseas campuses (OECD, 2004). "Cross-border higher education includes higher education that takes place in situations where the teacher, student, programme, institution/provider of course materials cross national jurisdictional borders… It encompasses a wide range of modalities, in a continuum from face-to-face (taking various forms such as students travelling abroad and campuses abroad) to distance learning (using a range of technologies including e-learning)" (OECD, 2005).

In general, the growth in CBHE has not been matched by developments in the quality assurance related to the activity although some countries have introduced suitable arrangements. In the case of exporting countries, the quality assurance agencies in Australia and the United Kingdom apply very similar procedures to exported and domestic provision while The Republic of South Africa and China (Hong Kong) are good examples of the importing countries that have introduced procedures that seek to assure the quality of higher education provided in their countries by overseas institutions.

The UNESCO/OECD guidelines, entitled "Guidelines for Quality Provision in Cross-border Higher Education" (OECD, 2005), are a response to the growth of cross-border higher education. They address the following six groups:

- governments,
- higher education institutions/providers,
- student bodies,
- quality assurance and accreditation bodies,
- academic recognition bodies,
- professional bodies.

While it is not adequate to describe the guidelines here in detail, it is worth of mentioning those addressed to quality assurance and accreditation bodies, as they capture the main spirit and intentions of the document as a whole:

- Ensure that its arrangements cover CBHE in all its forms (see Tables 11.8 and 11.9 below).
- Sustain and strengthen the existing regional and international networks of quality assurance and accreditation agencies and seek to establish them in regions where they do not exist.
- Establish links to strengthen the collaboration between the bodies of the sending and receiving country and enhance the mutual understanding of different systems of quality assurance and accreditation.
- Provide accurate and easily accessible information on the assessment standards, procedures, and effects of the quality assurance mechanisms on the funding of students, institutions or programmes as well as on the results of the assessments.
- Where feasible, consider undertaking experiments in international evaluation or peer review of quality assurance and accreditation bodies.
- Consider procedures for the international composition of peer review panels, international benchmarking of standards, criteria and assessment procedures and

undertake joint assessment projects to increase the comparability of the evaluation activities of different quality assurance and accreditation bodies.

The 2008 INQAAHE survey indicates that a good number of agencies are not as yet covering all forms of CBHE (see Tables 11.8 and 11.9). However, the gradual implementation of the guidelines may lead to a transformation of some quality assurance practices and contribute to its further internationalisation and, possibly, to a further harmonisation in practices.

Table 11.8. **Does an agency have policies and procedures in place relating to exported higher education (2008)?[1, 2]**

	Has a policy		Matter under review	Answer "Not Applicable"	Answer "No"	No answer	Total
	Same as domestic provision	Other					
Europe (excluding the United Kingdom)	6	2	5	8	1	6	28
Australia, Canada, *New Zealand* and the United Kingdom	5	2	1	5	1	1	15
Asia (excluding the Middle East)	1	0	1	4	4	3	13
Others	3	3	2	5	1	4	18
Grand totals	15 (20%)	7 (9%)	9 (12%)	22 (30%)	7 (9%)	14 (19%)	74 (100%)

1. Higher education provided by institutions under its remit overseas.
2. Europe includes Israel. The "Others" category includes countries from African, Caribbean, Pacific, Middle eastern and Latin American region as well as the United States, since information is available only on three of the 14 US agencies. See Annex for details on countries.

Source: INQAAHE (*www.inqaahe.org*).

Table 11.9. **Does an agency have policies and procedures in place relating to imported higher education (2008)?[1, 2]**

	Has a policy		Matter under review	Answer "Not applicable"	Answer "No"	No answer	Total
	Same as domestic provision	Other					
Europe (excluding the United Kingdom)	9	4	4	6	0	5	28
Australia, Canada, *New Zealand* and the United Kingdom	4	4	0	3	1	3	15
Asia (excluding the Middle East)	0	3	1	3	2	4	13
Others	4	5	2	1	2	4	18
Grand totals	17 (23%)	16 (22%)	7 (9%)	13 (18%)	5 (7%)	16 (22%)	74 (100%)

1. Higher education provided in its own country by overseas institutions.
2. Europe includes Israel. The "Others" category includes countries from African, Caribbean, Pacific, Middle eastern and Latin American region as well as the United States, since information is available only on three of the 14 US agencies. See Annex for details on countries.

Source: INQAAHE (*www.inqaahe.org*).

The growth of regional networks of quality assurance bodies

When first established external quality assurance agencies, for very understandable reasons, tended to look inwards while they developed their own policies and procedures and established relationships with the national higher education institutions and other major stake holders. With the founding of INQAAHE in 1991 the emerging agencies did have a forum for the interchange and experience but the next major step was the establishment of regional networks of quality assurance bodies.

The first of these was the European Association for Quality Assurance in Higher Education that was set up in 2000, it was originally called the European Network for Quality Assurance hence its acronym ENQA which it has retained to this day.

Since then a number of other regional networks have been formed covering, for example, the Asia Pacific region, the Asia Pacific Quality Network, the Arab States, the Arab Network for Quality Assurance in Higher Education, Africa, the Association of African Universities, the Caribbean, the Caribbean Area Network for Quality Assurance in Tertiary Education, Eurasia, the Eurasian Quality Network, central and eastern Europe, the central and eastern European Network of Quality Assurance Agencies in Higher Education, Scandinavia, the Nordic Quality Assurance Network in Higher Education and South and Central America, Red Iberoamericana para la Acreditación de la Calidad de la Educación Superior (RIACES). North America is a special case in that both the United States and Canada are federal countries, and while the federal governments are not without power and influence, from a Quality Assurance perspective the countries exhibit some of the characteristics of the regional groupings.

Most of the regional networks are at this stage largely concerned with the enhancement of quality assurance and the exchanges of staff and of experience.

ENQA is the exception that may well have a powerful influence on the development of quality assurance. While ENQA's membership is not restricted to the European Union (EU) the network was set up with EU support and has been supported by it ever since. What is special about ENQA is that it has helped establish European standards for both internal and external quality assurance and for the operation of the external quality assurance agencies themselves.

One big question is whether other regions will establish their own standards and, if so, whether they will then get together to establish international standards. While a number of the networks are very young it is already evident that their members are working together to establish common standards across their regions. While it is perhaps too early to do anything other than speculate about a search for truly international standards there are indications of both a growing need arising from both the growth of cross-border higher education and the increased mobility of those holding higher education qualifications and of a political willingness of both individual agencies and regional networks to cooperate with their counterparts across the world which suggests that the search may not be long delayed. International co-operation is also being encouraged by the work of international agencies such as OECD and UNESCO.

The recently established UNESCO portal provides access to information about HEIs recognised or otherwise sanctioned by competent authorities in participating countries. As of now it is left to each country to decide on who are the competent authorities but it does seem likely that initiatives such as this will in time encourage convergence in national approaches to recognition.

Another interesting question is whether or not it is possible that national quality assurance agencies will disappear to be replaced by regional agencies or even by a single global body. It is probably too early to predict the death of the nationally based agencies. What is more likely is that the practices of agencies within economic regions will converge driven by the needs of the labour market and the wishes of graduates to have their qualifications recognised outside their national borders. But this convergence will not necessarily be restricted to regional groupings. There is also evidence that this will also occur at the global level.

For example, INQAAHE has issued Guidelines for Good Practice for External Quality Agencies. A good number of members coming from different parts of the world at different stages of economic development have indicated that they comply with the Guidelines. A survey of the INQAAHE website in August 2008 indicated that of the 74 members, who answered the questions of whether they had reviewed their policies and procedures against the INQAAHE Guidelines and, if so, whether they believed that they were operating in compliance with them, 44 (60%,) said that they were.

The guidelines are at present simply suggestions but there are already pressures to turn the Guidelines into Principles and to make adherence to the Principles a condition of full membership. So while it is unlikely that in the foreseeable future a single global agency will replace national agencies it is possible that in some parts of the world regional agencies may start replacing national ones. Should present trends continue, it is possible that the practices will converge, unless different attitudes are taken as to whether quality assurance in higher education should be "harder" or "softer".

The international market for quality assurance

While in the very majority of cases HEIs still have no choice in who will quality assure or accredit them, the position is beginning to change. In a number of countries including Germany, Japan and the United States, there is more than one recognised national quality assurance body, which means that institutions can chose their agency.

In Europe a number of agencies are operating over national boundaries, although they often operate in specific linguistic areas. For example the Accreditation, Certification and Quality Assurance Institute (Acquin) operates in Germany, Austria and Switzerland while the Nederlands-Vlaamse Accreditatieorganisatic (Accrediting Organisation of the Netherlands and Flanders) was established by a treaty between the Netherlands and Flanders and operates in the two territories.

The establishment of common standards across a region, especially when accompanied as is the case of Europe with a register of recognised quality assurance agencies, would seem it more likely that the practice of institutions that are subject to regulations that require them to be "externally quality assured" being given the ability to choose their own quality assurance agency, and not to have to have that choice restrained by national borders, will spread. The ability of such institutions to be able to satisfy their regulatory obligations by selecting agencies outside of their region is likely to depend on the agreement of international standards.

What may prove to be significant step towards a situation where institutions will have the freedom to select to be subject to an agency based in another country was the recommendation made the European Parliament on 15 February 2006 that any institution may select any quality assurance or accreditation agency that is on the European Register of Quality Assurance Agencies so long as this is compatible with national legislation and is permitted by the national authority.[19]

The matter is one that falls outside the powers of the Parliament and hence cannot be more than a recommendation. It is too early to speculate on the impact of the recommendation but it is likely that a number of countries will be reluctant to give up national sovereignty and the influence that they can exercise over their national agencies.

France, for example, has confirmed that it will not permit its institutions to bypass the national agency but this may of course change in the future, especially, if other countries are content to encourage the development of an open market in quality assurance.

Voluntary participation in quality assurance is another matter and institutions do not infrequently seek recognition from overseas agencies. This is especially true in the case of professional or specialised accreditation. For example, a number of Middle East universities have obtained accreditation from the US Accreditation Board for Engineering and Technology.

Management, perhaps more specifically MBA programmes, provides the best example of a discipline where international accreditation has taken firm route and has had an impact on the way in which management information is provided in many countries. The AACSB[20] even changed its name (but preserved its acronym) from the American Assembly of Collegiate Schools of Business to the Association to Advance Collegiate Schools of Business and now accredits Business Schools in very many countries from (on an alphabetical basis) Argentina to Venezuela. With its origins on the other side of the Atlantic EQUIS – The European Quality Improvement System accredits schools in 33 countries (of which 15 are outside Europe) including Argentina and Venezuela. Given the spread of globalisation it does seem possible that other disciplines, especially those with a vocational basis, will follow where management has led.

Voluntary participation in cross-border accreditation also occurs at institutional level. An institution might wish to come within the ambit of an overseas agency if its national system is not well developed or, possibly, not well respected, but they might be other reasons. An institution that wishes to be seen as an international player may seek approval from overseas agencies even if its "home" agency is well respected. For example the UK Open University is, on a purely voluntary basis, accredited by the US Middle States Commission. Voluntary cross-border accreditation may also drive further globalisation in quality assurance and higher education.

11.7. A possibly more fundamental change – the end of, or the redefinition of, higher education

A reasonable generalisation is that, across the world, the quality assurance of higher education is done differently from quality assurance at other levels of education, which is generally far more inspectorial and governmentally directed. This reflects the very special place that higher education has, or possibly had, in society such that in many countries it was thought that there was nobody with sufficient authority to review its small and very elite higher education systems.

But the world has changed and will change and it may well be that as a result higher education will lose all vestiges of the special place that it held in most societies up to about the middle of the twentieth century. The changes and likely future changes include the following:

● greatly increased participation rates in higher education, already around 80% in some developed countries;

● the growing gap between the content of bachelor (and in some cases masters) degree and the "frontiers of knowledge"; and

● the perhaps inevitable consequence of the first two points that a very much smaller percentage of those engaged in teaching undergraduates will be engaged in research or even advanced scholarship or consultancy.

Traditionally, in terms of the age of the participants, higher education started at the age of about 18 so that it was perfectly acceptable for a student of 18 years and three months to be taught by a school teacher while at 18 years and nine months it was expected that the student be taught (or have their learning assisted) by a scholar researching at the frontiers of his or her discipline. This has already changed in many institutions with the growth in the use of teaching-only contracts and the reliance on the use of graduate teaching assistants. In addition nowadays much undergraduate learning is taking place in institutions that do not have research responsibilities such as the US Community Colleges. It is likely that these trends will be intensified in the first decades of the twenty first century and that by 2050 the traditional model will be found in only a few, highly unrepresentative, institutions.

It is therefore by no means impossible that the higher education/rest of education divide will shift towards the masters' degree and, while the change may be more implicit than explicit, it is nonetheless likely that severe pressures will be placed on the "collegiate" approach to quality assurance and that governments will want to have a much greater influence which is likely to result in the spread of the harder more inspectoral model.

The changes postulated here are not going to come about with a "big bang" but will be gradual and accumulative such that the position at the end of this century will be very different to that which now prevails.

Moreover, in many developed countries a significant proportion of higher education students are not of the traditional mode, that is young students studying on a full-time basis. Many are studying part-time and an increasing number are distance learning students while a small, but growing, number of students are gaining academic qualifications or, more usually credits towards academic qualifications from employment based studies. The need to increase the number of higher education students in the less well developed countries is well recognised and it is likely that this growth will to a large measure be in the number of non-campus based students.

What impact will this have on the development of quality assurance systems? In the case of part-time and even distance learning students not all that much. Because of the changes that have been referred to earlier in the paper, in particular the move away from an input-based approach that was to a large extent based on the traditional face to face model to an output-based quality assurance, agencies have discovered that their revised approach can quite easily accommodate part-time education and even distance learning.

The issue of new sorts of providers whether they be "for profit" private colleges or employers does raise different issues. It does seem that an effective quality assurance system needs to be able to accommodate both well established higher education institutions where the emphasis will be quality assurance for enhancement, and new providers where accountability is far more important and where it may be appropriate to adopt a harder, more inspectorial approach.

11.8. Summary

External Quality Assurance in Higher Education has arrived and will not go away. But it will change.

There is an apparent commonality in approach with virtually all agencies seemingly adopting the same overall approach, while some of the major changes identified in this paper including the move to outputs and the greater use of generally explicit statements of expectations is affecting all countries to a greater or lesser extent. In addition the breaking down of national boundaries such as, at the political level, the creation of "Higher Education Spaces" and at the operational level the growth in importance of the Regional Networks and the increasing use of overseas reviewers would seem to be leading to greater convergence of practice across the world.

But yet there are considerable differences in approach that are not disappearing such as the differences between the notion of audit found in countries such as Australia and the institutional assessment approach found, for example, in the United States where, to use the words of the Higher Learning Commission quoted earlier, "an institutional accrediting body evaluates an entire institution …". Another seemingly growing difference is between those agencies which do not believe in the dangers of a "compliance culture" and are, for example, happy to grade institutions and those organisations that would prefer to work in a manner more akin to a partnership with the common aim to sustain and enhance standards. It is likely that in the short term this difference will become sharper but it is possible that in the medium and longer terms the growing internationalisation of practice will result in adoption of a more uniform approach.

And whatever the agencies and the institutions think there is always the government. The indications are that governments will seek to have a far stronger influence than, at least in some countries, they had in the past. Some particularly significant examples are the United States, with the drive towards learning outcomes, and Europe, with imposition of common standards and the establishment of a register of agencies. While these tasks are not undertaken directly by governments, these developments are very strongly "guided" by governments.

There are many pressures and indicators that suggest that there will be a convergence of practice across the world so that all higher education institutions will face similar external quality assurance arrangements. But a fascinating question is whether different cultural approaches will prevent the adoption of an absolutely standard approach. Whether, to use the terminology of this paper, quality assurance becomes harder or softer depends on the interplay of two factors that pull in different directions. The soft pull comes from the increasing maturity of quality assurance with an increasing emphasis on quality assurance for enhancement. The hard pull is likely to come from increased numbers and the replacement of an elite system by a more democratised one, with a larger range of participation.

This tension does provide a challenge for those concerned with the development of quality assurance. How to retain the virtues of the soft approach while satisfying the growing demands that will be placed on the system by governments and others? These demands will likely be reinforced by the growth in absolute numbers that will be a feature of many higher education systems and the greater diversity of provision that will be a feature of most higher education systems.

Notes

1. For ease of expression for the term quality assurance should be interpreted as quality assurance in higher education unless stated otherwise.

2. Those interested in a more detailed discussion of terminology should consult the Analytical Quality Glossary that can be accessed *via* the website of INQAAHE's website at *www.inqaahe.org*. Another useful source is the Council for Higher Education Accreditation (CHEA) website *www.chea.org/international/inter_glossary01.html*.

3. It is recognised that in many countries much higher education is provided outside the universities but for simplicity the term 'university' will be used to include all types of institutions of higher education.

4. The term programme is used to mean programme of studies, that is the set of units or courses or modules that have to be taken by a student to gain his or her award.

5. The use of a few people from outside the programme or institution where the activity is organised by insiders and where most of the reviewers are insiders does not of itself make it an external event.

6. There were already four universities in Scotland, but none in Wales.

7. About half of the countries are from Europe, North America or Oceania (29, 3 and 2, respectively); 15 are from eastern Asia; the other regions of the world are represented, but to a lesser extent (see annex for further details).

8. In a number of countries, such as the United Kingdom, quality assurance were first applied to the lower status non-university side of the so called binary divide but in almost all instances the whole higher education sector is now subject to some form of external quality assurance.

9. See the members' section of *www.inqaahe.org*.

10. The other three objectives are to examine: 1) the effectiveness of arrangements for maintaining appropriate academic standards and enhancing the quality of postgraduate research programmes; 2) the effectiveness of an institution's approach to build systematically upon the outcomes of their internal quality assurance procedures, on the findings of reports of external reviews, and on other information such as feedback from students, graduates and employers; and 3) the accuracy and completeness of the information that an institution publishes about the academic standards of its awards and the quality of its information. Note that with the exception of the last point, the focus is on the effectiveness of the arrangements and approaches rather than an evaluation of the outcomes of applying the procedures.

11. Performance Indicators at *www.hesa.ac.uk*.

12. *www.oecd.org/dataoecd/62/21/37032873.pdf*.

13. *www.ecaconsortium.net*.

14. Austria, Denmark, France, Germany, the Netherlands, Belgium (Flanders), Norway, Poland, Spain and Switzerland.

15. Austria, Belgium, Denmark, Germany, Ireland, Italy, the Netherlands, Norway, Spain, Sweden, Switzerland and the United Kingdom.

16. *http://tuning.unideusto.org/tuningeu/*.

17. *www.enqa.eu/files/ESG_v03.pdf*.

18. *http://aei.dest.gov.au/AEI/GovernmentActivities/BolognaProcess/SeminarProgramme.htm*.

19. *Official Journal of the European Union: http://eur-lex.europa.eu/LexUriServ/ LexUriServ.do?uri=OJ:L:2006:064:0060:0062:EN:PDF*

20. *www.aacsb.edu*.

Bibliography

AUQA (2008), *Audit Manual version 5.0*, Australian Universities Quality Agency, Melbourne.

Brown, R. (2004), *Quality Assurance in Higher Education*, Routledge, London.

Campbell, C. and C. Rozsnyai (2002), *Quality Assurance and the Development of Course Programmes*. Papers on Higher Education Regional University Network on Governance and Management of Higher Education in South East Europe Bucharest, UNESCO.

CHEA (2001), CHEA website, *www.chea.org* section on "International Quality Review", CHEA *Glossary of Terms*.

CHEA (2003), *Statement of Mutual Responsibilities for Student Learning Outcomes: Accreditation, Institutions, and Programmes*, Council for Higher Education Accreditation, Washington, DC.

Department of Education (2006), *A Test of Leadership*, US Department of Education, Washington, DC.

El-Khawas, Elaine (2001), *Accreditation in the United States*, International UNESCO Institute for Educational Planning, Paris.

ENQA (2005), *Standards and Guidelines for Quality Assurance in the European Higher Education Area*, European Association for Quality assurance in Higher Education, Helsinki.

Haug, (2003), *Quality Assurance/Accreditation in the Emerging European Higher Education Area: A Possible Scenario for the Future* European Journal of Education, Vol. 38, No. 4.

HEC (2003), *Handbook of Accreditation*, Higher Education Commission, Chicago.

OECD (2004), *Quality and Recognition in Higher Education: The Cross-border Challenge*, OECD Publishing, Paris.

OECD (2005), *Guidelines for Quality Provision in Cross-border Higher Education*, OECD Publishing, Paris, *www.oecd.org/dataoecd/27/51/35779480.pdf*.

OECD (2008), *Tertiary Education for the Knowledge Society, OECD Thematic Review of Tertiary Education: Synthesis Report Volume 2 Assuring and Improving Quality*, OECD Publishing, Paris.

QAA (2003), *Handbook for Institutional Review: Wales*, Quality Assurance Agency, Cheltenham.

QAA (2006), *Handbook for Institutional Audit: England and Northern Ireland*, Quality Assurance Agency, Cheltenham.

Salmi J. and A. Saroyan (2007), "League Tables as Policy Instruments: Uses and Misuses", *Higher Education Management and Policy*, Vol. 19, No. 2.

Silver, H. (1994), *External Examining in the UK: How Did it Start?* in HEQC "External Examining in Focus", November 2004.

Stella, Anthony (2002), *External Quality Assurance in Indian Higher Education*, Paris, International Institute for Educational Planning (IIEP).

Vlăsceanu, L., L. Grünberg, and D. Pârlea (2004), *Quality Assurance and Accreditation: A Glossary of Basic Terms and Definitions* (Bucharest, UNESCO-CEPES), Papers on Higher Education, *www.cepes.ro/publications/Default.htm*.

ANNEX 11.A1

The INQAAHE website (*www.inqaahe.org*) contains a section that contains details of such matters as the type of entity, ownership, governance, sources of funding and mode of operation of its member organisations.

For the purposes of this paper a survey of the information contained in the returns from members was carried out in January 2008. For the purpose of survey, agencies that act as professional or specialised agencies were excluded, as were members whose responsibilities were confined to the recognition of quality assurance agencies. This, as is indicated in the table below, left 148 full members from 77 countries.

Some members had only supplied minimal information while others had not completed the new Database form that was introduced in 2004. These members were excluded from the analysis as were a number of very newly established agencies who had not been in a position to complete the form when they joined the Network. These counted for 74 of the potential sample of 148. The exclusion rate varies over the different geographical regions, which means that the findings of the survey are not based on a statically valued sample but they do provide some guidance as to existing practice.

It was thought better not to group countries strictly on geographical criteria but to take account of shared traditions and models of higher education. The groupings used are:

- Europe, excluding the United Kingdom but including Israel;
- Australia, Canada, New Zealand and the United Kingdom;
- Asia;
- Others, comprising Africa, Caribbean, Middle East, Pacific, South and Central America and the United States.

Number or countries, members and entries used in 2008				
Regional grouping	Country	Number		
		Countries	Full members	Entries used	Entries not used
Europe	Albania		1	1	
	Austria		3	3	
	Belgium		2	1	1
	Croatia		2		2
	Cyprus		1	1	
	Czech Republic		1	1	
	Denmark		1	1	
	Estonia		2	1	1
	Finland		1	1	
	France		2	1	1
	Germany		3	1	2
	Hungary		1	1	
	Iceland		1	1	
	Ireland		2	1	1
	Israel		1	1	
	Italy		1		1
	Latvia		1		1
	Lithuania		1	1	
	Netherlands		5	2	3
	Norway		1	1	0
	Poland		2	1	1
	Portugal		1		1
	Romania		1	1	
	Russian Federation		2	1	1
	Serbia		1	1	
	Slovak Republic		1	1	
	Spain		2	2	
	Sweden		1		1
	Switzerland		1	1	
	Total	29	45	28	17
Anglo-Saxon	Australia		3	2	1
	Canada		7	7	
	New Zealand		4	3	1
	United Kingdom		3	3	
	Total	4	17	15	2
East and Central Asia	China		11	6	5
	India		3	1	2
	Indonesia		1	1	
	Japan		3	1	2
	Kazakhstan		1		1
	Kyrgyzstan		1		1
	Malaysia		2		2
	Maldives		1		1
	Mongolia		1	1	
	Pakistan		1		1
	Philippines		3	2	1
	Sri Lanka		1	1	
	Thailand		2		2
	Vietnam		1		1
	Total	14	32	13	19

Regional grouping	Country	Number or countries, members and entries used in 2008			
		Countries	Full members	Entries used	Entries not used
	United States Total	1	14	3	11
	Egypt		2		2
	Jordan		1	1	
	Kuwait		1	1	
Middle East	Oman		1		1
	Palestine		1	1	
	Saudi Arabia		1		1
	UAE		1	1	
	Bahrain		1		1
	Total	7	7	4	3
	Botswana		1		1
	Ethiopia		1	1	
	Ghana		1	1	
	Kenya		1	1	
Africa	Mauritius		1	1	
	Namibia		1		1
	Nigeria		1		1
	Rwanda		1		1
	South Africa		2	1	1
	Total	10	13	6	7
	Argentina		1	1	
	Chile		5	1	4
	Colombia		2		2
Latin America	Costa Rica		1	1	
	Ecuador		1		1
	Mexico		2		2
	Total	6	12	3	9
	Bahamas		1		1
	Barbados		1		1
Caribbean	Jamaica		2	1	1
	Trinidad and Tobago		2	1	1
	Total	4	6	2	4
	Fiji		1		1
Pacific	Samoa		1		1
	Total	2	2		2
Total		29	40	15	25
Grand total		**77**	**148**	**74**	**74**

Regional grouping: Others

Source: INQAAHE (*www.inqaahe.org*).

OECD PUBLISHING, 2, rue André-Pascal, 75775 PARIS CEDEX 16
PRINTED IN FRANCE
(96 2009 04 1 P) ISBN 978-92-64-05660-2 – No. 56957 2009

4808119

Made in the USA
Lexington, KY
04 March 2010